W9-BYA-635

Unlocking the Scriptures for You

MATTHEW

LeRoy Lawson

ANDREW UNIVERSITY
BERKELEY
Χριστός πρωτεύων

STANDARD
BIBLE STUDIES

STANDARD PUBLISHING
Cincinnati, Ohio   40101

The author gratefully acknowledges that the publisher has allowed him to use, with very little change, material from his previously published book, *The Lord of Parables* (© 1984), for comments on the following passages: Matthew 13:1-23; 20:1-16; 21:33-46; 25:1-46.

Unless otherwise noted, Scripture quotations are from the *Holy Bible: New International Version,* ©1973, 1978, 1984 by the International Bible Society. Used by permission of Zondervan Bible Publishers and the International Bible Society.

Sharing the thoughts of his own heart, the author may express views not entirely consistent with those of the publisher.

Library of Congress Cataloging in Publication data:

Lawson, E. LeRoy, 1938-
  Matthew.

  (Standard Bible studies)
   1. Bible. N.T. Matthew—Commentaries. I. Title.
BS2575.3.L38   1986   226'.207   85-27698
ISBN 0-87403-161-3

Copyright ©1986, The STANDARD PUBLISHING Company, Cincinnati, Ohio. A division of STANDEX INTERNATIONAL Corporation. Printed in U.S.A.

CONTENTS

INTRODUCTION

A Word From the Author

This is not your typical Bible commentary. I know, because I read many of them as I prepared this volume. There are several excellent reference works available to the preacher or Bible scholar who wishes to dig deeper into the meaning of certain Greek words or theological concepts. This is not one of those books. There are also several volumes of quality expositions of Matthew by noted scholars of every theological persuasion. This is not one of them, either.

A modest purpose called this book forth, one that I hope I have fulfilled. I have written with the faithful layperson in mind, that indispensable saint who has to put together a weekly Bible lesson for a Sunday-school class or a home Bible study. Neither Bible scholar nor preacher, the dedicated teacher needs a little help interpreting a difficult passage here and there, but could also use some assistance in getting hold of the larger issues of Matthew: the themes in the Gospel, what they meant in the first century and now mean to ours, and how the events and literature that define our contemporary experience are anticipated and reflected in the Scriptures. As I said, I hope I have been of some help. The result of my effort has been a commentary that has at least these four characteristics:

It is very simple. Not that I don't think my hypothetical teacher could understand something much more difficult. Understanding isn't the issue here, but time is. If you are the typical church teacher, you put in a forty- or fifty-hour work week on your job, then have to attend too many church and civic meetings and tend to far too many chores around the house to have much time left over for serious research. Your family needs some of your time and so do your friends. You would like to devote far more preparation time than you do, but you can't. For you, then, I have tried to keep my comments simple and my illustrations to the point.

It is devotional. My study of Matthew has forced me repeatedly to

7

my knees. The Gospel is a masterpiece whose matchless hero is the Living Lord. You can't walk along Galilee with Him or sit at His feet during the Sermon on the Mount and remain unmoved, unless your reading of Matthew is merely an academic exercise, something that the writer of this magnificent Gospel could never have anticipated. He is introducing you to his Lord, not to some antiquarian object to titillate your scientific curiosity.

It is contemporary. In fact, it is doubly so. That is, I have tried to provide some insight into the time and culture into which Jesus came while at the same time borrowing heavily from writers and happenings in our own day in order to indicate the timelessness of the essential Gospel. It speaks to any society, even ours, complex and confused though it be. I have deliberately not limited my illustrations or analogies to typically Christian ones. Jesus came to all men everywhere, and this truth is applicable to saints and sinners alike. We have often made the mistake of speaking about "Christian truth." There is no such thing. If we had Christian truth, we should have to have un-Christian truth, an impossibility. Truth is truth. We can find examples and illustrations of the truth Jesus taught, then, on every hand. Just as the Lord could see the love of God in a shepherd's search for a lost sheep, so the alert Christian can find parables of Christian doctrine in the most common circumstances or quite "secular" literature.

It is personal. You might even call it eccentric. I have studied many of the scholars, but in the end it is my own reading of Matthew that you have before you. You'll often disagree with me. That is to be expected, even invited. My desire is to stimulate your own engaged reading of the Gospel, not to convert you to mine. Then, when you share what you have learned in your study with your class or discussion group, it will be *your* insight that they hear from you, and not the second-hand views of an amateur like me. (By the way, I don't apologize for my amateur standing. An amateur, you remember, is one who pursues an art or science just for the love of it. That's what I have been doing.)

Some Words About the Gospel of Matthew

The New Testament opens with the four Gospels of Jesus Christ, of which the Gospel according to Matthew is first. If you read Matthew, Mark, Luke, or John expecting a traditional biography, you'll be disappointed. Most of the details you look for in a person's life story are missing. You'll learn a little about the events surrounding Jesus' birth, one incident of His childhood (His visit to the temple when He was twelve), and nothing at all of His youth and early manhood until He commenced His ministry at thirty years of age. Even then the writers are quite stingy in the data they give you from His next three years. Only His last week is given much attention.

Obviously, a Gospel is not a biography. Then what is it? The word, as you know, means good news. The Gospel writers have one overriding purpose: they are announcing the good news that the reign of God has come to earth in the person of Jesus Christ, who brought with Him the possibility of forgiveness of sins and the gift of eternal life. At a decisive moment in history, in a particular geographical area called Palestine, to a specific people called the Jews, God penetrated human history in the person of Jesus, who lived, healed, taught, and died for men that, as God raised Him from the dead, they, too, might have eternal life.

To tell this story is Matthew's objective. Writing specifically to the Jews, he takes pains to prove that Jesus is the fulfillment of Old Testament predictions of a Messiah (an Anointed One) from God. At least sixty-five times Matthew relates events in the life of Jesus to Old Testament prophecies. No other New Testament book presents Jesus as faithful to Old Testament law as Matthew does, even as Jesus seeks to teach the real intent—as opposed to a legalistic observance—of the law. For Matthew, Jesus is no revolutionary or troubler of Israel, but the long-awaited Messiah who came to save His people.

The Jews have been a people of the covenant. In presenting his two major themes, Matthew insists that God continues to have a covenant people. But now that the Messiah has come, God's people belong to a new kingdom and serve a new King. No longer are they automatically members of God's people by virtue of their birth; now they become members through faith and citizenship in the kingdom of Heaven. Membership in God's covenant community has always been important. Now, however, Jesus has mediated a new covenant, so Israel has been succeeded by the kingdom. Gone are the days when Jews can make exclusive claims on God; Gentiles and Jews alike can become members of the kingdom of Heaven. What matters is not that they have Jewish blood in their veins, but that they have been saved through the blood of Jesus, their King.

Matthew leaves no doubt that Jesus is King. From His royal genealogy (Son of David—a title used nine times in Matthew, three times more often than in Mark and Luke; John does not use it at all) and the visits of the three Magi bearing gifts befitting royalty, to His triumphal entry into Jerusalem and the title nailed on Jesus' cross, to

His final regal commission ("All authority . . . has been given to me"), Jesus is the Messiah as Monarch.

Matthew is equally clear that the King rules in a kingdom. This is the theme of Jesus' preaching and teaching: "Repent, for the kingdom of heaven is near." "The kingdom of heaven is like . . ." Never precisely defined, the kingdom emerges from Matthew's pages as the supreme reign of God on earth; the church is its most visible manifestation. The kingdom comes in with Jesus, but it remains on earth following Jesus' ministry; hence the importance Jesus places on leadership training. His disciples will have to carry on His saving ministry in His absence; they will teach and heal and cast out demons and do everything else Jesus has instructed them, in His name and power.

Their ministry will not be limited to Jews, either. This most Jewish of the Gospels pulsates with concern for Gentiles. Matthew carefully notes in the genealogy that some of Jesus' progenitors were not Jews. The Magi, the first to acknowledge the new King of the Jews, were also Gentiles. Some of Jesus' miracles were performed "outside the camp" of Jews as His travels took Him beyond Israel's borders. Several of Jesus' most famous parables teach that God has wearied of waiting for the Jews to produce God's will on earth, so He will turn to others, instead. The climax of the Gospel has Jesus commissioning His apostles to go to all the peoples of the world; the love of God encompasses everybody. Membership in the people of God has been thrown wide open, even to Gentiles.

Matthew's themes of the King and His kingdom cannot be mistaken in a Gospel so filled with Jesus' teaching. It has often been pointed out that Mark's is the Gospel of action and Matthew's is the Gospel of teaching. The latter includes five great sections in which the author has collected sayings of Jesus and arranged them according to theme:

1) The Sermon on the Mount (5-7) (How citizens of the new kingdom conduct themselves),
2) The Powers and Problems of the Kingdom's Ambassadors (10),
3) Parables About the Kingdom (13),
4) Greatness and Forgiveness in the Kingdom (18), and
5) The Return of the King in Judgment (23, 24).

In addition to these major sections, Matthew sprinkles his narrative liberally with other words of the King. Matthew is a thorough writer.

The completeness of Matthew's Gospel, in fact, is probably one reason that it stands first in the New Testament. It includes practically all of the narrative material in Mark as well as information concerning Jesus' birth and resurrection not found in Mark. As noted above, Matthew also includes the most complete collection of Jesus' ethical teaching. John, writing much later, added to our treasure of Jesus' instruction. But as a later writer, he could not displace Matthew from his preeminence among the Synoptic Gospel writers.

Matthew, Mark, and Luke have written what we now call the *Synoptic* Gospels. The technical term simply indicates that the writers "see together." They have the same point of view, cover the same ground, and share much of the same material. John, on the other hand, charts his own course. While the Synoptics relate only the northern work of Jesus and the final week of His ministry in Jerusalem, John makes it clear that Jesus had earlier ministries in the Holy City before returning there for His crucifixion.

For centuries, Matthew was considered the oldest of the Gospels, although many modern scholars tend toward the opinion that Mark wrote first and that Matthew and Luke both leaned heavily on him when writing their own accounts. In the first centuries of the church, however, Matthew was considered the first written and the most thorough of the Gospels. It was certainly the most frequently quoted by Bible scholars in the early Christian centuries, not only because of its priority in time, but also because of its apostolic authorship.

In those days, there was no doubt that the author was Matthew the apostle. Respected early Christians like Papias, Irenaeus, Origin, and Eusebius lent their authority to the authenticity of Matthew's claim to this Gospel. From them we also learn that the Gospel was probably written first in Aramaic (in whole or in part), and then translated or rewritten in Greek.

From within the Gospel, we learn a little about the author. His Jewish background is obvious, as is his purpose of persuading Jewish readers that their Old Testament prophecies find their fulfillment in Christ. The writer is a systematic person, a trait quickly discerned as you read through his Gospel and see how neatly he clusters his material according to theme. (Note also his love of numbers. Count the times he speaks of persons or events in twos, threes, and sevens.) Some scholars insist that the author could not have been an eyewitness of events; others are just as adamant that the inclusion of so much teaching argues that he must have heard Jesus personally.

What can we conclude? I like the conclusion of W. F. Albright and C. S. Mann in the *Anchor Bible Commentary* on Matthew. They contend that the characteristics of this Gospel, namely its conservatism, its frequent references to traditional oral law, its multiplied

11

confrontations with lawyers and Pharisees, and its traditional position concerning the future, argue persuasively that the author was a member of the priestly clan, that is, a Levite. (A comparison of the lists of the apostles in the three Synoptics suggests that Matthew and Levi are the same person. Was Levi a "nickname" for "the Levite"?) Albright and Mann believe that "the Levite Matthew" satisfies the conditions for authorship that the Gospel's characteristics dictate better than any other candidate the New Testament offers. The debate over who wrote the first Gospel is being conducted by scholars far more able to present an argument than I am. For our purposes in this devotional commentary, there is no reason to seek further than Matthew the apostle.

CHAPTER ONE

Roots

Matthew 1

Historical Roots (1:1-17)
(Luke 3:23-38)

What new students of the Bible, determined to start at the beginning of the New Testament and read clear through, have not stuttered, stumbled, and finally given up on the first page? The "begats" have defeated them. The New International Version has substituted "the father of" for "begat," which is an improvement, but courage is still required to plod through the formidable list.

"The book of generations," the lists are called in older versions. The NIV calls them "a record of the genealogy of Jesus Christ." You probably wonder why Matthew starts his account of Christ's life by tracing His descent this way. He may have had several purposes, which our study should bring to light. You notice that he divides his list of Jesus' ancestors into three sections of fourteen generations each. The sections roughly correspond to three Old Testament periods: (1) from the beginning of the Hebrew nation with Abraham through the patriarchs and judges to the consolidation of the kingdom; (2) from King David through the period of the kings to the exile of Israel; (3) from the days of Israel's captivity to the coming of the liberator, Jesus Christ.

Matthew says "there were fourteen generations" in each section. A comparison of his list with Old Testament records, however, shows some discrepancies. Several generations have been omitted from the second section, and the third list is missing a generation.

Matthew appears to have arbitrarily arranged his sections to have fourteen generations because he is conveying something more important than the names alone indicate. He states his purpose in the first line: "A record of the genealogy of Jesus Christ the son of David, the son of Abraham." He wants his readers to understand from the beginning of his Gospel that this is a book about a person with traceable historical roots; He actually lived. Human blood flowed through His veins. He did not appear as a phantom out of nowhere, but as the legitimate issue of Jewish lineage. The genealogy traces Jesus' roots back to two of the most important leaders in Jewish history, their founder and their greatest king. He is son of David, son of Abraham. He is no accident of history, but the one whom God promised to send to His people. Further, if we hope to comprehend this Gospel, we must read it in light of the Old Testament. Matthew repeatedly quotes Scripture to satisfy any lingering doubt that Jesus is the Messiah.

Jesus is "son of David." God promised David that He would establish a kingdom of which there would be no end, that he would have a son who would continue his father's rule (see 2 Samuel 7:25ff; 1 Kings 8:22ff; and Acts 2:29-36). David's son Solomon seemed his likely successor in this eternal kingdom, but Solomon could not live up to his father's high hopes. Solomon's reign began with high promise when he asked God for wisdom to rule (1 Kings 3:9), but with the passing years, the king proved himself to be less than infallible. At least from our perspective, it does not seem the epitome of wisdom to marry 700 wives and add another 300 concubines for good measure. The Bible does not give Solomon high marks (1 Kings 11:1-3). He seems more the typical Oriental despot than a divinely inspired ruler. Luxury and sensuality weakened his court. He is not the son of David through whom God's promise would be fulfilled.

Jesus is also "son of Abraham." God called Abraham and established a covenant with him so that He could bless Abraham and use him as a channel to bless all the families of the earth (Genesis 12:14). Like David centuries later, Abraham also had a son who at first seemed, but then proved not to be, his true successor. His son Isaac had two sons, Jacob and Esau. Jacob sired twelve sons, and with them, the descendants of Abraham became the nation of Israel. But in spite of Israel's special relationship with God, the nation did not prove to be the channel for blessing the world that God had envisioned in Abraham. Something—or Someone—else was needed.

Matthew will seek to prove in his Gospel that the Someone else God has long had in mind is Jesus. The author will repeatedly quote the Old Testament to demonstrate that God's promises to Abraham and David, indeed to judges and prophets and the nation, have come to pass in Jesus, son of David and of Abraham.

As you check out Jesus' ancestors in the Old Testament, you may be surprised at what you find. They are not a thoroughly respectable lot. Some were famous, like Solomon, David, Abraham, Isaac, and Jacob; some, on the other hand, were more infamous than famous. And in an amazing departure from custom, Matthew even includes some women! Of course, everyone has female ancestors, but the Jews never mentioned them in genealogies. They never, never traced their lineage through a woman, since women did not count legally. Jesus would do more than anyone else in history to change the status of women, so Matthew subtly hints here at the change to come.

At the very end of the list, Matthew carefully avoids saying that Joseph was the father of Jesus. Instead he writes, ". . . Matthan the father of Jacob, and Jacob the father of Joseph, the husband of Mary, of whom was born Jesus, who is called Christ." Jesus is the son of God, not of Joseph. Since Matthew is writing his book to Jewish Christians, however, all of whom traced their lineage through their fathers, he includes Joseph's ancestors. A genealogy that read, "Jesus, the son of God," would not have satisfied Matthew's readers. They wanted to know about Joseph's family.

So Matthew follows convention—but not slavishly. When he lists the women, he announces his independence from convention. He has something so important to say that he will not scruple to bend genealogical rules to say it. And such women he mentions! "Judah the father of Perez and Zerah, whose mother was Tamar" (verse 3). Tamar the deceitful, who seduced her own father-in-law in order to have a child (twins, actually) by him (Genesis 38). A strange inclusion. Drop down to verse 5: "Salmon the father of Boaz, whose mother was Rahab." Rahab of Jericho was a prostitute. When Joshua sent his spies into Jericho to check the place out before leading the Israelites into their Promised Land, the spies made their bed at her house (Joshua 2; 6:15ff).

The next line introduces Ruth, the mother of Obed, whose father was Boaz (see Ruth 1—4). Ruth was an admirable woman. We still sing her beautiful song, "Whither thou goest, I will go . . ." from Ruth 1:16. She was an ancestor of whom one could be justifiably proud, but she was not Jewish. She was a Moabite woman, and Deuteronomy 23:3 decrees that no Moabite shall come into the congregation of Israel, down to the tenth generation. Yet here is Ruth, a forebearer of Christ.

We dare not overlook Bathsheba (verse 6). King David was the father of Solomon by this woman, who had been Uriah's wife. Their story reads like a daytime television soap opera. (See 2 Samuel 11.) A lust-smitten king orders his faithful subject to be assassinated so the king can legitimize the fantasy he has indulged with the subject's wife.

Jesus' family tree is not entirely an admirable group, and even the most respectable members are not without their blemishes. The genealogy makes you a little less ashamed of your own heritage, doesn't it? That is undoubtedly Matthew's point. He foreshadows here some changes that Jesus will make, including among them a new respect for women and a heightened appreciation for the full embrace of God's saving love, an embrace that gathers to God Israelites and non-Israelites, heroes and rascals, society's leaders and society's lower-enders. In fact, all males and all females. Later, the apostle Paul will write that in Christ "there is neither Jew nor Greek, slave nor free, male nor female, for you are all one in Christ Jesus" (Galatians 3:28). Christ does not recognize a second class of citizens in the kingdom of God. Even a Gentile woman, a prostitute like Rahab, is within the reach of God's love and Christ's saving grace.

In Matthew's genealogy, then, the range of human frailties and possibilities is suggested. And Jesus, whose name means "God saves," has come for just such people. God wants to save people like Jesus' ancestors, like our ancestors, like us.

Divine Roots (1:18-25)

Matthew narrates the birth of the baby from the husband's point of view. (See Luke 2 for the wife's.) This just man must have tossed many sleepless nights over the pregnancy of his intended. Had he not been a "righteous" man of unusual courage, he would not have borne the shame that fell upon him when in the public eye Mary's condition was explained as (l) a breach of their betrothal—intercourse should have waited until the actual marriage, or (2) a pregnancy caused by Mary's dalliance with some other man. The neighbors could not have conceived of a third alternative. But this remarkable carpenter of Nazareth, who could claim royal blood in his veins (verse 20), acted regally in his unusual predicament.

Joseph could have exposed Mary by dragging her into court; that was certainly his right. At the least, he could have divorced her privately by handing her a writ of divorce (this is how binding a pledge—or betrothal—of marriage was). In his kindness, he chose the quieter means. The extent of his righteousness, however, is revealed in his acceptance of the angel's reassuring word that Mary was not to be faulted. The Holy Spirit selected her for a great, if temporarily discomforting, honor.

"This is how the birth of Jesus Christ came about. His mother Mary was pledged. . . ." The word is *betrothed,* which means engaged but is a stronger, more binding tie than our modern engagements. The betrothal period was for one year. Once betrothed, the man and woman were like husband and wife (even using these terms) except that they did not live together or enjoy sexual intercourse.

"But before they came together," sometime during their betrothal year, "she was found to be with child through the Holy Spirit." (See Luke 1:26-38.) Joseph could never have guessed this explanation for Mary's condition. An angel calmed his fears: "Joseph son of David [see above comments on 1:1-17 for the importance of this title to Matthew], do not be afraid to take Mary home as your wife, because what is conceived in her is from the Holy Spirit." "*God* is responsible for Mary's condition, and the child who is to be born comes from the creativity of God himself. He will be Son of Man and Son of God."

The child in Mary's womb was God's promised Messiah. For centuries, Israel had eagerly awaited the day of His arrival. Modern Jews, who reject Jesus as Messiah, still pray to God for the Messiah to come. He will bring peace, establish justice, and reward the Jews for their patient obedience through long centuries of persecution. Jews are not alone in looking for some kind of Messiah. Many people are adherents of a religion that claims to adore some kind of coming Savior. The most bizarre in recent times is found on the little island of Tanna in the New Hebrides. Some inhabitants there claim to be awaiting one; they already know who he is. A religious cult born in the 1960s proclaims Prince Philip of England as their Messiah. They teach that he was actually born on their island but was somehow spirited away. They believe he left by ship and will return the same way one day. When he comes back, he will cure all disease, reverse old age, and bring paradise on earth to their little island.

These quirkish believers raise a pertinent question: Who is *our* God? What do we look for in God's Anointed One (Messiah)? The answer to the question, of course, depends upon the authority we trust. The Tannan cult members "adopted" their Messiah on their own authority; we Christians accept Jesus on the authority of the Bible. Contemporary Jews reject Jesus because they have rejected the New Testament as God's revealed Word.

The Bible's teaching on the incarnation shows us that God understands the plight of the little boy whose mother could not calm his fear of the storm outside. She told him that God would be with him, but he said he wanted a God with skin! In the same way, God also sympathized with the needs of His people Israel for "a God with skin." So God appeared on earth in skin (Philippians 2:5-11). Mary was God's chosen instrument for bringing Him into the world. Joseph had no need to fear, because the Holy Spirit was responsible.

The Holy Spirit is the power of God working on earth to accomplish God's purposes. Through the Spirit, the world was created (Genesis 1:2; Psalm 104:30). Through the Spirit, God's covenants are fulfilled. Matthew is at pains to present Jesus' story as the realization of what God promised through His prophets. "You are to give Him the name *Jesus* ["God saves"] (Matthew 1:21). "They will call Him 'Immanuel'—which means, 'God with us'" (Matthew 1:23). Even His names indicate God's holy activity among His people. Not that His given name, Jesus, is unique. At least one other New Testament person wears it (Colossians 4:11), and Joshua, the Hebrew form of Jesus, is a well-known Old Testament name.

What a story this is! Because Christians have grown up with the Christmas story, we take its marvels for granted. But think of it: the omnipotent God on the one hand; an impotent little baby on the other. Matthew says that in that baby, man meets God. He is with US! In the incarnation, as G. Campbell Morgan has written, God "stooped into an actual identification with human nature, and by that stoop lifted human nature into the spacious fellowship with God."

What is central to this event is the presence of God, not the virgin birth. Matthew is utterly convinced that Mary was a virgin when she conceived Jesus, but is like the other New Testament writers in not building the case for Christ on the virgin birth. Other religions have claimed a virgin birth for their founders, and pagan mythology was filled with such stories; so Christianity cannot base its uniqueness on the circumstances of Christ's birth. It never tries to. What is unique to the Christian faith is that Jesus Christ rose from the dead. Upon that assertion its case stands or falls. Only Matthew and Luke refer to Mary as a virgin, and the Gospels of Mark and John and the epistles present powerful cases for Jesus as the Christ of God without reference to His virgin birth.

Matthew quotes Isaiah 7:14. The prophet was predicting a stupendous miracle—one that was not fulfilled in Isaiah's time. Isaiah anticipated the birth of a child who was to be the savior of the world: "And he will be called Wonderful Counselor, Mighty God, Everlasting Father, Prince of Peace" (9:6). A limited application of Isaiah's prediction came in the birth of Hezekiah, the righteous son of King Ahaz. Hezekiah observed the Mosaic law, he destroyed the worship of idols, and he recalled his people to the worship of the true God. (See 2 Kings 18:4-6.) But genuine fulfillment awaited the birth of Immanuel, whose name is Jesus.

CHAPTER TWO

A God of Surprises
Matthew 2

Turning the World Upside Down (2:1-12)

Halford Luccock claims that he bumped into a department store Santa Claus. This one had no cotton whiskers or red coat. In fact, he was a she, overloaded with gifts for the children and the relatives and just about everybody else. As Luccock picked up the packages and offered his apologies, she grumbled, "I hate Christmas, anyhow. It turns everything upside down."[1]

It certainly does, as least in the visit of the Wise-men. What a story: a king defeated by a baby, a throne overthrown by a manger, power drained of its strength by weakness, craftiness outsmarted by innocence, ambition ambushed by selflessness!

"We Three Kings"

Magi, from which we derive our word *magician,* were the most respected wise men of their culture. They were astrologers, forerunners of today's astronomers. You will observe that Matthew's narrative differs markedly from the cherished traditional story that circulates at Christmas. Matthew does not say there were three of them and he does not call them kings. He doesn't give their names as Melchior, Caspar, and Balthasar, either. Tradition has assumed three because of the three gifts.

Astrology had evolved into a pseudo-science in the century before Christ, an understandable development in an uncertain world torn by famines and plagues and wars. When trouble was certain and circumstances weren't, people looked to the stars to find a sense of order missing in their otherwise chaotic lives. A violation of the heavens' orderliness, like a falling star or comet or a star rising in the East, could be interpreted as an omen fraught with grave significance.

---

[1]Robert E. Luccock, *Halford Luccock Treasury* (New York: Abingdon, 1963), p. 380.

These Magi were probably Babylonian astrologers, then, admirable in their search for truth. As their undertaking of this expensive and dangerous journey to Jerusalem indicates, they were prepared to pay a high price in their search for knowledge.

How refreshing their curiosity appears beside the mental laziness of many believers in the Lord who have no curiosity about His Word. They claim to love God, Christ, the Church, and even the Bible, but remain contentedly ignorant of His eternal truths. We turn quickly from their smug complacency to applaud the virtue of these devout, if sometimes misled, students of truth. As astrologers, they sought their answers in the wrong source; yet that source led them to the Scriptures. An extraordinary phenomenon lighted up their sky. They had to find its meaning. They trusted Hebrew Scripture enough to travel to Jerusalem in search of the newborn King of the Jews.

We don't know exactly what they saw in the sky. Scholars have guessed a comet or a nova or a conjunction of Saturn, Jupiter, and Mars. Not everyone saw it. In fact, the star is mentioned nowhere else in the Bible. The Magi saw it because they were constantly scanning the sky. They had prepared themselves to perceive what others could not see.

Christmas cards showing the star and shepherds together are wrong, as are those that put the shepherds and the Wise-men in the same scene. Much time elapsed between the shepherds' visit to the Christ child (Luke 2) and the later arrival of these travelers from the East.

Herod, the Puppet King

This story presents a conflict of cosmic proportions: King Herod versus King Jesus. They could not have been more different. Herod, in the last year of his reign, was a disturbed old man of approximately seventy, crazed with jealousy and fear. A puppet king, Herod was presented his throne by the Roman emperor. His tenure depended on the emperor's satisfaction, which Herod did everything in his power to supply. He was a superb politician. Maneuvering adroitly with armed force and clever guile, the Idumean (from the country of Edom) king kept his Jewish subjects in check. They feared and hated him, but they could not topple him. Herod systematically destroyed anybody he suspected of treachery, including his beautiful wife Mariamne, his own mother Alexandra, and three of his sons, Antipater, Aristobulus, and Alexander. He did not scruple to kill his own flesh and blood to save his throne.

He was no worse than most kings of his era—or any era, for that matter. And like most tyrants, he was keenly aware of his subjects' hatred. William Barclay reports than when Herod was in his last year and sensed he was dying, he left Jerusalem for his most beautiful city, Jericho. There he ordered several city leaders arrested and jailed with orders that the minute he expired, they too should be killed. He had to satisfy himself that there would be tears at his death.[2]

This is Herod, a disturbed but determined old man. The slaughter of the children you read about in Matthew 2:16 is very much in character. If he can't destroy the baby born to be king of the Jews, he will kill all the boys up to two years of age to guarantee that none of them can succeed to his throne!

What disturbs today's reader is the fact that Herod is not unique in history. Our century has produced its own Herods in Joseph Stalin, the infamous liquidator of Russians; Adolph Hitler, who slaughtered six million Jews and wiped out hundreds of thousands of enemies in war; Idi Amin, the crazy tyrant of Uganda; Ayatola Khomeini, the religion-mad dictator of Iran; and many, many more. Such is the perverting power of a throne.

But we can't blame the throne. Some parents have been known to kill their children emotionally if not physically; husbands and wives have often been charged with spouse abuse; corporations have flouted safety standards to protect profits at the expense of workers' lives. Then we could mention politicians who do anything and promise everything to stay in office, without thought of the consequences to others. Nor should we overlook petty gossips who destroy reputations of others in order to make themselves feel more secure on the social ladder. Herod is not at all unique. Would that he were! His is our sinfulness in the extreme.

So this deceiving old tyrant plots his strategy. He summons the Sanhedrin (the chief leaders and counselors of the Jews) to learn where this alleged king is to be born, according to their holy writings. When he learns that it is in Bethlehem, just five or six miles southwest of Jerusalem, he dispatches the travelers with the request that they return and report to him if they find the Child. He says he wants to worship, also, but Herod is not about to bow down to anyone else. He just wants the information; he will deal with the Baby King in his own practiced way.

---

[2] William Barclay, *The Gospel of Matthew*, Volume 1 (Philadelphia: Westminster, 1956), p. 20.

But this disturbed, determined, deceiving old man is about to be overruled. You can be as stubborn as you want to, but when you are up against the will of God, you will be defeated. So God warnsd the Wise-men in a dream to avoid Jerusalem on their way home, and they return in safety. And in triumph!

Jesus, the Real King

The Wise-men had found the one they had traveled so far to see. To Him, not to the puppet king, they gave their gifts appropriate for royalty: gold, always acceptable to a king; frankincense, sweet-smelling incense used in temple worship; and myrrh, ointment for anointing the body of the dead for burial. Their gifts honored Him as king, God, and one destined to die.

If Herod represents the worst in us, Jesus exemplifies the best. Even at birth, His very being divided people, righteous from unrighteous, sheep from goats, God-lovers from God-haters. The prophet Micah, confronting evil authorities in eighth-century (B.C.) Samaria and Judah, looked longingly toward a future when the humble village of Bethlehem would give birth to a different kind of ruler for Judah (Micah 5:2). He would not be another Herod, frantically clutching His throne at any cost, but a shepherd loving His sheep, protecting His people. Unlike worldly rulers, so ready to lay down the lives of their people on battlefields of doubtful purpose, He would instead lay down His life for the sake of His people. This is the contrast: Herod slaughtering babies; this Baby grown to manhood saving His people. Herod: You die so I can live. Jesus: I'll die so you can live. Herod grasping, Jesus giving. Wise men know before which one they should bow.

God Will Take Care of You (2:13-18)

When President Anwar Sadat flew from Egypt to Israel on November 19, 1977, he shocked the whole world. His journey was unprecedented in modern times. It was unheard of that an Egyptian leader should leap the barriers of prejudice to personally petition Israel for peace. We moderns have forgotten, however, that Egypt and Israel have not always been enemies. When Joseph and Mary took refuge in Egypt from the hateful Herod, they were following a well-established precedent. Throughout Israel's history, Israelites had fled to Egypt for protection or for food. Theirs is a long and honored love-hate relationship.

In Matthew's record of Joseph's flight to Egypt with his family are heard echoes of the Old Testament. Matthew deliberately reminds his readers that Egypt had held ancient Israel captive. "Out of Egypt I called my son" (Matthew 1:15; Hosea 11:1) causes our memories to flash back to Moses and the nation he led out of Egypt, or to an even earlier time when first Joseph and then his extended family entered Egypt.

Joseph did not move voluntarily. The son of his father's old age and of his father's favorite wife, Joseph was the favorite. Jacob doted on him, distinguishing him from his older brothers with the gift of a coat that only the wealthy could wear. Joseph further alienated himself through his incredible gift of analyzing dreams—and telling his analyses. In one of his dreams, he stood as the rest of his family bowed before him. It was not a dream you want to tell the whole family about. His jealous brothers, fed up with Joseph's boasting, waited for a chance to get rid of him. That chance came when they were in Shechem tending their sheep. Father Jacob sent Joseph to check up on them. When he found them, they captured him and sold him into slavery to the Midianites, who in turn made a profit when he was purchased for the household of the Pharaoh's captain of the guard (Genesis 37).

Joseph's uncanny way with dreams, which got him into so much trouble, also promoted his career. Through his dream interpretations, he in time became the assistant to the Pharaoh himself. When the famine that Joseph had predicted struck, he had the privilege of feeding his own family and saving their lives (Genesis 39—47). He invited his aged father and his brothers and all their families to come to Egypt, where he could take care of them.

But then the day came when a Pharaoh arose who did not know Joseph. By then, Joseph's family had become an enslaved people (Exodus 1:8). God looked upon His suffering people with pity and commissioned Moses to lead them to the promised land. "Out of Egypt I called my son" is Hosea's (11:1) succinct description of Israel's liberation.

Matthew's account of the sojourn of Jesus and His parents in Egypt suggests a retracing of Israel's odyssey. Jacob's family went there to escape almost certain death in their own country; so did Jesus'. This Son of God would also be called out of Egypt and, like a latter-day Moses, would lead His people to freedom. As God took care of His people in that earlier day, so would He take care of them in this crisis.

The other prophet Matthew quotes is Jeremiah (31:15), who

ministered in the period of the Babylonian captivity. In the eighth century B.C., Assyria defeated and carried the northern kingdom of Israel into captivity. In the south, Judah managed to hang onto its sovereignty a little longer. However, its precarious freedom finally dissolved in 586 B.C., when Babylon's King Nebuchadnezzar overwhelmed the weak king Jehoiakin and carried Judah into captivity.

Eight miles to the north of Jerusalem was a place called Ramah. There, centuries earlier, Jacob's favorite wife Rachel, the mother of Joseph, was buried. As Jeremiah watched in anguish the slow processional of his defeated people, he envisioned Rachel rising from her grave, as it were, weeping for her dispossessed children.

Matthew quotes only part of Jeremiah's prophesy, the saddest part. The context, however, is one of rejoicing. God will take care of His departing children:

> "Restrain your voice from weeping
>   and your eyes from tears,
> for your work will be rewarded,"
>   declares the Lord.
> "They will return from the land of the enemy.
>   So there is hope for your future,"
>   declares the Lord.
> "Your children will return to their own land."
>   —Jeremiah 31:16, 17

Herod may slaughter the children, evil may claim its victory, Ramah's Rachel may weep. But only temporarily. As God liberated the captives in Egypt and brought the captives back from Babylonia, so God now calls His own from wherever and by whatever they are held in bondage.

Dietrich Bonhoeffer, the famed German theologian who died in a Nazi concentration camp around Christmas time, compared life in a prison cell to Advent (the coming of Christ). He wrote in his diary, "One waits, hopes, does this, that, or the other—things that are really of no consequence—the door is shut and can be opened only *from the outside*."[3] Israel in Egypt could be released only from the outside; Judah in Babylon could not free itself—it had to be granted freedom from the outside. Likewise, persons held captive by their own stupidity, sinfulness, and guilt complexes, their very humanness, can be freed only by a power outside themselves.

---

[3]Dietrich Bonhoeffer, *Letters and Papers from Prison,* ed. Eberhard Bethge (New York: The Macmillan Company, 1972), p. 135.

A favorite song among Christians begins, "The love of God is greater far." Often the publishers put an asterisk by the title to call attention to a footnote that explains that the third stanza of the poem was found on the wall of an insane asylum. An inmate, cut off from society, found his comfort in God:

"Could we with ink the ocean fill,
And were the skies of parchment made,
Were every stalk on earth a quill,
And every man a scribe by trade;
To write the love of God above
Would drain the ocean dry;
Nor could the scroll contain the whole,
Though stretched from sky to sky."[4]

The man who penned these lines was locked up, but he received his help from the outside.

A minister spent some time with a sixty-year-old woman who was quite distraught. She did not belong to his congregation, but while visiting her children in his city she regularly attended his worship services. After some time, he had the privilege of baptizing her into Christ. When she returned to her own home, she sent him a gift of money for the church and this personal letter:

"Please accept this small gift from me. I'm deeply grateful to you for taking the time from your busy schedule to listen to me. Our pastor did not understand what I was going through. I really did not care to live. I'm not blaming him. No one knows what other people are feeling. The baptism and you talking to me helped me out of the trauma I was in. . . . Thank you so much for bringing me back to life."

He didn't, of course. He just told her about the God who would take care of her, who could lead her from captivity into freedom and joy. He explained that she did not need to be dismayed, recalling the truth in this final stanza of another well-known Christian hymn,

"No matter what may be the test,
God will take care of you;
Lean, weary one, upon His breast,
God will take care of you."

---

[4]Frederick M. Lehman, "The Love of God" (Copyright 1917, renewal 1945, by Nazarene Publishing House; used by permission).

God Where You Least Expect to Find Him (2:19-23)

The Christmas story bursts with surprises: angels talking to shepherds, the Son of God in the womb of a virgin, a king in a manger, Wise-men kneeling before a baby, the holy Messiah in a carpenter's shop, the long-expected descendant of King David growing up in a laborer's home.

You would have expected Him to be returned to Jerusalem, not exiled in Nazareth. Jerusalem was the holy city, the capital of the nation, the font of all wisdom, the center of rabbinical studies. Surely, Jerusalem was more qualified to nurture the Lord than was a non-descript place like Nazareth. But when the heat was off, Joseph led his little family from Egypt to Galilee, the province of his hometown Nazareth. It was still not safe to return to the capital. Herod the Great was dead, but his son Archelaus had succeeded him as puppet king. At first, it seemed that conditions would be safer with the mad king gone. Archelaus appeared more temperate; at first he wanted to please the Jews. Within months, however, the Jews' optimism vanished when he suppressed a Passover riot with such brute force that 3,000 Jews were killed.

Jerusalem was not safe for the rumored King of the Jews. God may have had other reasons as well for selecting Nazareth. Jerusalem was dominated by the Pharisees and scribes. The environment was legalistically religious, just the kind of surroundings that Jesus, who would free people from legalism and the strictures of religious traditionalism, did not need. Besides, everybody thinks God can be found in the holy city, but God likes to appear in unusual places, where you'd least expect to find Him.

Christ is more than the Lord of the church, sanctified, well-dressed, respectable, safely sanitized and ritualized. He is Lord of life. Jesus mingled with all kinds of people and enjoyed it. He would never appeal to His disciples to be more "religious," in that term's traditional sense. His enemies accused Him of many offenses, but they never charged Him with being stuffy, or even respectable.

What did Nazareth do for Jesus? For one thing, His hometown gave Him a poor reputation. "Nazareth! Can anything good come from there?" (John 1:46). It was a small, unimportant town, fifteen miles from the Sea of Galilee to the east and twenty from the Mediterranean to the west. Snuggled against the Galilean hillside, having a limited water supply, Nazareth had never achieved prominence. It is not mentioned in the Old Testament or by the great Jewish historian Josephus or by any other major Jewish writer.

But real people lived in Nazareth, the kind Jesus came to save. Nazarenes were held in contempt by society's best people, like the leaders in Jerusalem. In fact, Jerusalem's rabbinic circles looked down on the whole of Galilee. "Galilee of the Gentiles," they called it, sniffing that it was tainted with foreign trade, commercialism, and the sweaty physical work of its residents. When the Jewish leaders rebuffed Nicodemus' efforts on Jesus' behalf, they were just venting the current prejudice: "Are you from Galilee, too? Look into it, and you will find that a prophet does not come out of Galilee" (John 7:52).

Nazareth derives from a root meaning *sprout* or *shoot.* We think immediately of Isaiah 11:1—

> A *shoot* will come up from the stump of Jesse;
> from his roots a Branch will bear fruit."

And Isaiah 53:2, 3—

> He grew up before him like a tender *shoot,*
>   and like a root out of dry ground.
> He had no beauty or majesty to attract us to him,
>   nothing in his appearance that we should desire him.
> He was despised and rejected by men,
>   a man of sorrows, and familiar with suffering.
> Like one from whom men hide their faces
>   he was despised, and we esteemed him not.

Jeremiah 23:5, 6 uses the same root:

> "The days are coming," declares the Lord,
>   "when I will raise up to David a righteous *Branch,*
> a King who will reign wisely
>   and do what is just and right in the land.
> In his days Judah will be saved
>   and Israel will live in safety.
> This is the name by which he will be called:
>   The Lord Our Righteousness."

The Messiah will not be able to boast of His handsome appearance nor of His "connections." His character will be sterling and His judgments will be sure, but His mission will be to suffer for His own; He will be a humble leader raised up from humble beginnings. The prophets grasped the significance of His humility, but when the Messiah actually arrived, "he came to that which was his own, but his own did not receive him" (John 1:11). They rejected Him with such force that on one occasion His fellow Nazarenes drove Him out of town and threatened to throw Him over a cliff (Luke 4:28-30). Since they subscribed to the prevailing opinion about Nazareth, they could not believe that someone like them, from their town, could really be what Jesus appeared to be claiming for himself.

That Nazareth gave Jesus a poor reputation seems ironic to historians, since Jesus permanently elevated Nazareth's fame. Two thousand years after He grew up there, every Christian in the world knows about and appreciates the town that nurtured their Lord. No Holy Land tour is complete without a stop in Nazareth. What Jesus did for His town is but a hint of what He has done for mankind. He raises whatever He touches.

This brief passage is a valuable reminder that the gospel is not about what we do for Jesus, but what He does for us. Here is God among men, where you least expect Him. Nothing on earth helped Jesus. His earthly origins were as common as possible: an outdoor shelter for a birthplace, a sojourn as a refugee in a foreign country, a despised city for a hometown, childhood and youth far from the center of culture and religion. His upbringing was commonplace, a Jewish youth helping His father in a carpenter's shop, sweating over His craft, hitting His thumb, learning the hard way, forced to accommodate picky customers and prickly neighbors. No human advantages.

He is one of us. It is so tempting to think, "If only I had been born and reared someplace else, in the right city, on the right side of the tracks, with a better school system. If only I had gone into a different occupation, or had married better, or had a few breaks, then I might have become somebody, too." But Jesus has none of these supposed advantages, so that God can convince us that He is able to lift anyone out of unsavory circumstances by His grace. What God does for Jesus of Nazareth, He can do for all men and women everywhere who live in their own Nazareths and long for a better future. Through Jesus, God makes of a city of poor reputation one of the world's most famous towns. In Jesus, God reveals not only what He is like, but also what human beings can become. God appears to us where we least expect Him; through His appearing, any circumstance can be overcome.

CHAPTER THREE

John the Baptist

Matthew 3

Preparing for Change (3:1-12)
(Mark 1:1-8; Luke 3:1-17; John 1:19-29)

John the Baptist is the messenger of change. He paves the way for Christ, who will surpass John to become the greatest change agent in the history of the world. To prepare the people for what—and Who—is coming, John demands a radical turn-about in his listeners.

Radical Appearance

He looks like what the people thought a prophet should look like. He wears a garment of camel's hair, cinched up with a leather belt. He scorns the robe and phylactery of a religious leader. His goal is not to impress by his appearance; his message takes priority with him.

Matthew compares him with Elijah (see 2 Kings 1:8). Before John's birth, an angel announced to his father Zechariah, "Many of the people of Israel will he bring back to the Lord their God. And he will go on before the Lord, in the spirit and power of Elijah, to turn the hearts of the fathers to their children and the disobedient to the wisdom of the righteous—to make ready a people prepared for the Lord" (Luke 1:16, 17). In appearance, clothing, and prophetic message, John/Elijah will prepare the way of the Lord.

John is the son of the priest Zechariah and his wife Elizabeth, a descendant of the priestly family of Aaron. Born in the hill country of Judea about six months before the birth of Jesus, John has lived as a Nazirite (having taken a vow of separation and abstinence), emerging into public view with his ministry at the Jordan River. With his stern demeanor and unyielding sermons, John looks like, sounds like, and speaks with the honesty of Elijah, preferring to eat locusts and wild honey with the truth to banqueting at the tables of compromise.

In antiquity roads were not paved with asphalt. To ease the way of a traveling king, servants were often sent before him. They would literally lift the valleys and make low the high places to smooth his ride. John is such a servant, readying the way for the Lord.

John's message is both timely and timeless. It penetrated the consciousness of his day as it pierces the pride of our own. "Repent, for the kingdom of heaven is near" (Matthew 3:2). *Repent* has lost much of its punch, because in its unadulterated form, it offends easy consciences. We have redefined it to mean "feeling sorry." It does connote sorrow, but it means much more besides. *Repentance* is a change of mind that leads to a change of behavior. It is turning around, doing a 180-degree about-face. To the prophets, it meant turning back to God with your whole being. It is what Joel described (Joel 2:11, 12),

> "The day of the Lord is great,
>   it is dreadful.
>   Who can endure it?
> "Even now," declares the Lord,
>   "return to me with all your heart,
>   with fasting and weeping and mourning."

Isaiah pleaded in the same vein (Isaiah 55:7),

> "Let the wicked forsake his way
>   and the evil man his thoughts.
> Let him turn to the Lord, and he will have mercy on him,
>   and to our God, for he will freely pardon."

The prophets took their call for repentance terribly seriously. They would not have smiled at the playfulness of Ogden Nash, who notes (in his *Hearts of Gold)* that some people "are very resourceful at being remorseful." Unfortunately, they are. But if their remorse does not lead to reform, they are still unrepentant. The prophets demanded nothing less. They warned of the judgment of God in order to inspire the turnaround that would permit God to save. He takes no delight in judgment, but in redeeming. (See Ezekiel 33:10, 11.)

This is John's message. His hearers, unfortunately, are of two minds, very much like us. We want to hear the Word of the Lord, but we are afraid of what He'll say. We want to be cleansed while at the same time, we keep on heading for the pigsty. We want to obey God, but we don't want anybody to think we are peculiar. We desire God's way and we desire our way. To such as us, John thunders, "Repent!"

From the American Revolution, we have received an excellent example of repentance. John Callendar, who was a captain of the Massachusetts militia, panicked and ran from the famous battle of Bunker Hill. When George Washington became the Supreme Commander of the newly formed United States Army, one of his first duties was to order the court martial of Captain Callendar. "It is with inexpressible

Concern, that the General upon his first Arrival in the army, should find an Officer sentenced by a General Court Martial to be cashier'd for Cowardice—A Crime of all others, the most infamous in a Soldier, the most injurious to an Army, and the last to be forgiven." His career as captain was over. But his story isn't. As soon as he had been sentenced, Callendar turned around and re-enlisted as a private in the Union army. Later, in the Battle of Long Island, he exhibited such courage and exemplary fighting skill that Washington publicly revoked the sentence and reinstated him as a captain.[5] This is repentance. He was sorry for his earlier cowardice, sorry enough to change his mind *and* his behavior. He proved himself a different person.

"The kingdom of heaven is near." Throughout Matthew's Gospel, we'll be tracing the implications of the kingdom. Matthew mentions it more than thirty times. Basically, it refers to the rule of God.

"Repent, for the kingdom of heaven is near" means that the Messiah is coming.

"Repent, for the kingdom of heaven is near" means that God is coming into your life and wants to take control of it.

"The kingdom of heaven is near" means God will rule us if we will let Him, in a kingdom so superior that nothing else on earth can be compared to it (Matthew 13:44-46).

So turn toward God and let Him rule in your life. This is John's radical message.

Radical Actions

Repentance leads to action. The initial action is *baptism.* As his listeners hear and believe John's message, they confess their sins and guilt before God. But words aren't enough. They need to do something to prove their sincerity. John provides an opportunity right then and there to cleanse themselves. They repent, they confess their sins, and they are baptized. A little boy, watching a similar action in church one Sunday morning, tried to describe the baptisms for his aunt, who had not been in the service. "First the preacher preached," the boy told her. "Then he put on another suit, and he walked down some steps into some water, and he rinsed out four people." He's theologically pretty accurate, isn't he? (See 1 Peter 3:21.)

Well-known Argentine preacher and author Juan Carlos Ortiz, taking his understanding of baptism from Romans 6:1-10, has made

[5]Harry Emerson Fosdick, *On Being a Real Person* (New York and London: Harper and Brothers, 1943), pp. 67, 68.

baptism a never-to-be-forgotten moment for his people. Just before lowering the candidate into the water, Ortiz tells him, "I kill you in the name of the Father, and the Son, and the Holy Spirit and I make you born into the Kingdom of God to serve and please Him."[6] This is very close to what John is accomplishing in his baptism. John's is not yet Christian baptism, as he himself makes clear, but it is a killing of the guilt of sin and a preparation for the coming kingdom. However, the full baptism that Ortiz practices awaits the Messiah.

Baptism is associated in John's mind with *separation* of the past from the present. For this reason, he accosts the Pharisees and Sadducees, who stand aside, watching but not participating in the baptisms. The Pharisees cling to the past, they clutch their rules and regulations, and they congratulate themselves on their righteousness. The Sadducees are even more conservative doctrinally than the Pharisees, accepting no Scriptures later than the Pentateuch (the first five books of the Old Testament). Politically, they support the Roman government and compromise their principles (in the opinion of the Pharisees) to enjoy the favors of their overlords. To John, they are equally worthy of scorn. As long as they treasure the *status quo,* they are lost. The kingdom of Heaven is not for them. Even now, God is preparing judgment ("the ax is already at the root of the trees," Matthew 3:10— see Isaiah 5:1-7) and neither their pedigree (as descendants of Abraham) nor their religious propriety will do them any good.

What John pleads for is *results.* "Produce fruit in keeping with repentance" (Matthew 3:8). Israel has failed to yield the results God wanted from it (verse 10). Judgment is coming.

John places his work in the context of Christ's larger ministry. His own work is corrective and preparatory. He can baptize in water for repentance, but another one is coming who is far greater, and the Lord's baptism will be in the Holy Spirit and with fire. It will empower and purify and separate. He will judge by His Spirit and ignite by His fire. He will fulfill the promise of the prophets for a new, Spirit-filled day (Joel 2:28; Isaiah 44:3; Ezekiel 36:26, 27; 37:14; 39:29). It will be a glad and terrible day, for there is promise and threat in the prophet's vision (Malachi 3:2, 3; 4:1), both of which remain to this day. For the faithful, the Lord's coming brings Spirit-filled joy; for the fruitless unrepentant, however, a fiery destination awaits.

---

[6]Quoted in Madeleine L'Engle, *Walking on Water* (Wheaton, IL: Harold Shaw Publishers, 1980), p. 64.

Why Was Jesus Baptized? (3:13-17)
(Mark 1:9-11; Luke 3:21, 22)

Jesus' Request

Why *was* Jesus baptized? If He was sinless, as Hebrews 4:15 says, and if John the Baptist was baptizing people for repentance, then why was Jesus, the sinless one with nothing to repent, baptized?

John had the same question. He had a clear sense of his calling as the one to prepare the way for the Lord (Matthew 3:11; John 1:24-34). He recognized the Lord's superiority to him. Thus, when Jesus requested baptism, John's judgment was instantaneous: an inferior should not baptize his superior.

Every preacher identifies with John. Who has not hesitated before administering the sacred rite for someone whose character has humbled him? But the minister baptizes anyway because, as John is made to understand, the baptizer is not the conveyor of grace but merely God's agent by which baptism is accomplished. He does not by his own goodness or supposed spirituality impart any blessing. That's the Lord's doing. Jesus sweeps away John's objection.

Throughout the early chapters of Matthew, the humility of Jesus is a source of wonder. The Gospel writer presents a marvelous Lord who has emptied himself of His Heavenly glory and presented himself to mankind in the form of a human being, the lowest of human beings, a servant of those He came to save. His baptism is but one example of that humility. (See also Philippians 2:5-11.)

What a contrast between Jesus and some other candidates for baptism! This simple act exposes a great deal about people. If examined from a strictly physical point of view, it is not a beautiful rite. At the Jordan River, there were no dressing rooms to insure privacy. The water was not filtered, as in the lovely baptismal pools modern churches have installed. You could not stand on your dignity with the baptist. His baptism was intended to be an act of humiliation, as the repentant sinner humbled himself before God and man. No room for pride. That's the point: you cannot be proudly penitent.

In sinless humility, Jesus insists that John baptize Him: "Let it be so now; it is proper for us to do this to fulfill all righteousness." Then John consents (Matthew 3:15).

Jesus' Reason

We are not certain what Jesus means. We do know that God is the God of righteousness (Psalm 50:6) and that the promised Messiah would be a Lord of righteousness (Jeremiah 23:6). Jesus here presents himself to John, then, as the obedient Son of a righteous Father. We discern three motives:

(1) To identify with the people He came to save. When a Christian is baptized, it is into Christ. "In the name of Jesus," the Scriptures say (Acts 2:38). Jesus is here doing the reverse; He is being baptized into us. He identifies with the sinners John was challenging to repent. As He will later carry their (and our) sins to the cross, He here takes their (and our) humanity upon himself. He who was the King of Glory became a babe in a manger to identify with us; He who was innocent of all crime was crucified as a criminal in identification with us. He who was sinless was baptized to identify with sinners like us.

(2) To separate himself from His past. Baptism is often called "the water that divides." Our baptism separates us from our past. In the water, we bury our past so that we may start life again, new-born. Even for Jesus, the water divides. This is the ordination service for His new ministry. Up to His baptism, Jesus has been living at home, working at His carpentry, and caring for His mother and brothers and sisters. He has had family obligations to care for; He has preparations to make before He can launch full-time into His life's purpose. Finally He is ready. He steps into the dividing waters, never to return to His old way of life.

(3) To unite with the whole purpose of God. For Jesus and for the rest of us, baptism cannot be an assertion of individuality. It is entry into a shared ministry with God's people. Jesus assumes His place in carrying out God's purposes for the people of God, purposes that have remained constant since God called Abraham to become a blessing to the families of the earth (Genesis 12:3). Jesus will now complete Israel's assignment. His baptism buries whatever selfish purposes Jesus might have entertained and unites His will with the Father's. That is what our baptism signifies, also. We were baptized into the people of God, the church. We can no longer live solitary lives. To be in Christ is to be in His body, to dwell with His people, and to work with fellow Christians to accomplish God's purposes.

At Jesus' baptism, then, He is not stepping into a holy little circle of sanctified people. Just the opposite. He is stepping out of His protected past into a new vulnerability, one in which He opens himself to attack and persecution and even death for the sake of God's purposes. He now proclaims himself servant of God and servant of people. His baptism is His way of declaring His solidarity with the workers of God on behalf of sinners.

Although Jesus does not explain how His baptism fulfills righteousness, the subsequent testimony of the Spirit and the voice of God (Matthew 3:16, 17) prove that He was acting in obedience to God's will for Him. "All God's revelations are sealed until they are opened to us by obedience," Oswald Chambers has written. "The tiniest fragment of obedience, and heaven opens and the profoundest truths of God are yours straight away. God will never reveal more truth about Himself until you have obeyed what you know already."[7]

Even that most secular old rascal Montaigne promotes the virtue of obedience:

> The first law that God ever gave to man was a law of pure obedience; it was a naked and simple commandment about which man had nothing to know or discuss; since to obey is the principal function of a reasonable soul, recognizing a heavenly superior and benefactor. From obeying and yielding spring all other virtues, as from presumption all sin.[8]

Until you are willing to do what God has already told you, He is not going to tell you any more. Until you prove yourself willing to heed what He has already said, why should He let you in on any more of His secrets? Dietrich Bonhoeffer says it more simply: "Only he who believes is obedient, and only he who is obedient believes."[9] We do not know everything Jesus understood about His baptism, but we can clearly see that His is an act of obedience to His Father. Righteousness demands it.

God's Witness

"This is my Son, whom I love; with him I am well pleased." (Matthew is hearing Old Testament overtones again: "This is my son," from Psalm 2:7; ". . . in whom I am well pleased" from Isaiah 42:1.) The voice and the descendant dove prove to Jesus and the witnesses that He has done what His Father expected. The proof is necessary, because by placing himself in John's hands, Jesus was distancing himself from what the accepted religious leaders had been teaching as

---

[7]Oswald Chambers, *My Utmost for His Highest* (New York: Dodd, Mead and Company, 1935), p. 284.

[8]*Essays,* II, 12, "Apology for Raymond Sebond." From *The Complete Essays of Montaigne,* tr. and ed. Donald M. Frame (Stanford University Press, 1971).

[9]Dietrich Bonhoeffer, *The Cost of Discipleship* (New York: Macmillan Publishing Company, 1937), p. 69.

the way to please God. God's declaration of pleasure in Jesus will encourage His departure from Pharisaism and Sadduceeism as well. Righteousness has more to do with faith, repentance, and obedience than with temples and rituals and religious rites. Before Jesus' ministry has run its course, the temple will be replaced and the priesthood will be broadened. Every ritual that people have relied on as substitutes for faith in God will be declared unnecessary. God is ushering in His new age.

> "The Spirit of the Lord will rest on him—
>   the Spirit of wisdom and of understanding,
>   the Spirit of counsel and of power,
>   the Spirit of knowledge and of the fear of the Lord—
> and he will delight in the fear of the Lord. . . .
>   Righteousness will be his belt
>   and faithfulness the sash around his waist" (Isaiah 11:2, 3, 5).

Dwight L. Moody's conversion cannot be compared with this magnificent moment in the life of Christ, but the language with which Moody describes it makes it pertinent here. Moody was a shoe salesman when Edward Kimball, a teacher in the Mt. Vernon Congregational Church Sunday School, placed his hand on his shoulder as Moody was wrapping a package of shoes. "Dwight, don't you think it is about time you gave your heart to the Lord?" Reminiscing about his acceptance of Kimball's challenge forty years later, Moody wrote,

> I remember the morning on which I came out of my room after I had first trusted Christ. I thought the old sun shone a good deal brighter than it ever had before—I thought that it was just smiling upon me; and as I walked out upon Boston Common, and heard the birds singing in the trees, I thought they were all singing a song for me. Do you know I fell in love with the birds? I had never cared for them before. It seemed to me that I was in love with all creation. I had not a bitter feeling against any man, and I was ready to take all mankind to my heart.[10]

Many Christians can offer the same testimony. What God did for Christ in the Spirit and the voice, He does for us. The Spirit has been promised (Acts 2:38), and His entire published Word assures us that when we are obedient in faith, repentance, and baptism, we are His children, too (Romans 6:1-10; 5:1, 2; Luke 15:7, 10).

---

[10]This widely quoted episode is here taken from Clarence Edward Mac-Cartney, *The Wisest Fool* (New York and Nashville: Abingdon-Cokesbury Press, 1949), pp. 162, 163.

CHAPTER FOUR

God or Satan?

Matthew 4

How to Overcome Temptation (4:1-11)
(Mark 1:12, 13; Luke 4:1-13)

Jesus' temptation in the wilderness has provided comfort for many a discouraged Christian. It is too bad there is a chapter division between Matthew 3:17 and 4:1 because it separates two events that should be kept close together. Jesus' baptism was a glorious experience. The heavens opened, the Spirit of the Lord descended, and God declared His pleasure in Jesus. Then, abruptly, the light became darkness: "Then Jesus was led by the Spirit into the desert to be tempted by the devil."

How could this event bring comfort to Christians? Because it demonstrates that the temptations that befall newly baptized Christians are to be expected. They should not become discouraged with themselves or disenchanted with Christianity when the thrill of their conversion gives way to the struggle against sin. The devil strikes immediately, and he strikes hard. The Lord himself did not escape. But neither did He succumb. His victory gives us hope.

Jesus' battle is twofold. He resists Satan as the Son of God, as His adversary keeps reminding Him: "*IF* you are the Son of God . . ." He resists also as the Son of Man, Jesus' usual name for himself. He is very much a man as He struggles with our temptations.

The word here is *tempted* ("*peirasthenai,*" to be tempted, tested). Its Hebrew equivalent is used in the Old Testament for what happened when God ordered Abraham to sacrifice his son Isaac. "God *tested* Abraham" (Genesis 22:1). God wanted to prove what Abraham was made of. In this same sense, the devil is checking out Jesus.

To be temptable is flattering. As William Barclay has written, "Temptation is not the penalty of being a man; temptation is the glory of being a man."[11] Only a human being has a choice to make in who

---

[11]Barclay, *Gospel of Matthew,* p. 56.

he is and what kind of person he will become. He has intelligence to be applied, some values to be lived up to, and a will to be exercised. Temptation proves his potential.

Jesus' three temptations are basic to human experience. The first is to misdirect His ability in order *to take care of physical needs.* "If you are the Son of God, tell these stones to become bread" (Matthew 4:3). "You have been isolated in this wilderness for forty days. Surely You are hungry. There can't be anything wrong with feeding Your starving body."

The devil may be even more subtle. Since Jesus has come to minister to the needs of other people, the devil may be suggesting, "Look, if You make all of these stones here [and stones are plentiful in Palestine] into loaves of bread, You can feed all the hungry people in Your country. Think of the good You can do. Imagine how quickly You can accomplish Your mission on earth and please Your Father."

For most people, this test alone would have been overwhelming. When a body screams in hunger, the mind can think of little else. Physical urges and drives are almost overpowering. How, then, could it be a sin to make a little bread for the body, or other bodies? Yet Jesus sees through the tempter. His own needs and those of humanity at large can never be satisfied by placing the priority on the physical. More—the Word of God—is required.

The second temptation touches another basic drive: *to gain approval or attention.* "'If you are the Son of God,' he said, 'throw yourself down.'" "It is a drop of 450 feet. What a thrill it will be for the watching crowds. They will applaud and hail You as a great miracle worker. Think how this little feat can help You fulfill Your mission. People will follow You anywhere. Besides, when the angels come to Your rescue, that will be proof to everyone of Your special status with God." With what an insatiable appetite most of us are driven to gain the applause of people important to us! Compliments, praise, awards, ovations—we grovel for them. But Jesus will not put God to such a test. He will not play magician to bedazzle the crowds.

The final temptation concerns a need so essential that at least one psychologist calls it one of the two motivating factors of human existence. *It is the need for power.* The devil offers Jesus sovereignty over all the world in exchange for Jesus' allegiance. "Now listen to me, Jesus. God sent You here to establish the kingdom of God on earth. You see, I already control the kingdoms of this earth. I can help You do what God wants You to do." Notice the insidiousness of this temptation? "I can *help* You do what God wants You to do. I'll give

You all these kingdoms so You can report to Your Father, 'You see, I have done everything You wanted of Me.' I'll make it easy for You. What I want in return is insignificant enough: just bow down and worship me."

Power over people *and* fulfillment of God's purpose. The best of everything. Who does not want such power—at the office, at home, or wherever? Why else are we so desperate to earn titles or to make money? Whether the power we seek is political or military or monetary or whatever, something there is within us that yearns to be able to tell at least someone else what to do or where to go.

So what Jesus is wrestling with in His wilderness is the struggle of the human soul, the drives to satisfy the cravings of the body for nourishment, of the ego for applause and special treatment, and of the will for power over others.

Jesus conquers the temptations and shows us how to overcome ours. We can isolate four principles for overcoming the devil.

Know Who You Are

Satan tries to cause Jesus to doubt himself. Jesus has just heard His Father's voice: "This is my Son." Satan picks up on these words and toys with them. "Okay, *if* you think you *really are* the Son of God, prove it to me and to yourself. Make bread. Throw yourself down. Prove it." Jesus withstands Satan's taunts only because He is secure in His knowledge of His relationship with God. He will answer Satan's challenge, all right, but on *His* terms, not Satan's. "Yes, I am the Son of God, but because I am, I will not demean Him nor myself by playing little tricks to satisfy you. I know who I am."

The Christian's knowledge that he is an adopted child of God (Galatians 4:4-7) is his first line of defense against humanity's common sins. Confucius said that there are three things that the superior man guards against: "In youth he guards against his passions, in manhood against quarrelsomeness, and in old age against covetousness." A Christian recognizes even more lures (Galatians 5:16-21), but is even better prepared to fend them off, because the Holy Spirit fights with him (Galatians 5:22-25). He enjoys a special relationship with God, also, and he will no more defame the name of God than Christ will.

Know the Word of God

"Man does not live on bread alone, but on every word that comes from the mouth of God" (Matthew 4:4). This and the other quotations Jesus takes from Deuteronomy (8:3; 6:16; 6:13). The devil uses Scripture, also (Psalm 91:11, 12), but for his own evil purposes. He quotes it, leaves out a clause, misinterprets it, and tries to trip up the Son of God by the Word of God. Jesus could have been a pawn in the devil's hands except for His thorough knowledge of both the words and the meaning of Scripture.

"A distinguishing feature of maturity," Robert C. Leslie writes, "is the refusal to act purely on the basis of expediency; each act is decided upon by reference to principle."[12] He is correct, but upon what do we base these guiding principles? Jesus answers plainly, "On every word that comes from the mouth of God." With our air filled with such a conflicting array of philosophies, a principled life can result only from deliberate, disciplined study of the best of thoughts. The very best come from God.

After suffering a mysterious illness for many years, a woman was finally informed by her allergist that she would have to move to a less industrialized part of the country. The very air that she breathed was gradually poisoning her. She had to move or die. This diagnosis comes as no surprise to a scientist who has studied the pollutants in the atmosphere of certain cities, nor does it surprise students of ideas that there is poison in certain combinations of words or in the entertainment of demonic ideas. The only antidote for such poison is here: "Man does not live on bread alone, but by every word that comes from the mouth of God."

Admit Your Weakness

Jesus does not confess, "I am weak," to the devil. But His dependence upon the Word of God is an implied admission that self-reliance in this critical moment is inadequate. This is in stark contrast to the Sermon on the Mount, in which Jesus frequently stands on His own authority: "You have heard . . . but I tell you" (Matthew 5—7). People are amazed at His singular authority when He preaches. When confronting the devil, however, He does not rely on His strength alone. He leans on the strength of God's Word.

Nothing is more dangerous for disciples of Jesus than failure to admit weakness. We may be very able, but we are never self-sufficient. In fact, the greater our ability, the greater the temptation,

---

[12]Robert C. Leslie, *Jesus and Logotherapy* (Nashville: Abingdon Press, 1965), p. 13.

especially the temptation to believe in our invincibility. Adam and Eve, remember, did not fall because they thought too little of themselves, but because they thought too highly. (See also Romans 12:3.) Exaggerated self-confidence is a rich source of trials. Self-confidence is healthful; arrogance leads to a fall.

Helmut Thielicke laments that man "is constantly on the point of becoming unfaithful to God and making himself into God; he constantly desires to be free of God." Thielicke names this wish to be free of God "the deepest yearning of man. It is greater than his yearning for God."[13] The Son of God, however, does not presume. He answers God's great adversary with God's own Word.

In admitted weakness, the apostle Paul found God's strength in him. Plagued by some disability he called his "thorn in the flesh," he pleaded with the Lord three times to take it away. God wouldn't. Instead, He comforted Paul, "My grace is sufficient for you, for my power is made perfect in weakness" (2 Corinthians 12:9). His lesson learned, Paul then boasted "all the more gladly about [his] weaknesses, so that Christ's power may rest on me.... For when I am weak, then I am strong" (9, 10).

When applied to moral as well as physical strength, the principle is the same. A well-worn story from the days of slavery in America summarizes it. An old black Christian suddenly changed for the better in his behavior. Something good had obviously happened to him. One of his white friends remarked on the new man. "Well, Sam, I see you've got the mastery of the devil at last." Sam humbly answered, "No suh, boss, I ain't got the mastery of the devil. No man can do that. I's got the Master of the devil." Admitting his weakness, he appropriated the Lord's strength.

Serve the Lord

This is Jesus' basic choice: "Will I serve God or the devil? Am I for God or against Him?" The tempter pretends to be offering assistance to Jesus for doing God's will in exchange for Jesus' worship of him. But worship means service, adoration, allegiance. The devil is serving up an impossibility. Christ cannot serve His Father *and* the prince of this world. He has to choose.

It is the subtlety of these temptations that makes them so hard to

---

[13]C. C. Barber, trans., *The Thielicke Trilogy* (Grand Rapids: Baker, 1958, p. 24.

fend off. We are better at handling direct confrontations with the evil one than when he comes flattering, or offering assistance (usually justifying the means by the end), or suggesting ways to do what we really want to do. Then we are in danger. In *Donal Grant,* George McDonald describes a character who claims his only fear is of the devil, not so much as enemy but as pretended friend. He is afraid of his "creeping in." This is exactly Satan's strategy with Jesus. Creeping in. Pretending friendship. Offering help. Quoting Scriptures.

Jesus' struggle comes down to this: Will He adhere to the kingdom of God or will He join the kingdom of this world? Will He serve God or the prince of this world? Will He be God's person or will He let the devil remake Him? Will He do God's will in God's way, or will He alter His instructions just a little, adopting the devil's means to accomplish the Father's end?

How to Serve God (4:12-25)
(Mark 1:16-22)

Matthew has omitted several months of Jesus' ministry. John 1:29—4:42 fills in the blanks for this period. Matthew moves swiftly from Jesus' baptism by John, followed by His fierce period of testing in the wilderness, to the beginning of His ministry in Galilee. Jesus began openly preaching, Matthew reports, after Jesus learned of John's imprisonment by Herod Antipas. (See Matthew's account of this miscarriage of justice in 14:1-12.)

Leaving His hometown of Nazareth (for an account of the inhospitable reception He received there, see Luke 4:14-30), Jesus moved to Capernaum, which then became headquarters for His Galilean ministry. Again Matthew turns to the Old Testament to explain Jesus' decision.

Jesus' Commission: From God (12-16)

God was at work in Jesus, fulfilling His purpose in history. The regions of Zebulun and Naphtali had suffered grievously under the Assyrian siege of 730 B.C. Located at the upper extremity of Israel, they bore the brunt of the attack. Isaiah the prophet could not protect Israel from Assyria, but he could promise better days ahead:

> Nevertheless, there will be no more gloom for those who were in distress. In the past he humbled the land of Zebulun and the land of Naphtali, but in the future he will honor Galilee of the Gentiles, by the way of the sea, along the Jordan (Isaiah 9:1).

Speaking of future deliverance as having already occurred, Isaiah had visions that

> The people walking in darkness
> have seen a great light;
> on those living in the land of the shadow of death
> a light has dawned (9:2).

Now, Matthew confides, that great light has surely appeared. His name is Jesus. God has kept His word.

Jesus' Message: The Kingdom of Heaven (17)

Jesus begins where John the Baptist has left off: "Repent, for the kingdom of heaven is near." (See Mark 1:15.) This brief sentence summarizes Jesus' teaching ministry. He came to preach ("*kerussein*"—to herald, to deliver an important message). He came to introduce God's reign to people suppressed by tyrannical lords of this world. He came to shine the light of God on the darkness, to make visible His grace and goodness, and to deliver a new and superior covenant written in God's love for anyone who would accept it. He came to establish a new kingdom expressing a new covenant, like the one Jeremiah predicted, to replace the broken old agreement (Jeremiah 31:31-34). This one will be "in their minds" and "on their hearts," and all of the covenant-people will know the Lord.

A full description of the kingdom founded on God's New Covenant cannot be reduced to a few sentences, or even a lengthy treatise. But it can be experienced. Jesus' life, ministry, death, and resurrection embody the kingdom in action. We study the Gospel accounts of Jesus to discover how a citizen of the kingdom lives. Early in Matthew's account, we have had to adjust our thinking. Jesus is no ordinary person; His values and insights are not those of His contemporaries. What God is doing through Him marks Him as unique in His time—and in all times. Yet He repeatedly calls His disciples, even now as then, to follow Him.

Jesus lives His life in kingdom terms, so that through Him God can reveal what human life is like at its highest. He invites us up to His level.

We latter-day disciples may not entirely understand the kingdom about which Jesus spoke, but at least we have learned that it is more permanent than any other government this world has ever seen. It has outlasted them all. The church, which continues Jesus' ministry, has often been twisted nearly out of shape, driven before countless armed

43

foes, perverted from within by leaders observing the letter but not the spirit of the New Covenant, vilified from the left and the right, but as the one body on earth dedicated to kingdom work, it has proved indestructible. (See Matthew 16:18.) As Jesus stood alone against everything His enemies could throw at Him, so the kingdom of which He preached has stood the test of time.

No one enters the kingdom except through repentance. In this respect, Jesus builds on John the Baptist's precedent. John baptized in the Jordan, offering sinners this means to give evidence of repentance. In the waters, they could bury their sins and rise to new innocence.

That innocence is required for the kingdom of Heaven. The child becomes its symbol. (See Matthew 18:1-4; Luke 18:15-17.) A convert begins life again, like a baby. The kingdom belongs to those on whose hearts God has written the New Covenant, and God cannot write on the heart controlled by sin. So repentance opens the doors of the kingdom for the believer.

Jesus' Means: Discipling Others (18-22)

"Come, follow me." From the beginning of His ministry, Jesus is the rabbi, the great teacher, calling to himself persons willing to dedicate themselves to completing His commission. He is a rabbi with a difference, however. He calls disciples, not in order to make life-long scholars of them, nor to make future rabbis (they would always remain disciples), but to prepare them to become heralds and examples of the kingdom. Simon Peter and Andrew, ordinary fishermen before Jesus transforms them into fishers of men, are called from the crowd so that one day, they will be prepared to return to the crowd to lead others into the kingdom.

They do not hesitate. Undoubtedly they have previously heard of the Master. They may have been disciples of John the Baptist (we know Andrew was—John 1:19-42) and may even have been present when Jesus presented himself for baptism (Matthew 3:13-17). They would not have followed blindly. Still, their willingness to walk away from their business speaks loudly of Jesus' magnetism.

His challenge to become "fishers of men" typifies His administrative abilities as well. He takes what we have and turns it into a valuable asset in the kingdom. He never expects of His followers something they cannot give. Rather, He employs what we have and what we are to the best advantage. He already knows of our ability; what He wants is just our availability.

44

Churches sometimes make the mistake of expecting every church member to conform to institutional expectations. Every leader must be able to preside at meetings or in worship services; all faithful members must become Sunday-school teachers. But not everyone is so gifted. Jesus does not insist that every member become like every other member. He does not want duplicate copies; He wants originals. What He wants most of all is discipleship.

Jesus' Demonstration of the Kingdom (23-25)

Look at Matthew's verb forms: Jesus went teaching, preaching, and healing. He has seized the initiative. His ministry is launched.

Teaching. In synagogues, along country lanes, beside the sea— wherever He can gain a hearing, Jesus teaches. From formal exposition of Scriptures to simple narratives, Jesus presents kingdom insights. Although the masses hear Him eagerly, learned scholars stir restlessly in the crowd, finally growing resentful of this uncertified teacher of such penetrating intelligence. We shall trace their increasing hostility through Matthew's Gospel.

Preaching. Preaching differs from teaching as a breathless messenger differs from the relaxed classroom professor. Gospel preaching is limited in scope. It is about good news (which is what *gospel* means). When today's preachers are actually preaching, they are speaking about Jesus and His redemptive ministry. (See 1 Corinthians 15:1-3.) Jesus the preacher brings the exciting news that God is fulfilling His long-standing promise to deliver His people from bondage. At first, the people will only partially understand His message; full comprehension will have to wait until after His death and resurrection. In the meantime, though, they can share His excitement that God is at work on earth to overthrow their bondage and establish a new kingdom.

Healing. His healing is dramatic proof that the new kingdom will be better than the current situation. God desires His people well. Where God is truly in charge, there is "healing of every disease and sickness." Wherever Jesus walks, people bring Him their sick—in Galilee, in the region to the East of the Jordan River called the Decapolis (Ten Cities), in the southern province of Judea and even in its capital city, Jerusalem. The word travels ahead of Him: "Jesus can heal!"

For the most part, Jesus confines His ministry to Jews, although Matthew's summary statement (verse 25) indicates that He also ventures into non-Jewish territory. He speaks frequently in Jewish synagogues, because His commission from God is to concentrate on "the lost sheep of Israel" before sending His disciples into all the world (Matthew 10:6; 28:18-20).

Preaching, teaching, and healing form Jesus' ministry. As Joseph Pulitzer once told journalists that the task of a newspaper is to "afflict the comfortable and to comfort the afflicted," so Jesus comforts men and women upon whom a hostile world treads and challenges the calloused ease of the religiously and politically comfortable. Great crowds flock to Him because He meets their needs. Churches that follow Jesus today adopt the philosophy expressed by Ken Chafin, pastor of Houston's South Main Street Baptist Church, who reports that his church has a group of "Formerly Marrieds" whose motto is, "We have to take anyone who is hurting and love them back to health." Chafin's church learned this ministry from Jesus.

So here they are, the deaf, the disabled, the demoniacs, the epileptics, and the paralytics. Today, we would add others for whom Jesus is concerned: the formerly married, the never married, the married but troubled, the aged, the parentless, the childless, the poor, the helpless, the war victim, the crime victim, and the criminal. Of such is the kingdom of earth. From such is the kingdom of Heaven.

CHAPTER FIVE

The Beatitudes:
Handbook to Happiness

Matthew 5:1-12

"Happiness is what it's all about, man!" From the street child to the philosophy professor, everybody wants to find happiness. The rich young ruler asked Jesus, "What good thing must I do to get eternal life?" (Matthew 19:16). His question is more typical of the first century than it is of ours. Eternity is too far off. We want what we want now. Happiness, not eternity, is what we'd ask Jesus for.

The quest is even built into the American *Declaration of Independence:* "We hold these truths to be self-evident, that all men are created equal, that they are endowed by their Creator with certain unalienable Rights, that among these are Life, Liberty and *the pursuit of Happiness.*" Happiness is not a privilege; it's a right!

If we grant that rather dubious truth, then another question demands an answer: "What *is* happiness?" Several answers have been proposed.

(1) Happiness is **equality.** George Orwell took great delight in puncturing the Communistic myth of equality in his famous *Animal Farm.* Rebellious farm beasts take over the farm in protest against their unequal treatment by the farmer. "From now on," they declare in the story that closely parallels events in Soviet Russia since 1917, "all animals are created equal." That should guarantee universal cheerfulness in the barnyard. What actually occurs, of course, is that the declaration must eventually be amended to fit the truth: "All animals are equal, but some animals are more equal than others."[14] That equality is even possible is a naive hope, let alone a political possibility. Whoever equates happiness with equality dooms himself to disappointment.

---

[14]George Orwell, *Animal Farm* (New York: Harcourt, Brace and Company, 1946), p. 112.

(2) Happiness is **prosperity.** Political dreamers may envision happiness in equality, but the rest of humanity acts as if only material prosperity matters. The Great American Dream consists of large bank accounts, exclusive addresses, and all the rest of the good things money can buy. Maurice Sendak exposes the folly of this fantasy in a little story of a pampered dog who had her own pillows, comb and brush, wool sweater, and two windows to look out of and two bowls to eat from. All this and a master who loved her unreservedly. Still, the dog whimpered, "I am discontented. I want something I do not have. There must be more to life than having everything."[15] There is.

(3) Happiness is a **good marriage and satisfying family life.** "If only I can find the right girl. . . ." "Someday my prince will come. . . ." Such is the stuff of fairy tales. Yet each new generation has to learn the hard way that reality seldom resembles the fantasy. "They were married and lived happily ever after . . ." is the perfect ending of the story in the book. Marriage is just the beginning in life, and the ending cannot be predicted.

Happiness is _____ .

That God is interested in our happiness surprises many people who have only a casual knowledge of Him. The peerless body of teaching we call the Sermon on the Mount begins, however, with a handbook for happiness (the Beatitudes). Jesus signals God's interest in our well-being from the beginning. His word *blessed* is *makarios,* which means *happy* or *fortunate* or even *supremely happy.* The Greeks used the word to speak of the happiness of their gods, especially as they contrasted life among the gods with the general state of mankind on earth. In the Beatitudes, Jesus offers specific guidelines so that His disciples can realize the full joy (a more precise word than happiness for what Jesus has promised—see John 15:10, 11).

Blessed (makarios) originally referred to outward prosperity, but came in time to take on the overtone of moral quality or of high character. Jesus traces the source of joy to spiritual characteristics like humility, sensitivity, and hunger for justice. Not in externals, but in attitudes, is happiness to be discovered. It has to do with people, not things; with giving, not receiving; with humility, not pride; and with becoming, not with having. Jesus departs from Aristotle's famous teaching that "Happiness is something final and self-sufficient and

---

[15]Quoted by Morris B. Parloff, "The Me Degeneration" *Psychology Today* (December, 1979), p. 92.

the end of all action." No, Jesus counters, happiness is not a goal and certainly is not self-sufficient. It is a by-product, and it depends upon one's religious values. From his studies of Jesus' teaching, C. S. Lewis rightly concluded that "joy is the serious business of heaven."[16] So the old man in the Southern train station answered correctly when a man stepped off the train and asked him, "Uncle, do you find anyone around here enjoying religion?"

"Them's as got it is," he replied.

Jesus' "Handbook for Happiness" is for "them's as got" enough interest in religion to listen to Him seriously.

Blessed Are the Poor in Spirit, for Theirs is the Kingdom of Heaven

Only the poor can fully appreciate wealth. Only by admitting your poverty can you hope to overcome it. If you want to achieve happiness, you must begin by confessing you do not have it and have not found the way to get it. Of yourself, you are poor. You need help.

With this admission, you are ready to receive. It is the lesson Paul learned when he begged God to take away his physical affliction. God refused; instead He assured Paul, "My grace is sufficient for you, for my power is made perfect in weakness." When Paul learned this, he began to boast, not of his strength, but of his weakness, "for when I am weak, then I am strong" (2 Corinthians 12:9, 10).

As long as you are convinced that you are self-sufficient, you impair God's ability to help you. Your pride will prevent true worship. What is true of the individual is true of the church: the congregation that boasts that its members are the city's leading citizens, the most highly educated, and most influential and wealthiest will not be able to hear this Beatitude.

Jesus commends those who have nothing to boast about. Pride is not their besetting sin, for they can point with pride to nothing. A well-known football coach, addressing a sportswriter's convention, for a while sounded anything but poor in spirit. He began his speech by quoting from a letter he had just received: "You are the greatest football coach in the world. You are better than Frank Leahy, Knute Rockne, or Bud Wilkinson. And not only are you the greatest coach, you are also the wisest and most handsome." The sportswriters were

---

[16]C. S. Lewis, *Letters to Malcolm: Chiefly on Prayer* (New York: Harcourt, Brace and Company, 1963), p. 93.

stunned by this apparent arrogance. Then he continued. "Incidentally, the letter is signed, 'Mother.'" He was not deceived.

In a memorable exchange between Glendower and Hotspur in Shakespeare's *Henry IV Part I,* the conceited Glendower boasts about his birth:

> Glendower: I say the earth did shake when I was born.
> Hotspur: And I say the earth was not of my mind,
>   If you suppose as fearing you it shook.
> Glendower: The heavens were all on fire, the earth did tremble.
> Hotspur: O, then the earth shook to see the heavens on fire,
>   and not in fear of your nativity.

Glendower, comfortable at the center of his own universe, had no trouble imagining that heaven and earth announced his birth. Of such is not the kingdom of Heaven!

The pride of Glendower, which contrasts in every respect with the poverty of spirit Jesus encourages, is a subtle serpent. In our insecurity, we grasp anything that will promote our egos above our competitors. We will boast of anything, even our humility. During the early days of Christianity, it was common for a new woman convert to cast off her jewelry and fine clothing and adopt the dress of peasants. Women fancied this would mark their contempt for the things of this world. Even this seemingly noble gesture could be motivated by far less than noble reasons, however. Jerome, an early church leader, warned distinguished Roman matrons against going to such an extreme. "Let it not produce pride in you that you have despised the pride of the world; take care lest, since you have ceased to wish to attract notice in garments full of gold, you seek it in sordid attire."

Jerome uncovers the obstacle to becoming poor in spirit: are you *still* attracting attention to yourself? The poor in spirit feel themselves unworthy of notice. They concentrate on the things of God. It is this concentration that gives them the presence of God in their lives.

"The kingdom of heaven" is a Matthean synonym for God. As a good Jew, Matthew frequently substitutes *Heaven* for *God,* a name too holy to profane with overuse. The poor in spirit enjoy the fellowship of God because their attention is on Him and not on themselves.

Blessed Are Those Who Mourn, for They Will Be Comforted

If you have never mourned the death of a loved one, this Beatitude will seem like nonsense. If you have, its wisdom is immediately apparent. Mourning deepens, strengthens, and sensitizes the mourner. No one who has truly loved and lost can ever be the same again. If the love was pure, unadulterated by fear or jealousy or unhealthy dependency, the mourner will be grateful for how much richer his life has become through his relationship with the loved one.

This is not to suggest that we should suffer death gladly. It is rather to hint that Paul speaks with the insight of experience when he writes "that in all things God works for the good of those who love him" (Romans 8:28), even in death. Against the backdrop of God's providential care, Jesus encourages His disciples to learn what sorrow means if we would be fully happy.

Blessed are those who mourn the death of a loved one. They will be comforted. The fraternity of those who have lost a father or mother or child or spouse to death is close and sympathetic. They do not need words to communicate: the deep look into one another's eyes, the tender touch, the catch in the voice when they express condolences, and the quiet "being there" say it all.

Blessed are those who mourn for a world in trouble. How many Scriptures tumble to the front of our minds here:

"For God so loved the world that he gave . . ." (John 3:16).

"Dear friends, let us love one another, for love comes from God. . . . Dear friends, since God so loved us, we also ought to love one another" (1 John 4:7, 11).

"Go and make disciples of all nations . . ." (Matthew 28:19).

"As for you, you were dead in your transgressions and sins, in which you used to live when you followed the ways of this world and of the ruler of the kingdom of the air" (Ephesians 2:1, 2).

"You see, at just the right time, when we were still powerless, Christ died for the ungodly" (Romans 5:6).

Jesus mourned for a world dead in sin. And He did something about it. Abraham Lincoln once said, "I am sorry for the man who can't feel the whip when it is laid on the other man's back." He felt it, and he did something about it. When Jesus visited the tomb of His friend Lazarus, He wept for him (John 11). Then He did something about it. When He sat overlooking Jerusalem, His heart cried out for the city about to be left desolate (Matthew 23:37, 38). He mourned for the city. Then He did something about it—on a cross.

Jesus could not remain aloof from the world in trouble. That is the origin of the gospel. Jesus' disciples will see with Jesus' eyes and feel with Jesus' sympathy. The hunger pangs of the starving, the longings for freedom of the imprisoned, the loneliness of the abandoned, the darkness of the superstitious, the lostness of the lost are always the concern of disciples. They mourn as Jesus mourned. Then they do something about it.

Blessed are those who mourn for themselves. When they confess their desperate plight apart from God's grace, when they acknowledge their sin, then they are ready to receive the comfort of the gospel. "For what I received I passed on to you as of first importance: that Christ died for our sins . . ." (1 Corinthians 15:3). Here is what the Lord wants from us:

> You do not delight in sacrifice, or I would bring it;
>   you do not take pleasure in burnt offerings.
> The sacrifices of God are a broken spirit;
>   a broken and contrite heart,
>   O God, you will not despise (Psalm 51:16, 17).

When the broken-hearted person returns to God, He comforts him.

Blessed Are the Meek,
for They Will Inherit the Earth.

As strange as this Beatitude sounds to our ears, Jesus is not saying anything new. The psalmist had sung centuries earlier,

> A little while, and the wicked will be no more;
>   though you look for them, they will not be found.
> But the meek will inherit the land
>   and enjoy great peace (Psalm 37:10).

This optimistic vision follows the psalmist's plea for peaceful behavior:

> Be still before the Lord and wait patiently for him;
>   do not fret when men succeed in their ways,
>   when they carry out their wicked schemes.
> Refrain from anger and turn from wrath;
>   do not fret—it leads only to evil.
> For evil men will be cut off,
>   but those who hope in the Lord will inherit the land (verses 7-9).

Jesus' meekness must not be confused with weakness. Disciples of Christ are often tempted to skip this Beatitude, because they hold weakness in contempt. They recognize that often mild-manneredness is not so much a matter of Christian character as of fortunate genes. They are built like that. Others of more tempestuous temperament cannot hope to imitate them, and they don't want to.

Such disciples need to consider Moses. He was a man among men, strong of arm and quick of temper. In a fit of righteous indignation, he killed an Egyptian and had to flee for his life. On another occasion, he discovered his people turning from God to idol-worship. In anger he threw to the ground the stone tables of the law, which he had just received on the mountaintop. Yet the Bible describes Moses (in Numbers 12:3) as a "very humble man, more humble than anyone else on the face of the earth." In the Revised and King James versions, the word is "meek." It obviously must not be defined as weakness or spinelessness.

Aristotle is some help here. He defined every virtue as the midpoint between extremes. In this case, meekness is the mean between excessive anger and absence of anger. A meek person reacts, then, with emotion appropriate to the occasion. He exercises self-control, and self-control implies strength. So we might say, "Blessed are the meek, for they have the strength to be humble." This is the sense in which Jesus referred to himself as "gentle and humble [meek] in heart" (Matthew 11:23). See Him before Pilate, receiving those slaps on His face, the spittle running down His cheeks, the cruel mockery assaulting His character—without uttering a word or making a move in His own defense. See Him in the Garden of Gethsemane, pleading to be released from the agony to come, but adding, "Yet not as I will, but as you will" (Matthew 26:39). See Him in the temple with the whip of cords in His hand, driving out the money-changers and tradesmen. See Him on the cross, breathing out His final word, "It is finished." There is only one conclusion: meekness is born of strength.

E. Stanley Jones has described the meek as people who cannot be tempted or bought, since they do not serve themselves. They enjoy the serenity of humility. Their peace comes from an absence of selfish ambition. They have no desire to promote themselves above others. They do not have to be the star of the show or at the head of the line. They do not indulge in their society's shoving to get ahead, because they trust the Father to watch over them.

Their serenity is not to be confused with tranquility. They have not been anesthetized against injustice or cruelty. They fight against evil in any form. Their peace is more like the quiet in the eye of a hurricane. The meek believe with a childlike faith. They trust that the Lord has a purpose for their lives, and they mean to accomplish it. They obey the Christian ethic; they follow the example of Christ; they carry out the Lord's commission.

They are, in other words, God-controlled. Like little children, they are without pretense. Even the scientist T. H. Huxley, who did not believe in God, understood the principle of childlikeness. Without it, no scientific achievements are possible. Huxley wrote to Charles Kingsley one time, "It seems to me that science teaches in most unmistakable terms the Christian conception of entire surrender to the will of God. Science says, 'Sit down before the facts as a little child, be prepared to give up every preconceived notion, be willing to be led to whatever end Nature will lead you, or you will know nothing.'" This is meekness in science. The same meekness is required of faith— the surrender of self to the data of truth.

So Christians surrender to Jesus, the way, the truth, and the life (John 14:6). We have taken our choice. The Bible presents only two alternatives: surrender to Christ or surrender to sin (Romans 6:1-18). In this self-surrender, we achieve self-control, although it is not we but the Spirit of Christ who controls us.

"Blessed are the meek," for meekness means strength, serenity, surrender, and self-control. Such persons will outserve, outlove, and outlast everyone else. They will inherit the earth (and all the other blessings of God).

Blessed Are Those Who Hunger and Thirst for Righteousness, for They Will Be Filled

Hunger is not a common occurrence among most readers of this book. Oh, we have gone without a meal now and then, or have panted for a cold lemonade on a hot day, but we have not been nearly starved nor parched from extreme thirst. We've stared with sympathy at many pictures of little children with stomachs bloated from starvation, but our own bellies are usually comfortably satisfied. Protected as we are by unemployment compensation and welfare benefits, living in a country rich in agricultural production, we can easily miss the real import of Jesus' fourth Beatitude: "Blessed are those who are desperate, who are starving, who will do anything for righteousness."

The Palestinians, to whom Jesus spoke, quickly grasped His meaning. Life was precarious for them. Crops were unpredictable. Water was precious in that desert climate.

Though we don't give them much thought, hunger and thirst pangs are among our most beneficial sensations. Our bodies naturally need water and nourishment; they die without them. Neither, Jesus asserts, can our souls be healthy without the ingredients of righteousness. The soul has, as Kierkegaard has said, "a God-shaped void that only God can fill." Blessed are those who crave God and the kind of life God designed us for with as much intensity as the hungry and thirsty crave food and drink.

An appetite for righteousness has to be cultivated. It is in some respects an acquired taste. Righteousness values relationships as top priority. In the New Testament, the most important relationships of all are based on covenants (agreements) between God and His people. Whatever acts to preserve or enhance these covenant relationships is righteousness. Blessed are you, then, when you yearn with your whole being to be right with God according to the covenant He made with you in Christ. You will be satisfied, because God wants nothing more than to be your God, protector, and friend. You will be satisfied, because nothing compares with pleasing God, and nothing pleases God more than that you should live up to the terms of the covenant, thus becoming everything God wants you to be.

Augustine wrote, in the fourth century after Christ, "Two verbs have built two empires, the verb *to have* and the verb *to be.* The first is an empire of things, material possessions and power. The second is an empire of the Spirit, things that last." Gathering material possessions comes naturally to us; desiring *to be* is an acquired taste.

So cultivate your appetite that you can sing with the psalmist,

> As the deer pants for streams of water,
>   so my soul pants for you, O God.
> My soul thirsts for God, for the living God.
>   When can I go and meet with God? (Psalm 42:1, 2).

Warning: Don't kill your appetite. **Sinful pleasures** can do that. When the apostle Paul began his strenuous ministry, he had a young colaborer named Demas. But Demas didn't last. Paul wrote his biography in nine words: "Demas, because he loved this world, has deserted me" (2 Timothy 4:10).

Sometimes the love is secret. A woman nearly died of malnutrition. She had a small fortune in the bank, but she was not able to feed herself. Her physician had once prescribed that she take a little wine upon occasion to settle her nerves as she was nursing her dying husband. She did as instructed and developed such a dependence upon the wine that after a while, it replaced her food. She lost her appetite for a nutritious diet and almost lost her life. For a long time, no one knew of her problem; she drank in secret.

In addition to the pleasures of this world, the old enemy **self-sufficiency** can also kill your appetite for righteousness. Again, humility is important. The person who boasts of his independence, who glories in his achievements, and who parades in his fine apparel has little longing to change his ways to get right with God or people. It is of just such empty braggarts that Revelation 3:17 speaks: "You say, 'I am rich; I have acquired wealth and do not need a thing.' But you do not realize that you are wretched, pitiful, poor, blind and naked."

Take care not to kill your appetite, but feed yourself a balanced diet of spiritual nutrients. Here are some simple suggestions:

(1) Bible reading. Get a good new version of the Bible and read it. Don't start with Genesis and trudge through the Old Testament books in order. You'll bog down. Start with the Gospel of John, then read Paul's letters to the Philippians, then the rest of the Gospels, and so on. You'll find it the most exciting reading you have ever undertaken. Read it aloud in family gatherings; then discuss what you have read.

(2) Become a part of a Bible study group, preferably one that fosters discussion. You'll find many others who share your hunger.

(3) Develop your prayer life and times of quiet meditation. Pray quietly by yourself. Pray with the family. Pray simply, without undue concern for proper religious vocabulary or English grammar. Just let God know what is on your heart. Then wait upon Him in stillness.

(4) Be a faithful member of the church. Righteousness involves right relationships, remember. You are a Christian, a member of the body of Christ, important to other members and to the Head of the church. Be in attendance on the Lord's Day.

(5) Become a faithful steward of your money. The tenth (tithe) is minimal. It symbolizes your trust in God and desire to serve Him.

(6) Help others to know the Lord. God wants to save them, too. He wants you to help Him do so.

For further insight into righteousness and how to satisfy our craving for it, see Romans 3:23; 4:18-25; 6:15-23. Since we have sinned and failed to achieve righteousness on our own, God has made our relationship with Him right for us (2 Corinthians 5:16-21). He has given us what we could never achieve on our own. "It is by grace you have been saved" (Ephesians 2:5, 8).

Blessed Are the Merciful,
for They Will Be Shown Mercy

Aesop's ancient tale illustrates this Beatitude. A lion was sleeping in his lair when a mouse accidentally ran across the mighty beast's nose and woke him up. Instantly, the lion snatched the mouse in his paw and made ready to dispatch him. Begging the lion's mercy in most pitiable tones, the mouse apologized for offending him and persuaded him that so insignificant a prey was unworthy of his honorable paws. Smiling at the little fellow's fright, the lion generously released him.

Now it happened, as it often does in these tales, that the two were to meet again. The lion, ranging the woods in search of prey, fell into a snare set by some hunters. He was hopelessly trapped. The whole forest trembled at the lion's frightened roar. The little mouse recognized the voice, ran to the spot, and without so much as a fare-thee-well commenced to gnaw through the knot in the cord that bound the beast. He quickly freed the lion.

Aesop's moral: There is no creature so much below another but that he may have it in his power to return a good office.

Mercy is better described than defined. Several Scriptures come to mind:

"Praise be to the God and Father of our Lord Jesus Christ! In his great mercy he has given us new birth" (1 Peter 1:3).

"Speak and act as those who are going to be judged by the law that gives freedom, because judgment without mercy will be shown to anyone who has not been merciful. Mercy triumphs over judgment!" (James 2:12, 13).

"But because of his great love for us, God, who is rich in mercy, made us alive with Christ even when we were dead in transgressions— it is by grace you have been saved" (Ephesians 2:4, 5).

"I desire mercy, not sacrifice" (Hosea 6:6; Matthew 9:13).

"Let us then approach the throne of grace with confidence, so that we may receive mercy and find grace to help us in our time of need" (Hebrews 4:16).

Taken together, these Scriptures describe mercy as a withholding of punishment, a refusal to give someone his "just deserts." Mercy implies compassion, which is not just a feeling of pity, but feeling plus action. It is sympathy that leads to assistance. Mercy is the gracious act of a superior (in strength, title, social position, and/or resources) toward an inferior. God's mercy is most clearly demonstrated in His willingness to send Christ to die for sinful man (Romans 5:8).

The merciful "will be shown mercy." Jesus will return to this theme later when He teaches His disciples to pray for forgiveness (Matthew 6:12). He insures that they will not minimize how essential forgiveness and mercy are: "For if you forgive men when they sin against you, your heavenly Father will also forgive you. But if you do not forgive men their sins, your Father will not forgive your sins" (6:14, 15). For the same reason, Jesus' disciples are not to judge (7:1-5).

Without God's mercy, the Bible repeatedly stresses, you and I have no hope of salvation. Without our showing mercy to others, there is little hope for us. Jesus' parable of the unmerciful servant (Matthew 18:21-35) teaches that unless we are willing to forgive small offenses against us ourselves, we can't hope to expect God to forgive our much graver sin against Him.

The general confession in the Book of Common Prayer is rich in its understanding of God's mercy:

> "Almighty and most merciful Father; We have erred, and strayed from thy ways like lost sheep. We have followed too much the devices and desires of our own hearts. We have offended against thy holy laws. We have left undone those things which we ought to have done; And we have done those things which we ought not to have done; And there is no health in us. But thou, O Lord, have mercy upon us, miserable offenders. Spare thou those, O God, who confess their faults. Restore thou those who are penitent; According to thy promises declared unto mankind in Christ Jesus our Lord. And grant, O merciful Father, for this sake; That we may hereafter live a godly, righteous, and sober life, To the glory of thy holy Name."

Charles Haddon Spurgeon, the famous nineteenth-century London preacher, captured the essence of God's mercy in one of his famous illustrations. A benevolent person had given Mr. Rowland Hill one hundred pounds to pass on to an impoverished minister as an anonymous gift. Mr. Hill thought it best not to give the entire amount at once, so he sent five pounds in a letter which said only, "More to follow." In a few days he sent another five pounds, with the same message. After another day or two came the third, then the fourth, and so on until the entire amount had been received. Having told the story, Mr. Spurgeon added,

> Every blessing that comes from God is sent with the self-same message, "And more to follow." "I forgive you your sins, but there's more to follow." "I justify you in the righteousness of Christ, but there's more to follow." "I adopt you into my family, but there's more to follow." "I educate you for heaven, but there's still more to follow." "I will uphold you in the hour of death, and as you are passing into the world of spirits, My mercy shall continue with you, and when you land in the world to come there shall still be *more to follow*."[17]

---

[17]D. O. Fuller, ed., *Spurgeon's Sermon Illustrations* (Grand Rapids: Zondervan, 1942), pp. 56, 57.

Mercy does not anticipate, because it does not deserve, what it will receive. It does not keep score, it does not withhold itself. It most certainly does not adopt the ethic of the little schoolboy who wrote on his classroom blackboard, "Do one to others as others do one to you." Shakespeare describes it best:

> The quality of mercy is not strain'd;
> It droppeth as the gentle rain from heaven
> Upon the place beneath: it is twice bless'd;
> It blesseth him that gives, and him that takes.
> 'Tis mightiest in the mightiest.[18]

Blessed Are the Pure in Heart, for They Will See God

This is the Beatitude of self-examination. No one else really knows, except God, whether we are pure or not.

The word is *katharos,* which means "pure, unadulterated, clean, and unmixed." It connotes transparency and innocence. One who possesses a pure heart serves without mixed motives or ulterior purposes. He is what he seems to be; he does what he does for the reasons he gives. There is an absence of worldly sophistication about him, an almost childlike innocence to him, similar to the quality Jesus calls for when he insists that "unless you change and become like little children, you will never enter the kingdom of heaven" (Matthew 18:3).

Christianity is an inside-out faith. Hating hypocrisy, it teaches that the inner person must conform to the outer. Persons who "appear to people as righteous but on the inside ... are full of hypocrisy and wickedness" may "look beautiful on the outside but on the inside are full of dead men's bones and everything unclean" (Matthew 23:27, 28). Purity of heart, therefore, can never consist simply of performing certain rituals or carefully regulating diet. "Don't you see that nothing that enters a man from the outside can make him 'unclean'? ... What comes out of a man is what makes him 'unclean' (Mark 7:18-23).

Among God's most precious promises is this one to Israel: "I will give you a new heart and put a new spirit in you; I will remove from you your heart of stone and give you a heart of flesh" (Ezekiel 36:26). A new heart. In this day of heart transplants and artificial heart

---

[18] William Shakespeare, *The Merchant of Venice,* Act IV, Scene 1.

machines, this promise takes on new meaning. As the heart pumps lifeblood to the body, so the "heart" in Scripture represents the center of life itself: the emotions, will, and thinking. Proverbs 23:7 (KJV) puts it best: "As he thinketh in his heart, so is he." Purity in the center of one's being, then, is what Jesus commends here. It is the reverse of what God observed in the days of Noah, when "every inclination of the thoughts of [man's] heart was only evil all the time" (Genesis 6:5). Blessed is the person whose "inclination" is toward purity.

This Beatitude removes the test of character from observable actions to hidden inclinations. No wonder Jesus warns against judging (Matthew 7:1-5); we can observe actions but only guess at what motivated them. God, who sees the secrets of the heart and will one day judge them through Jesus Christ (Romans 2:6), is alone competent to judge. He can't be fooled. We can.

> If we had forgotten the name of our God
>   or spread out our hands to a foreign god,
> would not God have discovered it,
>   since he knows the secrets of the heart? (Psalm 44:20, 21).

Purity begins with the *mind*. If thought is "the soul of the act," as Browning says, or "the seat of action" and "the ancestor of every action" as Emerson has written, then it is imperative to think right. What feeds the mind controls our thoughts. The magazines and books we read, the television programs we watch, the movies we view, the jokes we listen to and repeat, and the environment we inhabit all program our minds and form our thoughts. Bombarded with sexual enticements, educated to grub for money, prodded to seek political or career advancement, scorned into serving self above anything or anyone else—to people like us, any talk of *purity* of thought sounds like Victorian prudery, simply too old-fashioned for this sophisticated age. Yet this is precisely what Jesus commends.

Paul helps our understanding a bit. He exhorts us to bring our thoughts under control, focusing them on "whatever is true, whatever is noble, whatever is right, whatever is pure, whatever is lovely, whatever is admirable" (Philippians 4:8). Fleeting thoughts move too fast for us to control them, but we can control what we concentrate on.

Purity is expressed in *behavior*. Habits of personal hygiene, physical fitness, and avoidance of addictives assist here. Refusal to endanger the body with drugs or drinks or promiscuity is a form of purity. Remember that God made man just "a little lower than the heavenly beings and crowned him with glory and honor" (Psalm 8:5). Some things are beneath such a being. He cannot justify his cheating on God's standards by claiming that he is "only human." To be human, in God's eyes, is to be the best earth has to offer. To live life impulsively, "doin' what comes natcherly," pleading helplessness over one's lusts, is to deny one's divine origins.

Everyone's *feelings* can be purified. A true disciple of Christ will not feel good when he has disappointed God. He will have strong feelings about the importance of his home and family, about his church, about what's right and what's wrong. He will subscribe to the wisdom of a certain father whose son asked, "When will I be old enough to do as I please?" With the insight of experience, the father answered, "I don't know, son. Nobody ever lived that long." So his feelings won't be hurt when he doesn't get his way. What matters more is that God gets His way.

To be pure in heart is "to will one thing," Kierkegaard has written somewhere. Blessed is this pure person. God will reveal himself to such a one. (See Hebrews 11:27 and 1 John 3:2.)

Blessed Are the Peacemakers, for They Will Be Called Sons of God.

This is the Beatitude we love to misunderstand. We tolerate many intolerable situations because, we say, we just want peace. But Jesus does not say, "Blessed are those who desire peace," but, "Blessed are those who *make* peace." Many a home has been led to war by passive parents who "just want some peace and quiet in this house."

The word Jesus uses (*eirene* in Greek, *shalom* in Hebrew) means far more than absence of war or trouble. As the Jewish greeting "Shalom" implies, it connotes everything that makes for a person's highest good. *Peace* is a relationship word, signaling that everything is good between you and God and between you and those whom you greet and with whom you live—family, friends, countrymen, your fellow man. Blessed are you if you contribute to peaceful relations.

Tourists have often written about the twenty-six-foot-high statue of Jesus that stands high in the Andes along an important pass between Argentina and Chile. He holds a cross in His left hand while raising His right hand in an appeal to travelers passing by. The statue is a symbol of peace. Many years ago, the two nations nearly went to war over a dispute. Armed conflict was averted when leaders of both nations recalled what Christ had done for them. This led the nations to melt down their bronze cannons and cast from them a statue of

Christ—from the symbols of destruction to the emblem of peace. They inscribed these words on the base of the statue: "Sooner shall these mountains crumble into dust than Argentines and Chileans break the peace to which they have pledged themselves at the feet of Christ the Redeemer."

Would that such a statue could guard the peace between all nations of the earth! Especially in this nuclear age, the world needs Christian peacemakers. Prospects of an all-out nuclear war horrify peace-loving people everywhere. The world is well on its way to destruction, with instruments of annihilation piled ever deeper in the weapons stores of hostile nations. Otherwise normal human beings dedicate themselves to finding surer and cleverer ways to wipe each other out. This neo-cannibalism infects even the most advanced civilizations and threatens a revival of savage barbarism. Warmakers are everywhere. Where are the peacemakers?

A few years ago, a lavish new resort opened in the Caribbean. The owner, an incurable perfectionist, fussed over every detail. One of his problems was with sliding doors he had installed in the hotel. People kept running into the clear glass. His solution was to order the word *PEACE* etched on the glass. But to solve one problem was to pose another: should *PEACE* be read from the outside or the inside?

He raised a good question. The Bible reads it from both directions. First from the outside. The Prince of Peace had to be sent into this hostile, warring world from the outside. Since then, Christ—who has become our peace (Ephesians 2:14)—dwells inside His disciples, who are one in Him. Their internal peace makes for interpersonal peace that can lead to world-wide peace.

The peacemaker enjoys peace within himself (Psalm 23:1-3), a condition so intertwined in his peace with God as to be inseparable. He is also at peace about his physical well-being and financial security. He agrees with the apostle Paul, who had "learned to be content whatever the circumstances," and could "do everything through him who gives me strength" (Philippians 4:11-13).

A stoic philosopher would have called such contentment the secret of true wealth. Such a truly rich person is prepared to make peace, because his inner contentment prevents his warring with family or neighbors; in fact, it encourages his involvement with them in their struggles. The peacemaker has conquered the selfishness that fosters competition between people. Such a person can genuinely rejoice when others prosper.

The peacemaker has prepared himself to pay the price of peace. In one of his books, E. Stanley Jones warns that peacemakers are often persecuted. Quakers have been hounded by patriots who would not be deprived of their wars. Gandhi was repeatedly tossed into jail for his nonviolent demonstrations on behalf of India's outcasts. Jesus was nailed to the cross by a bloodthirsty mob that preferred almost anybody else to a peacemaker.

Blessed are the peacemakers, for they try the nearly impossible. They search for the best in other persons. They admit their limitations and are slow to find faults in others. Hesitant to condemn but quick to understand a brother's weaknesses, the peacemaker offers grace and forgiveness in place of vengeance. Yet he is bold enough to stand against evil, disciplined enough to insist on order, compassionate enough to embrace even the guilty offender.

It is not easy work, peacemaking. Devotion to the God of peace, honesty with the God of truth, and love for the God of mercy require total commitment from the maker of peace. But peacemakers shall be called sons of God, because they carry on the mission of His only begotten Son. (See 2 Corinthians 13:11; Ephesians 2:14; 1 Corinthians 14:33; and Romans 5:1.)

Blessed Are Those Who Are Persecuted Because of Righteousness, for Theirs Is the Kingdom of Heaven

The Beatitudes abound in paradoxes. When we ask Jesus what we must do to be happy, His replies puzzle and confuse us at first." Be poor," He says. "Be meek, be hungry and thirsty for righteousness, be in mourning." The last is perhaps the strangest of all: "Be persecuted." You should not only accept persecution, but persecution that comes because you have done something right!

What does the disciple do that seems to invite trouble? *Persecution* refers not only to physical brutality, such as Christian martyrs have suffered through the ages, but every form of action that punishes Christians for being Christians.

In the first place, Christians earn violent disapproval through their *stand against the status quo.* There would be no gospel if God had been satisfied with the ways of the world. He would not have sent His Son on a rescue mission if human beings had not been malfunctioning. The gospel is God's attack on the *status quo.* It offends everyone who likes things as they are (1 Corinthians 1:23). Nobody likes being told that he is in the wrong, or that he works for things that are unimportant, or that his god is not the true God. When Jesus' disciples preach the gospel, they can't help making enemies. The partisans

63

of this world counterattack, labeling the disciples misfits, scoffing at their quaint morality, attacking their prudery, impugning their motives, and, in extreme instances, ridding the world of their irritating presence. Persecution in some form is almost inevitable.

Since the majority of people follow the prince of this world (Ephesians 2:1-3), Christians are a minority group. The Christian ethic, with its stern stance regarding honesty, for example, cannot tolerate the "taking" ways of a moral code that justifies this or that breach of honesty because, "after all, everybody's doing it." The Christian sexual ethic, which unites love and sex and marriage, opposes the easy immorality of the Playboy philosophy in its various guises. The Christian who follows Jesus cannot tolerate hatred or jealousy or selfishness in his own life, so without ever preaching to anyone, he becomes a living rebuke to the me-first-ness that is so prevalent. Whoever bucks this *status quo* cannot expect to be accepted.

In the second place, Christians invite persecution by their *advocacy of strange values.* They are not only opposed to current trends but are strong for opposing ones.

"Every one who wants to live a godly life in Christ Jesus will be persecuted, while evil men and imposters will go from bad to worse, deceiving and being deceived" (2 Timothy 3:12). The godly life is what Jesus lived. He was greeted with misunderstanding, envy, scorn, rejection, and finally death. You can count on something of the same, except from those who are likewise striving for godliness. "A student is not above his teacher, nor a servant above his master" (Matthew 10:24).

Why do Christians pursue values that virtually guarantee some form of persecution? Because they choose to give themselves to something eternal. ("Godliness has value for all things, holding promise for both the present life and the life to come"; 1 Timothy 4:8.) When you study Paul's contrast of the works of the flesh and the fruit of the Spirit in Galatians 5:16-24, the choice seems obvious.

But so do the consequences, which will be all the more severe for Christians who *stand up under attack.* Of course, there would be no persecution without resistance. What infuriates the enemy more than the resistance is the Christian's attitude. "Consider it pure joy, my brothers, whenever you face trials of many kinds, because you know that the testing of your faith develops perseverance. Perseverance must finish its work so that you may be mature and complete, not lacking anything" (James 1:2-4). Because he looks for his rewards beyond this life, the Christian can endure anything here. Even tyrants can't bully Christians into submission. James VI of Scotland tried to silence Andrew Melville, the Scottish reformer. In extreme anger, the king threatened to imprison Melville, who calmly instructed his monarch,

> I must tell you, there are two kings, and two kingdoms in Scotland; there is Jesus Christ, the king of the church, whose subject King James VI is, and of whose kingdom he is not a king, nor a lord, nor a head, but a member. . . . We will yield to you your place and give you all due obedience; but again I say, you are not the head of the church; you cannot give us eternal life, which even in this world we seek for, and you cannot deprive us of it."

Melville escaped imprisonment for a while by fleeing to England, but he later was locked up in the Tower of London for five years for boldly resisting the king's interference in the work of the church. He would not buckle under attack.

Exhorting besieged Christians to "be strong in the Lord and in his mighty power" (Ephesians 6:10), Paul encourages us to prepare for inescapable spiritual warfare. "Therefore put on the full armor of God, so that when the day of evil comes, you may be able to stand your ground, and after you have done everything, to stand" (6:13). Stand when your employment is threatened, when you are socially ostracized, when your financial security is at stake, when your family misunderstands, and when you wonder whether you have the strength to take any more. Stand.

Early Christians needed this encouragement. They were slandered and reviled, often with the most absurd charges. Their enemies accused them of cannibalism, because they "ate the body and drank the blood" of Jesus Christ in Communion. They reviled them for sexual immorality, certain that the disciples were meeting for weekly orgies they called Love Feasts. They hated Christians for splitting up families, which, in fact, did sometimes happen when one member became a Christian and was disowned by the rest of the family. And, of course, there was always the charge of treason, since Christians claimed to belong to another kingdom and refused to worship Caesar as God.

To endure so much abuse, Christians relied on Jesus' promise of a great reward. Jesus assured them that "theirs is the kingdom of heaven," and "great is your reward in heaven."

It was reward enough to be numbered among "the prophets who were before you." Christians no less than Jews honored Elijah, Isaiah, Ezekiel, and the many other faithful spokesmen of God.

Courageous and indomitable, dedicated to the truth whatever the cost, these giants of the faith frequently paid for their devotion to God with excruciating suffering. God's truth tellers seldom endear themselves to office holders at any level, but later generations esteem them highly. To be named among them is an honor indeed.

Jesus mentions the fellowship of the prophets because Christians share with them the charge of proclaiming the message of hope to a lost world. Since the world hated them, and hated Jesus (John 15:18, 19), it will hate Jesus' chosen ones.

Inherent in the reward is *the knowledge that we belong to God.* He is our King, and our King reigns above all others. Thus, in periods of persecution, we may seem to be losing, but only temporarily. In the end, God's kingdom will triumph. It is not limited by time and space; it holds sway over Heaven and earth, over life and death. His kingdom is forever, and in His kingdom there is neither hunger nor thirst nor pain nor suffering anymore (Revelation 7:15-17; 21:1-4).

CHAPTER SIX

Living the Gospel;
Fulfilling the Law

Matthew 5:13-48

Disciples Are Influential (5:13-16)

When you ask yourself who made you as you are, you discover something fascinating about the power of human personality. Leaving aside for the moment such obvious answers as God or parents or schoolteachers, think instead of those people in your past who changed your thinking on some subject, or who guided you for a while, or who left you richer than you were before they met you. What you'll find is that your life has been shaped not so much by the famous or powerful persons of this world, but rather by quiet persons who probably have no idea they had any influence on you.

Albert Schweitzer, musing on this subject, thought of many people in his youth who had given him something or were something to him without even realizing it. Some of them had never uttered a word to him, others he had only heard of, yet they touched his life in significant ways. "Much that I should otherwise not have felt so clearly or done so effectively was felt or done as it was, because I stand, as it were, under the sway of these people."[19]

To measure the power of personality, think of a newborn baby. When our firstborn came into our family, we quickly learned what real power is. She couldn't talk. We held no animated conversations. She spoke no orders, although she certainly motivated us. She did not consciously try to influence our decisions, yet little in our household remained unchanged when she assumed command from her cradle.

This inherent power explains why God, when He wanted to change the world, did not resort to bombs or bulldozers, or even billions of dollars. He sent a baby.

That baby was special, but in a little different way, so is every baby.

---

[19]Charles R. Joy, ed. *Schweitzer Anthology* (Boston: Beacon Press, 1956), p. 151.

Every personality can affect others for better or for worse. It is this power of personality to influence that informs Jesus' teaching about salt and light. This is a discomforting passage because we can't get around it. You can read the Great Commission (Matthew 28:18-20), for example, and excuse yourself because there is no way, you tell yourself, for you to become a missionary. (This is not what the Commission says precisely, but you can always rationalize your way out.) There is no escape from this portion of the Sermon on the Mount, though. These words are for us. Jesus wants His disciples to exert a powerful influence for good wherever we are. Since we are already influential, He challenges us to be a positive, and not a negative, force.

Like Salt

Our word *salary* comes from the Latin *salarium,* salt. Before refrigeration, salt preserved food. In arid Palestine, meat could not have been kept without salt. It meant the difference between life and death. So important was it that *salarium* literally meant "salt money," which Roman soldiers received as part of their pay.

Salt is still used as a *preservative.* Fishermen salt their catches; housewives salt their pickles. Its *penetrating* quality makes it ideal for use on icy roads and sidewalks. Its *purifying* quality is good medicine, as its use in salt-water gargles proves. Visit the Dead Sea in Palestine, so saline that no organic life can be found in its waters.

Christians can influence others by *preserving* the best traditions and morality of their society. Their motive is to preserve lives, to rescue the perishing. They do this by *penetrating* into the heart of cultures and into the hearts of individuals, and into the core of any issue that affects the welfare of mankind. They never content themselves with surface living or superficial loving. Theirs is a *purifying* presence. Seeking holiness for themselves, they become the cause of more ethical behavior in others. What would our society be like without the hospitals, schools, rescue missions, legislation, churches, and other benevolent institutions fostered by Christian activists?

Salt is also a *seasoner.* It makes insipid food palatable. It brings out the natural flavors. Christians are to be such salt. Contrary to ill-informed critics, Christ does not take the zest out of living. He makes it even more enjoyable. He does not encourage a dismal, gray existence. He inspires joy and challenges His followers to become infectiously joyful. There is radiance in Christian living. Its serenity stands out in bold relief against the pessimism of the world; its laughter abounds, its singing uplifts, its hope encourages wherever it exists.

Jesus is not speaking here of the *musts* or *don't*s that people some-times mistakenly attribute to Christianity. Rather, He suggests that His disciples season society because they accentuate the positive. They are affirming, life-loving people. They have said yes to God and yes to whatever constitutes abundant life. They are by no means escapists. Although they anticipate a future in Heaven with their Lord, that hope does not lead them to abandon earthly joys; it just prevents their taking anything strictly earth-bound too seriously. They have no need for artificial stimulants or depressants to get their kicks or to calm their nerves. They love life, they love God, and they love people. The earth is improved by their living on it.

Jesus provides the example, as always. Study Him closely as you read through Matthew. You'll see Him surrounded by crowds of peo-ple who are attracted by His vitality. Their lives are trapped in dreary routine. His is obviously different. He stands for something; He is going someplace. He offers an exciting alternative to their humdrum existence. He is the original Salt.

Like Light

He is also the original Light. "While I am in the world," He re-minds His disciples, "I am the light of the world" (John 9:5). Since He is no longer here, He has passed His illuminating duties on to His disciples. "You are the light of the world [now], a city on a hill [that] cannot be hidden" (Matthew 5:14).

You disciples are to be obvious. You are to light the way for others. In an adult Bible discussion, the class debated the relative effective-ness of the married Protestant minister and the Roman-Catholic celi-bate priest. The minister leading the discussion livened the argument by presenting what he thought was a pretty convincing case for celi-bacy, citing such matters as the additional time an unmarried religious leader could give to the church, the fewer stresses he would have regarding finances and personal decisions, and so on. Finally, a mem-ber of the class offered this rebuttal: "No, you have chosen the harder but more important way. Those of us who live in the world, who have families to take care of and jobs to perform and time clocks to punch, need someone who is in the same boat we are to show us how to succeed. We need to see him overcome obstacles so that we will know how to do it ourselves."

Someone to show the way. Someone to light the path.

When Jesus told His disciples that He was the light of the world, He was preparing to heal a blind man (John 9). He violated the

Sabbath to do so and stirred up yet another controversy. His enemies tried to force the formerly blind man to give them evidence that would condemn Jesus for breaking the law. "We know this man is a sinner," they told him.

"Whether he is a sinner or not, I don't know," the man answered. "One thing I do know. I was blind but now I see" (John 9:24, 25).

He was just doing what Jesus asks all His disciples to do. Jesus doesn't expect us to answer all the theological or philosophical problems posed by skeptics, but we can tell what we know: once we were blind to the Lord, blind to life, blind to the worthwhile in life, blind to the right, blind to the transforming power of God, blind to our own sinfulness, and blind to so much that makes life meaningful— but now we see! And we want to help others see. We who were darkness have become light. (See also Ephesians 5:8, 9; Philippians 2:14, 15; Psalm 27:1; 1 Peter 2:9.)

Dr. Viktor Frankl's moving account of his days in a Nazi concentration camp during World War II proves that one's light can shine even in the most extreme circumstances.[20] He describes the horror of being stripped of everything: of home, family, clothing, wedding ring and precious things, even of hair, left in stark nakedness with no hope of escape. Then to be tossed some dirty rags recently stripped from a corpse. Then sent to work for the enemy. Dr. Frankl asked himself how men could continue to live in such depraved conditions. What gave their life meaning? And what made some rise above others, seemingly more able to withstand the pressures on them? His prison experience taught him that men and women can have everything else taken from them, but they still retain a choice of action. He saw some heroic behavior. He observed great souls who comforted others, even to giving away their last meager piece of bread. There weren't many like this, but there were enough of them to prove that although one has nothing else left, nobody can rob you of your right to choose your attitude. That's always yours.

What you do depends on what's within. P. T. Forsythe is right, "If within us we find nothing over us, we succumb to what is around us."[21] If what is within is from the Father, we can be salt and light wherever we are.

---

[20]Victor Frankl, *Man's Search for Meaning* (New York: Washington Square Press, 1963).

[21]P. T. Forsythe, *Positive Preaching and the Modern Mind* (Grand Rapids: Baker Book House reprint, 1980), p. 47.

Do Not Misunderstand Jesus (5:17-20)

Jesus is easily misunderstood. Sometimes He sounds like a revolutionary set on overthrowing the traditions of His religion and nation; at other times, like this one, He presents himself as the strictest defender of "the smallest letter," "the least stroke of a pen" of the law. Sometimes He encourags His disciples to ignore the fussy rules of the Pharisees (9:14-17), but here He demands greater attention to rules than even the Pharisees observed. What is He up to?

We must remember who these Pharisees and teachers of the law are. The Pharisees are members of the strictest, the most "religious" sect of Judaism. Teachers of the law are the strictest of the strict, the most learned members of the Pharisaic sect. They know the law and observe it. To the average Jew, then, the Pharisees and teachers not only explain the sacred writings, they live them. Their conduct is the essence of holiness. They can tell you how many positive and negative commands are in the law, how these commands have been interpreted by generations of scholars, and how they are to be rightly obeyed. And they obey them! Yet, Jesus insists, His disciples must be even more righteous than they.

"The Law or the Prophets" (Matthew 5:17) refers to the entire Old Testament. The Jews had more instructions than these, however, because centuries of scribes had added their interpretations of the larger principles. They specified, for example, what was, or was not, work on the Sabbath. These explanations were called the Oral Law, and were handed down from generation to generation by the scribes. Finally, in the middle of the third century A.D., these interpretations were summarized, written, and codified. This written form is called the Mishnah (in English, it forms a book of almost 800 pages). Later Jewish scholars provided commentaries now known collectively as the Talmud. The legalistic mind is forever defining and refining laws.

Strict adherence to the laws, however, is not what Jesus means by righteousness. He appeals for right conduct with God and man. Jesus pronounces blessing on one "who hungers and thirsts for righteousness" (Matthew 5:6). Righteousness is not religiousness or legal punctiliousness. The last thing Jesus wants from His disciples is closer attention to the niceties of ritual conduct or greater expertise in the trifles of legalism. Instead, He commends the person whose appetite can be satisfied only by good relations with God and other people. Moral conduct and personal relationships are what the law is really about. God has always been more concerned about the way we get long with one another than about the religious acts we perform.

This was the invarying theme of the prophets. Let Amos speak for all of them:

> I hate, I despise your religious feasts;
>   I cannot stand your assemblies.
> Even though you bring me burnt offerings and grain offerings,
>   I will not accept them.
> Though you bring choice fellowship offerings,
>   I will have no regard for them.
> Away with the noise of your songs!
>   I will not listen to the music of your harps.
> But let justice roll on like a river,
>   righteousness like a never-failing stream! (Amos 5:21-24).

God's primary concern is not in how properly or how often we bow to Him. Not that bowing is wrong or irrelevant; it is neither. But what God desires more than proper ritual is that His people be righteous, and as Amos' preaching explains, righteousness means justice. We cannot be holy before God and unjust in dealings with others.

In this, then, our righteousness is to surpass that of the Pharisees and teachers of the law. They may outstrip us in their grasp of Scripture and performance of ritual, but they neglect the weightier matters of the law like "justice, mercy and faithfulness" (Matthew 23:23). Jesus appeals to His disciples to be salt and light. This requires us to be righteous, but never self-righteous.

Self-righteousness hurts God's kingdom on earth. Some people seem so "religious" that they ruin religion for others, like some teetotalers who drive others to drink, or pacifists who make you angry enough to fight. George Bernard Shaw's *Man and Superman* cleverly distinguishes between true and false righteousness. An old woman has died and gone to hell. This surprises her, for in life she had been a respectable church member and had gone regularly to confession. She loved confession. She enjoyed it so much that she confessed sins she hadn't even committed. But when she arrived at her eternal destination, she complained, "Oh! and I might have been so much wickeder! All my good deeds wasted! It is unjust." Hers was self-righteousness, with little attention to good relationships.

Reading Matthew 5:17-20 immediately following Jesus' teaching on salt and light leads to the conclusion that what Jesus most wants from us is that we light up *others'* lives. His own ministry demonstrates how to do it. He lived for others. He ate at a tax collector's table; He broke bread with a prostitute; He worked among the sick like a good physician; He endured criticism for keeping bad company.

72

Like salt, which has to be sprinkled around to be useful, Jesus and His disciples mingled with people of all kinds, for *their* sakes.

Righteousness does not fuss over accumulating points toward a reward for good behavior. Righteousness lights up others' lives. It is the human conduit through which God can express His love. Any rules that obstruct the flow of love must be abolished. Any person who cares more about observing the rules than about passing on God's love becomes such an obstruction. This is behind Jesus' running battle with Pharisees and teachers of the law who, in their self-righteousness, turn others away from the love of God.

No, Jesus did not come to abolish the law. He came to fulfill it, to bring it to completion, to make unmistakably clear what God intended when He revealed the law in the first place. We shall therefore not play fast and loose with God's revelation, but shall observe its intent to the fullest. In the verses to follow, Jesus shows us how.

How to Light Up Others' Lives (5:20-48)

This long passage should be kept together. It is like a book in six volumes, held in place on the shelf by two bookends. One bookend (Matthew 5:20) reads, "Unless your righteousness surpasses that of the Pharisees and teachers of the law, you will certainly not enter the kingdom of heaven." The other one, at the end of the passage, is one of Jesus' most disturbing utterances: "Be perfect, therefore, as your heavenly Father is perfect" (Matthew 5:48).

Perfection connotes completion or fulfillment of design. When applied to persons, it means that the perfect one has attained maturity, has fulfilled his or her potential, and has fleshed out God's original design for the person. Putting one bookend beside the other helps us understand that Jesus expects His disciples to stop holding up teachers of the law and Pharisees as the examples of religious perfection; they must imitate someone higher, the Perfect One himself. Religious leaders may be fine examples of external behavior, but God looks on the inside, and hopes to find His reflection there.

Each of the six volumes of the book of righteousness begins with something like, "You have heard that it was said to the people long ago.... But I tell you...." Then Jesus introduces His better way.

Volume One: Do Not Murder—Do Not Even Be Angry With Your Brother (20-26)

Murder is just the last step, the physical application of the anger that motivates it. First comes the insult (or supposed insult), then the

73

taking of offense (or the perception of being cheated, or whatever), followed by the anger. Anger mixes with bitterness, hatred, fear, and a whole complex of dangerous emotions. They lead to murder. The Pharisees would certainly agree with Jesus that murder is wrong. They can boast of never having killed anyone. But Jesus hopes His disciples will be able to claim even more, that they have never been angry enough to want to kill.

Raca is an Aramaic term of contempt. Jesus forbids contemptuous language that lowers another person's self-esteem or causes him to lose face in the eyes of others. Contempt is a kind of soul-murder. Your anger kills any relationship you might have with the person. The old saw, "He is a very even-tempered person—angry all the time," sounds humorous at first. But only at first. Such a person is his own worst enemy. He is gradually committing suicide by making life-sustaining relationships impossible.

Since you cannot be on good terms with God when you are on bad terms with your brother (1 John 4:20), you cannot in good conscience offer any gift to God, who cares as much about your interpersonal relationships as the one you desire with Him. So first heal the breach between you and your brother; then return to worship.

Lawsuits are to be avoided. Why should anyone need to sue you, since you bear ill will to no one? You cannot enter into bitter litigation without its taking its toll on your attitude. If you have refused to do everything possible to be reconciled to your brother before court proceedings begin, you who refused to extend grace cannot now expect anything less than the full weight of the law to fall on you. You who earlier castigated your brother in anger, in contempt *("raca")*, and with insults ("You fool!") have invited the consequences of hell itself. Anger is a most serious offense to the God of righteousness.

Volume Two: Do Not Commit Adultery — Do Not Even Lust (27-30)

No verses more decisively separate Jesus' ethic from our easy modern morality. Many counselors in matters sexual and moral flatly disagree with Jesus. "Sex is not a moral question," they argue. "There are no absolutes," they comfort their counselees. "The question should not be, 'It is morally right or wrong to have premarital or extramarital sex?' but, 'Is it socially acceptable, is it personally rewarding, does it enrich human life, or does it harm anyone?'" From the stern admonitions of our Victorian predecessors to the soothing prescription to be certain to make your sex life "meaningful"—how far we have come in this century!

When Jimmy Carter was running for the Presidency of the United States, he confessed to a reporter that he had occasionally looked at a woman lustfully. The secular press laughed at his naivete. Surely no one takes a harmless "look" seriously. But Carter was taking Jesus seriously, and his fellow Christians understood.

A Pharisee can boast, "Why no, I've never committed adultery. I have never been unfaithful to my wife." His pride is without consequence as far as Jesus is concerned, however. "If you have committed adultery with your eye, you have, in fact, committed adultery in every way except physically." What you call pure behavior may be only failure of nerve. Given different circumstances, if you thought you would not be found out, you may have given in to your lustful eye.

Behind Jesus' injunction is His high regard for women. How He must shudder at today's proliferating pornography industry with its cruel debasing of women. He can be no more pleased with the popular relaxed standards of sexual behavior, but not for the reason that most men will attribute to Him. They think He's against sex. He's not. He is against sexual exploitation.

A woman went to see her minister in deep distress. She and her husband lived in a neighboring community in one of the city's most luxurious suburbs. A sophisticated upper-class couple, they frequently attended the many neighborhood parties that, more often than not, ended in wife-swapping. Her husband enjoyed himself immensely, she said, but she just felt cheap. She wanted to keep her husband but couldn't stand what was becoming of her. She was losing her last bit of self respect. It was evident her husband had no respect for her. She was a victim of the new morality.

Jesus will have none of it. Adultery violates the sanctity of the marriage bond. Two cannot really be one if a partner wanders from bed to bed. Nor, Jesus correctly observes, can the two be one if a partner's mind is wandering into mental adultery through unchecked ogling. He fails to pay proper respect to his wife, and he turns the other women he leers at into mere sex objects.

This temptation is so powerful for normal men, though, that even more powerful restraints are needed. It is better to lose part of your body than your whole soul!

Volume Three: Do Not Divorce Without a Certificate — Do Not Divorce at All (31, 32)

Volumes Two and Three cannot be separated. Jesus' respect for women and for the institution of marriage go hand in hand. He raises marriage from a mere legal arrangement to the level of mutual commitment.

Jesus was not the first to speak against divorce. His fellow Jews were respected by other nations because of their high view of marriage at a time when Greeks and Romans divorced in huge numbers. Nevertheless, even the Jews made dissolving a marriage relatively painless. A simple writ of divorce (initiated by the husband, not the wife) could finish the marriage (Deuteronomy 24:1). The charge was "uncleanness." Scholars debated what uncleanness in the wife meant. Some agreed with the school of Shammai that only unchastity could be meant. Others, siding with the school of Hillel, allowed almost anything that displeased the husband to be called "uncleanness." What was not ever questioned was that the man, not the woman, had legal standing. In the eyes of the law, she was property, not person.

Jesus seems to advocate the cause of the wife here. He notes that a man who divorces his wife "*causes* her to commit adultery." The husband is forcing her to break her marriage promises. Whether she has been guilty of anything or not, her standing in society will be as one who has committed adultery. She cannot become a "single adult" or a "career woman" in our modern sense. (The only career women in Palestine were prostitutes.) Further, any other man who might marry her will, in effect, be committing adultery, since she really belongs to another man.

Jesus' argument is not so much *against* divorce as *for* the permanence of marriage. As He explains later, "What God has joined together, let man not separate" (Matthew 19:6). God has never been in favor of divorce. He allowed Moses to permit it only because men's hearts are hard (Matthew 19:8). In this respect, as in others in this six-volume book, Jesus is upholding perfection, "as your heavenly Father is perfect."

His example is the first marriage. The couple in Eden (Genesis 2:18ff.) were made for each other. God concluded that it was not good for a man to be alone, so He created woman. Clearly, marriage is more than than physical union, more than joint housekeeping, more than a mechanism for propagating the race. It is even more than companionship. It is the spiritual fusion of two persons into one, each being completed in the other. The union is symbolized in, and in part achieved through, sexual expression. The pure union can only be harmed, then, by sexual indulgence elsewhere or through the deliberate wrenching apart of the partners.

76

When divorce rends the marriage, the personal growth and nurturing that is realized through pledged faithfulness to each other also stops. Nothing calls out the best in us like loyalty to vows to be true and faithful "for better or for worse, for richer or for poorer, in sickness and in health." Perhaps Humpty Dumpty had this wisdom in mind as he advised Alice in Lewis Carroll's famous story,

> "I never ask advice about growing," Alice said indignantly.
> "Too proud?" Humpty Dumpty inquired.
> Alice felt even more indignant at this suggestion. "I mean," she said, "that one cannot help growing old."
> "One can't, perhaps," said Humpty Dumpty, "but two can."

Jesus holds up marital fidelity as an essential in achieving a righteousness that exceeds that of Pharisees and scribes. It is a must if we would be perfect "as [our] heavenly Father is perfect." One further word: Throughout these six volumes, Jesus teaches a very high standard for His disciples. He does not whitewash sin. He does not compromise anything in order to make His teaching more palatable. But neither does He make failure to attain any one of these standards an unforgiveable sin. He does not even hint that if you commit divorce, you are forever excluded from the kingdom of Heaven, any more than He teaches that taking oaths or committing murder is unpardonable. It is sin, yes. Unforgiveable? No.

Volume Four: Do Not Break Your Oath—Do Not Swear at All (33-37)

If you always speak honestly, you won't have to utter a special oath to make people believe you. When you say yes, they'll know you mean yes. From the child's "Cross my heart, hope to die; stick a needle in my eye" to the adult's swearing in court "to tell the truth, the whole truth, and nothing but the truth," oaths are supposed to convince the hearers that this time, at least, the speaker is being truthful. The prevalence of oaths testifies to the scarcity of honesty. Jesus wants disciples who are so transparently honest that people can always count on their word. Such integrity involves punctuality, dependability, financial integrity, and keeping promises. It requires a certain precision in choice of vocabulary. When movies that used to be merely stupendous, daring, and sensational are succeeded by others that are super stupendous, extra-daring, spectacularly-sensational, you can hardly blame people for their skepticism about advertisements. A gasoline customer, to take another industry, noticed that the service station was charging a little more per gallon than on his last stop there. "Oh," the hardened attendant explained, "they've added another adjective."

Oaths become required operating procedure when even top executives believe lying is necessary in business. In the *New York Times* a few years ago, a new ruling by the National Labor Relations Board was published. It stated that it was now permissible for either union or management to lie to workers when trying to persuade them to vote for or against a proposed contract. Here's the ruling: "Exaggeration, inaccuracies, partial truths, name calling, and falsehoods, while not condoned, may be excused as legitimate propaganda before a union representation election." Even the *Times* editors were upset. They editorialized, "If respect for the commandment, 'Thou shalt not bear false witness' lapses, there will be no hope of maintaining a free society of self-governing men." Without a certain modicum of honesty, no democracy or republic can exist.

Jesus does not promise that if you live an honest life, everything will go well for you. He would probably not agree with the pragmatic cynicism of Benjamin Franklin's dictum, "Honesty is the best policy." He wants more from us than a policy designed to get us ahead in the world. He desires integrity that tells the truth whether it gets us something or not. (See Leviticus 19:11, 12; Exodus 20:7, 16; Numbers 30; 1 Peter 1:22; Psalm 25:5; 51:6.)

Volume Five: Eye For Eye—Do Not Resist an Evil Person (38-42)

The Old Testament ethic of an eye for an eye was, in its time, a giant step forward. It vastly improved upon the older blood feud ethic, which held that if you do anything against any member of my clan, it becomes the duty of my entire clan to retaliate against you and your whole clan. Carry things far enough, and you will quickly solve the world's problem of over-population. Exodus 21:20-25; Leviticus 24:19, 20; and Deuteronomy 19:21 offer a better way. They limit vengeance to the value of the object taken or damaged. They hint of mercy. And they were seldom applied literally, being quickly supplemented by a fine system based on approximate value. An injury was evaluated in money, and recompense was paid in currency. A similar system still operates in civil justice today.

Jesus expects more of His disciples, however. In their reach for perfection, they will imitate God, who returns good for evil. If He did not, where would we be?

"If someone strikes you on the right cheek, turn to him the other also." If someone insults you, He means, since a slap on your right

78

cheek would come from the back of your adversary's hand. He doesn't mean to hurt you so much as to shame you. How should you respond? With restraint, not revenge.

A certain minister applied Jesus' instruction—almost. Before entering seminary, he had been a rounder. A large, muscular man, he had sincerely dedicated himself to the Lord's ministry and tried his best to live up to the standards of the Sermon on the Mount. But one day, he was confronted by one of his old opponents who, just learning of his clerical status, crossed the room and with all his might let the minister have it on the right cheek. The minister did not defend himself. Instead, he turned the other cheek. His opponent let him have it on that one, too. With that, the preacher said, "Right there my instructions end." Then he floored the man.

Jesus is not to be taken so literally. His point is to meet insult with restraint and to go to some trouble to do good to those who abuse you. This instruction had specific meaning for Jesus' early disciples, because they lived in occupied territory. Roman soldiers could actually take their tunic or force them to carry the soldiers' gear for a mile. In Persia, citizens could be compelled to ride a horse from one place to another to carry mail in an emergency. Every country has similar duties that officials can impose. Jesus teaches us to do more than we are compelled to do. Do not insist on your rights. Insist rather on your responsibilities as citizens of the kingdom of God. You are to do everything possible to break down hostility among men and to foster good relations.

"Always return good for evil," Mark Twain has counseled. "It will drive them crazy." This is not what Jesus has in mind. Rather, He does not wish the conduct of His disciples to be dictated by others. They must act, not react. Theirs should be the philosophy of the city businessman who bought his newspaper at the same newsstand every morning. Without fail, the grumpy news vendor growled about this or that or something else. Every morning, the businessman cheerfully greeted him with a friendly, "Good morning," made his purchase, thanked him politely, and left with, "Have a good day." A friend was with him one morning. Observing the exchange, he asked as they left, "How can you be so cheerful when that guy is such a grouch?"

"Why should I let him dictate my behavior or ruin my day?" his friend explained.

Jesus concerns himself more with inner attitudes than with outer behavior, remember. So live that your attitude toward others is one of good will, even if theirs is not. Be determined that you will do good to all people, even when they do not return the favor. Give your best, your most, even when your efforts are spurned. Somebody, somewhere, has to break the cycle of human hostility.

Mark Twain's classic *Huckleberry Finn* includes a section satirizing the senseless but long-standing feud between the Shepherdsons and the Grangerfords. It's a masterpiece. By this time in the two clans' histories, they have been fighting for generations. They have forgotten what sparked the feud, but they know that their family honor depends on getting even for something. Twain ruthlessly exposes their childishness and helps us laugh at ourselves as well. At this stage in human history, we can no longer afford to marshall our energies in getting even with anybody. Maturity—perfection—demands that we act in freedom and not in slavish reaction to what someone else does to us.

If an illustration of the necessity for Jesus' teaching is wanting, it can quickly be found in the Middle East. So long as Palestinians and Israelis execute their senseless plans to get even with each other, there can never be peace. Someone must call a halt to the cycle of revenge, go the second mile, and give to the one who asks. In the last analysis, there is no alternative to Jesus' ethic here—except mutual annihilation. We must respond with restraint when insulted, with respect when threatened, with more than is asked, with generosity rather than greed—with good and not evil. This alone is the way to peace. And to perfection.

Volume Six: Love Your Neighbor—Love Your Enemies (43-47)

Be like your Heavenly Father, who does good even to those who hate Him. He causes the sun to shine on the just and unjust. He does not discriminate against them when they despise Him. So when you are hated, remember how your Father treats His enemies. If they hate, love. God so loved the world, the good *and* the bad, that He gave His Son. Christ died for all.

Jesus is not quoting any particular Old Testament verse here. Nowhere in the thirty-nine books can you find, "Love your neighbor and hate your enemy." This is, instead, the teaching of later interpreters of the law. In several instances, the Old Testament instructs Israelites to help their enemies: Exodus 23:4, 5; Proverbs 25:21, 22. So Jesus is not introducing something never heard before. Jews have long known they are to help their enemies, but Jesus adds a new dimension: Love your enemies. *Love* in the New Testament is the English translation of several Greek words. Here the word is *agape,* the highest and noblest form of love. *Agape* is used when the writers speak of the love of God for man and of man for God. This love is neither romantic nor sentimental; it is not dependent on feelings. An act of the will, love works for the very best on behalf of the one loved, no matter how the loved one responds.

Love for neighbor or kinsman is relatively easy. Love for an enemy or stranger or persecutor is the supreme test of Christian maturity. Jesus would only be fully understood after His death on the cross. That death is what love does. When Jesus healed the high priest's servant, who was among the mob arresting Him in Gethsemane (Luke 22:51), and when He forgave His killers as He was dying on the cross (Luke 23:34), He defined *love* for all time. His enemies wielded their military and political power over Him, but regardless of what they did to Him, He assumed moral command of the situation. He would love in spite of everything.

Love does not seek vengeance. It prays for the enemy. A young minister learned this truth the hard way. There was a movement under way to oust him from his pastorate. He had inadvertently offended a strong church leader, who then went to work to have the young man dismissed. For a while, it seemed that he would have his wish.

Nursing his abused feelings, the minister became bitter. He could not understand why the respected older leader had turned on him. He had done nothing to deserve this treatment. In spite of his theological training, the younger man gave way to anger and resentment. Surely the Lord did not expect him to take such abuse.

In the midst of this hassle, the minister still had to prepare his weekly sermons. The text he had much earlier assigned himself for the next Sunday was this one: "Love your enemies and pray for those who persecute you." He tried to rationalize that this text did not need to be taken literally in his own situation. But he couldn't convince himself. Jesus' words would not leave him alone. They haunted him by day, they kept him awake at night. Finally, he yielded to the Lord's command. "I clinched my fist, gritted my teeth, and began praying for the louse," he later recalled. "Then the strangest things began to happen. I discovered that you can't pray for somebody and go on hating him. Your hatred turns to tolerance, your tolerance to understanding, your understanding to compassion, your compassion to forgiveness, and your forgiveness to love. No, we never did become great friends, but it wasn't my fault we didn't. I forgave him. He was no longer my enemy."

Nothing demands more trust in the Lord than praying for those who persecute us. Such prayer requires humility, but it can turn an enemy into a friend. How many marriage difficulties could be overcome, how many church divisions healed, how many international tensions eased through such prayer!

The Final Bookend: Be Perfect, Therefore, as Your Heavenly Father Is Perfect

"Be imitators of God, therefore, as dearly loved children," Paul exhorts the Ephesian Christians (Ephesians 5:1). How then shall we imitate Him? Paul continues, "Live a life of love, just as Christ loved us and gave himself up for us as a fragrant offering and sacrifice to God." He died for all of us, just as the sun rises "on the evil and the good." God is no respecter of persons (Acts 10:34), so Christians do not expect special treatment for themselves, nor do they grumble when they see nonbelievers seeming to prosper. God does not withhold the sun and rain from His enemies. Then we should not reserve our love only for those we like. That's how pagans behave. We have a higher standard. We have to do more than others.

In the early days of the labor movement in America, union leader Samuel Gompers adopted as the workers' slogan, "More." One word said it all. That's what they wanted. "More" could be the Christian's slogan, also. But this "more" is not what we want to get but what we are willing to give.

Jesus has often been charged with impracticality, especially in the Sermon on the Mount. "He taught fine ideals," some of His critics charge, "but they won't work in the real world. These are good rules for the kingdom of Heaven [the so-called 'kingdom ethic'], but you have to be a lot tougher-minded to survive in this dog-eat-dog world of ours." Perhaps. But the real world does not seem to be prospering too well as it is, does it? Frankly, one would be hard put to find an ethical system any more practical than what Jesus proposed here. His respect for human life and personality, His regard for women and marriage, His insistence upon the truth, His belief in the power of good over evil, and His practice of love to replace the practice of hate are genuinely enlightened ideals. If you do these things, you will light up others' lives.

An old rabbi was asked by one of his disciples, "What's the worst thing an evil urge can achieve?"

"To make a man forget that he is the son of a King," the rabbi wisely answered. Remember, disciples of Jesus, that you are children of the King. Let your bearing be royal.

CHAPTER SEVEN

Worship and Worry

Matthew 6

How to Worship Men (6:1-18)
(An Overview)

Jesus has not finished developing His theme of a righteousness that surpasses that of the scribes and Pharisees (Matthew 5:20). Unless you remember the larger context, you could mistakenly conclude from this text that Jesus opposes public worship. Jesus' own worship practices prove otherwise. He regularly attends the synagogue on the Sabbath (Luke 4:16) and faithfully goes to the Temple when in Jerusalem. He observes the stated feast days. He does nothing to discourage, either by example or precept, assembling to worship God. What He attacks here is staging a performance of religious devotion that does not come from a worshiping heart.

What we call worship of God may be more accurately termed worship of men. "Be careful not to do your 'acts of righteousness' before men, to be seen by them" (Matthew 6:1). The English phrase "to be seen by them" translates the Greek *theathenai,* which has entered our language as "theatrical" or "doing theatrics." Its cousin is Jesus' word "hypocrites" (verses 2, 5, 16), which derives from the Greek word for actor. "Do not practice your religion 'theatrically,' for the applause of an audience." To do so is hypocrisy, play-acting. Whether giving to charity or praying or fasting, worship God and not the approval of men. Sound no trumpet to announce your offerings, indulge in no long showy prayers to impress others with your piety, and refrain from disfiguring your appearance so everyone will admire your discipline of fasting. You may fool your audiences, but God is not taken in by your charades.

What makes your religious performances so dangerous is that success is guaranteed. You want people to see you. They see you. Period. That's the end of it. You have received what you wanted. Sadly, you have not wanted enough.

Three times Jesus says, "They have received their reward in full" (verses 2, 5, 16). They wanted attention, they got attention. They have been paid in full. Nothing else is coming to them. Many timid but well-meaning parents teach their children that the opinions of other people should govern their behavior. "What will the neighbors think?" is their guideline. So what other people think dictates their choices of clothing, cars, houses, clubs, recreation, and church. They would deny this charge, of course, but they are worshiping men, not God.

If we are serious about wanting to please God, then we will serve Him with quiet giving, with honest prayer, and with secret self-denial.

With Quiet Giving

Jesus takes it for granted that His disciples will be generous in giving to the needy. He just wants us to be quiet about it. The Bible does not separate righteousness from generosity. We help those who cannot help themselves. But we must not call attention to ourselves. Our goal is not to have our names engraved in some monument, or to be honored at an appreciation banquet. We give just as much, but we give to help.

With Honest Prayer

When you want to talk seriously with a friend, you don't stand on the street corner and shout at one another. Since prayer is intimate conversation with God, street corners are hardly an appropriate setting, even for silent prayer. Respect the privacy of the conversation. Treat God as you would an intimate friend. In the privacy of your room, He can hear you.

During America's Civil War, the United States Senate chaplain irritated many senators by his habit of advising them on the conduct of the war. His prayers turned into sermons. In disgust, Senator Saulsbury of Delaware moved this resolution (which was not passed):

> Resolved: That the Chaplain of the Senate be respectfully requested hereafter to pray to and supplicate God in our behalf, and not to lecture Him, inform Him what to do, or state to Him, under pretense of prayer, his (the said Chaplain's) opinion in reference to His duty as the Almighty; and that the said Chaplain be further requested, as aforesaid, not, under the form of prayer, to lecture the Senate in relation to questions before the body.

The parson was apparently praying to be heard by men. He was paid in full.

Genuine prayer, as we shall note in more detail in the sections to follow, is private but not selfish. Jesus prayed in the plural: *"Our* Father," "Give *us* today *our* daily bread," "Forgive *us our* debts," and so on.

It is never *to* oneself, either. In Woody Allen's *Love and Death,* Napoleon enters his lady's room with the comment, "I heard voices."

"I was praying," she replies.

"I heard two voices."

"I do both parts."

She is not alone in praying both parts. Many pray-ers claim, before they embark on this or that dubious enterprise, that they prayed to God about it. What they do not go on to admit is that they have usually supplied both the question and the answer.

Prayer is not so much seeking to get something from God as seeking to be with God. Oswald Chambers said that spiritual lust makes us "demand an answer from God, instead of seeking God Who gives the answer." He adds, "The meaning of prayer is that we get hold of God, not the answer."[22]

"Getting hold of God" requires no formal language or lofty, lengthy sentences. Young Christians can easily trip themselves up on the *thee* s and *thou* s of King-James English. The King James Version of the Bible was published in 1611, just five years before William Shakespeare died. In those days, the English language used two forms of address: the formal *you* or *yours* and the more intimate *thou, thee,* and *thine.* Language evolves, and over the years, the intimate form of address was dropped and *you* became the second person pronoun for all seasons. Except religious. Because of the KJV, *thee* and *thou* took on special significance. It did a flip-flop. Where once it could be used only among intimates, it now took on new dignity as the formal, proper form to use when addressing the Almighty. Prayer, which once had been regarded as conversation with a close friend *(thou)* became, through the passage of time, a formal address to a superior. Intimacy was banished.

Yet if Jesus is to be believed, we ought to think of God as a Father, intimately and simply. Thus, the proper language for prayer is the the vocabulary of respectful family conversation.

With Secret Self-Denial

Fasting is like being a young suitor too much in love to eat, or a

---

[22]Chambers, *My Utmost for His Highest,* p. 38.

writer too wrapped up in his novel to stop for supper, or a scientist who loses track of time in his pursuit of a solution. Such fasting is joyous deprivation. It is a temporary rejection of anything that gets in the way of the object of your happiness. There is nothing self-conscious about it. You don't call attention to your fast—you are hardly aware you are doing it.

When you fast, then, do your usual cosmetic job. Shave, comb your hair, take your bath. Don't announce by an unkempt appearance that you are doing something spiritual. Just get on with your devotion.

According to Madeline L'Engle (in *Walking on Water)*, Hawaiians gave the white man their name *haole* because of their impatience in worship. It seems that before missionaries arrived on the islands, the Hawaiians used to sit outside their temples meditating and preparing themselves for a long time before they eventually crept to the altar to pray. Then they would once again sit outside the temple for a long while, "breathing life" into their prayers. The missionaries, on the other hand, would just get up, utter a few sentences, say a hasty amen, and be done with it. They acted like *haoles,* people "who failed to breathe life into their prayers." They were in too big a hurry to meditate before or listen to God. They seemed to pray in order to be seen praying—by other men.

Whether praying, giving, or fasting, what matters is what *God* sees.

The Lord's Prayer (6:9-15)

When we approach this prayer that Jesus taught His disciples to pray, we approach on our knees. Nothing else quite like it has ever been uttered. In a few brief words, Jesus changes the pattern of prayer forever. Pious Jews of His day are accustomed to offering eighteen petitions to God three times daily. They are long and complicated.

Jesus' prayer is brief and simple, almost childlike in vocabulary but profound in implication. The doctor of philosophy and the child kneeling by his bed can both pray this prayer. Before God, every believer becomes a child.

Jesus' prayer expresses the freedom of a child. It takes liberties; it frankly asks for things and expects to get what it asks for. Yet it is not presumptuous. It puts first things first: first we adore God; then we ask. It is not a theological, but a personal, utterance. We learn little here of the nature of the divinity. We just assume that God is and that God loves.

Our Father

This is the only verse in the New Testament in which Jesus says, "Our Father," instead of, "My Father," or, "The Father." His own relationship with God was unique, of course. But Jesus here draws His disciples into that relationship as far as possible, encouraging God's adopted children to claim their family status.

As a member of the family, the Christian prays with his brothers and sisters in mind. He is never, for the Christian, just "My God." He is ever "Our God." John Donne, the famous seventeenth-century English poet, was right: "No man is an island, entire to himself." We can never pray as if we were the only ones in the universe. There is no hint of exclusiveness in this prayer.

A few years ago, the meaning of "our" became uncomfortably clear to some American farmers. Drought hit their section of the States, raising an outcry from the truck farmers there. The cause, they claimed, was that some fruit growers, in order to keep the seasonal hail from destroying their fruit, had ordered cloud seeders to disperse the clouds before the rain and hail could do any damage. But the truck farmers needed those same clouds to water their crops. How should they pray? The God of truck farmers is also God of fruit growers.

Abraham Lincoln reminded Americans that both the South and the North read the same Bible and prayed to the same God. They should both have begun their prayers, *"Our* Father. . . ." How inclusive was their *our?* Can union laborers pray "our" without including the welfare of management in their prayer, nor management without thinking of the benefits to labor? Can any nation pray "our" without recognizing another nation's best interests?

Father

Father is as much an Old Testament as it is a New Testament word for God. In the Old, however, He was perceived as Father of the nation more than of individual persons. The Israelites did not use "Father" as a common address in prayer and never employed it with the sense of intimacy that Jesus gives it. The Hebrews clothed the word with the authority and love of the Creator for His creation, but not with the patience of the forgiving father of a prodigal son (Luke 15).

Yet Jesus does not propose that "Father" should conjure up the image of a physical man in a business suit with gravy stains on his tie. God is Spirit, and Spirit cannot be caged in time and space. Jesus

87

certainly does not propose that we are praying to a flesh-and-blood God. He merely borrows human language to suggest to our limited imaginations something of what God is like. He relates to us personally and lovingly, as a good father to a child.

The language bothers some modern believers. "It's sexist," they protest. Why not God the Mother instead of, or as well as, God the Father? Certainly God Almighty is neither masculine nor feminine as human beings are, if He is Spirit. To raise the question is to betray a misunderstanding of how language works. Beyond any doubt, the word *Father* does not tell us everything about God. Certainly, His love incorporates those elements of love usually attributed to the father, but also those more often thought to be motherly. The language may even have been intended to connote the sterner, more objective love more often associated with fathers than with mothers. Mothers often think their husbands demand too much of little children; fathers tend to criticize their wives for coddling the little ones. Has it always been so?

Whatever the reasons, the fact remains that the Biblical word is *Father,* not *Mother.* Traditionally, the male parent has been the family provider, disciplinarian, and source of comfort and security. Perhaps these are the controlling ideas to be attached to the word. For thousands of years, no one thought to criticize Jesus on this point. In modern industrialized cultures, however, women are entering the business and labor force in unprecedented numbers. Even so, the norm is still that the father is the chief provider. We are not amiss, then, in following Jesus in speaking to God as our Father, the source of every good and perfect gift. Yet like a good father, who wants the best for his children, God does not "shell out" on demand. That would spoil us. He is on "our side," if by that we mean that He wants us to win in life. He is not on "our side" if we man that He always approves of what we do, just because we are His offspring. He is best described by the writer of Hebrews:

> "My son, do not make light of the Lord's discipline,
>   and do not lose heart when he rebukes you,
> because the Lord disciplines those he loves,
>   and he punishes everyone he accepts as a son.
>   —Hebrews 12:5, 6

In Heaven

Jesus is not, as some would have it, describing the geographical location of God's mansion. God is Spirit (John 4:24) and cannot be cabined in a temple in Jerusalem or atop a mountain in Samaria or astride a planet orbiting in some solar system. In May of 1962, Russian cosmonaut Gherman S. Titov orbited around the earth. When he came down, he reported, "In my travels around the earth . . . I saw no God or angels." Does this mean that God does not exist, or only that Mr. Titov was given the wrong map for locating Him? America's astronaut John Glenn answered Titov's quip, "The God I pray to is not so small that I expected to see Him in space."

Paul wrote in Ephesians 1:3, "Praise be to the God and Father of our Lord Jesus Christ, who has blessed us *in the heavenly realms* with every spiritual blessing in Christ." Did he mean that we have been blessed geographically? Hardly. He means that we have received the highest conceivable blessings. In His prayer, Jesus indicates that God occupies the highest levels of our conceptual powers. We can't imagine all there is to God, and what we do imagine stretches our minds to the maximum. Before the world was created, God was. He is more than the world He made, and He will still be after the world is no more.

Here is something of the magnitude of the universe. Our sun, three million miles in circumference, is 92 million miles away from earth. Our moon, never wavering from its schedule of 27 days, 7 hours, 43 minutes, and 11 seconds, circles the earth. Our planet itself hurtles through the solar system a distance of 550,000,000 miles in 365 days, 5 hours, 48 minutes, and 49 seconds. All the while it is turning at a speed of more than 1,000 miles an hour, revolving completely once every 23 hours, 56 minutes, and 4 and 1/9 seconds. Yet our earth and its solar system are out on the edge of a great galaxy in a universe of millions of galaxies. In our immediate neighborhood are 40,000 stars, each like our sun only larger. And there are multiplied millions of galaxies, each with hundreds of thousands of stars. This we can grasp with our intelligence. God transcends it all.

Look in another direction. Scientists suggest there may be as many as 500,000,000 organisms in a single drop of water. Increasingly powerful microscopes reveal additional worlds we had never before dreamed of. Atoms, which we used to think were the smallest bit of matter, are now divided and subdivided. We have discovered a world below us as immense and complex as the universe above us. We are forced into singing,

> How many are your works, O Lord!
>   In wisdom you made them all;
>   the earth is full of your creatures.
> There is the sea, vast and spacious,

teeming with creatures beyond number—
living things both large and small (Psalm 104:24).

And "our Father" made them all.

Hallowed Be Your Name

"Make it holy and cause us to keep it holy."

Names indicate relationship, in most cultures with the father: Larson, son of Lars; Johnson, son of John; or in the best style of Russian novels, Ivan Petrovich, son of Peter. Sometimes names signify occupation, as in Shoemaker, Carpenter, Weaver, or Baker. Sometimes they designate a region or district, like the Chesters or Hartbergs or Newkirks. They may also point to social class or caste. In Boston, for example, your family name may rank you on the social register. There is that old joke that in Boston the Cabots speak only to the Lodges, and the Lodges speak only to God. The Kennedys, being Johnny-come-latelys from Ireland, can't get a word in edgewise.

God's name is to be honored as holy. *God* is an English word derived from the Anglo-Saxon word for good. It points to His nature. He is the Good One, the essence of goodness, the cause of goodness in others. Somebody explained God this way: "All conceptions of God which are incompatible with a movement of pure charity are false. All other conceptions of Him, in varying degrees, are true."

"Let Your name be held in reverence, because Your name is good." If so, the only way we can hallow the name of God is through our devotion to whatever is good, through good—or godly—living. Even the words of our mouths and the meditations of our hearts must be acceptable to the One who is the standard of all goodness. (See Psalm 19:14; cf. Philippians 4:8.)

"Let our works honor Your name." The Muslim turns toward his mosque several times a day to pray, "God is great." Christians have no such ritual. A sterner demand rests on us: our work and our play must kneel in reverence. Advertising, business practices, politics, friendships—everything we do must honor His name. "So whether you eat or drink or whatever you do, do it all for the glory of God" (1 Corinthians 10:31).

"Hallowed be Your name." You are the Creator and Sustainer of life. We pray to You, we yield to You, we ask You to accept us, we ask You to help us in our every endeavor to bring honor to Your name.

Your Kingdom Come

A kingdom has both a ruler and subjects. The positions are fixed;

they are not interchangeable. A king is not elected, so he is not subject to the will of the people. He rules either by hereditary right or armed might. Subjects obey him or overthrow him, but they do not dictate to him.

"Your kingdom come." When I pray these words, I mean, "You, Lord, are sovereign in my life. As You rule Heaven, I want You to rule earth, especially me. I pray these words as a Christian and a member of Your church. Take control of the church, Lord." When the citizens of Heaven pray this prayer, they mean, "Lord, we have entered into Your permanent kingdom and we submit to Your everlasting reign." When the citizens of the kingdom of Heaven on earth pray it, they mean, "Lord, we too have come into Your permanent kingdom and also submit to Your everlasting reign. Rule us on earth as You will rule us in Heaven. Help us to live in all things as Your subjects."

God's kingdom is not, like other sovereignties, characterized by taxes and armies and office holders, but by the freedom and continuing personal growth of His subjects. Christ said, "Do not be afraid, little flock, for your Father has been pleased to give you the kingdom" (Luke 12:32). We have not earned our citizenship, but God granted it to us so we could be with Him forever (John 10:28).

As an undeserving citizen of this kingdom, I want to be the best possible representative of my Sovereign, so I ask Him to help me to live up to the honor He has bestowed on me. I have learned that living in the kingdom is so wonderful that I am willing to give up everything else I possess for its sake (Matthew 13:44-46). It cannot fully be described, even by Jesus, who tells many parables to give us a glimpse into it (Matthew 20:1-16; 22:1-14; 25:1-13, among many others). It is free from Satan's clutch (Matthew 12:28), and available to those of childlike faith (Matthew 18:1-5) and humble readiness to obey the Lord. I have also seen it in the person of Jesus, who embodies the healing, caring, restoring, loving qualities of the kingdom in His ministry.

The kingdom is experienced personally, among and within the Lord's disciples (Luke 17:20, 21). Through new birth (John 3:3), by loyal submission to Christ as Lord, by seeking first a right relationship with God and others (Matthew 6:33), the subject enters into the security of God's kingdom, a security that nothing, not even death, can destroy (Romans 8:38, 39). Life in the kingdom "is not a matter of eating and drinking, but of righteousness, peace and joy in the Holy Spirit" (Romans 14:17).

Five centuries before Christ, the great Greek philosopher Plato dreamed of an ideal society. He recorded his dream in *The Republic*. He believed that society should be ruled by philosopher-kings, who would be specially educated to rule wisely and to benefit mankind. He took it for granted that these men would be so concerned for the less enlightened of mankind that they would make any sacrifice to save them from their delusions and lead them to enlightenment. A very Christian idea, isn't it? His vision resembles Jesus' prayer, "Your kingdom come."

Like the enlightened philosopher-kings, Christians have been granted a glimpse of a higher reality. We do not rule but are ruled by the King himself, who sets us free and empowers us to fulfill our potential. We have more things, more knowledge, and more hope than most of this world's people. We cannot fully enjoy our privileges, however, so long as other people are deprived. So we pray to God to spread His kingdom, His gracious rule, all over the earth. Our prayer implies our readiness to help.

Your Will Be Done

This petition restates "Your kingdom come" and is equally personal. To pray these words is to ask God to realize His will in the life of the pray-er. "Your will be done" means "Take over here. If I want the world to obey You, then I must be the first to obey. If I ask You to reform the world, then You must start by reforming me."

Christians often confess that they are confused about God's will. The Bible employs the term only in connection with God's love and His desire that all people should be made whole through Christ. God's will has nothing to do with the so-called "acts of God" that insurance papers describe.

A telephone pole fell on a man's car during a severe storm. In the accident, the man's back was broken. He sued the telephone company for damages. In defense, the company argued that the accident was an "act of God." God willed the pole to fall and break the man's back, the lawyer said. Fortunately, the Pennsylvania Supreme Court, which ruled against the company, suggested that it was time to abandon this defense plea (which dates back to 1581). Justice Michael A. Musmanno wrote in his opinion,

> The loose use of the name of Deity in the realm of the law should not be a matter of our approval. There is something shocking in attributing any tragedy or holocaust to God. The ways of the Deity so surpass the understanding of man that it is not the province of man to pass judgment upon what may be beyond human comprehension.

In many ways, God surpasses man's understanding, as the judge declared, but in some things, He has spoken clearly. He wills that men and women should be saved. He wills that we should become like Christ. He wills that our lives should exhibit the fruit of the Spirit and not the works of the flesh (Galatians 5:16-23). He wills that we be salt and light in the world (Matthew 5:13-16).

We pray, "Your will be done," with full knowledge that, as Paul writes, we are "God's fellow workers" (1 Corinthians 3:9). We will assist Him to accomplish His will. David Livingstone, pioneer missionary in Africa, prayed, "O Jesus, fill me with Thy love now, I beseech Thee, accept me and my service, and take Thou all the glory." This was his way of praying, "Your will be done."

Give Us This Day

Up to this point, Jesus' lofty prayer addresses the Father in His magnificence. It holds His very name in reverence while aligning the pray-er with His purposes on earth. Here Jesus shifts abruptly from spiritual to physical concerns. We have bodies that need nourishment. Without embarrassment, Jesus teaches us to ask God to take care of these bodies.

Give. God is the source of everything. "The earth is the Lord's, and everything in it" (Psalm 24:1). Whether we acknowledge His ownership or not, every human being is dependent upon God's largess. Jesus encourages us to ask from Him alone who can give.

Matthew's version uses the aorist tense, *dos,* "give in one act." Luke uses the present, *didou,* "be giving, give continually"*(Luke 11:3). Someone has suggested that Matthew touches the readiness, and Luke the steadiness, of God's giving. Matthew's verb translates, "Give us this* day," and Luke's, "Give us *each* day." Either way, we rely upon God one day at a time, neither worrying nor hoarding for tomorrow, like the Israelites depending daily on just one day's manna from Heaven (Exodus 16).

Give us. Strange, isn't it, that in teaching His disciples a personal prayer to a personal God, Jesus does not say, "Give me"? Whether the Lord intended this effect or not, His prayer never allows one of His disciples to pray for himself alone. We pray to *our* Father for *our* needs. As we are fellow recipients of God's grace, so we concern ourselves with one another's welfare. We need God, and we need each other. Almost always, God answers our prayers for daily bread through other people. We cannot eat without farmers, transporters, processors, and merchants. We cannot build without loggers or oilmen, laborers, truckdrivers, electricians, plumbers, and, unfortunately, tax assessors. Since we depend upon cooperative effort for our livelihoods and meals, we always pray with others in mind.

In Archibald MacLeish's play *Panic,* a woman watching a news bulletin reporting predictions of depression and unemployment prays, "Forgive us our daily bread." She offers what should be the prayer of a nation, which, with remarkable disregard for most of the world, builds up food surpluses in the face of world-wide hunger. "Give *all* of us our daily bread."

Give us this day. Jesus reveals what He thinks of hoarding and covetousness in His parable of the rich man who built bigger barns to store his surplus crops (Luke 12:16-21). He died anyway. Nothing we store up for tomorrow can push away our date with death indefinitely. The only time we have is now. Tomorrow is an act of faith, not a possession in fact. With the world's superpowers aiming more and meaner missiles of destruction at each other, only a fool would try to predict whether there will even be a tomorrow.

So it doesn't do a bit of good to worry about the future (Matthew 6:25-34). Instead, trust God for each day's provisions, and with them be content. We are asking for bread, not caviar. And bread doesn't keep. (Of course, you can bring up refrigeration. That's true and it's not true. Most of the world's people do not enjoy the use of electricity, let alone refrigerators or freezers. Anyway, even if you freeze it, thawed bread suffers by comparison with freshly baked, homemade bread, doesn't it?) The point is to pray for *daily* bread, not a lifetime of foodstuffs.

Give Us This Day Our Daily Bread

This line reminds us that it is unwise to live just for today. People who do are always in financial trouble because they haven't planned for the rainy day. Is the problem that they have failed to plan or that they have wasted their money on so many other things than bread? This is a simple prayer for basic needs. Elsewhere Jesus has some things to say about planning ahead (Luke 14:28-32).

This is a prayer of trust. Jesus would be able to sing our hymn, "Be not dismayed whate'er betide, God will take care of you." He can be compared to the father of a young daughter, both of whom were swimming in the Atlantic. They enjoyed themselves so much that neither realized that with the changing tide, they had been carried far out from the shore. When he became alert to their peril, knowing that his daughter could not swim the long distance to shore and that he did not have enough strength to take her in, he very calmly told her their problem, then added, "You just float on your back. You can rest that way. I'll swim back to get a boat. Then I'll come back to get you. It will seem that I'm gone a long time, because it is so far for me to swim. But don't be afraid. I'll come back."

She said she'd do what he said, and he started for the shore. It took him over an hour to swim against the tide, considerably longer to get someone with a boat. Unable to secure a motor boat, he frantically rowed toward her in a fourteen-foot rowboat. It was more than two hours later when he and his companion picked her up. The other man was amazed that she was still alive. He had thought the father crazy for leaving her.

"Weren't you afraid to be out here alone?" he asked her.

"No," she replied as she hugged her father. "Daddy said he would come."

Jesus teaches us to pray with such trust. Ask for *daily* bread.

Forgive Us Our Debts

In July, 1962, a Buddhist monk and herbalist named Talduwe Somarama mounted a prison scaffold and was hanged in Colombo, Ceylon. He died for the 1959 assassination of his country's Prime Minister Solomon W. R. D. Bandaranaike. In a confession he later retracted, Somarama said he killed the prime minister for favoring western medical techniques over oriental herbal medicine. Prison officials reported that twenty-four hours before he was hanged, Somarama submitted himself to Christian baptism so that he could ask God for forgiveness. There was no forgiveness for him in his Buddhist religion.

He was wrong to kill but he was right to believe that the heart of the Christian gospel is forgiveness.

We owe *debts* we cannot pay. (The translation, "Forgive us our trespasses" is the inaccurate translation of the old official prayerbook of the Church of England. The word is *debt*.) We owe something to God, we owe something to others with whom we have not always traded fairly. We even owe ourselves.

Following the Lord's Prayer, when Jesus explains forgiveness, He uses a different word. Here it is *opheilemata,* "debts." In 6:14, it is *paraptomata,* "trespasses." Sin is both a debt owed and a trespassing into territory where we don't belong. In Luke's account (Luke 11:4), the word is *hamartia,* "missing the mark." Sin then, is a debt owed, a trespassing where you don't belong, and a failure to meet the goal or standard. No matter which word you use, Jesus offers forgiveness—provided that you are also willing to forgive.

Martin Luther once had a dream in which he stood on the Day of Judgment before the throne of the Judge. Satan was there to accuse him. When the books were opened, he pointed to sin after sin of which Luther was guilty. Luther despaired. Then he remembered the cross.

Turning to the devil, he said, "There is one entry which thou hast not made, Satan."

"What is that?" the devil asked him.

"It is this: 'The blood of Jesus Christ his Son cleanseth us from all sin'" (1 John 1:7).

At the heart of the gospel is forgiveness, but for the gospel to do its cleansing work in the sinner, in his heart must also be a readiness to forgive. This is a hard saying. Some people refuse to forgive. They say they can't. They protest that they are sorry to be that way, but that's just how they are. They are victims of their unconquered pride. The famous General Oglethorpe is reported to have said to John Wesley, "I never forgive." Wesley properly retorted, "Then I hope, sir, you never sin."

Forgiveness shines through almost every page of the New Testament. Paul writes to the Ephesians, "Be kind and compassionate to one another, forgiving each other, just as in Christ God forgave you" (Ephesians 4:32). Stephen, the first Christian martyr, demonstrates how it is done: "Lord, do not hold this sin against them" (Acts 7:60). His words echo those of his Lord, who prayed from the cross for the people who were killing Him, "Father, forgive them, for they do not know what they are doing" (Luke 23:34).

When we fully accept the Lord's forgiveness of us, we are no longer so quick to fix blame on others. (See Matthew 18:21-35.) The effect of Jesus' teaching is this: "Don't try to blame someone else for your sins. You don't have to. I'll forgive you, if you'll confess them (1 John 1:9). Then, when I have forgiven you, you can do the same for anyone who has offended you. Pass it on."

Imagine, if you can, an unforgiving neighbor whose memory has stored up every wrong or imagined wrong the man next door has ever done to him. Then listen to him recite the Lord's prayer:

> "O God, I have sinned against Thee many times;
> I have been often forgetful of Thy goodness;
> I have broken Thy laws;
> I have committed many secret sins.

Deal with me, I beseech Thee, O Lord, even as I deal with my neighbor.

He hath not offended me one hundredth part as much as I have offended Thee, but I cannot forgive him.

He has been very ungrateful to me, though not an hundredth part as ungrateful as I have been to Thee, yet I cannot overlook such base ingratitude.

Deal with me, O Lord, I beseech Thee, as I deal with him.

I remember and treasure up every little trifle that shows how ill he has behaved to me.

Deal with me, I beseech Thee, O Lord, as I deal with him."

And Lead Us Not Into Temptation

But does God actually *lead* us to do wrong? No. In our idiom, this would sound more like, "And keep us out of trouble." We acknowledge our bullheadedness, our impulsive jumps beyond good judgment, our adolescent curiosity to dally in dens of iniquity. Help us overcome these baser instincts.

Jesus pricks our consciences here. Don't we much more frequently pray, "Deliver us from sickness" than ". . . from temptation or evil"? Yet the sickness we would be delivered from can be a road to spiritual health. It might not be all bad. Evil is.

And don't we pray regularly for deliverance from fear? Or from poverty? Or from unpopularity? Yet temptation should be our more consistent concern.

Temptation to go along with the crowd. In Charles Dickens' *Oliver Twist,* the young orphan Oliver must undergo his indoctrination in pickpocketing. He is a poor student. He refuses to steal. The good Dodger, his youthful instructor, rationalizes his occupation in these comfortable terms: "If you don't take pocket-hankerchers and watches, some other cove will; so that the coves that lose 'em will be all the worse, and you'll be all the worse too, and nobody half a ha'p'worth the better, except the chaps wot gets them—and you've just as good a right to them as they have." Dodger artfully applies the old twist on the Golden Rule, "Do unto others as you would before they do it unto you." It's the rule of the crowd. Don't fall for it.

Temptation to procrastinate. This is the greatest labor-saving device known to man. For a while. It is also a time-tested pacifier of troubled consciences. "Tomorrow I'll reform." "Tomorrow I'll start applying Christian principles."

Temptation to shift the blame. William James in *Essays in Pragmatism* reduces this habit to absurdity: "A man confessed to murder at Brockton. To get rid of the wife whose continued existence bored him, he inveigled her into a desert spot, shot her four times, and then, as she lay on the ground and said to him, 'You didn't do it on purpose, did you, dear?' replied, 'No, didn't do it on purpose,' as he raised a rock and smashed her skull."

Then whose fault was it?

Temptation to be indifferent. "It doesn't matter" should be said of many things, but never of fundamental values nor of the effect of our influence on others, nor of the truths the Scriptures teach. Walt Whitman forcefully reminds us of the impact that even little things have on a growing child.

> There was a child went forth every day,
> And the first object he look'd upon, that object he became,
> And that object became part of him for the day or a certain part of
>   the day,
> Or for many years or stretching cycles of years.
>
> The early lilacs became part of this child,
> And grass and white and red morning-glories, and white
>   and red clover, and the song of the phoebe-bird. . . .
> And the water plants with their graceful flat heads, all became part
>   of him.[23]

Whitman sings on and on about the little things that go into the making of a child. Things we scarcely notice become a part of us. Lord, deliver us from the temptation to be indifferent to these little things that go into us or to the bigger things that come from us.

Jesus is not alone in His concern about temptation. Here are some other, if somewhat less profound, thoughts on the subject:

> "Many men have too much will power.
>   It's won't power they lack"—John A. Shedd.
>
> "It is easier to stay out than get out"—Mark Twain.
>
> "Honest bread is very well—it's the butter that makes the temptation"—Douglas Jerrold.
>
> "How oft the sight of means to do ill deeds
>   Make deeds ill done!"—Shakespeare.

---

[23]Walt Whitman, *Leaves of Grass.*

For Yours Is the Kingdom and the Power and the Glory Forever. Amen

This doxology (hymn or verse of praise to God) is not found in the earliest manuscripts. Later copyists may have added it to bring the prayer to a conclusion more useful in public worship. One source may be 1 Chronicles 29:11.

> Yours, O Lord, is the greatness and the power
> and the glory and the majesty and the splendor,
> for everything in heaven and earth is yours.
> Yours, O Lord, is the kingdom;
> You are exalted as head over all.

Andrew University
1821 Catalina Ave.
Berkeley, CA 94707

Second Timothy 4:18 is another Christian doxology:

> "The Lord will rescue me from every evil attack and will bring me safely to his heavenly kingdom. To him be glory for ever and ever. Amen."

Christians feel we have even more reason to praise God than our Israelite ancestors had, since Jesus died for us and arose from the grave and has gone to prepare a place for us. Praise God! For ever and ever. Amen.

The Fine Art of Fasting (6:16-18)

We have already commented on these verses, but a little more needs to be said. Although it sounds as if Jesus and His disciples fasted regularly ("*when* you fast"), they were more conspicuous by the absence than by the presence of the practice (Matthew 9:14; 11:19). Apparently, Jesus was not given to long periods of fasting, nor did He insist that His disciples do so regularly. This was unprecedented in a Jewish religious leader. Most Jews observed five or six fasts annually, and the stricter Pharisees fasted twice a week, commemorating Moses' ascent and descent at Mt. Sinai. On those days, they made their deprivation obvious by their unwashed faces, drawn looks, bare feet, and ash-covered heads.

Jesus does not concern himself here with the niceties of fasting; He speaks more to its purpose, which is self-denial before God. This may explain His choice of "when" rather than "if." Fasting *per se* may be optional, but self-denial is basic to Christian living. To fast is to deny oneself food and drink for a specific period, a good spiritual discipline. Jesus' brief instruction recalls Isaiah's interpretation of fasting's real meaning (Isaiah 58:1-8). To exercise the discipline properly requires neither sackcloth and ashes nor hunger pains and dry tongue. Rather, a conscious and conscientious denial of self for the sake of another is what constitutes fasting. It is identifying with the miserable, the hungry, the thirsty, and the naked.

These are not easy words. Even fasting, which of all religious practices seems the most individualistic, cannot be undertaken for purely selfish rewards. Meditation can become mere introspection that leads to self-worship. Ralph Waldo Emerson wrote a century ago, "Henry Thoreau made last night the fine remark that as long as a man stands in his own way, everything seems to be in his way—government, society, and even the sun, moon and stars, as astrology may testify." As Jesus observes, fasting can be practiced in the name of God but for the purpose of attracting attention. In that case, the person who is fasting stands in his own way.

Self-denial must be genuine. Your regular routine should be observed as far as possible. Self-denial that calls attention to itself cancels itself out. Genuine humility never goes on display. It is for God's eyes only.

How to Quit Worrying (6:19-34)

Dr. Paul Tournier reports hearing heart specialist Professor Laubry discussing the case of a divorced woman suffering from a functional heart ailment. "There is always some reason for a woman to have nervous troubles; when she's unmarried, it is because she wants to get married; when she is married, it is because she wants a divorce; and when she is divorced, it is worse still."[24] The professor has discovered a very common affliction: if you've made up your mind to worry, you'll find something to worry about. One woman worried so much about her worries that she began to keep a record of them. She found that forty percent of the things she worried about never happened, thirty percent were old decisions she couldn't alter, twelve percent were criticisms that other people made of her, mostly untrue, ten percent were about her health—which worsened as she worried about it, and only eight percent were what she called legitimate. (Life does have some real problems.) Her biggest discovery was how much energy she was needlessly expending on her worries.

Most people worry too much. All worriers need to pay close attention to this section of the Sermon on the Mount, because it reads like

---

[24]Paul Tournier, *The Healing of Persons* (New York: Harper and Row, 1965), p. 82.

Jesus' prescription for overcoming worry. His advice contains four great principles for anxiety-free living.

First, Invest in What Cannot Be Destroyed or Stolen (6:19, 20).

If what you value most in this world can be broken or stolen, of course you are going to worry. The greater our affluence, the more we have to worry about. Anxiety grows in relation to wealth. Yet Alexander Pope observed a couple of centuries ago,

> If then to all men happiness was meant,
> God in externals could not place content.

Consider the lock. It has been called the new symbol of American life. A generation or two ago, in most American towns, few people locked up anything. Perhaps they didn't have anything worth stealing. Now our houses and apartments are chained, dead bolted, and wired with security systems, and electric alarms and hookups to police stations. We have all the latest hardware for making ourselves secure, but we are more afraid than ever. We think we have effectively locked the criminals out, but in reality, we have locked ourselves in.

Our present federal administration plans to spend two trillion dollars on national defense in five years in a gigantic, desperate bid to make the United States secure. But the strategy won't work. Whenever we learn that Russia has built another missile, we panic. We already have weapons enough to kill everyone in the world hundreds of times over, yet we press for more. A nation dedicated to destroyable, stealable, rustable, corruptible treasures is consumed by worry. What happens when you buy something new? You're afraid somebody might touch it. So you accumulate things to worry about, then feel guilty for worrying. Seems rather foolish, doesn't it?

Francis Bacon said, "Seek not proud riches, but such as thou mayest get justly, use soberly, distribute cheerfully, and leave contentedly." Even Dennis the Mennis understands the principle. Leaning over his back fence, watching Mr. Wilson mow his lawn, Dennis spies Mr. Wilson's heavily-laden apple trees. He tells Mr. Wilson that he bets he'll have "about a million apples to worry about" now. From what we know of Mr. Wilson, we'd guess that Dennis will win his bet.

If you would give up worrying, invest in what cannot be destroyed or stolen.

Second, Serve God and Not Money (6:22-24).

The bluntness of the New International Version is refreshing. Older translations read, "You cannot serve God and *mammon,*" meaning the same but softer in its impact. Jesus doesn't attack the use of money as currency, but the worship of it as an end in itself. Do not be enslaved by it, do not bow down before it. Money can be stolen and the things money buys can be destroyed, so there is no genuine security in money.

Security is in the Lord. The apostle Paul viewed himself as a prisoner of the Lord no matter which side of the bars he was on. Since he turned his life over to Christ, he was satisfied to be used in any way the Lord desired (Ephesians 3:1; Philemon 9; Romans 16:7). He could write to the Philippians, "I have learned to be content whatever the circumstances" (Philippians 4:11). He could be acquitted and freed, or found guilty and executed, but he would not worry about it. To die would be to live in the presence of the Lord; to be set free would mean to live on earth with his friends. Either way, he would win. He had nothing to worry about because he served God.

When King Henry VIII of England was leading his nation from Roman Catholicism (with its allegiance to the Pope in Rome) into nationalistic Anglicanism (with its loyalty to the King), two recalcitrant monks vigorously opposed him. Henry threatened to tie them in a sack and throw them into the Thames River if they would not obey him. They remained unmoved. "The road to heaven lies as near by water as by land; and therefore it is indifferent to us which way we go thither." When your treasures are in Heaven, so is your heart. You don't have to worry, even about death.

Third, Be Served by God and Not by Money (6:25-33)

Serve God and He'll serve you. Can anything your money can buy compare with the laughter of a little child who loves you, or the forgiveness and loyalty of a spouse who hangs on to you when you're not worth it? Can it compare with peace that passes understanding, or the touch of love, the embrace of compassion, the warmth of acceptance, or the assurance of Heaven? If you would escape worrying, be served by God and His treasures. "Do not worry about your life."

Don't even worry about your clothes. In the Orient today, holy men express devotion to their god through contempt for their clothing. They wear nothing or perhaps a dirty loin-cloth. They want to prove literally that abundance of life cannot be found in a full clothes closet.

And don't worry about your food. Birds don't sow or reap or store their surplus, but they eat quite well. God feeds them, and we are more valuable than they are.

Of what value is worry over such things, anyway? It can't make you taller or able to live longer. Football heroes "Mean Joe" Greene and Craig Morton were preparing for a television interview when the man who would be hosting them asked what it takes to be a great professional quarterback. Morton identified the first qualification as the ability to relax under fire. Then "Mean Joe" added that a "pro" defines relaxing as "staying in control." No panic under fire. Not a bad definition, is it? It's not a bad goal, either, to trust God so much that you don't panic under fire.

Clarence Macartney repeats an oft-told tale of a young English farmhand who offered the farmer who hired him only one qualification for employment. He could sleep when the wind blows. Although the farmer interviewed several other candidates, he finally settled on this gangly, awkward-looking youth named John with the strange credentials. The first time a terrific storm blew up in the middle of the night, the farmer learned his hired hand's value. He ran to the bottom of the attic stairs to get John to help him. Then he ran on ahead and found, to his surprise, the stable doors locked, the horses safe in the barn, the cattle secure in the stable, stacks of grain and hay already tied down, and all the cows, pigs, and sheep safely inside. John, by the way, never left his bed in the attic. He could sleep when the wind blows.[25]

The Christian who serves God has prepared himself for windy nights. He knows that as he serves the Lord, the Lord will serve his needs. He can trust Him.

Fourth, Live Each Day to the Fullest (6:34)

Do not drag along yesterday's baggage. Do not borrow trouble from tomorrow. Jesus does not encourage us to make no provision for tomorrow. That would be foolhardy. Preparation makes it unnecessary to worry about tomorrow. Those who worry most about the future are those who have least prepared.

"Each day has enough trouble of its own." This is another instance of Jesus' realism. He does not promise that each day will be glorious, or that if you are a Christian you will have no problems, or that you

---

[25]Clarence Macartney, *Along Life's Highway* (Grand Rapids: Baker, 1969), pp. 68-70.

will be immune from heartache. There will be trouble, so don't add to the inescapable load you will have any unnecessary burden from the past or the future.

Two American Presidents provide a perfect commentary on Jesus' injunction here. Franklin Delano Roosevelt and Warren G. Harding both confessed to friends what a day in the White House was like. Roosevelt said, "At night, when I lay my head on the pillow . . . and I think of the things that have come before me during the day and the decisions I have made, I say to myself, "Well, I've done the best I could—and I turn over and go to sleep." He lasted as President into his fourth term.

Harding did not finish one term. He is reported to have blurted out to a friend, "I listen to one side and they seem right, and then . . . I talk to the other side and they seem just as right, and there I am where I started. . . . God, what a job!" Had he appealed to God in prayer rather than profanity, he might have survived.

"God, what a job. Help me do the job so that I can sleep when the wind blows. So that I can say each morning, 'This is the day that the Lord has made, I will rejoice and be glad in it.' So that I can say when the day is over, 'I have done my best. It may not have been as good as somebody else could have done, but I've done *my* best, and I have trusted the Lord.' So tonight, when the wind blows, I shall sleep. I shall sleep, Lord, thanks to You."

CHAPTER EIGHT

Real Disciples

Matthew 7

Real Disciples Are Different (7:1-14)

In this section, Jesus continues an all-important Sermon on the Mount theme: "My disciples are to be different." Citizens of the kingdom of Heaven are not like citizens of this world. They enter through a narrow gate; they avoid the broad road that leads to destruction. They have strength to overcome the pressure to conform. They have conquered their normal fear of being peculiar. They are growing better as they grow older.

Oswald Chambers has summarized Jesus' intent in the Sermon in these words: "The Sermon on the Mount is not a set of rules and regulations; it is a statement of the life we live when the Holy Spirit is getting His way with us."[26] When God takes over, we change. Because we are Christians, there are some things we won't do—and some others we must do. These differences distinguish disciples of Christ from those who walk the broad road toward destruction.

What We Won't Do

We won't judge. Jesus has already warned that the unforgiving person cannot receive forgiveness (Matthew 6:15). Here He adds that the judgmental person invites similar judgment upon himself. He insists that you must "first take the plank out of your own eye, and then you will see clearly to remove the speck from your brother's eye" (Matthew 7:5).

Jesus has the order right. We are most judgmental when we are most conscious of our own shortcomings. I judge you because I don't like me. I punish myself in you. My bad temper is the overflowing of self-contempt.

Or of self-righteousness. (See Luke 18:9-14.) A Scottish pastor with

---

[26]Chambers, *My Utmost for His Highest,* p. 207.

a reputation as a fine Bible teacher also achieved a certain notoriety by his obvious use of cologne. He explained his habit as protection against offending anyone when he came down from the pulpit. That explained Sunday, but he wore it the other six days as well. One day, he visited a Christian bookstore run by a very pious lady. Arching her eyebrows, she sniffed, "Sir, you wear perfume."

"Madam," he sniffed back, "you don't."[27]

You probably have heard the unforgettable exchange between Winston Churchill and Lady Astor. Said the lady to gentleman, "Winston, if you were my husband, I should flavor your coffee with poison." "Madam," said the gentleman to the lady, "if I were your husband, I should drink it."

Clever repartee like this seems harmless. But not infrequently, a more deadly motive exists. Tom Cahill, a reporter and editor, once wrote an article about the famous swimmer Mark Spitz, in which he suggested that whereas in the water Spitz was wondrous to behold, he was perhaps not the brightest of men. A fan of Spitz wrote Cahill and accused him of slandering the greatest swimmer of all time. He warned him that God would kill him for his impertinence. Cahill put the note on the bulletin board and didn't think much about it until several days later. Then he learned that on the day it was written, its author had killed an entire family just north of San Francisco.

Judgment is but a step removed from murder. (See Matthew 5:21-26.) Jesus returns here to His treatment of anger and killing. Don't be angry with your brother, don't call him a fool, don't judge him, because your anger can so quickly turn to action. What begins as a seemingly harmless spirit of criticism can overtake you in slavery to your passions. When you judge, you betray your anger, insecurity, bitterness, fear, sense of inferiority, and lack of self respect. You aren't in control of yourself when these feelings take over. So don't judge.

Another warning is in order here. You are doomed to be disappointed if you think that, when you have learned to overcome your critical spirit, you won't be criticized any more. You can count on it— if you are doing anything worthwhile, you'll get into trouble for it. When you do, remember G. K. Chesterton on the subject: "I believe in getting into hot water. I think it keeps you clean."[28]

[27]Russell T. Hitt, *How Christians Grow* (New York: Oxford University Press, 1979), p. 41.

[28]Masie Ward, *Gilbert Keith Chesterton* (Sheed and Ward, 1943), p. 156.

When you pursue a goal, do not be sidetracked by your critics. Expect them to disapprove. Expect them to spot your imperfections and then spotlight them. Don't let them stop you; you are not working for their approval, but God's. Jesus could not satisfy His critics, either. His reputation among Jewish leaders was poor, but He had something more important to accomplish than establishing a good name: He came to seek and to save the lost. He succeeded. When John Wesley's brother begged him to defend himself from his critics, Wesley refused. "Brother, when I devoted to God my love, my time, my life, did I except my reputation?" When God gets all, critics get nothing.

You have no need to judge. God will take care of the task for you.

We won't "give dogs what is sacred" (7:6). While discouraging a judgmental spirit, Jesus nonetheless encourages a discerning one. Certain critical judgments must be made: between good and evil, or better and best. You can't help noticing that the opinions of some persons are not worthy of your attention. So Jesus, borrowing words that a Jew would use to describe an unclean dog, urges His disciples to protect what is precious to them. It is similar to His counsel to the disciples to shake the dust off their sandals at an inhospitable home (Matthew 10:14). "Don't give pigs and dogs what is holy." They don't know what to do with it. Plato's *Timaeus* says that "to find the maker and father of this universe is a difficult task; and when you have found him, you cannot speak of him before all people." They can't hear you. They are too insensitive.

Once again, Jesus presents himself as extremely practical. His optimism is not unbounded. He encourages discernment, but warns against allowing it to make you a critical, judgmental, condemning person. This you must not do.

What We Do

We pray, believing. "Ask and it will be given you" (Matthew 7:7). We can expect satisfaction from God in the same manner that our children have a right to expect good things from us. John Bisagno was at work when his five-year-old girl disturbed him, coming into his study to ask her daddy to make her a dollhouse. He promised he would. She left and he was again quickly engrossed in his studies. After a while, he glanced out the window and saw her walking across the backyard, carrying her toys, dishes, and dolls to a little pile of goods she was building up. He called out to his wife to ask what little Jan was doing. "Oh, you promised her a dollhouse," she replied, "and she believes you. She's just getting ready for it."[29] He quickly closed his books, hurried to get supplies, and started building. His motive was less because she had asked for it or deserved it than because he had promised. He had to keep his word. So has God.

For this reason, Jesus encourages disciples to pray persistently, consistently, stubbornly, if you please. Ask, seek, knock. Don't give up. On another occasion (Luke 11:5-10), Jesus told a story of a man whose neighbor banged on his door at midnight, needing food to feed some unexpected company. The neighbor, disturbed and unhappy, told him to leave him alone. The noisy man just kept banging, though, until the man had to get up in order to get some rest. He fetched the food for his neighbor, and got some peace and quiet. Jesus stresses the moral of His story. The man did not give because his neighbor deserved it but because the neighbor wouldn't leave him alone until he gave. "Pray like that," Jesus says. Both passages reach the same conclusion: "For every one who asks, receives; he who seeks, finds; and to him who knocks, the door will be opened."

We practice the Golden Rule. This makes us different, also. People love to claim they live by the Golden Rule (Matthew 7:14), but their promise outstrips their practice. The saying has been around a long time before Jesus comes on the scene. But He changes it for the better. It used to be stated in the negative: "Do not do to others what you do not want them to do to you." Negative and quite convenient. "I'll leave you alone if you'll leave me alone." That wasn't good enough for Jesus. (A street-wise member of one church put it like this to his minister, "I learned it this way: Do unto others *before they do it to you."* This is a popular version, but it is not what Jesus says.)

It's tough for people who have been brought up to put their own interests first to live by this Rule. We are willing to *not* do to others what we don't want them to do to us, but to become actively, assertively, sacrificially doers of good, no thanks. That's not our style nor our morality. But it *is Jesus' command.*

Here Greek philosophy and Christian morality part company. Socrates taught, "Daily to discourse about virtue . . . is the greatest good of man." "Not so," Jesus says. It profits no one for students to discuss what is good or not good. Jesus says, "I have taught you what is good. Now do it." And if you will, you will be distinguished from

[29]John Bisagno, *The Power of Positive Praying* (Grand Rapids: Zondervan, 1965), p. 24.

the vast majority of humanity stumbling along on the broad way that goes to the wide gate that leads to destruction. This saying of Jesus, as someone has said, puts the Lord's Prayer into overalls and sends it to work. Brendan Gill of *The New Yorker* would not agree. Convinced that everything will end badly for humanity, "in the inescapable catastrophe of death," he prescribes two rules of life: first, "have a good time," and second, "hurt as few people as possible in the course of doing so." Then he adds, "There is no third rule."[30] Gill is most uninventive. This is nothing more than the old saw, "Let's eat, drink and be merry, for tomorrow we die." It's not only pagan, it's cruel. It assumes that some will have to get hurt while I'm having a good time, but that's all right, if there aren't too many of them and if I am having a really good time. It's the law of the jungle.

Speaking of which, in a little village in Africa, an anthropologist trying to learn about the people asked a native the difference between good and evil. It was all very simple, he discovered. Evil is when somebody steals my wife and cattle; good is when I steal somebody else's wife and cattle. The law of the jungle—and of most human society. Do unto others before they do it unto you.

But Christians will be different. You'll treat others as you want to be treated, you'll take the first step in kindness, you'll go the last mile in patience. You'll grow better as you grow older, not judging, but discerning, while praying with a faith that knows God will answer with good for you.

What Real Disciples Look Like (7:15-29)

Discipleship is more than learning correct doctrine: It is energetically **doing** Christ's teaching. It is not just thinking right; it is right doing based on right thinking. Throughout the Sermon on the Mount, Jesus stresses the imperative of doing from the heart the things that make for righteousness. Discipleship is the will of God expressed in the actions of Christ's disciples. In these final verses of the Sermon, Jesus presents a series of contrasts that leave no doubt about the level of life He expects His followers to achieve. The Christian life is not for sluggards. Jesus wants us to bear fruit, to do God's will in all things, and to practice what Christ teaches so that we can survive life's inevitable storms.

---

[30]Brendan Gill, *Here at the New Yorker* (New York: Berkley Publishing Corp., 1975), p. 52.

Disciples Not Only Promise—They Produce

False prophets promise; true prophets produce. Like Israel before it (Deuteronomy 13:1-5; Jeremiah 8:1-15), the church will be confused by the demands of conflicting leaders who claim to be speaking for God. False prophets, dressed up like legitimate spokesmen for God in their sheep's clothing (the garments shepherds wore when guarding their flocks), promise a future that pleases their gullible listeners:

> From the least to the greatest,
>   all are greedy for gain;
> prophets and priests alike,
>   all practice deceit.
> They dress the wound of my people
>   as though it were not serious.
> "Peace, peace," they say,
>   when there is no peace (Jeremiah 6:13, 14; 8:10, 11).
> (See also Ezekiel 13:10; 22:28; Zephaniah 3:4).

The apostle Paul warned the elders of the Ephesian church to beware of "savage wolves" who would arise from within the congregation. They would "distort the truth in order to draw away disciples after them" (Acts 20:29, 30). Jesus also alerted His disciples to the "false Christs and false prophets [who] will appear" in the last days to deceive the elect (Matthew 24:24). And the epistles supply ample evidence that from its earliest days, the church suffered the fulfillment of these predictions: 2 Corinthians 11:13, 14; 1 John 4:1; 1 Timothy 4:1-5. The last passage even includes some of the specific false doctrines: "They forbid people to marry and order them to abstain from certain foods" (1 Timothy 4:3).

What do these deceivers have to gain? From their warped point of view, everything: power, money, self-esteem. From ancient Babylon comes this good example, which incidentally shows that false prophets abound everywhere. ("For wide is the gate and broad is the road that leads to destruction"; Matthew 7:13.) A messenger was sent to Memphis to summon the renowned Egyptian physician Hermes, who returned with the messenger to call upon the stricken Zadig. After examining him, Hermes declared that Zadig would lose his eye. He even specified the day and hour it would happen. A pity, too, he told his adoring audience, for "had it been the right eye, I could easily have cured it, but the wounds of the left eye are incurable." All Babylon mourned the fate of Zadig's doomed eye, which, two days later, healed itself when the abscess broke. Not to be undone by the appearance of facts, Hermes proceeded to write a book to prove that the eye should never have healed. We are told that Zadig did not read the book.

Returning to more familiar religious grounds, we should mention the unending stream of prophets who major in identifying the date of the second coming of Christ or the end of the world or the arrival of the Antichrist. In the sixteenth and seventeenth centuries, many tracts and sermons were written predicting that 1666 was "the year of the beast," when the Antichrist would be destroyed. While England trembled with political upheaval in the 1640s and 1650s, people's convictions regarding 1666 hardened. But when 1666 passed into 1667, false prophets did not apologize for misleading the masses; they simply offered other dates to keep the speculation—and their popularity—alive. The year of the beast is still the subject of religious prognosticators today.

Futurist magazine for October 1982 reprinted an article that first appeared in *The Ladies' Home Journal* in December, 1900. The author of that article claimed to have surveyed "the wisest and most careful men in our great institutions of science and learning" and then presented his findings in a scenerio of the next one hundred years. Among other things, he predicted the demise of the city house and the outlawing of building in blocks. The letters *c, x,* and *q* would disappear from the English alphabet, since they are unnecessary. Automobiles would be cheaper than owning a horse in 1900. Rats and mice would exist no longer, having been exterminated when humanity declared war on them. *Evangelical Newsletter* (December 10, 1982) takes up where the *Futurist* reprint leaves off, quoting some misguided predictions compiled by Chris Morgan and David Langford in "Facts and Fallacies." They attribute one quotation to an English clergyman of the mid-nineteenth century, Dr. Dionysius Lardner: "Rail travel at high speed is not possible because passengers, unable to breathe, would die of asphyxia." Astronomer and mathematician Simon Newcomb has never been forgotten because of his 1902 opinion, "Flight by machines heavier than air is unpractical and insignificant, if not utterly impossible." For sheer quotability, however, it's hard to beat Dr. Richard Wooley, Britain's Astronomer Royal, in 1956: "Space travel is utter bilge."

False prophets, some of them with apparently sterling credentials, are everywhere. They are all over Wall Street where, with pompous certainty, they sell their advice to nervous gamblers on the big boards. (Warren Buffett, an investment genius in the 1960s, refers to investor gullibility as "the seersucker syndrome": "As long as there are seers, there will be suckers.") Even though no one can predict the future, and everyone claims to believe that no one can predict the future, the world teems with people who still fall for the man who claims he can predict the future.

This accounts for the strong following astrologers command. A recent study concluded that every day, over 50 million Americans consult their astrological readings in 1200 newspapers. Estimates claim that 10,000 full-time astrologers work in this pseudo-scientific field. People are driven to extremes to find out what their future holds. Their motivation seems to be a desperation to absolve themselves of any responsibility for their situation. They are what they are, and they will be what they will be, because that's what is written in the stars.

No wonder false prophets abound. And since religion is the foundation of human life, no wonder religious false prophets are, and always have been, everywhere. Biblical prophets had a hard time of it when they came up against false ones, because they couldn't play to the crowds. They had to tell the truth, a more difficult assignment. They were called to be God's spokesmen; the future was not their primary concern. (They were content in their belief that God could manage the future as well as He had managed the past.) Their real concern was ethical living in the present. Further, God's prophets would never grant their people the easy way out; they couldn't blame the stars or the fates or anything else for their condition. The prophets held them morally responsible for themselves.

Such prophets are never honored at court, because they attack rather than support the cherished program of the current government or political parties. The *status quo* is their enemy. In fact, the chief concern of the prophets of God was not God or the worship of God, but how God's people were treating their fellow human beings. Social justice, not religious status, was their burden. True prophets preached justice, righteousness, and mercy; they themselves were usually very poor, and they refused to make themselves rich, because they would have to compromise themselves to do so. They did not preach for money, they sought no offices, they were greedy for nothing but God's will on earth. They didn't promise to satisfy their audiences; they produced the fruit of God's goodness. They called their people back to the true faith and promised a new world when their people produced the fruit of righteousness.

You can test prophets, Jesus tells His disciples, by their results.

Judge them by the Word of God: do they produce what God's prophets have always sought to produce, true servants of the living God? If not, they are like a fig tree that refuses to bear. Their destination is the same (Matthew 7:19; see also Luke 6:43-45; 13:6-9; Matthew 21:18-22). Disciples of Christ, whom Jesus has trained as the new generation of God's spokesmen (prophets), will likewise produce, as the following verses make so clear.

Disciples Not Only Produce—They Obey

Jesus wants more than promises, even more than producing. He desires nothing less than obedience. Success in producing marvelous deeds is not the criterion by which Jesus' disciples will be judged. What is so special about the ability to work miracles, after all, when there are many besides Jesus' disciples who can perform them? Such productions prove nothing. Prophets and exorcists and miracle-workers can cast their spells, and even use the name of Jesus to do so, but still be far from Him.

Jesus does not mention here why the kingdom will be barred to some who protest their faith in the Lord. Their razzle-dazzle doesn't thrill Him. He thinks they are evil-doers.

He is still thinking of the false prophets. Although false prophets may produce results, good deeds turn to evil in their hands, for their hearts are black. They do good for bad reasons. They let their light shine before men—but not so that men will praise God (Matthew 5:16). They use their special powers for selfish purposes. They do not obey the Lord. Their words are hollow.

After the famous battle of Thermopylae between the Persians and the Spartans, Simonides penned an epitaph that John Ruskin called the noblest group of words man has ever uttered:

> "Go tell the Spartans, thou who passest by,
> That here, obedient to their laws, we lie."

They paid more than lip service to their country; in obedience they gave everything.

Jesus repeatedly speaks of His own obedience to the Father: "For I have come down from heaven not to do my will but to do the will of him who sent me" (John 6:38). He demands the same submission in His disciples: "If anyone loves me, he will obey my teaching" (John 14:23). He asks nothing more than what He performs himself: "The world must learn that I love the Father and that I do exactly what my Father has commanded me" (John 14:31).

113

The parable of the wise and foolish builders summarizes the entire Sermon. Jesus has been teaching His disciples to do from the heart the things that make for righteousness. Promising (like the false prophets) certainly falls short of His standard. Even producing marvelous works is not good enough, if the heart is disobedient. Hearing everything Jesus teaches is of no avail either, if the teachings are not put into practice. Hearing must be quickly followed by doing. "Our chief want in life is somebody who shall make us do what we can," Emerson has written. Unfortunately, that person does not exist. Even God won't force us, since He prefers to invite rather than compel obedience.

Deliberately applying Jesus' teaching is rare, even in the body of Christ. Juan Carlos Ortiz, a highly respected Argentine pastor, startled his church members and ministerial colleagues when he decided to take Jesus' parable literally. Instead of the usual churchly fare of teaching on prayer at the Tuesday-evening prayer meeting, on Nehemiah at the Thursday-evening Bible study, on the Tabernacle in Sunday school, and on another topic (holiness, for example) in the Sunday-morning sermon, and yet another (the second coming of Christ) in the evening sermon, Ortiz decided to concentrate on one lesson until his people put it into practice. He felt they would profit more to listen to one message and not even return to church until they had put it into action than they would from hearing multiplied messages on multiplied subjects. Under the new program, he taught only four or five lessons a year. He says it revolutionized his church. Christians were actually practicing what Jesus preached.

When they did, the church was built on the solid rock.

Paul called Jesus the solid rock (the "sure foundation") upon which the church and Christian life are based (1 Corinthians 3:11). No threatening tempest can destroy what is built on Christ (Matthew 16:18; Romans 8:38, 39; Isaiah 26:4; Psalm 31:3). When disciples do what Jesus teaches, they build solid lives.

Amazement

Never have the people heard such teaching. Instead of quoting ancient authorities or referring to the opinion of this rabbi or that scribe, Jesus has with simple authority said, "I tell you. . . ."

Whether their amazement will translate into action remains to be seen. We may try flattering the Lord with confessions of amazement, but He is not fooled. He wants results!

CHAPTER NINE

Faith, Commitment, and Power

Matthew 8:1—9:8

The Faith That Heals (8:1-17)
(Mark 1:29-31, 40-45; Luke 4:38; 5:12-16; 7:1-l0)

As Jesus leaves His place of teaching on the mountain, much of the crowd follows Him. He has amazed them with His authoritative teaching; and He continues amazing them by His extraordinary healings. In chapters 8 and 9, Matthew records three clusters of various kinds of miracles as proof of Jesus' authority.

In this first cluster (Matthew 8:1-17) are miracles of healing; the second consists of demonstrations of power over nature—including another healing (8:18—9:8), and the third is another series of healings (9:18-34). Always concerned to present Jesus fulfilling Old Testament prophecies, Matthew (8:17) places these healings in the context of Isaiah's prediction (53:4): "He took up our infirmities and carried our diseases." (The RSV says, "Upon him was the chastisement that made us whole.")

The Gospels frequently relate sin to sickness. In this passage, Matthew records three such instances. As sin and sickness are often intertwined, so are faith and health. Three persons are healed here, a leper, a centurion's servant, and Peter's mother-in-law. With each person, the physical illness has other than physical consequences.

The leper is affected socially; his leprosy has forced him from society. He has become an outcast. The centurion is a Roman, another kind of outcast as far as the Jews are concerned. Having long been an object of Jewish prejudice, he knows better than to invite Jesus into the home of "a Roman dog." He may represent the ruling government of Rome, but to an orthodox Jew, the Roman and his servants are unworthy of notice.

Peter's mother-in-law is a woman in a culture that gives little official stature to women. What's so impressive about Jesus—among other things—is His tenderness with women. In touching her, He heals more than her illness; He elevates her self-regard. As always, He heals the whole person.

115

"Lord, if you are willing, you can make me clean." The leper confesses faith in Jesus. So does the centurion: "Just say the word, and my servant will be healed." His remarkable faith, expressed by a non-Jew, impresses Jesus: "I tell you the truth, I have not found anyone in Israel with such great faith." In response, Jesus does say the word, "and his servant was healed at that very hour."

This emphasis on faith in healing is a helpful antidote to our modern prevailing, almost magical, belief in medicine. We demand miracles of our physicians, leaning on them with a trust that previous generations never granted their medical men. We have transferred faith in God to faith in medicine and its practitioners. Yet it is passive faith. We expect to contribute little to the healing process.

Writing about glandular disorder in his *Physiological Psychology* , Dr. Starke R. Hathaway says that "the effects of personality upon glands are more impressive and easier to illustrate than are the effects of the glands upon personality."[31] Christian missionary E. Stanley Jones tells of reading somewhere that if glandular secretions were upset, a person's moral character would change. Concluding that this placed morality in a person's glands, Jones realized that preachers then should proclaim "the gospel of good glands" instead of Christ. He consulted a doctor about the power of glands, asking, "What kinds of states of mind and emotion upset the glands?" As the physician named them, Jones noted that every one was "unchristian."

Then he asked, "Suppose a person's glands were normal and suppose the person would live in a truly Christian way, would his glands function well?"

"Perfectly."

"Then, doctor, we have Christian glands," Jones concluded.[32]

The leper's faith was not unrelated to Jesus' healing of him. The effects of faith were experienced in the "glands." As everybody knows, "Sometimes it is more important to know what kind of a fellah has a germ than what kind of a germ has a fellah."

An elderly man of eighty-four years was crossing a street when he was hit by a truck and killed. During the autopsy, the doctor discovered that the old man had suffered ulcers, kidney trouble, lesions from tuberculosis, and serious heart trouble. "This man should have

---

[31]Quoted in Fosdick, *On Being a Real Person,* p. 7.
[32]E. Stanley Jones, *A Song of Ascents* (New York: Abingdon Press, 1968), p. 167.

been dead thirty years ago," the doctor reported. He asked the man's widow how he had managed to live so long. "My husband always *believed* he would feel better tomorrow," she said.[33]

Faith like this man's is enormously effective. Yet to say that faith healed these three "patients" of Jesus is to misread the passage. Something—that is, Someone—more than faith is involved.

Christ Restores Health

Jesus heals the three, not faith alone. Matthew's emphasis is on Jesus, not on their faith. In fact, the centurion's servant was healed with no expression of faith by the servant. And Peter's mother-in-law made no confession of faith at all. These are not instances, then, of what we have come to call "faith healing." This is Christ-healing.

Just about every Christian has a testimony of the effect of Christ's healing touch on him. Here's A. B. Simpson's, the pioneer of the Christian Missionary and Alliance Church. As a young Presbyterian minister of extraordinary promise, he established his reputation in Kentucky and was soon called to a New York church where he attracted immense crowds to his tabernacle. After only a little more than a year, his heavy load brought on a physical breakdown. His heart was weak, and he seemed on the verge of a nervous collapse. His physician advised him to quit the ministry entirely. Though only thirty-seven, he walked like a tired old man.

While in this condition, he visited Old Orchard, Maine, where he attended a testimonial meeting in which many Christians spoke of their healings by Christ. On a painful and slow afternoon walk in the woods, he knelt and prayed. God touched him. He later recalled, "Every fiber of my soul was tingling with the sense of God's presence." He once again committed himself to Christ's ministry. A few days later, he took a long but painless walk across the countryside and, in another day or two, climbed a 3,000-foot mountain. For thirty-five more years, he labored with all his might in Christ's service, with never another hint of heart trouble. He always believed that Christ had restored his health.

As the leper kneels before Jesus, he looks to the Savior for healing. He has been unable to cure himself; others have had no affect on his disease. Only Jesus can. The centurion likewise believes that Christ can heal. Luke describes the Roman officer (the commander of one

---

[33]Norman Vincent Peale, *The Amazing Results of Positive Thinking* (New York: Prentice-Hall, 1959), p. 170.

hundred men) as a worthy man who loves Israel and even built a synagogue for the Jews (Luke 7:1-5). He is sensitive also to Jewish feelings about Gentiles, and will not require Jesus to cross the boundaries of social propriety to enter his Gentile home. His is a faith Jesus has seldom seen among His fellow Jews. But the faith is not generalized; the centurion believes specifically, completely, in Christ. And that faith in Christ is what will one day bring Jew and Gentile together (see Ephesians 2) while some Israelites, who refuse to believe, will be lost (Matthew 8:12).

Christ Restores Full Humanity

Implicit in these healings is the fact that Jesus grants the "patients" more than health. He gives them back their full humanity. The leper is no longer an outcast. Jesus instructs him to obey Old Testament law directing that a recovered leper show himself to a priest, who could then officially pronounce him clean and offer appropriate sacrifices for him (Leviticus 14:1-32). He belongs among people once more!

The centurion's servant and Peter's mother-in-law are also restored to their rightful places. The servant returns to his service and the mother-in-law takes her place once again in Peter's home.

The Lord cares for more than physical health. He desires wholeness. It is possible for a person to have a body that functions quite satisfactorily but still fail as a person. Perhaps this is why God does not always choose to grant physical healing to those who call upon Him. If He did, the whole world would quickly become Christian, but for the wrong reason. What would happen to such virtues as patience, mercy, long-suffering, and bearing one another's burdens?

This is not to suggest that God deliberately inflicts His children with cancer, polio, or heart disease in order to foster such virtues. Most of our suffering can instead be traced to human folly or cruelty: drunken driving, homicide, child abuse, divorce, and poverty can more often than not be traced to human causes. Even certain diseases, we now realize, stem from our dietary choices or our propensity for polluting our habitat, or our strange addictions. In fact, in 1981, the Surgeon General of the United States declared, "Seven of the ten leading causes of death in the United States could be substantially reduced through common-sense changes in the life-style of many Americans."[34]

-----

[34]Sam E. Stone, "Taking Care of the Temple," *Christian Standard* (May 24, 1981), p. 3.

Christ's healing has to do with more than physical functions, then. He touches our values, our attitudes, and our habits. He teaches us how to relate to one another in helpful, healthful ways. He instructs His church to be a healing community, in which members of the body affect each other for their mutual health. "Upon him was the chastisement that made us *whole* " (Psalm 53:5, RSV).

What It Costs to Follow Jesus (8:18-22)
(Luke 9:57-62)

The Impulsive Disciple

"Teacher, I will follow you wherever you go." The man is a scribe, an Old Testament expert. He has listened to Jesus' teaching and observed His power. Because of his familiarity with the books of the Law, the Prophets, and the Writings, he can interpret Jesus in light of prophecy. When he promises to follow Jesus, he means what he says.

He is ready, but can he pay the price? Is his commitment deep enough? As a scribe, he has been a respected representative of the "party in power." As a disciple, he will incur the disapproval of the very people he has belonged to. Can he take it? He is intelligent and religious, but is he prepared to offer Jesus more than superficial allegiance? Will he really follow Jesus wherever He goes, even to the cross?

Jesus' cause will always be plagued with hangers-on. Superficial faith abounds; what Jesus needs are disciples with deep faith.

Jesus' Warning

"The Son of Man has no place. . . ." To follow Jesus is to venture into alien territory, to become a stranger and sojourner among your own people, and to give up everything, even home. Foxes and birds are better off than the Son of Man. Count the cost.

When missionary William Walker and his family returned to the United States, they did so with great reluctance and sorrow. Mrs. Walker was dying of cancer. They had no choice. A fellow minister with no experience living abroad asked Bill, a few months after their return, what effect living in Japan had had on their children. More specifically, what did the children call home? Walker said, "We've taught our children that this side of Heaven, they have no home."

> "This world is not my home, I'm just a' passing through,
> My treasures are laid up somewhere beyond the blue.
> The angels beckon me from heaven's golden shore,
> And I can't feel at home in this world any more."

Christians enjoy singing this popular chorus, but they probably do not realize the import of their words any more than this impulsive disciple realizes what he is promising Jesus.

When George Vins was exiled to the United States from Soviet Russia in 1979, he had already spent seven out of the preceding fifteen years in Siberia. A strong, uncompromising Christian, Baptist preacher Vins had been willing to submit to the state on all civil matters, but he would not bend his neck to the government in matters of faith. In these, he would submit to God alone.

Just before his departure from Moscow, a political officer notified Vins that he had been stripped of his citizenship. He warned that after a brief period of popularity in America, he would soon be forgotten by his adoptive country. Vins' fate was a sad one, he added. Vins was not shaken. "The God in whom I believe will decide that." He was prepared to be an alien for the rest of his life, since this world—whether in Soviet Russia or in the United States of America—was not his home. He would pay the price of discipleship.

The Reluctant Disciple

"Lord, first let me go and bury my father." Has his father just died? Possibly. If so, he is asking permission to perform a priority duty. Even a priest, who ordinarily had to avoid any defiling contact with the dead, was permitted to bury his father (Leviticus 21:2, 3).

Or is the reluctant disciple implying that he will follow Jesus sometime in the future, after his father has died? He is a loyal son with obligations to the family. When he is no longer under his father's authority, then he will be free to follow Jesus. If this is what he means, then he is serving notice that he considers service to his family more important than to his Lord.

Jesus' Command: Order Your Priorities

"Follow me, and let the dead bury their own dead." Do not, when you are considering Jesus' call to discipleship, allow any other pressures to turn you aside or cause you to hesitate. The dead will be buried in good time. But now is the time to give yourself to Christ. No excuses. Jesus wants the truth from us. When we say we'll follow Him, we must mean it.

When on another occasion Jesus said, "Anyone who loves his father or mother more than me is not worthy of me" (Matthew 10:37), He was again insisting on an ordering of priorities. Do not let anyone, even your closest relatives, come between you and your Lord. If you are His disciple, He comes first.

Jesus' call to discipleship is not an invitation to comfort. Nothing will be easy. There will be tough decisions, personal sacrifices, and problems. Obedience is seldom easy, but it is always necessary.

Molly Anness, an Indiana housewife who loves the Lord, penned her "Housewife's Lament" to express the difficulty of trying to be a true disciple today while surrounded by luxury:

> "I'm all wrapped up in my machines
> I push a button, my clothes are clean;
> I push another and so are my jeans.
> How can I find Jesus, where does it say On?
> It must have been easy for Peter and John
> For they didn't have their TV turned on,
> So when you called them, they just got up and went.
> But what did they leave? Just their fishing net.
> I've worked so hard for all I own,
> Now you're trying to tell me it's only a loan?
> I would answer your call, Lord, and give up all I own
> If you could only reach me through my telephone.
> How can I find Jesus, where does it say On?
> I'd follow you too, Lord, wherever you go
> If I can just bring along my transistor radio.
> But please don't come during my TV show.
> How can I find Jesus, where does it say On?

The Power That Heals (8:23—9:8)
(Mark 4:35—5:20; 2:1-12; Luke 8:22-39; 5:17-26)

This is the second of three sets of three miracles each that Matthew clusters together in chapters 8 and 9. In the first group, Jesus heals a leper, the servant of a Roman centurion, and Peter's mother-in-law. Now Matthew turns our attention from Jesus' ability to heal the sick to His power over nature and the consequences of sin.

His Power Over Nature (23-27)

The Sea of Galilee is not really a sea, but a lake, and not a very large one at that. Nestled in a basin so deep that its surface is 680 feet below sea level, it is about seven miles across and approximately thirteen miles from north to south. The dramatic contrast between Galilee's depth and the height of Mt. Hermon, rising to the north over 9,000 feet above sea level, accounts for the severe air turbulence that often afflicts the region. Visitors to the Holy Land are often treated to one of these sudden, violent storms that Matthew describes. Lord Byron could well have had Galilee in mind when he wrote *Childe Harold's Pilgrimage.*

"Roll on, thou deep and dark blue Ocean, roll!
Ten thousand fleets sweep over thee in vain;
Man marks the earth with ruin, his control
Stops with the shore; upon the watery plain
The wrecks are all thy deed. . . .

He sinks into thy depths with bubbling groan,
Without a grave, unknell'd, uncoffin'd, and unknown.

Several of the disciples are fishermen. They fear the lake with a respect born of experience. They would never volunteer to sail the lake in a storm like this one. Nature inspires such awe by its brute force that more than one philosopher has concluded that God and nature are one. Others, with more Christian insight, agree with Pascal: "Nature has some perfections to show that she is the image of God, and some defects to show that she is only His image." The fishermen-disciples in Jesus' boat do not worship nature as God, but they quickly admit their helplessness and their ignorance before the elements.

We have not, for all our impressive scientific advances, banished ignorance to this day. In a recently published compendium of scientific gaps entitled *The Encyclopedia of Ignorance,* leading researchers confess how much they don't know. One article, for example, discusses the genetic system. After describing the grouping of genes in a hierarchical system, showing how some genes control the timing of the activity of other genes or the formation of hormones that, in turn, activate other changes in a baffling complex of interacting regulators, Sir Vincent B. Wigglesworth finally concludes, "To say that the body form is controlled by the genes is hardly more illuminating scientifically than to say that it is controlled by God.[35] To speak of genes sounds more scientific than to speak of God; in fact, however, we are still painfully ignorant in this branch of science—as ignorant as we are in others.

Like meteorology, for example. Jesus' disciples could quickly admit their helplessness before natural forces they could neither explain nor control. We have a little more difficulty admitting our inability to control the winds and rains, but we are no less helpless, as faithful attendance to the television meteorologist's weather forecasts testifies. In desperate faith, the disciples rouse Jesus from His sleep. He

---

[35]Ronald Duncan and Miranda Weston-Smith, eds., *The Encyclopedia of Ignorance* (New York: Pocket Books, 1977), p. 252.

must save them. Their appeal is no less urgent than a drowning man's prayer. What they expect Jesus to do is not clear, but they obviously do not expect what He does.

Jesus' immediate control of the situation reminds us of Archbishop William Temple's well-known statement on prayer. He could not explain it, he admitted. But "when I pray, coincidences happen. When I don't, they don't."

Rebuking the winds and waves, Jesus restores peace to the waters. But He troubles His disciples. "You of little faith, why are you so afraid?" They have enough faith in Jesus to petition Him for help. But they don't have enough to sleep in the storm. His rebuke implies that faith in God banishes fear. If you believe in God's power over life and death, if you believe He is sovereign in the universe, if you hold Him to be stronger than nature, and if you believe that God cares for you, you should be able to sleep in a crisis.

His Authority Over Demons (28-34)

Gospel writers had no doubt that there were demons on the earth. Here Jesus confronted two demon-possessed men. (Mark's and Luke's accounts concentrate on just one of them; Mark 5:1-17; Luke 8:26-37.) They lived in the region along the northeast coast of the Sea of Galilee. We are uncertain about the precise location, but this is the general area. There, in the precipitous limestone cliffs, are numerous caves that were used as burial places. These formed a natural lunatic asylum. It afforded a dwelling place among the dead for the living dead.

These are violent demoniacs, known to attack unsuspecting travelers. They are society's rejects. But they are not dull. Instinctively, they sense the superior strength of Jesus. They can terrorize anyone else, but before Him they cower. He can torment them, if He wants, but He doesn't.

What are these demons, superior to man but inferior to the power of the Lord? The Bible speaks of them as spirit-beings, without body or permanent form, yet alive and obedient to "the ruler of the kingdom of the air, the spirit who is now at work in those who are disobedient" (Ephesians 2:2). Several aspects of their "personality" are noted in Scripture: they recognize Jesus (here and Mark 1:24), acknowledge His power (Mark 5:7), plead with Him (Luke 8:31), obey Him (Matthew 8:16), deceive others about the Lord (1 John 4:1-3), and are aware of their eventual destruction (Matthew 8:29). They are unclean or evil (Matthew 10:1; Acts 8:7; Revelation 16:13), and they can be the cause of such physical illnesses as blindness (Matthew 12:22), insanity (here), deformities (Luke 13:11-17), muteness (Matthew 9:32, 33), and convulsions (Mark 9:22). They are sometimes free spirits (Ephesians 6:11-12) and sometimes imprisoned in bodies (as with these demoniacs) or in the Abyss (Luke 8:31; Revelation 20:1-3).

Of one thing we can be certain: these demons believe in Christ. (See James 2:19.) Fearing what He can do with them, they plead for a reduced sentence. Jesus grants their wish, transferring them to the herd of pigs, which so madden the animals they plunge down the bank to their watery destruction. The pigs could not sustain the torment that had plagued the men. For the former demoniacs, a great calm follows the tempest. Thanks to Jesus, they have nothing to fear from the demons.

Nor do any followers of Christ, "because the one who is in you is greater than the one who is in the world" (1 John 4:4). Christians have no need to fear demons. We label our demons differently today, but they still take possession of the unwary. Alcohol controls some, drugs others, the lust for power or popularity still others. Normal sex drives can be perverted into demonic lusts; paranoia or other fears can take charge of a person's life. It is terrifying to lose control of oneself, yet nothing is more common. For all the disdain of demons in modern culture, we have not escaped the need for some kind of exorcism.

A missionary in Africa took exorcism literally not too many years ago. Skilled in medical and psychiatric techniques, he was asked to undertake the treatment of a patient that nobody else could cure. She had been diagnosed as a katatonic schizophrenic. Dr. L. Arden Almquist, the missionary, discovered that the woman came from a village whose people believed she had an evil spirit. That discovery sent him to his New Testament, where he read again that Jesus had empowered His disciples to cast out demons (Matthew 10:1). He called the patient's family, and in their presence, he spoke to the woman as he felt a first-century disciple of Christ would have done in order to exorcise an evil spirit. She was quickly restored to her normal self and worshiped the next morning with her family in the mud and thatch chapel of the mission.[36]

You would think the whole neighborhood would rush to praise

---

[36]"Medicine and Religion—A Missionary Perspective," *Occasional Bulletin from the Missionary Research Library,* April 1967.

Jesus for delivering the demoniacs. They rush to Him, all right, but to hustle Him out of their area. He has disturbed their peace and upset their economy. Just think of how much money the owners of the pigs have lost! They prefer living dead men to dead pigs. Pigs are valuable, you see.

You can count on it! The world teems with people who prefer to protect their pigs rather than be out any expense to make people whole. God may consider persons infinitely valuable, but unregenerate man prefers to traffic in pigs. What can we say to people who criticize the church for failing in its mission but do not raise a whisper against a tobacco industry that attacks people's health or a liquor industry that takes people's lives or a drug industry that dulls people's senses or the various perversions of capitalism that reduce the masses to slavery to feed the insatiable appetites of the privileged few?

Jesus towers above His Gadarene critics: they grumble about lost pigs while He dramatizes the value of human life. If one of these men had been your son, would you not have been willing to sacrifice a herd of swine to save him? That's what a soul is worth to God.

His Power Over the Consequences of Sin (9:1-8)

Returning to Capernaum, Jesus continues His teaching. People throng to Him even in the house where He is staying. As He teaches them, a paralytic is lowered from the ceiling to recline on the floor immediately in front of the Master. (See Mark 2.) His friends have brought him for healing.

He is a paralytic, but his sickness is more than physical. Once again indicating that sickness often has its source in sin, Jesus wastes no time treating superficial symptoms. He removes the cause: "Your sins are forgiven." As far as Jesus is concerned, that is the same as saying to the man, "Get up, take your mat and go home." To heal is to forgive; in this case, to forgive is to heal.

"This fellow is blaspheming," the teachers of the law mutter to themselves. They accuse Jesus of assuming authority only God has, for only God can forgive sins. If Jesus were not God's Son, their charge of blasphemy would be true.

What hurts in this incident, however, is their attitude. Ignoring the plight of the paralytic, they attack Jesus for transgressing the law (not just the law of Moses, but that and the rest of the written Scriptures and oral traditions of the elders that interpret the Scriptures). Only an expert could keep up with all the demands of what the scribes mean by "the law." Jesus is not playing by the rules of their religious tradition. They are more offended that one of their rules has been broken than by the man's paralysis. They never seem to catch on to the fact that God loves people, not rules.

Even though the subject has already been discussed, we would be remiss not to point out the relationship of sin and sickness, at least briefly, here. Jesus' treatment of the paralytic's real problem provides a helpful antidote to today's propensity for dispensing pills for every ailment. Most illness does not have a physical cause, but a moral or spiritual one. Guilt cannot be cured by a pill; neither can the host of physical ailments that may be traced to other than physical causes (like some forms of arthritis, cancer, heart trouble, and so on). Physicians speak of psychosomatic (soul-body) sickness. They appreciate the medical implications of Jesus' healing technique here. Jesus wanted the man to be whole, so He had to kill the root of the paralysis.

C. J. Jung, in his *Psychology of the Unconscious,* states that "the domestication of humanity has cost the greatest sacrifices. We do not realize against what Christianity had to protect us.... We should scarcely know how to appreciate the enormous feeling of redemption which animated the first disciples, for we can hardly realize in this day the whirlwinds of the unchained libido which roared through the ancient Rome of the Caesars. In the past two hundred years Christianity has erected barriers of repression which protect it from the sight of its own sinfulness."[37] In spite of these barriers, however, paralysis too frequently occurs. Explanations are sought everywhere but in the paralytic's sin. Mental hospitals try to cope with their overloads, prescribing group therapy, injecting tranquilizers, and theorizing about this or that probable cause. But the analysts don't blame sin.

Jesus does. And He wastes little time defending either His diagnosis or His authority for drawing such a conclusion. He just exercises His power to save. Without explaining His ability or the process by which He has diagnosed, He just tells the man to get up. Note that He does not require the man to become morally perfect so that He can heal him; instead, He heals the man so that he can become what God intends. The paralytic's friends had been unable to free him from his affliction; he had been unable to cure himself. No medicine was available that could enable him to walk again. Only the Lord who forgives sins could heal him.

---

[37]Quoted in Ralph G. Turnbull, *A Minister's Obstacles* (Grand Rapids: Baker, 1972), pp. 183, 184.

CHAPTER TEN

The Joy of Discipleship
Matthew 9:9-34

A Reason to Celebrate (9:9-17)
(Mark 2:13-22; Luke 5:27-39)

In the Christian life, celebration is routine. When Jesus invites you to follow Him, and you accept His invitation, celebration commences. Even if you are nothing but a tax collector!

Salvation Is for Sinners (9:9-13)

To his fellow Jews, a tax collector was scum. A tool of Rome, a servant of hated King Herod, handler of filthy lucre (stamped with pagan inscriptions and pagan images), a tax collector usually deserved his reputation as a corrupt money-grubber. Yet Jesus, with His astonishing disregard for reputation, invited just such a social pariah to follow Him. He did not even demand that Matthew change his ways first. He knew the change would come later.

People often misunderstand Jesus here. They believe they cannot come to the Lord until they have reformed themselves. This is a demand Jesus never makes. In His order of events, first comes the invitation to discipleship, then the reformation of character.

Immediately Matthew leaves his collection table and follows Jesus. He is so pleased to be included in Jesus' crowd that he throws a party. When you give a party, whom do you invite? Your friends, of course. But if you are a tax collector, who are your friends? Other persons of equal social demerit, like fellow tax collectors and prostitutes and, in general, society's outcasts.

The Pharisees, strict religious separatists who pride themselves on their holiness, cannot accept Jesus' disregard of social convention. How can He, a teacher, consort with riff-raff? "Because," He defends himself and His company, "for just such people I came to this earth. You, righteous persons that you are, do not need My ministrations. At least, you think you don't. These people do. So here I am."

Wise words for the church, aren't they? Every congregation is part of the body of Christ, continuing Jesus' ministry on earth. As such, the church is the only human organization that exists for the sake of people who are not yet in it. Christians do not assemble to congratulate themselves on their religious achievements; instead they meet to worship God and encourage one another as together they rescue the perishing. To rescue or assist the lost, we have to walk with those among whom Jesus walked, not "the righteous, but sinners."

"Pastor," an enthusiastic lady asked, "do you have a visitation program in this church?" The preacher assured her that the church had one that was probably the best of any church in the world.

"Really?"

"Yes, we do, and you're it." When she volunteered the information that she had a list of names of persons she wanted him to visit, he handed the list back as her assignment. Since she knew and cared about them, no organized program was needed. She represented the Lord and the church to them. She could bring the Physician to the sick as well as the pastor could. Better than he could, in some instances.[38]

Similar advice was offered by a most dignified Episcopalian preacher, in a story that has been making the rounds for some time. After he had challenged a crowd to active Christian living, a lady gushed, "Oh, Dr. Hern, I'm so excited; my cup runneth over. Whatever shall I do?"

"Why don't you go slosh on somebody?" he asked her.

When you become a disciple of Christ, you cannot keep your excitement to yourself; it spills—or sloshes—over. You tell others, you alert your friends to the new life possible for them, too—you throw a party. If your friends are among society's "less desirables," so much the better. They are the very people Jesus seeks. *Salvation is for sinners.*

Christ Is the Reason for Celebrating (9:14-17)

The disciples of John the Baptist, that austere prophet of repentance (Matthew 3:1-4), were as devoted to the pious acts of prayer and fasting as the Pharisees were. They thought there was no more authentic expression of religious fervor. Jesus and His disciples, on the other hand, were remarkable in their abstinence, but from fasting, not food. While Jesus certainly did not disapprove of fasting, He

---

[38]J. Cook, *Love, Acceptance, and Forgiveness* (Ventura: Regal, 1979), pp. 105, 106.

did teach that the discipline should be pursued in private, without calling attention to oneself (Matthew 6:16-18). John's disciples were puzzled by Jesus' departure from tradition.

More than once, Jesus must have had to answer this question. On another occasion He countered His critics, "For John came neither eating nor drinking, and they say, 'He has a demon.' The Son of Man came eating and drinking, and they say, 'Here is a glutton and a drunkard, a friend of tax collectors and "sinners"'" (Matthew 11:18, 19). In this as in so many other ways, Jesus did not fit the stereotype of a religious leader.

He offers three brief statements in defense.

"How can the guests of the bridegroom mourn while he is with them?" You don't fast at a wedding or any other celebration, do you? Jesus compares himself to a groom and His disciples to groomsmen. Self-denial when they are together would be like mourning at a wedding. There will be such a time later, when the bridegroom will be taken away (a veiled allusion to His crucifixion), but not now. Even at the end of His ministry, Jesus assures His "groomsmen" that He will always be with them, "to the very end of the age" (Matthew 28:20). Fasting, then, can never become the dominant mode of the Christian's life, since the bridegroom is always with him. Sackcloth and ashes are out of place in the company of men and women rejoicing and celebrating in their Lord.

"No one sews a patch of unshrunk cloth on an old garment." Jesus is saying, in effect, "You must understand that My ways will not fit into your traditional prescriptions for religious behavior. I am offering something quite different. Do not force My teachings into old forms. They are not designed to patch up your old-time religion. It would be as unwise to force what I bring you into the old ways as to sew new cloth that has not been pre-shrunk into an old garment. You'll ruin both the garment and the cloth. The gospel of grace cannot be patched into a religion of law or works. Grace cannot patch; it replaces."

"Neither do men pour new wine into old wineskins." If you try it, you'll burst the wineskins. Tough old leather isn't flexible enough to stretch with the fermenting wine. And the wine of Jesus' teaching is most effervescent. It will bubble out of any old containers. The new wine makes for bubbling imbibers, too. Bishop Fulton Sheen, popular television preacher of a generation ago, insisted that there could be no such person as a sad saint. His reasoning was this simple: "The fruit of the Spirit is joy." The ancient church father Tertullian

summarized the matter this way: "The Christian saint is hilarious." This is the faith that began with "tidings of great joy." Its best expression is celebration.

He Forges Wings (9:18-34)
(Mark 5:21-43; Luke 8:40-56; 9:14, 15)

This is Matthew's third cluster of miracles that attest to Jesus' authority. Additional details are given in corresponding accounts in Mark and Luke. Matthew limits himself to the essential facts.

We can grasp the sense of the miraculous that Matthew presents in this chapter by approaching the stories indirectly, by way of a childhood legend. It is just one of many stories that quickly grew up about Jesus' childhood. The Bible tells us so little about the first thirty years of Jesus' life that inventive minds filled in the blanks. One such legend reports that when Jesus was four years old, He made small birds out of clay. Then He blessed them and they quickened and flew away. The Greek novelist Nikos Kazantzakis, captivated by the image, borrowed it for his *Last Temptation of Christ*. In it, he depicts an aged rabbi, Simeon of Nazareth, talking to the young man Jesus. He tells Jesus that when the Lord was but a boy, the rabbi knew He would be special. He had seen signs, like the time when Jesus had taken some clay and fashioned a bird that seemed, as Jesus caressed it, to grow wings and fly away. The rabbi likens the bird to the soul of man which, in Jesus' caress, can take flight.

Kazantzakis could not get the image out of his mind. Much later in the book, Jesus is on the cross, hallucinating. In His delirium, Judas scolds Him for betraying His cause. He reminds Jesus what He had taught the disciples: that life on earth means eating bread and transforming it into wings, and drinking water and transforming it into wings. "Life on earth means the sprouting of wings." Then he recalls the night that Nicodemus came to see Jesus by night. He asked the Master who He was and what work He had come to do. "I forge wings," Jesus told him.[39]

The novelist has captured the essence of Jesus' ministry. Everywhere Christ went, He forged wings: wings of healing, wings of hope, wings of faith, wings to fly to eternity.

Matthew treats the first two miracles here almost casually, leaving

---

[39]Nikos Kazantzakis, *The Last Temptation of Christ,* P. A. Bien, tr. (New York: Simon and Schuster, 1960; Bantam edition, 1961), p. 484.

out much of the details found in the other accounts. He tells enough, though, for us to see Jesus forging wings for a synagogue official's daughter and a very ill woman.

That a synagogue official would beg help from Jesus is remarkable in itself. A leader in his community, a member of its upper class by virtue of his position if not his wealth, he risks his reputation to speak to this uncredentialed, itinerant healer. It is a gamble. If He fails, the man loses face.

His daughter's condition is grave. She is either already dead or very close to the end. Professional wailers, a cultural necessity in any Jewish home stricken by death, are already raising their mournful cries to the accompaniment of wailing flutes. When Jesus tells these professionals, who knew death when they saw it, that the girl is not dead but sleeping, they laugh at Him. Something about His bearing communicates authority, however, so when He tells them to stop, they stop. Gently taking her hand, Jesus speaks to the girl, and she gets up. He has forged wings for her flight to life from death.

His visit to her home was interrupted by a woman who had been victimized by an unstoppable flow of blood. For twelve years, she had hemorrhaged, a victim of her disease and a victim of the countless physicians and quacks who took her money but not her disease. Her misery was compounded by the social consequences of her ailment. The Old Testament decreed that a person in her condition was to be considered unclean and the cause of uncleanness in whomever she touched (Leviticus 15:15-30). So this woman was not welcome in polite society. Sick in body and heart, she reached toward Jesus, believing that even a touch of His garment could heal her. Impressed by her faith, Jesus forged wings for her to fly from her disease. "Your faith has healed you."

In a similar manner, He forged wings of sight for blind men. Condemned to beggary in an age that made no provision to rehabilitate the handicapped or pay any form of disability compensation, these men had no choice but to beg. From Jesus, they did not ask alms, but mercy. Not once, but repeatedly, they called to Him. They even followed Him into the house, persistence becoming rudeness in their desperation.

"Do you believe that I am able to do this?" He asked them. They believed. He believed their sincerity and gave them sight.

For the mute, Jesus forged wings of speech by exorcizing the demon that held his tongue. Chances are good that this man was illiterate. How, then, could he communicate, except by vague signs and gestures? When Jesus healed him, the man became a full participant in society.

Not everyone approves of someone who forges wings. You must understand that when someone goes about doing good, he will get himself into a lot of trouble. He will be resented for his meddling, especially by the powerful who are threatened by his greater power. As usual, the Pharisees were quick to criticize. "It is by the prince of demons that he drives out demons." This was not the first, nor would it be the last, time for Jesus to be denounced by enemies who could not deny what He had done but wanted to deny Him the right to do it. When you fly on the wings of faith, you can be certain that someone will do his best to shoot you down.

CHAPTER ELEVEN

The Kingdom and the World
Matthew 9:35—10:42

The Kingdom's First Mission (9:35—10:15)
(Mark 6:6-13; Luke 6:12-16; 10:1-16)

There is more to do than even Jesus can get to. Disease and every kind of infirmity press in on every side. Ignorance and religious confusion keep the masses in spiritual darkness. Everywhere Jesus walks, His heart goes out to the people. He touches, He heals, He teaches. He gives himself unreservedly, and still they come by the hundreds. Their eagerness to hear equals their desperation to be healed. "The harvest is plentiful," He tells His disciples. The people are ready for the Lord to lead them into the kingdom of God. But He can't do it alone.

He has been training His harvesters from the beginning of His ministry. The time has come for them to go on their own. It will be a kind of trial mission. They've been with Him for months. They've studied His every word and deed. He has decided they are ready to practice what He has been preaching. They need hands-on experience in the ministry. By going out at this time, they can learn while He is still around to evaluate their performance and correct their mistakes. Their permanent assignment will come later (Matthew 28:18-20).

Their practice run will be to their own people in Palestine. When they are more experienced, after Jesus has completed His saving work, the Lord will send them into the whole world. But as yet, they are too unsteady. They need more experience, and the evidence of Jesus' death and resurrection, before they can launch such an ambitious mission. For now, their own people will be challenge enough.

Jesus' instructions are basic, but their implications are profound. His disciples are about to become apostles.

Become Apostles

Jesus called them to be His disciples; here He sends them out as apostles (missionaries). Note the subtle change of wording between verses one and two:

"He called his twelve *disciples* to him and gave them authority to drive out evil spirits and to cure every kind of disease and sickness. These are the names of the twelve *apostles*. . . ."

"Disciples" are students, learners, or (preferably) apprentices. Jesus called them to learn from Him, the Master Builder of Lives, how they could impart life to others as He had.

They constitute a diverse group, these apprentices. Jesus has assembled some extroverts and some introverts, some brilliant stars and some shy plodders, some leaders and some followers. There are Peter, the impulsive leader, and his brother, the steady, loyal Andrew; deceitful Judas, patriotic Simon, doubting Thomas, and the others. An incongruous lot, but one He is transforming into a team capable of turning a world upside down. He does not want them to remain mere disciples forever; without ever leaving their apprentice status, they will soon be recognized as *apostles* (sent ones) as well.

Christian history has done a disservice to this good word. It has been fossilized as a title of honor for the limited number of Jesus' special disciples. From a term in motion, is has been transfixed in place and consigned to yesteryear. It originally meant "sent ones," "men on a mission," "missionaries." Jesus has been training His men to penetrate enemy lines and rescue captives. While the students (disciples) will never outgrow their Teacher, He expects them one day to become more than disciples. They are to be apostles.

Juan Carlos Ortiz explained the phenomenal growth of his church to a group of young pastors. At first, he said, his was a traditional congregation. Every week, he preached while his people sat and listened. After they listened, they sat. They enjoyed sitting and listening. They studied the sermon, they studied the preacher. They were good students. But they never graduated.

Ortiz was disturbed by these sedentary Christians. "It can't be right," he concluded, "that they just sit week after week." He searched the Scriptures to learn what he was doing wrong. Here's what he discovered: Jesus does not allow His disciples to remain apprentices forever. When the time comes, He turns them into apostles ("men with a message") and sends them out preaching and healing.

From then on, when Ortiz welcomed new members into the church, he taught them, surrounded them with Christian fellowship, and sent them back to their jobs and neighborhoods with their new knowledge of Jesus Christ. He charged them to be living testimonies to what Jesus had done for them. After a while, a new convert will tell him, "I have three or four people who have seen what has happened in my life and they want what I have. Will you teach them? Will you visit them?" Ortiz answers, "No, that's your job now. You know what brought you to Christ. You share that with them." Hesitatingly, the convert will then share his limited knowledge. In time, he will form a cell of people he is teaching. Then in time, some of them will start their own cells.

Ortiz' method is similar to that of Pastor Paul Yonggi Cho of the Full Gospel Central Church in Seoul, Korea, which at this writing has nearly 300,000 members. Pastors all over the world have asked how Pastor Cho can take care of so many members. He cannot, of course. His people meet in clusters of no more than 15 or 16 people all around the city of Seoul. Each cluster has a lay leader who teaches and pastors the members. Cho has encouraged his people to move from discipleship to apostleship (in this term's primary meaning).

Jesus provides the pattern for this shared leadership. From the wider number of followers He selects just twelve.

"Simon (who is called Peter)." Although Peter was not the first disciple whom Jesus called, his later prominence as the natural leader of the apostles places him at the head of the list.

"And his brother Andrew." Quieter and more self-effacing than Peter, Andrew will always be honored if for no other reason than that he led his more aggressive brother to the Lord. (See John 1:35-42; Mark 1:29; Matthew 4:18, 19; John 6:6-9; 12:20-23; Acts 1:13).

"James son of Zebedee, and his brother John." James is usually mentioned before John, suggesting that he was the elder of the "Sons of Thunder," their nickname, which hints at their impetuous personalities. James became a leader of the Jerusalem church and the first of the group to be killed for his faith (Acts 12:1-3). John is frequently mentioned with Peter in a leadership role in the early church, and the trio of Peter, James, and John seem to have been the closest to Jesus.

"Philip," like Andrew and Peter, came from Bethsaida (John 1:44). He is not to be confused with Philip the evangelist (Acts 6:5; 8:5-40; 21:8). Philip was probably a disciple of John the Baptist before becoming a follower of Jesus (John 1:43). He brought Nathanael to Jesus (John 1:45; see also John 6:5-7; 12:20-23; 14:8-14; Acts 1:13).

"Bartholomew." Although he is mentioned in all four lists of the apostles (Matthew 10:3; Mark 3:18; Luke 6:14; and Acts 1:13), nothing else is known of him. There are no other references to his name. Some Bible scholars guess that he is the same man as Nathanael, whom Philip led to Christ (John 1:45, 46).

"Thomas" was also called "Didymus" or "the Twin" (John 11:16; 20:24; 21:2). Most of our knowledge of him comes from John, who notes his bravery in the face of possible danger in Jerusalem (11:16), his question concerning Jesus' destiny (14:1-6), his insistence on proof that Jesus was resurrected (20:24, 25), and his belief when he saw the evidence (20:26-29; see also John 21:1-8 and Acts 1:13).

"Matthew the tax collector," also known as Levi (Luke 5:27), was the son of Alphaeus (Mark 2:14). Bible students still marvel that Jesus would dare to select a hated Jewish servant of Rome to be one of His trusted disciples. (See Luke 5:27-32.)

"James son of Alphaeus." We know his name but nothing more. He is usually identified with James the Little or the Less, the brother of Joses and son of Mary (Matthew 27:56; Mark 15:40). It is possible that James and Matthew were brothers, since Matthew is also a son of Alphaeus, although whether of the same Alphaeus is uncertain. (See Matthew 10:3; Mark 2:14.)

"Thaddaeus" is mentioned only here and Mark 3:18. The lists in Luke and Acts omit this name but include Jude or Judas, either a son or brother of James (Luke 6:16; Acts 1:13). We know nothing of him.

"Simon the Zealot" was also called "the Canaanean," which was a political rather than a regional nickname. He belonged to a party that aggressively sought the overthrow of Rome in Palestine. (He is also named in Acts 1:13; Luke 6:15; and Mark 3:18.)

"Judas Iscariot, who betrayed him." Judas' other name seems to derive from the Hebrew *Ish Kerioth,* the man of Kerioth, a town in southern Judah (Joshua 15:25). He served as treasurer of the disciples, although a not entirely honest one (John 12:1-6; 13:29). Judas had high hopes for Jesus, which were disappointed, so in the end, he turned traitor (John 6:64-71; Mark 14:10; Matthew 26:14-16; 47-50; 27:3-5).

Be Preachers and Healers

Jesus sends His apprentice-apostles out to multiply His own ministry, "to drive out evil spirits and to heal every disease and sickness." "Go to Jews only; no Samaritans or Gentiles. Preach as you go, heralding the same message you have heard: 'The kingdom of heaven is near'" (Matthew 4:17). Their healing and exorcizing will demonstrate the nature of the kingdom in which God rules, where Satan is helpless to harass and where the body is whole, where God is in charge and people love each other with a love that has the power to heal the sick and raise the dead.

The apostles must not separate preaching from healing. Jesus wants no do-goodism. To heal the sick without telling them of the Great Physician would be to condemn them to repeated illness. To cast out demons without introducing them to Him whose power is greater than the demons would leave them once again subject to demonic invasion (see Luke 11:24-26).

While touring a mission field with a non-Christian friend, Andrew W. Blackwood, Jr., had difficulty explaining the motive force behind the good works they were observing. "This I can understand," his friend said when they came up to the schoolhouse and hospital. "Here you are helping people." But at the chapel he protested, "Why do you have to drag in all this religion?"[40] Blackwood patiently explained that the missionaries did not leave home just to practice medicine or for the love of teaching. They could have done both more easily in their homeland. Their love for God compelled them to respond to Christ's commission; as a service to the Lord they were living in a hostile climate, among a people of strange culture, to bring healing and salvation to strangers they would have completely ignored had it not been for the Lord's express command. "Freely you have received, freely give," the Lord says. The roots of worldwide relief and rescue missions are in the love of God and nowhere else.

Elizabeth Elliot, widow of a missionary victim of the Auca Indians in Ecuador, contrasts two meetings of women interested in missions. The first was in a Mennonite church in Virginia, where in a matter of moments the women quickly volunteered to assume responsibility for meeting 119 different needs of missionaries. Miss Elliot was impressed.

The second meeting impressed her also, but negatively. It was a lecture on the campus of a prestigious divinity school. Most of the women attending were professor's wives. A nice man spoke on "The Search for a New Theory of Mission." Elizabeth Elliot was not quite certain what he said, but she knew for sure that in the discussion period following, one lady complained, "I never could see this business of going out and telling the whole world that your religion is better than theirs." Other heads nodded agreement.[41]

---

[40]Andrew W. Blackwood, *From the Rock to the Gates of Hell* (Grand Rapids: Baker, 1968), p. 72.

[41]Elizabeth Elliot, *Twelve Baskets of Crumbs* (Chappaqua, New York: Christian Herald House), p. 125.

The lady hasn't read Matthew 10. Jesus does not here, or anywhere else, dispatch His followers to peddle a better brand of religion. The proclamation is of the kingdom of Heaven, something superior to all religion. It is the kingdom of reality, operated according to God's rules, suffused with His love, making persons whole and liberating them from the trappings of legalistic, traditional religion.

Become Dependent

Even an apprentice missionary pays the price of practicing Jesus' ministry. Jesus orders His charges to take nothing along: no money, no bags of extra clothing, nothing. They are worthy of their keep; hospitable God-lovers will take care of them. When they are cordially received, they are to accept what is offered without looking for better provisions elsewhere. When they are refused food and lodging, they are to employ an unmistakable signal: "Shake the dust off your feet." God will note, on Judgment Day, who has turned away one of the Lord's emissaries.

It must have been nearly as difficult for Jesus' close circle of friends to give up their independence as it would be for us. Jesus insists that the beneficiaries of His men's services should support them. It is a double blessing He sought, one for the giver and one for the receiver. It is also a lesson in walking by faith for His disciples. As it had been the duty of every Jewish community to support its rabbi, so it has become the duty of the Lord's followers to support the Lord's missionaries (apostles).

The New Testament church clearly understood this principle. Paul instructed the Galatians to "carry each other's burdens," including the fact that "anyone who receives instruction in the word must share all good things with his instructor" (6:2, 6). Timothy was to see that ruling elders in his churches received double honor, which refers to the pay they received as well as the respect they deserved (1 Timothy 5:17, 18). "The Lord has commanded that those who preach the gospel should receive their living from the gospel" (1 Corinthians 9:14).

A missionary preparing to leave his home church for mission service in Indonesia reminded the congregation of Luke 8:1-3, which reveals that Jesus and His disciples were financially supported by Mary Magdalene, Joanna, Susanna, and many others who contributed out of their private means.

"Do you mean that Jesus, with all His abilities to perform miracles, needed help? He could feed thousands, but not himself?" the

138

missionary asked. "Apparently not," he answered his own question. He then told his brothers and sisters that when Jesus committed himself to His Father's service, it cost others greatly. He mentioned Jesus' family's embarrassment, and Simon of Cyrene, who was yanked out of the crowd and forced beneath Jesus' cross, and the extreme suffering of His mother Mary. When Jesus obeyed His Father, others helped pay the cost.

Ona Liles, the missionary, admitted that his human pride wanted to protest, "But I am independent. If I can't do this alone, I won't do it at all." His decision to leave America several years earlier to teach in Ethiopia had already cost his family many things: mental torture during the last year before the Communists finally forced them out of the country, the loss of everything they left behind, the further loss of $80,000 income they would have made in the States.

Then he listed the costs to be assumed in the new mission. The children would be torn from their peers; they would be educated alone, without the help of Sunday school or youth group. His wife would never have a home as beautiful and convenience-filled as those among the church families. They would be separated from friends, families, and the grandmother who may not see her grandchild again. And their supporting home church would have to raise at least $30,000 annually to support the family of five so far away.

It is precisely this dependency that Jesus asks of His obedient ambassadors. His disciples have been independent, also: fishermen, businessmen, breadwinners. They will find it no easier to give up that freedom than the missionary found it. Christ's mission demands a walk in dependency, however; His apostles can trust their own devices no longer. They will go out, trusting in the Lord and His people to meet their needs.

Woe to the Lord's people upon whom His missionaries *cannot* depend. On the day of judgment, their sentence will be worse than the ones received by Sodom and Gomorrah. Sodom cannot be found today. A nineteenth-century study called *The Land and the Book* speculated it was probably located in what is now the southern end of the Dead Sea; later speculation has pointed to the northern end of the Sea, but no one knows. Sodom and Gomorrah, which have become the symbol of vice for subsequent history, were destroyed when God sent fire from heaven during the days of Abraham and Lot. (See Genesis 19.) An even worse fate awaits Israel if the nation fails to receive Jesus' disciples.

What Disciples Can Expect in a Non-Christian World (10:16-33)

What can disciples of Jesus expect in a non-Christian world? Trouble, that's what!

Jesus continues His instructions to His disciples-becoming-apostles. He has told them where to go (to "the lost sheep of Israel" only) and what to do ("preach," "heal the sick, raise the dead, cleanse those who have leprosy, drive out demons") and how to do it ("freely you have received, freely give"). Then He cautions them to expect trouble.

Some Bible scholars believe that Matthew has here compiled a number of Jesus' teachings on various occasions. There are references, for example, to the persecution that they would face in their future but not necessarily on this limited mission (verses 17-23). With His customary realism, Jesus undoubtedly frequently alerted His men to the danger they were in because of their association with Him.

Jesus never raises false hopes. If you are a Christian, you must not expect to be exempted from the suffering that is the lot of humanity. On the contrary, you must expect more than your share, since you will be taking your stand for God in a hostile climate.

War is fraught with hardship. The Christian has declared war, along with his Lord, against Satan. The battle will be hard fought. Jesus steels His warriors against hardship, like any successful general. Garibaldi, after the siege of Rome in 1849, cheered his badly beaten forces with the promise of prolonged struggle. "Soldiers, all our efforts against superior forces have been unavailing. I have nothing to offer you but hunger and thirst, hardship and death; but I call on all who love their country to join with me." They stepped forward by the hundreds. Winston Churchill challenged his British countrymen in the darkness of their apparent imminent defeat by Hitler. He could not promise victory; he could not even promise a fair fight. Blood and toil and tears and sweat would be extracted from every English patriot. The British won the admiration of the world by their courageous response to Churchill's challenge.

You Can Expect Hostility in the World (10:16-20)

Soldiers in Christ's army do not have it any easier. "I am sending you out like sheep among wolves," unarmed except with innocence and a Spirit-led power of persuasion, bereft of even the customary basic provisions (vs. 9, 10). Don't be foolish; use your intelligence. "Be as shrewd as snakes and as innocent as doves." Be alert to the tactics of your enemy, who will drag you before hostile authorities.

140

Jesus' words are not fulfilled on this trial mission, but they come true with a vengeance later. Christ himself leads the way. Arrested in Gethsemane, falsely accused and improperly tried, condemned in a mistrial of justice, brutally flogged and crucified, Jesus advances over the enemy territory His troops will have to traverse. Then, in the early days of the Christian church (Acts), the apostles will be hauled into court time and again, falsely charged, beaten and imprisoned, and ordered to keep silent. The Holy Spirit will indeed speak through them. The good news about Jesus will be spread even through their suffering as Jesus' men obey God rather than men (Acts 4:20; 5:29). (And see the account of what just one apostle, Paul, underwent because of his service to Christ—2 Corinthians 11:24-28. Like other apostles before him, he rejoiced that he was counted worthy to suffer dishonor for Jesus; see Acts 5:41.)

Someone has said of Jesus that He did not so much go about doing good as getting himself into trouble. In this as in so much else, "a student is not above his teacher" (Matthew 10:24). But do not worry, even "about what to say or how to say it," for "the Spirit of your Father" will speak through you.

Most gospel ministers identify with the testimony one of them gave to a group of theological students. "Although I have never had to go to court for my beliefs, as the apostles did, I can testify that on many occasions, I have been informally accused and tried because of my faith in Christ. Without fail, the Holy Spirit has rescued me, and I have listened with amazement as my stammerings gave way to a persuasive argument on behalf of Christ. I have often said more than I knew and sounded wiser than I am. Somebody else was speaking through me."

You Can Expect Rejection in the Family (10:20-23, 34-38)

Persecution will come from every direction ("All men will hate you because of me"), but the most devastating blow will be your betrayal by members of your family.

History provides too many examples. During the Nazi regime in Germany, hatred and suspicion tore families apart. Children were forced to spy on their parents, brother spied against brother, neighbor against neighbor. America's Civil War wrought the same havoc, as members of families raised rifles against one another. Religious warfare wrenches families no less than political war does. Whenever you stand for Christ and the truth, you must anticipate that some, or perhaps all, of your family will oppose you, sometimes with great animosity. In practically every Christian congregation are members saddened by their banishment from blood relatives. Some have been officially declared dead. Others have been disinherited. Some have actually been beaten for God's sake—or someone's perverted interpretation of what they should do for the sake of God.

An unintentional effect of such rejection is to strengthen the bonds of love in the Christian family, the church. It is common for Christians to testify that they feel much closer to their brothers and sisters in the family of God than they do to their blood kin. It is their love in addition to the love of God that makes possible standing "firm to the end" (Matthew 10:22).

What end? "You will not finish going through the cities of Israel before the Son of Man comes." There are five possible interpretations of Jesus' meaning here:

(1) In this trial mission, the missionaries will not have completed their mission to "the lost sheep of Israel" before Jesus recalls each of them.

(2) Following His resurrection and ascension, Jesus' apostles and the other disciples of Christ will not have completed the Great Commission (Matthew 28:18-20) before the fall of Jerusalem in A.D. 70.

(3) Could Jesus have been referring to the demonstration of His eternal majesty when He was transfigured before a select group of disciples (Matthew 17:1-13)?

(4) Or was He here referring to the Day of Pentecost, when the Holy Spirit empowered the disciples to commence their ministries (Acts 2)? If so, Jesus here equated the Son of Man with the Spirit of Christ, suggesting the manner in which He would be with His disciples "to the very end of the age" (Matthew 28:20).

(5) His second coming. The conviction that Jesus would return soon to usher in the new age of the kindgom electrified the early church. Could Jesus have had this meaning in mind? (It is a little difficult to believe He intended His second coming, in light of His long delay.)

You Can Expect What Happened to Jesus (10:24, 25)

You are students and servants. You cannot expect better treatment than your teacher and master. You Lord has been insulted; do not expect compliments.

"Beelzebub" is indeed an insult of the lowest degree. "Lord of the flies," or "Lord of dung" is what the word means. You would hesitate to apply the epithet to Satan, yet Jesus' enemies freely nailed the title

142

on Him (Matthew 10:25; 12:22-28). You'll earn your own nicknames, too. Don't expect them to be flattering.

You Can Expect to Win (10:26-33)

This long chapter, with its warnings of peril ahead, is nevertheless more comforting than frightening. Jesus promises victory.

The truth will out (26, 27). What Jesus teaches His disciples in their private sessions will be disclosed publicly. Then the world will know the truth. Realistically preparing His followers for the suffering they can not avoid, He calms their fears. They do not need to be anxious. The truth will win.

They cannot kill the soul (28). So fear God, but do not fear people. Jesus' enemies can even go so far as to kill, but you are more than body. You are soul, and soul is beyond their reach.

A well-traveled minister was returning home one stormy evening. With his fellow passengers, he experienced some of the roughest moments he had known in his flying around the world. His seatmate was a lovely young woman of eighteen, who had never flown before. She was plainly scared, which brought out the protective father in the minister. As he calmly reassured her, another blinding flash of lightning brightened the dark sky outside. "There is nothing to worry about, my dear," he told her. He had traveled through enough storms to believe what he was telling her.

They were not in danger, but that knowledge did not bring peace to many of the passengers on board. Looking pale and frightened, they reached for their air-sickness bags and prepared for the worst. Everywhere the minister looked, he saw frightened eyes. He was surprised that he felt so calm, having never considered himself a particularly brave person. As he analyzed his situation and the peace he felt, he found that he was drawing his peace from two sources. (1) He had traveled by air enough to expect anything. He knew that if the plane went down, it went down. All his worrying could not keep it in the air. (2) He realized that he believed what he preached. The only One to fear is He who has power over life and death. If He really has that power, no one else does. If the plane went down and this were to be his last flight, he still had nothing to worry about. His body would be destroyed, certainly, but he was more than body. He was soul.

In that spirit, Jesus instructs His disciples. Your enemies can persecute you, ridicule you, riddle your body, and even knock the life out of it, but they cannot knock the life out of life. The soul they cannot kill.

Your Heavenly Father knows your worth (29-31). He designed you for eternity and endowed you with infinite value. He who watches over sparrows and counts the hairs on your head knows what you are worth. So don't worry. The Lord's appraisal is a powerful corrective of the prevailing derogatory opinion of humanity that is to be found in literary and scientific publications. For the most part, modern novelists seem agreed that their world is populated with beings who are not worth knowing. Most of their fictitious heroes and heroines are eminently forgettable.

We've descended frightfully from the early American appreciation of the common man. Thomas Paine, that fiery revolutionary, concluded the first part of his *Common Sense* with this ringing tribute:

> In England a king hath little more to do than to make war and give away places; which, in plain terms, is to impoverish the nation and set it together by the ears. A pretty business, indeed, for a man to be allowed eight hundred thousand sterling a year for, and worshiped in the bargain! *Of more worth is one honest man to society, and in the sight of God, than all the crowned ruffians that ever lived."*

Paine was militantly not an evangelical Christian, but he derived his opinion of human worth directly from Scripture (although God is a little more generous in His opinion of all men, even the kings and aristocrats among them, than Paine). He learned his view of humanity from the same place we do. The Christian ethic is based upon our infinite value to God. He created us to be important.

A middle-aged couple recently buried their two-year-old son. They have two older ones, one in college and the other in high school. The baby was a surprise, coming as he did so long after his brothers were born. A risk is involved when older parents have a baby. This baby suffered from that risk. He was a Down's Syndrome child. His parents could not have loved any child more than they loved him. Like Dale Evans Rogers, another mother of a mongoloid child, who wrote a book with this term as its title, they considered him their "angel unaware." They gave him everything they could—a secure home, food, an outpouring of love—but they could not give him health. He died before he reached his third birthday.

When the baby was born, some people said of his condition, "How terrible. How unfair." When he died, they said, "How terrible. How unfair." His parents grieved deeply when they had to give him up. He was still just a baby, a seriously flawed baby, but you would not have had to ask these parents what was the value of that baby. They would have sacrificed everything they had to keep him alive. They knew his worth.

Our Heavenly Father sacrificed His Son to keep us alive. We are maimed, imperfect creatures, but in the eyes of God, of eternal worth. So don't be afraid.

If you are true to the Lord, He'll be true to you (32, 33) The parents of the Down's Syndrome boy are Christian ministers. They did not escape hurt because they are in the ministry. Jesus never promised a painless existence to His disciples. What He did promise is that He will reward our faithfulness to Him with His own loyalty to us when He represents us to the Father. Whatever befalls us, then, we will win. He will personally guarantee our victory.

Alistair Cooke's account of *Six Men*[42] includes an indictment of the Duke of Windsor, England's former King Edward VII. Cooke recalls the fateful day when the king announced to his stunned subjects that he was abdicating his office in order to marry the woman he loved, the American divorcee Wallis Simpson. Cooke traces the succeeding years of their non-event-filled lives. You keep waiting for the author to praise the man for something, but he does not. Instead, he sums up the Duke in "the most damning epitaph" he can compose about "Edward as a Prince, as a King, and as a man." "He was at his best only when the going was good."

For Jesus' disciples, the going will not always, maybe not often, perhaps not ever, be good. He does not ask for heroics in the face of adversity, but He does demand loyalty. His loyal disciples can be certain that they will one day be received, on Jesus' recommendation, by the Father in Heaven himself.

A Demanding Virtue (10:34-42)
(Luke 12:51-53; 14:26, 27; 10:16; Mark 9:37)

As Jesus concludes His commissioning charge to His disciples-turning-apostles, He makes it impossible for His followers to misunderstand what He demands of them. They dare not believe He is leading them into a trouble-free utopia. "Do not suppose that I have come to bring peace to the earth. I did not come to bring peace, but a sword" (Matthew 10:34). In Ephesians 6:17, Paul calls the Word of God the "sword of the Spirit." This sword "penetrates even to dividing soul and spirit, joints and marrow" (Hebrews 4:12). Jesus is the Prince of

---

[42]Alistair Cooke, *Six Men* (New York: Alfred A. Knopf, 1956), p. 82.

Peace, but He is also "the way and the truth and the life" (John 14:6), and as every wise person has discovered, truth divides. (For a discussion of peace-seeking versus peace-making, see the commentary on Matthew 5:9, above.) Jesus correctly insists that what matters in discipleship is not your desire for peace, but your loyalty to your cause. The consequence of loyalty is peace within, if not necessarily without. Allegiance to Jesus has to come before any other commitment, even before family.

The Tests of Loyalty

Family takes second place to Christ. Jesus paraphrases the eighth-century prophet Micah (see Micah 7:6):

> "For I have come to turn
> a man against his father,
>   a daughter against her mother,
> a daughter-in-law against her mother-in-law—
>   a man's enemies will be the members of his own household"
>   (Matthew 10:35, 36).

Lest someone should miss the point, Jesus adds, "Anyone who loves his father or mother more than me is not worthy of me; and anyone who loves his son or daughter more than me is not worthy of me" (10:37). Nothing less than total commitment satisfies the Lord. The family must not reach any higher than second place in our hearts. To place it first is idolatry (Exodus 20:3; Matthew 12:46-50).

Jesus does not disparage family ties. From the cross, He arranged for the care of His mother (John 19:26). He scolded the Pharisees and teachers of the law for allowing calloused treatment of parents (Mark 7:9-13). He wants heightened, not lessened, love. He who loves the Lord first will love his parents more. He who is genuinely loyal to God will treat his wife, children, and parents better.

The test of loyalty is tough. A wife recently divorced her husband of more than twenty years. Now in her forties, it seems the woman had made up her mind many years ago that she no longer loved her husband but would stay with him for the sake of the children. Then, when the children were old enough, she would rid herself of him. Her commitment was temporary. Her attitude symbolizes the "me-first" or "children-first" loyalty that writes its own rules. If your allegiance goes no higher than your family, then your family will suffer the insecurity of knowing it can be dissolved when you feel it no longer satisfies your conditions.

"Anyone who does not take his cross and follow me is not worthy of me" (Matthew 10:38). Your professions of loyalty cannot be trusted as genuine until they have been tested and found true. Figuratively (and sometimes literally), you have to die first. To prove His obedience to His Father and His love for His Father's world, Jesus will later take up His cross and carry it to Golgotha. He has told His Father, "Your will be done." He has to prove He means what He says.

He means what He tells His disciples, also. He expects cross-bearing. In His case, a cross meant death. For His disciples to bear a cross could mean dying for the Lord; at the very least, it means standing firm for Him, working hard for Him, carrying your share of the load even when you don't want to. It certainly cannot mean treating the church like a social club, or relying on somebody named "George" to do all the work. A cross means sacrifice. Without a cross, a disciple is "not worthy" of Jesus.

In Revelation 2:10, the Lord predicts that "the devil will put some of you in prison to test you, and you will suffer persecution for ten days." Then He charges, "Be faithful, even to the point of death, and I will give you the crown of life." At the time Revelation was written, Domitian was emperor of Rome. He decreed that everyone in the Empire must obey an old law that he discovered and revived, requiring the Empire's citizens to address their Emperor as "Lord and God"! He did not force them to forsake their old religions, so long as they burned a pinch of incense and swore allegiance to him in addition to their other gods. Domitian had just commissioned statuary depicting his great general-father, Vespasian, former emperor; his dead brother Titus, conqueror of Jerusalem; and his sister. They were to be mounted over the caption, "We are your Gods."

Domitian seemed the incarnation of confidence. But he was terrified. He ordered stone mirrors to be set in the palace walls so that he would never be unable to see behind him. Knife blows come from the rear when you are emperor. He finally went mad, like a latter-day Nero.

Christians in his empire did not know this about their ruler, of course. They just knew that his orders were impossible for them to obey. In John's vision, Jesus comforts the church in Smyrna (Revelation 2:11), promising that "he who overcomes will not be hurt at all by the second death." Many of them will die because of the emperor's edict. But then they will live.

The Paradox of Loyalty

Memorize this Scripture: "Whoever finds his life will lose it, and whoever loses his life for my sake will find it" (Matthew 10:39). The paradox seems universal. If you would find it, you will lose it; if you would save it, you will lose it; if you will lose it, you will find and save it. "It" can be many things. Driven by desire to possess something, you will probably succeed in driving it away from you. You know people who want to be loved so strongly that nobody wants to love them. Others, lusting for power or position, clutch so tightly they cannot hang on to what they sacrificed everything to get. On the job, some employees will do just about anything to get a promotion—except earn it. Their wanting insures their losing. Some parents become terrible parents by trying too hard to be perfect parents. They hang on to their children tighter and tighter for fear they'll lose them. Inevitably, they lose them. Jealous husbands and domineering wives drive their spouses away, exactly what they do not want.

It is a fundamental principle of life, paradoxical though it sounds. You will lose what you most want if you want it too much. The person who says, "I've got to do my own thing," will probably never discover what it is. The one who says, "I've got to find out who I am," is not going to find out, at least not that way. No Scripture is more often forgotten or violated by Jesus' disciples than this one. Yet this lesson must be learned: the only One we can want so strongly, whom we cannot lose, is God himself. We shall not lose Him because He cannot be destroyed and will not be controlled by us. In our other relationships, intense desire leads to an attempt to control the one desired. But we cannot do that to God. We can love Him with all our being, with "heart and soul and mind and strength," in a way we dare not love another. Jesus, whose insight into the nature of love has never been surpassed, encourages His disciples to offer God that intense love, love that is really worship, but He never encourages us to love wife or husband or children or parents in this way. That would be idolatry, and it would destroy the relationship. Only God is worthy and only God can withstand the lover's attempts to overpower the loved one.

When I graduated from theological school and began my work as a pastor, my biggest worry was what the demands of my calling would do to my family life. After twenty-five years, however, I have found that my fears were groundless. In fact, I have had a richer experience with my wife and children than I ever thought possible. My wife gets the credit for making this possible, since she helped the entire family become part of the team ministry with me. Every child recognizes that the family's highest loyalty is to God, not to himself or herself or even to the family as a unit. I'm convinced now that if you serve God as a family, and not the family itself, God will reward your loyalty with blessings beyond anything possible otherwise.

A doctor in New York City suffered a nervous breakdown and was confined to a mental hospital for eighteen months. After his long treatment for schizophrenia, his doctors declared him sufficiently well to return to his medical practice. He confided to a friend six months later that he (the friend) could not remotely imagine what a battle it had been for the doctor to return to his daily task of seeing and helping patients. Every little difficulty made him look longingly back to the protection and serenity he enjoyed in the hospital. He said that the temptation to run away from his duties to find peace was at times almost irresistible. He had discovered the way to peace while he was a patient: retreat from life. Let others worry about the problems "out there." Turn over to someone else all responsibility for yours and everybody else's welfare. This is called "saving your life." You give up just about everything, but that's the way to save your life. The result? You lose it. Only by leaving the sanctuary of the hospital, where everything he did revolved around his welfare, to a problem-filled world where he was forced to forget himself as he helped others, could he find life again.

The Reward of Loyalty

The doctor had discovered what every mother already knows. How many nights she sacrifices her sleep to answer a child's cry, change soiled sheets and clean up the sickness, pace the floor to hold and comfort a fretful young one, or rush to the hospital for emergency care. No mother worthy the name ever raised a child without giving up a great deal. Why don't mothers quit? Because they know that in losing their lives, they find them. Life consists of hurting when others hurt, crying when they cry, running risks for them, doing things you don't want to do, going the second mile when you are already exhausted from running the first one. The paradox of complete loyalty is that what seems to be sacrifice turns out to be the only road to life.

Jesus does not blush to offer a reward for such loyalty. To serve Jesus is to serve the Father who sent Him (Matthew 10:40). Jesus' messengers can expect to be cared for; further, those who assist them can look forward to being treated in a manner worthy of the prophet or righteous man himself (just as an ambassador is treated with the respect due to the important official who sent him). You can be certain that the Son of Man will adequately recompense you for your sacrifices and will see to it that any kindness done to you because you are His disciple will also be rewarded. He who sees in secret will take note of what has been done (Matthew 6:4, 6, 18).

C. S. Lewis somewhere draws attention to the "staggering" rewards Jesus promises, and he suggests that the Lord seems to find our usual desires "not too strong, but too weak." We fritter away our opportunities by pursuing food and drink and sex and ambition when we could be taking advantage of Jesus' offer of joy and life. Lewis compares us to an ignorant child making mud pies in a slum, who keeps on with his meaningless activity because he cannot imagine what someone means who offers him a vacation at the beach. The child is far too easily pleased. So are we.

CHAPTER TWELVE

Faith, Repentance, and Rest
Matthew 11

Do You Doubt Jesus? (11:1-15)
(Luke 7:18-30)

It might seem surprising that John the Baptist should ask, "Are you the one who was to come, or should we expect someone else?" John had earlier spoken with such confidence about Jesus, hailing Him as "the Lamb of God" and baptizing Him (although admittedly with some reluctance, because of his awe of the Messiah). He had no doubt then that Jesus must increase even as he would decrease in power and influence (John 3:26-36). The question here sounds as if John is now not so sure. John is a great prophet, but he is still a man, subject to disappointment and depressions like the rest of us.

John's Doubt

John has high expectations of Jesus, and the Lord has not disappointed him. On the other hand, neither has He fully satisfied him. As John languishes in prison in the fortress of Machaerus by the Dead Sea (he has been arrested by Herod the Tetrarch of Galilee—see Matthew 14:1-12), his only source of information about Jesus is rumor. And many rumors there are, containing just enough truth about the growing number of Jesus' enemies and His failure to do anything about the burden of Roman rule to make John wonder. John must also be questioning Jesus' failure to do anything to bring about John's release. He has placed all his hope in Jesus. Has he hoped in vain?

Unrealized hopes are a frequent source of doubt. We tell the Lord what we want Him to do; when He fails to meet our expectations, we begin to wonder whether He is the Lord after all. "How can the Lord let me down like this? How can He let this happen? Why aren't my prayers answered?" Or, in Jesus' day, "If He is the Messiah, why hasn't He freed us from Rome?"

No wonder Jesus said, "Blessed is the man who does not fall away on account of me" (verse 6). None is immune to this temptation. One of Jesus' first disciples earned the nickname, "The Doubter." Thomas found his fellow believers' stories about Jesus' resurrection just too incredible to accept. He refused to go along with them, he said, until he could actually touch the nail marks in Jesus' hands. When Jesus later appeared to the disciples and let Thomas have his way, the disciple immediately confessed his belief (John 20:28). Jesus spoke beyond him to the millions who would not have have access to this physical proof, yet would trust Jesus anyway. "Blessed are those who have not seen and yet have believed." Jesus does not condemn doubt, even in Thomas. Nor do the Scriptures. They realize that faith implies doubt. We needlessly criticize ourselves for occasional doubts, but what we condemn is the force that impels us to search for the evidence upon which faith is built. Doubt is the stimulus to which faith, anchored on knowledge, responds.

Genuine faith is not easy. Believers speak of the passion in their hearts, the anguish of their minds, the uncertainty of intelligence, even, at times, of the near despair of their feelings. Like Jacob wrestling with his angel (Genesis 32:22-32), they have encountered the power of God and have limped away. They are humbler than before, less dogmatic than they were, but more trusting in the few essentials of their faith. Unlike those simpler souls whose faith is more in faith than in God, they believe with their whole beings in a God who refuses to conform to their expectations of Him. What matters is what He thinks of them! God feels no compulsion to be God on our terms. He writes His own job description. Not until we accept Him as He is can we be certain of Him.

Jesus' Answer

Jesus answers John's inquiry with evidence. "Go back and report to John what you hear and see: The blind receive sight, the lame walk, those who have leprosy are cured, the deaf hear, the dead are raised, and the good news is preached to the poor" (4, 5). Whether the response is satisfactory to John, the Scripture doesn't say. But Jesus is answering in His own terms. When He began His ministry, He read Isaiah 61 to His townspeople and told them that this would be His job description (Luke 4:16-21). Now to John He sends this report: "I am preaching good news to the poor, setting prisoners free, giving sight back to the blind, and releasing the oppressed. I am doing what I was sent to do. Yes, I am the one you are asking about. This is the evidence you seek."

He still provides evidence. A minister with twenty-five years of experience describes the difference between his early and his mature preaching. When he began, he was as faithful to God' Word as he knew how to be. He believed what he read, and he taught its meaning as accurately as his limited experience could afford. What he preached, however, he preached "on faith," because he had not yet seen the proof of the power of the gospel. A quarter of a century later, however, he preaches about peace of mind with deeper conviction, because he has attained it. He speaks of healing, because he has experienced it personally and observed it repeatedly. He offers new birth in the name of Jesus because he has been born again and has assisted many others to new life. He knows the power of the Holy Spirit, since the Spirit has taken over his life. He believes the Word because of the evidence! His earlier tentative faith, sprinkled generously with the doubts of youth, has yielded to knowledgeable faith which has overcome most doubts. He no longer demands that God meet his expectations; he tries now to meet God's.

E. Stanley Jones offers a good example of how this works. While the missionary to India was in the United States, he met a Chinese man who claimed to be without any religion. He had lost faith in his old one and had found nothing to take its place. He could not accept the divinity of Christ. Jones asked him what he did believe. The man admitted he thought Christ was the best of men.

Dr. Jones challenged him to begin right there. Since Jesus was his ideal, he should cut out of his life anything that his ideal could not approve of. Protesting that it would not be easy to do this, the man was nonetheless honest enough to admit that he could with integrity do nothing less. Without waiting to resolve all his intellectual difficulties, he determined to let Jesus into his life—as the most outstanding moral ideal he knew. Some time later, he sought Jones out. "I didn't know a man could be as happy as I am today," he told him. His questions and doubts about Christ were gone. He had stopped trying to be his own god, had accepted Jesus as Lord (even with his incomplete understanding), and acted.[43]

When doubts overwhelm us, it is usually not because they raise such large questions but because they have a paralyzing force. They render us indecisive, then inactive. Faith can only grow as it is expressed. You must lose the little you have, or even that will be taken

---

[43]E. Stanley Jones, *Victorious Living* (New York: Abingdon, 1936), p. 51.

away. Old-timers in the faith sometimes seem utterly reckless to younger believers. They are not really abandoning judgment, however. They are just living on evidence. They began acting years ago on the little bit of faith they had then, and the Lord has rewarded their little faith. So they have continued taking bigger and bigger steps, and the Lord has rewarded their bigger steps.

Jesus' Promise

As John's disciples leave, Jesus speaks about him to the crowd. He wants to reinforce John's reputation as a prophet and great man. The crowd should not misunderstand him, just because he has sent some questioners to Jesus. He is no "reed swayed by the wind." No, he is a prophet, of that they can have no doubt. Not only a prophet, but Elijah returned according to promise (Malachi 3:1; 4:5). He has heralded the way of the Messiah.

A great man. Yet, when compared with the citizens of the new kingdom of which Jesus speaks, he is like the least among them. John could only point to the one who would baptize with fire and the Spirit; citizens of the kingdom would be in His living presence forever. John is a lone voice crying in the wilderness; the kingdom's citizens would be a great host of people in fellowship with each other. You, then, are greater than John. The prophet is still bound by the law of Moses; you will be citizens of a new kingdom, free from that law but upheld by a higher one, the law of love. You will do greater things than John (greater even than Jesus, John 14:12)!

Thrust and Counter-Thrust (11:16-24)

From answering John the Baptist's inquiries, Jesus turns the conversation to the criticism both He and John have been receiving. The critics have rejected John, even though he is no less a person than the great prophet Elijah returned to herald the way for the Messiah. And they are now rejecting the Messiah (although Jesus does not use this title here).

Thrust (11:16-19)

The critics condemn John for his strict, ascetic life, and Jesus for his vigorous participation in society. They are like children in the marketplace (the *agora,* the public square where people gather for trade or talk—see Acts 17:17) who amuse themselves with games. First they play Wedding, which requires dancing and singing; then Funeral, with mourning and weeping. They decide the game, they make up the rules, then they urge others to play what they have decided in the way they dictate. When others don't dance to their tune or weep to their beat, they complain loudly.

Is Jesus suggesting that His and John's critics are making a game of their religion? Probably not, although it is tempting to develop the idea. Certain psychologists like to talk, in the language of Berne's book, about the *Games People Play*. Games-players do not relate to others as adults to adults, but assume either a parent or child role. Jesus, who urges His disciples to be childlike in their relation to God, chides His critics here for their childish petulance.

They disapprove of John's stern self-denial and his unyielding call for repentance. While great crowds responded to his ministry at the Jordan, there were the predictable persons who could not or would not accept John's message or repent and be baptized. They covered their hardness of heart with mockery. "He has a demon," they said. Jesus would hear the same charge (Matthew 12:24). Now, however, the charge He deals with is gluttony and drunkenness, a most predictable accusation to level against one who ministers among sinners wherever they feel most at home. Jesus, no less than John, preaches repentance; so Jesus, the same as John, must expect condemnation.

There is some truth in their charge, of course. Jesus is no "saint," in the ordinary religious meaning of the term. John qualifies, but Jesus doesn't. He keeps the wrong company, He speaks the truth even if it offends proper religious leaders, and He does not define righteousness in terms of what He eats or drinks, but in terms of service to God. His opponents cannot understand His alleged violations of religious propriety, but then, as Emerson has said, "to be great is to be misunderstood." (Emerson argues that being understood is not such a bad thing. "Pythagoras was misunderstood, and Socrates, and Jesus, and Luther, and Copernicus, and Galileo, and Newton, and every pure and wise spirit that ever took flesh.")

The world is full of people who know better what you should do than you do. When Fred Astaire took his first screen test, his evaluation was unforgettable: "Can't act. Can't sing. Balding. Can dance a little." This was said of the most famous American dancer in the twentieth century!

Jesus has no intention of changing to please His critics. "Wisdom is proved right by her actions" (v. 19). "The truth will out," we say. When you know you are serving the truth, let the critics carp. When Cesar Franck's Symphony in D minor was first performed, the audience greeted it with a roar of boos. Hector Berlioz, another famed

155

composer, was in the audience, leading the chorus. A friend of Franck's went backstage to console Franck and to ask the composer how the symphony sounded to him. He smiled gently and said that it sounded just as he had hoped it would. He was satisfied, because he was listening to a voice more authoritative than that of his critics. He served a higher truth.

Socrates asks Crito whether it is not better to follow the opinion of the one man who has understanding rather than the opinion of the many. The question still needs to be raised. Truth makes you free; submission to the dictates of the masses enslaves. Jesus will serve wisdom and be free to speak the truth. "Truth will out."

Counter-Thrust (11:20-24)

Jesus does not remain on the defensive. Now it is His turn. We think of His insistence that He did not come to judge but to save the world. Yet, the "very word which I spoke will condemn" the nonbeliever on the day of reckoning (John 12:47, 48). Truth is truth, and truth judges nontruth. Just as greatness is not at the critical mercy of shallow amateurs but is instead the judge of the critic, so the truth that Jesus speaks is not in question: the judgment of His critics is what is at stake.

With compassion, Jesus bewails the fate of the cities (and by implication, all people) that have rejected Him. They have refused to repent, in spite of Jesus' many miracles among them.

Korazin appears only here and in Luke 10:13. This is evidence that Jesus really did perform many other deeds that have not been recorded in the Bible. (See John 21:25.)

Bethsaida appears only here and Mark 8:22-26. More evidence.

Capernaum was the city that Jesus made His Galilean headquarters. There He performed many mighty signs. Perhaps the citizens of this town considered themselves superior to other cities because of Jesus' work there. If so, Jesus wishes to restore their humility.

Tyre, Sidon, and Sodom were considered heathen cities of the worst kind. Yet they would have been more receptive to Jesus than the cities of Israel were; so at the Judgment, they can expect to be treated more favorably than haughty Israel. Had they received the favors that Israel's cities received, their citizens would have taken to sackcloth and ashes (camels' hair garments made of the same tough material of the large sacks laid across the backs of beasts of burden, and ashes over the body to signal the deep distress of the penitent). They would have profited from the opportunities Israel is squandering.

So Capernaum and her sister cities can expect no Heavenly destination. Hades, the abode of the dead, will be the end of its journey.

(For Sodom, see Genesis 18:23—19:29. For Tyre, see Amos 1:9, 10; Isaiah 23; Ezekiel 26:3-7, 28:19; Jeremiah 25:22, 47:4. For Sidon, see Ezekiel 28:20-23; Jeremiah 25:22; 47:4.)

The Lifting Load (11:25-30)

Sometimes You Can Be Too Smart for Your Own Good

This is an ancient truism, honored more often in breach than in practice. To be smart or clever or sophisticated is a cherished goal of the ambitious. It is just expected that the rising young executive, for example, will be worldly wise, an expectation that a certain applicant for an executive position failed to meet. His credentials were superior to those of the other candidates, he was told, and he was considerably more experienced. His recommendations were excellent and his rapport with his associates was commendable. He was passed over, however, because in the opinion of several members of the selection committee, he did not seem "sophisticated" enough for the position.

The man felt complemented rather than insulted by this evaluation. He was a Christian, and he had already had his fill of the sophistication his society praised. He probably knew the meaning of the root word, *soph,* "wise." He may have also known that this root shows up in words like *soph*istry ("deceptively subtle reasoning, with intent to mislead") and *soph*omore ("wise fool"). He had read his Scriptures and heeded their advice to beware of those who think they are wise (1 Corinthians 1:18-31; Proverbs 3:7).

Jesus has no compliments for the worldly wise. He knows that prosperous and influential persons (and even cities, like those He has dealt with in verses 20-24) will not eagerly hear a word from the Lord. It does not worry Him that they reject Him; He prefers the company of innocence. "I praise you, Father, Lord of heaven and earth, because you have hidden these things from the wise and learned, and revealed them to little children" (verse 25). Sometimes you can be so smart you can't see what a child sees. Standing taller, you may see farther than a little child, but only when you stoop can you study the beauty that is the treasure of the observant little one. How good it is for us to see with a child's eyes and hear with a child's ears.

A child often "sees" truth that adults miss. A three-year-old girl blurted out to her father, in the midst of a conversation, "Daddy, talk like Jesus." Her father, a college dean, couldn't understand what she wanted. For her slow-learning father she explained. "You told me that Jesus lives in you. Now talk like Jesus." She's right, of course. She expects that her father, who claims to be Christian, will so comprehend his Lord that he'll even sound like Him.

John Gardner says somewhere that old dogs won't learn new tricks, not because they are unable, but because they are content with their mastery of the old tricks. Learning new ones is strictly for puppies, they think. Besides, they "are too busy paying off the mortgage on the dog house." A child isn't hasseled by mortgages or stagnated by conceit, so he can learn and do. The child's honesty makes it easier for him to confess that he is a little sinner and a little saint, capable of being very good and very, very bad. He is tractable in either direction. Thus the Lord can reveal to a child what a hardened adult refuses to learn. "I praise you, Father . . . because you have hidden these things from the wise and learned, and revealed them to little children."

The Son of God, Who Is Smarter Than We Are, Always Speaks the Truth

"All things have been committed to me by my Father. No one knows the Son except the Father, and no one knows the Father except the Son and those to whom the Son chooses to reveal him." So if we wish to know the truth about God or about life or the world or ourselves, we must listen to the Son through whom the Father reveals it. He tells the truth.

Not everybody does. When Jimmy Carter was running for the U. S. Presidency, he promised the American people that he would never lie to us. We greeted his pronouncement with a chorus of hoots. It was too late; we are too cynical. We long ago stopped believing politicians. What makes us so sure they don't tell the truth? We point out that their record speaks against them. We can't trust them; we also distrust lawyers, bankers, scientists, teachers, and even, sometimes, parents. We have caught too many of them distorting the truth. Lying is of the essence of sinful humanity. Whom can we believe?

Jesus: "If you hold to my teaching, you are really my disciples. Then you will know the truth, and the truth will set you free" (John 8:31, 32). Specifically, Jesus' truth will free His followers from the heavy burdens the Pharisees and teachers of the law were laying on the Jews. They demanded careful attention to the hundreds upon hundreds of regulations that they taught as the essence of religion. In place of the rules and "rulers," Jesus offers a relationship with himself, a partnership in which Jesus shares our work.

158

John's Gospel calls Jesus the *logos,* the *Word* or *Expression* of God (John 1:1). We have no "scientific" proof that John is correct, but we treat this claim to truth as we would any other claim: we use it until investigation or experimentation proves it to be untruth. After two thousand years of testing, Jesus' truth still holds. When we build upon his words, we build on a sure foundation (Matthew 7:24-27).

He Offers Us This Welcome Word of Truth: "I Give You Rest"

"Come to me, all you who are weary and burdened." Christ's words are for tired people. He has walked among the poor, lifted the oppressed, brought the outcast into His circle of love, and made life easier for every burdened soul. He has compassion on the people who crawl through their difficult days, scratching out enough to get by today, hoping there'll be something for tomorrow. Many are beyond poor; they are destitute.

Most of the readers of these pages do not experience such poverty. Your burdens are not financial nor physical so much as mental and emotional. You need rest more from social anguish than from physical sweat. In the 1960s, it became a cliche to call this the age of anxiety. People began admitting that life had become too much for them. They were—they are—scared.

The century is not ending as it began. In 1902, George Coe boasted in *The Religion of a Mature Mind* that "men have ceased to be afraid." He was only one among many seers who, peering over the edge of the new century, beheld Utopia. In the twentieth century, they believed, mankind would solve all its problems. No more fears, no more superstitions, no more wars, no more anxiety. Then came two world wars and police actions without number. Depressions and recessions, cold wars and hot ones, armed truces and broken disarmament treaties, spiraling incidents of homicide and suicide, breakups of homes and breakdowns of psyches. We have not ceased to be afraid. We major in worry.

Robert Frost quipped once that "the reason worry kills more people than work does is that more people worry than work." Work, in fact, is just the antidote to worry and weariness that Jesus offers. Instead of inviting His disciples into tranquil retirement, like some South Sea Island vagabond relaxing in his hammock and sipping his drinks, Jesus offers a yoke. "Take my yoke." This may not mean much to a city-apartment dweller, but every farmer for centuries could identify a yoke. Jesus refers to a double yoke, designed to assist two oxen to pull together. The yoke is a harness that makes work possible and eases its strain at the same time. Jesus' work is still work, but the strain and tension are gone. He's pulling with you.

Ralph Waldo Emerson discovered that "God offers to every mind its choice between truth and repose." You take your choice; you can't have both. Blessed, then, is the person who has found his truth and does it. His love of his work and the One for whom he works makes his work light.

Rest, defined as complete ease, is exactly what Jesus does not promise. Nothing damages mind and body like total withdrawal from meaningful labor. Visit a retired person who has found no creative activity to replace his employment, who has a live-in nurse or lives with a son or daughter or is in a nursing home so he won't have to do anything for himself. There you can study at your leisure what most people think they want: rest. Nothing to do but sleep, all your food brought to your bed, someone to care for your every need. That's rest. But it is not life.

True soul-rest comes from teaming up with the Lord in the care of others. It comes from loving someone else. That love draws out your potential. It helps you to please God. Thomas Huxley said, "A man's worst difficulties begin when he is able to do what he likes." Kierkegaard defined anxiety as "the dizziness of freedom." To be able to do what you want to when you want to because you want to will topple you. What you need more than freedom is a lifting load.

The joy of teaming up with Christ is that He takes the worry out of work. The worry belongs on His side of the yoke, not yours. When African pioneer missionary David Livingstone entered a village where his reputation had preceded him, six or seven thousand villagers rushed out to meet him, including the court herald, who shouted to Livingstone, "Don't I see the white man? Don't I see the comrade of Sebituane? Don't I see the father of Sekeletu? We want sleep. Give your son sleep, my Lord."[44] He solicited the missionary to grant the village protection from the neighboring Metabela tribe. His people could not sleep; they worried about attack. He believed Livingstone could protect the people from their enemies. Then they could sleep.

What the court herald wanted from Livingstone, Jesus freely gives His people. We can sleep. We will still work, often very hard, but without worry. Our Partner takes care of the worry.

---

[44]George Seaver, *David Livingstone: His Life and Letters* (New York: Harper and Brothers, 1957), p. 175.

CHAPTER THIRTEEN

The Authority of the Lord
Matthew 12

It Is Never Wrong to Do Right (12:1-14)
(Mark 2:23-3:6; Luke 6:1-11)

"On God and God-like men we build our trust," Tennyson wrote on the death of the English general Wellington. We can agree with the poet's sentiment, but we must add that we fear anyone who claims to be God-like. This passage justifies our fears. "The Pharisees went out and plotted how they might kill Jesus" (Matthew 12:14).

The Heartlessness of the Religious

An opinion poll of first-century Palestinian Jews would have concluded beyond doubt that the Pharisees were the most God-like men in the country. Yet these holy men could murder in the name of religion, and for no graver offense than violating the Sabbath law. Legalistic interpreters and upholders of the law, Pharisees could explain its every nuance. For example, they knew that it was ordinarily acceptable to pluck grain as you walked through your neighbor's grainfield. (Deuteronomy 23:25—"If you enter your neighbor's grainfield, you may pick kernels with your hands, but you must not put a sickle to his standing grain.") But when the Pharisees saw Jesus' disciples picking and rubbing the grain on the Sabbath, they were offended. That was work (reaping and threshing), and illegal (Exodus 20:8-11).

Jesus defends himself and His disciples by alluding to an Old Testament exception to the law. Young David, not yet king of Israel, had to flee for his life from the maddened King Saul. He and his men hid for some time in the wilderness. They naturally became hungry. David entered the tabernacle and received some of the consecrated bread (called "showbread") from the priest (1 Samuel 21:1-6). It was forbidden to eat the showbread, but the priest treated this incident as an extenuating circumstance, so he fed David's company.

If this exception was justified in David's case, Jesus implies, it is more than justified now, since "one greater than the temple is here."

Sometimes circumstances overrule the law. At any rate, God desires "mercy, not sacrifice" (Hosea 6:6).

Jesus appeals to another higher principle to explain His healing on the Sabbath. If plucking a few grains was work, certainly healing someone's illness was. *"Is it lawful to heal on the Sabbath?"* One such question deserves another, especially since Jesus perceives that He is being trapped. "Is it lawful to rescue a sheep?" They have no qualms about that! Then He applies His governing principle: "How much more valuable is a man than a sheep!"

Jesus almost sounds here as if He is against religion. In a real sense, He is. So are His disciples, if you will grant the distinction between being "religious" and being "Christian." From a Biblical point of view, you do not necessarily honor someone when you call him "religious." Religiosity and meanness frequently keep company. This is why Jesus repeats "I desire mercy, not sacrifice" (Matthew 9:13).

On this subject, John Ruskin offers a variation of the proverb (Proverbs 22:6). "To make your children capable of honesty is the beginning of education. Make them men first, and religious men afterwards, and all will be sound; but a knave's religion is always the rottenest thing about him."

This putting down of religion may discomfort you, but it is precisely what the prophetic message of the Bible has always done. God's greatest enemies often fight God in the name of God. Everytime Jesus opens His mouth or makes ready to heal somebody, it seems, a religious leader steps forward to obstruct the flow of mercy. These legalists would prevent healing by murder, if necessary. They would kill the Son of God in the name of religion.

Jesus responds to the heartlessness of the religious by asserting both His lordship and the value of persons.

The Lordship of Christ

"I tell you that one greater than the temple is here. . . . The Son of Man is Lord of the Sabbath" (Matthew 12:6, 8). His authority transcends temple and law. To prove that authority, He orders the man to stretch out his hand. He heals him.

When Pope John Paul II returned to his native Poland in June, 1979 (his first homecoming as Pope), he said almost nothing that directly criticized the Communistic regime there. He didn't have to, of course, since his very presence as a prominent representative of Christ was a rebuke against all ungodliness. When he spoke to a gigantic crowd in Warsaw, however, he aimed his argument right at the center of atheistic Communism. "The exclusion of Christ from the history of man is an act against man," he told his fellow Poles. When the Communists usurped the power over the people that belongs only to the redemptive Lord, they could then treat human beings as mere things. In removing Christ, they removed the world's greatest protector of humanity. In the Communist system, men and women are devalued. Even Jesus' disciples sometimes forget that it is because they believe in Christ that they believe in people; because they follow the Lord, they must carry on His work of healing and then uplifting maimed and pained mankind. Totalitarian governments can casually order them around and determine their fate without regard to needs. Disciples of Christ can never do that, even in the name of—especially in the name of—religion. They have only one Lord.

The Value of Persons

When Jesus asserts His Lordship, the effect is to raise the value of persons. What happens to the man's withered hand happens to the whole person. He is restored.

The history of graphic art in western civilization reveals what happens to humanity when a culture moves away from its Lord. Look at Gothic (medieval) paintings, for example. At first, the modern student is bored by them, since the faces of individuals are so stylized, looking the same from painting to painting. In many of them, it is the background that captures the viewer's attention. Back behind the main subject of the painting, Heaven and earth are depicted, because the artist has related the individual in the foreground to the world in which he lives and the God from whom he came.

Modern painting has no patience with background. Heaven has been eliminated. Gone are the angels and the cherubim and seraphim. Gone is the celestial light. Gone also is the stylized sameness of the Gothic, with its minimizing of persons as individuals and its glorifying of the God in whose image man is made.

Modern paintings, if they bother with persons at all, depict them as highly individualized, isolated, unique—and devalued. No God in the background. Property rules, money talks, and man is diminished. Then, in an even more recent period, man disappears, replaced by abstractions and suggestions, then splotches of paint sometimes thrown on canvas with apparent abandon. Man derives his meaning from God; remove God and you remove man. When God doesn't count, man doesn't count. Things become more important—like sheep.

The Pharisee who has lost the will of God in a tangle of laws and commentaries on laws, and the modern painter who has erased God from the background of his paintings, resemble one another more than either would care to admit.

From the American Civil War comes this story of the attorney who stood before a Vermont judge to appeal on behalf of a southern slave-holder that his runaway slave be returned. The judge turned down the request because, in his opinion, the evidence of ownership was insufficient. "What evidence does your honor require?" the lawyer asked him. "Nothing less than a bill of sale from God almighty."

The judge believed that God made the man to be a man, not a slave. He would not treat him as a thing. Abraham Lincoln treated this same theme when he spoke at the dedication of the new Whig party he helped form. "I read once in a law book, 'A slave is a human being who is legally not a *person* but a *thing.*' And if the safeguards to liberty are broken down, as is now attempted, when they have made *things* of all the free negroes, how long, think you, before they will begin to make *things* of poor white men?"

Slavery to laws, slavery to religious laws, slavery to the heartless who enslave in the name of religion, slavery to those who treat persons as things—against all of these Jesus takes His stand. God hasn't sold anybody into slavery; He still desires mercy.

Remember what Jesus did to the woman taken in adultery (John 8)? Do you also remember with what meanness her accusers spied, framed, defamed, and tried to destroy her? Do you recall what the father of the prodigal son did when his son returned home (Luke 15)? Can you hear the mean-spirited whining of the elder brother who could not bear the attention the prodigal was receiving? Think also of the prayers of the Pharisee and the tax collector—and which one Jesus justified (Luke 18). See Jesus at table with sinners (Matthew 9). What Jesus is up to here, healing this disabled man on the Sabbath, is simply more of the same. He is restoring a person to full humanity. He believes he is valuable, worth the trouble that is inevitable when Jesus breaks the Sabbath for him.

He believes we are all worth the trouble.

A Strategic Retreat (12:15-21)

Opposition to Jesus' healing and teaching ministry is growing. "Aware of this," that is, aware that the Pharisees are plotting to kill Him, He moves on into one of His periodic retreats. There is no escape from the crowd, however. He protects himself from His enemies, but there is no respite from His friends. Jesus is not reckless with His life. He trusts himself to neither His enemies who would kill Him nor the crowds who would try to protect Him.

In this withdrawal, Matthew sees another fulfillment of prophecy. He loosely quotes Isaiah 42:1-4, a passage that originally referred to the Persian King Cyrus, a gentle conqueror. Matthew, believing Jesus to be the Messiah, and the Messiah to be the embodiment of Israel's vocation as servant of the Lord, does not elaborate on Isaiah's description. Here is the Messiah:

He is *chosen:* "Here is my servant whom I have chosen."

He is *loved:* "The one I love, in whom I delight."

He is *Spirit-filled:* "I will put my Spirit on him."

He is *a preacher:* "He will proclaim justice to the nations."

He is *peaceable:* "He will not quarrel or cry out."

He is *submissive:* "No one will hear his voice in the streets."

He is *gentle:* "A bruised reed he will not break."

He is *victorious:* "He leads justice to victory."

He *gives the people hope:* "In his name the nations will put their hope."

This gentle, suffering Savior is described in Isaiah 53, the most famous of the Messianic prophecies. In Matthew's description of Jesus' final week, the Gospel writer details the extent of Christ's embodiment of Israel's Suffering Servant role. He will not lash out against His enemies, but will instead die for them. Just as He would not condemn the woman taken in adultery (John 8:11) but would instead take her condemnation upon himself on the cross, so He will not plot against the plotters against His life. Of Him, Thomas Dekker was justified in writing,

> The best of men
> That e'er wore earth about him
> Was a sufferer; a soft, meek, patient,
>   humble, tranquil spirit,
> The first true gentleman that ever breathed.

This "gentleman" lives forever as an example for His disciples:

> To this you were called, because Christ suffered for you, leaving you an example, that you should follow in his steps.
>   "He committed no sin,
>   and no deceit was found in his mouth."
> When they hurled their insults at him, he did not retaliate; when he suffered, he made no threats. Instead, he entrusted himself to him who judges justly. He himself bore our sins in his body on the tree, so that we might die to sins and live for righteousness; by his wounds you have been healed (1 Peter 2:21-24).

Are You For Me or Against Me? (12:22-37)
(Mark 3:20-30; Luke 11:14-23; 12:8-10)

A controversy rages, and Jesus is in the middle of it. "Who *is* this man and by what power does He do these mighty works?" the people are asking. Some firmly believe Jesus to be the Messiah; others even more firmly deny it. They won't stand for it!

His critics cannot deny His supernatural powers. They have seen the wonders with their own eyes. No ordinary person could do what Jesus does. Since the power is there, and since it cannot possibly have come from God, there is only one other source. "It is only by Beelzebub, the prince of demons, that this fellow drives out demons" (Matthew 12:24).

Jesus has heard this tired charge before. (See Matthew 10:25.) This time, He answers with seven statements.

(1) "Every kingdom divided against itself will be ruined" (25, 26). You cannot be right. Satan would not cast out Satan by the power of Satan. You are reasoning illogically.

(2) Since some Pharisees drive out demons also, they must likewise be casting out demons by Satan's power. Does this make sense? (27). What is the difference between My casting out demons and the exorcisms practiced by your own people?

(3) "If I drive out demons by the Spirit of God, then the kingdom of God has come upon you" (28). Now Jesus comes closer to the essence of His argument. In sending His disciples out on their first mission (Matthew 10), He charged them to "heal the sick, raise the dead, cleanse those who have leprosy, [and] drive out demons." "What you are witnessing in these exorcisms," Jesus answered His critics, "is evidence that the Spirit of God is at work through Me, bringing the kingdom of God very close. This is not Beelzebub's work, but God's."

A young minister in his first pastorate found himself hopelessly confused by the many conflicting doctrines of the Holy Spirit that were in print. Believing that he could read the Bible as well as some of the authors he had read on the subject, he put away his books and spent several weeks in Bible study, examining every reference to the Holy Spirit. He learned that whenever the Bible speaks of God the Father or God the Son, it is quite clear. However, when Biblical writers wish to speak of God at work on earth among men, they use the term "Spirit" or "Holy Spirit" in a way to indicate the power of God in action. There are over 300 references to the Holy Spirit, and almost all of them connote power. Jesus' power to drive out demons, then, is the Spirit of God, the same God who rules the kingdom of Heaven.

(4) I have bound Satan (29). Jesus speaks indirectly, but the implication is clear: He has entered Satan's domicile and bound him. Only by so doing could He carry off Satan's demons. Here Jesus touches on the war between the forces of good and evil (see Revelation 12:7-11).

(5) You must take your choice (30). On this issue, at least, Jesus and the Pharisees agree. You must be for Jesus or against Him. You must take your place on one side of this cosmic struggle or the other. You cannot be indifferent, since indifference itself is a choice. Humorist Sam Levenson loved to reminisce about his strict Jewish upbringing. His mother understood choices. She used to give her children two choices when they sat down to eat: they could take it or leave it.

The decision Jesus forces is infinitely more important, obviously. It has the urgency of James Russell Lowell's anti-slavery poem, "The Present Crisis":

> Once to ev'ry man and nation
> Comes the moment to decide,
> In the strife of truth with falsehood,
> For the good or evil side;
> Some great cause, God's new Messiah,
> Off'ring each the bloom or blight,
> And the choice goes by forever
> 'Twixt that darkness and that light.

Lowell has captured the moment of decision; Jesus urges its necessity. He does not allow temporizing. The Pharisees and all others whom Christ confronts must decide—will they be on His side or Satan's? Harvey Cox, pondering the Fall in Eden, submits the intriguing suggestion that Adam and Eve's sin was not pride but sloth. When they had to make the fateful decision, they deferred to the snake. Adam's sin was "not pilfering God's fire but abdicating his choice to the fork-tongued consultant."[45] His course was set from that moment. Church members defer to their pastor for decisions; clients keep counselors busy because they willingly pay someone else to make decisions for them—decisions a wise counselor refuses to make. No one else can make this decision: You are for Christ or against Him.

---

[45]Harvey Cox, *The Seduction of the Spirit* (Simon and Schuster: Touchstone Books, 1973), p. 64.

(6) The unforgivable sin is speaking against the Holy Spirit (31, 32). To speak against the Holy Spirit is to choose the wrong side. It is to reject the Holy Spirit and the One whom the Holy Spirit lifts up, Christ himself. It is to reject the power of God. The New Testament says we can grieve the Spirit (Ephesians 4:30), resist the Spirit (Acts 6:10), and quench the Spirit (1 Thessalonians 5:10).

A preacher who keeps very complete files on every Christian doctrine began preparing a sermon on "The Unpardonable Sin." He went to his file cabinet, pulled out the file on this subject, and found it empty. He concluded that his discovery was symbolic. For years, he had listened as his members confessed their fears that they had committed the unforgivable sin of blaspheming the Holy Spirit. Not once had anyone been guilty. They had already made their choice *for* Christ. They were guilty of disappointing God, but since they had no intention of deserting His side for Satan's, they had done nothing that could not be forgiven. It is unpardonable to choose Satan over God. You can't be forgiven if you refuse to let the power of God in the Spirit lead you to the grace of God in Christ.

All Christians know that every sin can be forgiven except one. But they differ in what they think that one sin is. Some consider that their excessive drinking has placed them beyond God's grace. Others seem to think divorce does it. No, what is unforgivable is the refusal to accept forgiveness. God sent His Son to tell us, "I love you and want you. I am prepared to forgive you. I know the deep, dark secrets of your heart, but I love you anyway. The blood of Calvary is proof of My love. Only if you reject Me will you be unforgiven."

The context of this verse clarifies its meaning. Jesus heals a demoniac and some of His critics attribute His power to Satan. They are denying God. That's blasphemy. If they persist in denying God, God will be helpless to save them. That's unforgivable.

What God wants more than anything else is to save. When we turn our backs upon the Son or the Spirit who leads us to the Son, what else can God do? Nothing.

(7) Your words will condemn or acquit you (33-37). As fruit betrays whether its tree is good or bad, so your words give you away. The mouth only utters what the heart tells it to. You Pharisees, so quick to attribute what I am doing to Satan, by your criticism are letting us know how well acquainted with Satan you are. You speak from an evil heart. Even you, who pride yourselves in your righteousness, will be judged by your words. They give away the truth about which side you are on. The fruit you produce is evil fruit.

168

"Give Us Proof—Then We'll Believe You" (12:38-42)
(Mark 8:11-13; Luke 11:16, 29-32)

To the Jews, a "sign" was a miracle or other remarkable event that signified divine power. A bona fide miracle worker must enjoy the approval of God, otherwise he would not be able to perform such marvels. Jesus' message is so radical that no self-respecting religious leader is prepared to accept it unless Jesus can prove by another miracle that His credentials are from God. The demand for a sign strikes us as quite unnecessary, since the Gospels are full of Jesus' miracles. But the Pharisees and teachers of the law are seeking a "sign on demand," as it were. "If you are authentic," they are saying, "perform a miracle right now. And not just your common, ordinary, run-of-the-mill variety, either, but something spectacular, so we'll know beyond doubt that we should believe you."

It is the same temptation Jesus faced down in the wilderness (Matthew 4:5-7). He would not then, nor will He now, turn magician just to impress His critics. If they were convinced by the miracle, they would follow Him, all right, but for all the wrong reasons. Miracle-seekers seek God in the abnormal; they do not know how to perceive Him in the everyday realities.

Dr. John Witherspoon was one of the signers of the American Declaration of Independence and president of New Jersey College (later Princeton University). One morning, a neighbor came excitedly to his home. "Dr. Witherspoon, you must join me in giving thanks to God for His providence in saving my life. As I was driving this morning the horse ran away and the buggy was smashed to pieces on the rocks, but I escaped unharmed."

"Why, I can tell you a far more remarkable providence than that," Witherspoon remarked." I have driven over that road hundreds of times. My horse never ran away, my buggy never was smashed, I was never hurt. God's providence has been for me even more remarkable than it has been for you." He was able to see God in everyday realities. He did not depend upon the abnormal.

Jesus will not cater to His skeptics' appetite for the extraordinary. "A wicked and adulterous generation asks for a miraculous sign!" They are "wicked" because they seek God where He has not promised to be found, and "adulterous" because they have left their covenant relationship with Him to follow the goddess Success or Respectability or Prestige. Only one sign will be given, and that will come in God's timing, not theirs. Jesus' resurrection will be the sign upon which all subsequent history will depend.

Jesus' sign will be greater than Jonah's (Jonah 1:1—2:10), as He is greater than the prophet who preached in Ninevah, and His sign will be greater than that of the Queen of Sheba's visit to the wise King Solomon (1 Kings 10:1-13), for one wiser than Solomon is now here. In fact, the sign is already present: Jesus himself is God's sign to the Jews. Their rejection of the Son of God invites the judgment of Ninevah's repentant citizens and of the Queen of Sheba upon the Jews. The Jews have spurned the one they would quickly have embraced.

When Goodness Is Negative (12:43-45)
(Luke 11:24-26)

Jesus is not accusing the Pharisees and teachers of the law of demon possession but of the kind of negative goodness that concentrates on sweeping away "badness" but does not replace it with positive "goodness." For example, these religious leaders would be horrified by adultery or theft or even failure to observe proper dietary or sabbath regulations but, as Jesus will point out later (in 23:23, 24) they do not fill themselves with attitudes that lead to justice, mercy, and faithfulness. They need to be inhabited by the positive virtues so their hollowness will not be occupied by evil. They may not be like "robbers, evildoers, adulterers—or even like this tax collector" (Luke 18:11, 12), but neither are they justified before God.

Walter Lippman has written that "virtue is really good and really relevant." He acknowledges that it is so frequently "encrusted with pious cries of foolish men and sour old women, that our generation has almost forgotten that virtue was not invented in Sunday schools but derives originally from a profound realization of the character of human life."[46] It is to this character that Jesus is speaking.

When Jeb Magruder, one of the Nixon men convicted in the Watergate scandal, appeared before Judge John Sirica to receive his sentence, he read a prepared statement: "I know what I have done, and your honor knows what I have done.... Somewhere between my ambition and my ideals, I lost my ethical compass. I found myself on a path that had not been intended for me by my parents or my principles or by my own ethical instincts. It has led me to this courtroom."[47] Up to Watergate, he had concentrated on not getting caught in minor violations. He had not pursued active goodness.

---

[46]Walter Lippman, *Preface to Morals* (New York: The Macmillan Company, 1929), pp. 226, 227.

[47]Quoted in *Time* (June 3, 1974), p. 14.

Jesus' wisdom is apparent when one studies current American sexual practices. We have virtually abandoned some of our most deeply held traditional beliefs about marriage and the family. Sweeping away the "evil spirit" of Victorian prudery in the name of honesty, we have watched as "seven other spirits more wicked" than the first have moved in, including a dramatic increase in one-parent homes, uncontrollable venereal disease, the rise in the number of unmarried couples living together, the frightening increase of divorce, and the reluctance of modern parents to sacrifice their selfish desires for the long-term good of their children. Perhaps Dennis the Menace summarized it best when he asked his father to read to him the bedtime story, "Snow White and the Seven Divorces." Dennis' confusion is understandable. His culture has brought it on itself. It is never enough to exorcise a wrong unless one is committed to replacing it with a positive good that will prevent even greater evil from moving in.

It does little good to drive out evil spirits unless the Holy Spirit then takes up residency.

The Real Family of God (12:46-50)
(Mark 3:31-35; Luke 8:19-21)

John 7:5 reports that Jesus' brothers did not believe in Him. They may have even subscribed to the circulating rumor that He was out of His mind (Mark 3:21). At any rate, when we meet them here, they are prepared to take charge of Him as if He were unable to be responsible for himself. His startling rebuff on this occasion will do nothing to ease their anxiety about Him. He seems to be disassociating himself from them: "Who is my mother, and who are my brothers?" (Matthew 12:48). That is not a normal question.

Jesus often seems to be saying strange things about family. Christians still puzzle over these words: "Anyone who loves his father or mother more than me is not worthy of me; anyone who loves his son or daughter more than me is not worthy of me" (Matthew 10:37).

In both instances, Jesus is not so much putting family loyalties down as lifting discipleship loyalties up. When you begin to take God seriously in your life, He becomes, in fact as well as in word, your Heavenly Father. His Fatherhood redefines all your other relationships. Your blood relatives are not squeezed out; your new relatives in Christ are invited in. Anyone with whom you share a common Father now becomes a brother or sister.

Your new family then, shares *a common Father*. You will no longer think of your blood family as "all I've got." You have a much larger set of relationships now. On the other hand, you cannot think of your church as primarily an institution, either. It is first of all a family. Of course, any large group will necessarily have some institutional trappings, but it is more than an institution. It is, as Elton Trueblood has nominated it, "the company of the committed." Its first commitment is to the Father, who holds His large and diverse family together by His love.

The family shares *in obedience to the Father's will.* Jesus had to do His Father's will, whether His blood family understood or not. (See Luke 2:49.) One thing we have learned by now in our study of Matthew is that it is a great mistake to think that God is chiefly interested in religion. His will is much broader than that. Jesus' ministry is proof of God's incredible concern for mankind. It is as if, when sending Christ to earth, the Father married Him to mankind "for better or for worse, for richer or for poorer, in sickness and in health." Jesus took us all on with the dedication of a groom taking a bride to himself. Even in Gethsemane, Jesus was true to His "vow," promising His Father, "Not as I will, but as you will" (Matthew 26:39).

The family shares *the Father's concern for all the children.* No member can ever dismiss another as unimportant. (See 1 Corinthians 12). Nor can he claim to believe in one holy infallible church, of which he is the only member. Like any family, this one is filled with quite fallible members. Further, these members need one another because the family resides as strangers and aliens in a foreign land. While here, we enjoy the hospitality of the land, we obey its laws, honor its governments, and do everything possible to help its peoples. We know our Father loves us. He also loves them, every one of them. His business is to save all of them if possible and we, His family, must be about our Father's business. His priorities are our priorities.

In a sense, the followers of Jesus are God's Exhibit A on earth. When a love-starved world seeks relief from its deprivation, it can find love in the church. While no country on earth can provide complete justice for its people, the church offers something better: mercy. As the world's survival becomes more questionable with its multiplying wars, the church offers peace within its borders. God's family is the world's primary hope for peace, joy, love, kindness, gentleness, and the other essentials for abundant life. We Christians will do our best to make these qualities available worldwide. It is our business to do so. We must succeed—the family honor is at stake.

CHAPTER FOURTEEN

Parables of the Kingdom
Matthew 13

"He Who Has Ears, Let Him Hear" (13:1-23)
(Mark 4:1-9, 13-20; Luke 8:5-15)

This is the first of seven parables of the kingdom of Heaven that Matthew clusters together in chapter 13. Four of them, ("weeds," "hidden treasure," "pearl of great price," and "net") are found only in Matthew. The others have parallels in Mark and Luke.

A parable (from the Greek *parabole,* literally a placing beside in order to compare) is a simple story told in order to illustrate a concept or principle. It usually has only one point, although sometimes it may be almost like an allegory, with several points of comparison between the story and what the story is illustrating. As used by Jesus, the parable is easy to understand immediately, but has such profound meaning that it rewards careful study. The parable can be used to make something very clear to the audience, or, as Jesus says here, sometimes the parable can seem to be simple when, in fact, it may mask a deeper message that only a few can understand. In the case of the parable of the sower, Jesus expects that most of His listeners will not grasp its full meaning, but His disciples, of whom He says, "Blessed are your eyes because they see, and your ears because they hear," will be able through His earlier teaching and His explanations here, to fathom it.

The central message of this parable is that the kingdom of God will take root and grow. Even though many to whom it is preached will reject it, or accept it for a while and then leave it, some will receive it and let it flourish. On such will the kingdom be built.

By this time in Jesus' ministry, the disciples are aware that not everyone hearing Jesus' message is accepting it and becoming a disciple. Some reject it immediately; others follow for a while and then desert Him. Jesus is not worried by their defection. He knows that many will remain faithful, for they genuinely want God to reign in their lives. They hear the word of the kingdom gladly, and their lives produce.

173

In a secondary sense, this parable is about listening. In Jesus' usual profoundly simple manner, He captures the complexity of the listening process by comparing hearers with various types of soil. The quality of the seed is assumed (the seed is "the message about the kingdom"); it will take root and produce in hospitable soil. The unpredictable element is the soil, or listener.

The first-century Palestinian farmer would first sow his seed on the top of the ground, then plow it under. His harvest would vary according to the readiness of the soil. Some seeds would fall on the hard surface of the path, failing to penetrate at all. Others would fall in rocky soil, where it might immediately begin to take root, but then die because their roots could not take hold (like hearers who would at first be intrigued by or at least interested in the message but would then desert at the first sign of trouble or persecution). Still others would fall among thorns, which would grow up and choke out the tender plants (like the "worries of this life and the deceitfulness of wealth" that choke out the message of the kingdom). Fortunately, some soil is hospitable enough to grow good plants that will produce out of proportion to their numbers. This is the hope of the kingdom—the few true disciples will be far more effective than their limited numbers would lead you to expect.

Jesus' disciples are good soil. Their eyes see and their ears hear. They have prepared themselves to hear and receive Jesus' word. They have left home and career, they have forsaken security and comfort, to give themselves completely to Jesus. They are not like the typical Israelites, whom Isaiah describes, "Though seeing, they do not see; though hearing, they do not hear or understand" (Matthew 13:13; see Isaiah 6:9, 10). Isaiah describes people who took God for granted. They rested secure in their special status as God's chosen people. Thinking they were hearing, they nodded agreement without fully comprehending. There was no true communication between them and their God.

What, then, does Jesus call for in the parable? At least three things: *Concentration, commitment,* and *application.*

Concentration

To concentrate is to banish distractions. It is to become so absorbed in the subject that you lose yourself and become a slave to the dictates of the one speaking, thus liberating yourself from captivity to your own ego. For the Christian, it is to achieve the goal of John R. Mott, who wrote in *Confronting Young Men with the Living Christ* that his dearest wish was "that by the time I come to my old age I may have so brought all thoughts into obedience to His marvelous captivity, that whenever my mind comes out of unconsciousness into consciousness it will revert naturally and inevitably to Jesus Christ." It is in the Bible that you meet Jesus Christ and in the study of the Bible that you really hear His voice. If you honestly listen, Bible study becomes a dialogue between the Speaker and the listener. The Word of God will come alive and speak with human voice, and your human heart will respond.

Commitment

Concentration demands commitment. You have to want the message to take root in you, or else the thorns (worries and deceitfulness of wealth) and rocks (trouble and persecution) can all too easily discourage you. You dare not listen to Jesus' message casually. No important conversation is relaxed. When you are talking with someone who really matters, you are alert, committed to the person and to the exchange of information. Every true lover learns quickly that there is no real communication in conversation without commitment to the loved one and concentration on the loved one's words.

Application

"Do not merely listen to the word, and so deceive yourselves. Do what it says" (James 1:22). Listening does not conclude with the beating of sound waves against ear drum. Biblically speaking, to hear means to heed, to do. Only when those hearing Jesus obey Him will they be productive. "You are my friends if you do what I command" (John 15:14). Not only will His disciples, His friends, do what He has commanded, but they will do far more. "I tell you the truth, anyone who has faith in me will do what I have been doing. He will do even greater things than these, because I am going to the Father" (John 14:12). From such people Jesus expects productivity that yields "a hundred, sixty or thirty times what was sown."

Jesus' disciples can fathom the meaning of Jesus' parables because they concentrate on His teaching, commit themselves to the Teacher, and apply His words and example in their own lives. Jesus can give them "the secrets of the kingdom of heaven," because they are worthy soil. Having some insight, they will receive much more ("an abundance"). Others, who have no insight (especially those who think they have some but actually do not), will lose the little they do have, because, lacking true commitment, they neither concentrate on nor apply Jesus' message. The Lord cannot teach those who will not learn nor heal those who prefer their illness. But He can work marvels with those who have ears to hear.

Jesus has spoken to them in parables both to teach and to withhold teaching (10-15). To His serious disciples, He imparts secrets of the kingdom; to the majority in the crowds, who by this time have proved themselves curious but not committed, ready to hear but slow to respond, He veils His meaning in stories He later interprets for His disciples. The others don't really want to know all the implications of His teaching about the kingdom, anyway.

Jesus' parables are not just nice little stories with a moral. He is talking specifically about the kingdom of Heaven. He cannot be completely understood by anyone who refuses to accept Him as the Messiah. Receptive soil involves belief in the "Sower" as well as hospitality to the "seed."

The Final Separation (13:24-30, 36-43, 47-50)

The parable of the weeds and the parable of the net are pictures of the final Judgment. Jesus does not dwell on the nature of the punishment the lost will suffer, but He leaves no doubt that there will be a final division of wheat from weeds or of good fish from bad; in other words, of kingdom citizens from aliens. These parables offer the same encouragement to Jesus' disciples as the parable of the sower. There are various kinds of soil receiving seed (the teaching of the Master), only some of which will be productive. In the early stages of growth, it is not always easy to tell which will produce and which will not. Eventually, the truth will be evident. Among the "sons of the kingdom" on earth will be some illegitimate pretenders. The disciples need not worry unduly about them—a final separation will purify the kingdom.

There will be a harvest. God is in charge of history and is working toward His goals. Just as time began when God spoke the world into being, so the age will close when His goals have been accomplished. Until then, wheat and tares, good fish and bad, will coexist. The Son of Man and His disciples will work in the meantime to insure a bountiful harvest for the Lord. (See Matthew 28:18-20 and Acts 1:8.)

But they are not the only ones interested in the harvest. The devil plants his own seeds to destroy God's plants. He plants darnel, which resembles wheat so closely in the early stages of growth that they cannot readily be distinguished. To try to weed the darnel out too soon would cause great damage to the wheat. It is better to let them grow side by side until harvesttime—then their differences will be plain.

Jesus does not accuse the devil of planting poisonous or inedible fish among the good ones in the net, but as anyone who has fished with a large net knows, the net will trap all kinds of sea animals, many of which have to be thrown back.

Both parables, then, speak of *the harvest as judgment*. The good will be claimed by the Son of Man, the rest will be cast away. The reader should remember that the "fiery furnace" is only one of several New Testament pictures of destiny awaiting the sons of the evil one. Here are some others:

> "Eternal punishment" (Matthew 25:46),
> "Punished with everlasting destruction and shut out from the presence of the Lord" (2 Thessalonians 1:9),
> "They will be destroyed" (Philippians 1:28),
> "There will be wrath and anger . . . trouble and distress" (Romans 2:8, 9),
> "Hell, where 'their worm does not die, and the fire is not quenched'" (Mark 9:47, 48), and
> "The lake of fire" (Revelation 20:14, 15).

The Biblical language of judgment is strong. It does not provide a literal description of the condition of the damned so much as convince the reader of the terribleness of life apart from God. We do an injustice to these parables if we concentrate more on the fate of the weeds and bad fish than on the prospects of the wheat and good fish. C. S. Lewis correctly warns of the two extremes to which we can erroneously go in our thinking about devils. One is to disbelieve and thus dismiss them, and the other is to believe and then take too much interest in them. What is said of devils is equally true of the abode of the devils.

Jesus insists that the culling responsibilities belong to the Lord and not to the Lord's people. We are not qualified. Human intelligence has grave difficulty separating wheat from weeds, especially since the world's most accomplished perpetrators of evil always cover their sins with a cloak of virtue. (Bernard Shaw in *Man and Superman* says through Don Juan that "Hell is the home of honor, duty, justice, and the rest of the seven deadly virtues. All the wickedness on earth is done in their name.")

Jesus does not even claim the right to judge. It is not He who judges, but the word He has spoken (John 12:47, 48). He has come to save, not to judge (John 3:17). To think of Him primarily as judge is to distort His ministry and forget His mission as Savior. When the final Judgment Day comes, the Lord will not arbitrarily assign some to Heaven and some to Hell. Those who stand before Him will have already decided their fate by their response to the word He has spoken. Since Jesus' mission is to deliver the saving message from God, "He who rejects me rejects him who sent me," Jesus says (Luke 10:16). How can anyone who rejects God be considered a citizen of His kingdom?

Until the final Judgment, *the kingdom will not be pure.* Even in the fellowship of believers there will be non-believers. Not all self-proclaimed disciples of Christ will be what they seem. We cannot expect a pure church, then. It has not been so from the beginning. (If the early Christian church had been pure, we would not have had the helpful letters of the apostle Paul dealing with so many church problems.) The earliest Christians followed Jesus' instructions. On the Day of Pentecost, three thousand persons were added to the church. Peter's invitation to his audience to "save yourselves from this corrupt generation" opened the church's door (Acts 2). No entrance test was required of the respondents to guarantee that only the pure were received into membership. They heard, they believed, they repented, they were baptized, and they were accepted. Although a spotless life was held before the members as the goal of Christian growth, perfection was not required for membership. The result was a congregation of persons almost as varied as humanity itself. Never, from the beginning, has the church's garden been weedless.

How the Kingdom Grows (13:31-35)
(Mark 4:30-32; Luke 13:18-20)

When Jesus compares God's kingdom to the growth of a mustard seed, or a bit of leaven transforming a lump of dough (or a seed producing a fully matured ear of corn—see Mark 4:26-29), He speaks with the authority of personal experience. From His own start as a baby born of unimportant parents in an outbuilding of an inn, He has grown into the leader of a spiritual revolution. Better than anyone else, Jesus knows God's way of turning the commonplace into the sacred. God chose a manger for a king's bed, a cross to be the key to Heaven's door. In the same tradition, Jesus foresees that His small band of ordinary men will initiate an extraordinary movement that will one day encompass the globe.

These little parables are veiled exhortations not to grow weary, but to face the future with hope. Even as Jesus speaks His men are misunderstood and despised, but if they endure their hardships, their present seemingly tiny influence will grow into a powerful instrument for God's purposes. Only eternity will reveal its full strength.

Today, Jesus might tell a parable of an airplane, like Orville and Wilbur Wright's at Kitty Hawk, North Carolina, which sputtered only a few feet in the air but led the way into space; or of a Colonel Harlan Sanders, whose fried chicken in his little cafe in Corbin, Kentucky, has become the famous Kentucky Fried Chicken found on almost every continent; or of the handful of believers in Seoul, Korea, who first met with Pastor Paul Yonggi Cho in the 1950s and have multiplied into to a church of more than 300,000 members today. Examples of big results from small beginnings are all around.

According to these parables, *God's kingdom grows toward God's goal.* God directs that growth to fulfill His desire for mankind. A man does not scatter seed because he is interested in observing the marvels of biological change from seed to blade to ear to grain, but because he wants a harvest. So does God (Matthew 9:35-38). Through their service to Christ, disciples participate in the will of a God whose purposes cannot fail. God's sovereignty over nature is taken for granted in these parables. He has created, He sustains, and He orders the world. As plants grow according to His design, so does His kingdom.

God's kingdom grows in partnership with men. Somebody has to sow the seed or to hide the leaven in the meal. While we do not make the leaven work nor make the seeds grow, God grants us the privilege of doing what we can to assist Him. The parables present neither the all-powerfulness of God nor the self-sufficiency of man, but a happy partnership between God's mysterious generative force and man's humble responsible labor.

God's kingdom grows by using the commonplace. Leaven and seeds are homely illustrations, the elements of everyday life, which is undoubtedly why Jesus selected them. God does not rely on the grand or spectacular to do His work. He does not subscribe to the American cult of bigness. He who changed the world with the birth of a baby does not need anything more extraordinary than a seed or leaven to prove His power. Nor does He require the services of extraordinary persons to help His kingdom grow. He seems to delight in selecting commonplace persons, undistinguished from their contemporaries, to be His representatives and kingdom-builders. What distinguishes them is not their personal attributes but their dual citizenship. They never forget their first loyalty to the kingdom of Heaven. They reside on earth as aliens, here for a while as they journey to their ultimate home.

One of the classic descriptions of these ordinary kingdom citizens is found in a second-century document, "The Epistle to Diognetus." The author and the recipient of the letter are unknown, but the description of Christians arrests our attention. For the most part, it could have been written of today's disciples.

> Christians are not distinguished from the rest of mankind by either country, speech, or customs; the fact is, they nowhere settle in cities of their own; they have no peculiar language; they cultivate no eccentric mode of life. Certainly, this creed of theirs is no discovery due to some fancy or speculation of inquisitive man; nor do they, as some do, champion a doctrine of human origin.

Is there then nothing special about these Christians? Yes, in spite of their conformity "to the customs of the country in dress, food, and mode of life in general," the letter praises "the whole tenor of their living."

> They reside in their respective countries, but only as aliens. They take part in everything as citizens and put up with everything as foreigners. Every foreign land is their home, and every home a foreign land. They marry like all others and beget children; but they do not expose their offspring. Their board they spread for all, but not their bed. They find themselves *in the flesh,* but do not live *according to the flesh.* They spend their days on earth, but hold citizenship in heaven. They obey the established laws, but in their private lives they rise above the laws.

They pay a price for their high standards:

> They love all men, but are persecuted by all. They are unknown, yet are condemned; they are put to death, but it is life that they receive. *They are poor and enrich many;* destitute of everything, they abound in everything. They are dishonored, and in their dishonor find their glory....[48]

Ordinary people, yet with extraordinary influence to make God's kingdom grow!

God's kingdom grows with power. That power is invincible,

---

[48]"The Epistle to Diognetus," *Valiant for the Truth,* David Otis Fuller, D.D., ed. (New York, Toronto, London: McGraw-Hill Book Co., Inc., co. 1961), pp. 9, 10.

inherent in the purposes of God. This is the central teaching of the parables. The kingdom grows inevitably, certainly, constantly. Like a fragile tree sapling forcing its way through solid rock, the kingdom will overcome every obstacle to its progress. God's power is with it.

Think of Jesus' church. First there was but a handful of followers, to whom Jesus opened the mysteries of the kingdom. Then, when He left them, He sent His enabling Holy Spirit to strengthen them. These Spirit-filled men and women gathered others around them, and the gathered Christians met in cells. Then they moved out into the dough of society, infiltrating it with the yeast of change, and before long, the little cells fermented a revolution in society.

This is how the kingdom works, like yeast, stealing quietly from person to person and group to group to transform them into Christlikeness. Fermentation takes time. The power in the kingdom seldom erupts in explosive violence. Explosions often leave piles of destruction. The work of the kingdom, however, is construction, and it takes longer to build than to destroy. But God is indeed building.

These parables are examples of the many that Jesus told the crowds (verse 34). In Jesus' teaching technique, Matthew finds another Old Testament prophecy fulfilled, quoting from Psalm 78:2 to hint that Jesus revealed through His parables truths that were being heard—or at least understood—for the first time. What an advantage we have over the disciples: they took His words concerning the kingdom's growth on faith; we have the accumulated evidence of two thousand years of Christian history.

The Joy and Price of Discipleship (13:44-46)

There is an old Spanish saying that must have derived from this passage: "Take what you want, said God; take it and pay for it." The parables of the Pearl of Great Price and the Hidden Treasure are about taking the best and paying for it. The best is citizenship in the kingdom of Heaven; the cost is everything else you have.

Discipleship is not for the moderately interested. In another context, but to this same point, Robert Heinlein has written, "To enjoy the full flavor of life, take big bites. Moderation is for monks." Jesus enjoins His disciples to bite on the finest God has to offer. He also warns that its cost is staggering. But what is gained is priceless, to be valued above everything else in this world.

The kingdom of Heaven is a treasure waiting to be found, sometimes by accident, like the man who discovers it while plowing the field, and sometimes after diligent search, like the pearl merchant who at long last has attained his goal. Some people who have never considered themselves to be "religious types" have been amazed when their privacy has been unexpectedly invaded by a messenger from God. Others have pursued God for years. The point of the parables is not in the method of discovery but in the availability and incredible value of the find. Paul calls the treasure "the riches of his glorious inheritance in the saints" (Ephesians 1:18).

The treasure is there, but not everyone will purchase it. The world is filled with people who, for whatever reason, turn their backs on genuine treasure. They do not esteem what is most valuable! They are like Yale coach Tad Jones, who cheered his 1924 team on as they went out to face their arch-enemies: "Gentlemen, you are about to play Harvard. You may never again do anything as important." Any sports fan can appreciate Jones' enthusiasm, but can beating Harvard in a football game seriously be the most important experience a young man could have? Is this a treasure worth dying for? We can sympathize with the frazzled father in the Harry Mace cartoon who, after fretting over the family finances, informs his wife and seven children, "I've taken another close look at the budget, and I'm sorry I'm going to have to let two of you go." If we thought he meant it, we would be horrified. His treasures are in the family; something else must be sold for their sake.

Purchasing what is of greatest value requires discipline and sacrifice. Jesus commends both the discoverer of the buried treasure and the pearl merchant for their quickness to give up everything else in order to possess what is most valuable. His is not rare advice. The world's wisest counselors have always taught that we must order our priorities and give preference to the most important. Confucius, for example, held that "a scholar whose mind is set on truth, and who is ashamed of bad clothes and bad food, is not fit to be discoursed with." He must not concern himself with dwelling or reputation in his single-minded devotion to truth. "A man should say, 'I am not concerned that I have no place—I am concerned how I may fit myself for one. I am not concerned that I am not known; I seek to be worthy to be known." Abstract truth, however, is not Jesus' highest good. The kingdom of God reigns supreme over all else; before it all else bows.

The kingdom of Heaven is not something you just believe in; it is something to which you give yourself, heart and soul and mind and strength—and financial resources. The result of your commitment is joy.

These parables raise two questions that are fundamental to human happiness: (l) *What do you really want in life?* (That is, what would make you happiest? Is the kingdom of Heaven, the rule of God in your life, your supreme treasure? (2) *What are you willing to give up in order to get what you say you want?* There is no fulfillment without sacrifice. Are you willing to sacrifice whatever is keeping you from this supreme treasure?

Shut Out at Home (13:53-58)
(Mark 6:1-6; Luke 4:16-30)

'Tis only when they spring to heaven that angels
Reveal themselves to you; they sit all day
Beside you, and lie down at night by you
Who care not for their presence, muse or sleep,
And all at once they leave you, and you know them!
Robert Browning, *Paracelsus*

Neither angels nor prophets can expect recognition in their hometowns. Perhaps it's because most hometowns are small places whose inhabitants are convinced of their insignificance. Nothing much has ever happened there and nothing much ever will, since everybody is pretty much like everybody else and nobody is particularly outstanding. Nathanael's opinion of Jesus' hometown ("Nazareth! Can anything good come from there?"—John 1:46) has been pinned on thousands of towns over thousands of years. Can anything good come out of anywhere?

Nazareth was not all that splendid a city when Jesus went there. It wasn't even important enough to merit mention in the Old Testament. Located in lower Galilee (near the modern en-Natzirah), Nazareth was a stopover place for Roman soldiers and for traders. Its reputation was fairly unsavory, as is that of most places that cater to soldiers and traders. Its citizens had no reason to expect much of their town or themselves. Mediocrity was their trademark. Nothing more was possible.

Or so they thought. Twice their complacency was shattered, and on both occasions it was the carpenter's son who shattered it. Early in His ministry, Jesus returned home (Luke 4:14-30). When He read from the scroll of the prophet Isaiah and applied the words concerning the Messiah to himself, He enraged His townspeople. They drove Him out of the city and threatened to kill Him for His blasphemy.

Their tempers must have cooled in the interim, because once more Jesus visits Nazareth (His last recorded appearance there), and once more He teaches in the synagogue. By this time, their rage has turned to cold indifference. They don't run Him out of town, but neither will they give Him a hearing. "They took offense at him" (verse 57)—that is, they were caused to stumble—because they could not accept Jesus' superiority.

"Where did this man get this wisdom and these miraculous powers?" (verse 54). They cannot deny, but neither will they accept, His superhuman abilities. They are like the myriads of skeptics today who reject outright what they cannot explain or imagine. Given the astonishing popularity of moving pictures today, it is amusing to read that producer D. W. Griffith pontificated in 1926 that "speaking movies are impossible. When a century has passed, all thought of our so-called 'talking pictures' will have been abandoned. It will never be possible to synchronize the voice with the picture." When Secretary of State William Seward purchased Alaska from Russia in 1867 for $7.2 million, his countrymen hooted his bargain as Seward's Folly or Seward's Icebox. They quit jeering in the late 1890s when gold was discovered there. Nazareth long ago stopped jeering about Jesus, if for no other reason than the gold of the tourist business that Jesus has brought to the little city.

"Isn't he one of us?" That is their real question. "He is the son of a carpenter; we know his mother and brothers and sisters, he grew up in this town, working like us, educated like us, having no apparent advantages over us. How can he do these things?" Their questions betray genuine confusion. They also give away the questioners. They are offended, envious. They cannot admit that one of themselves could do what none of them had even thought of trying. They ran Him out of town for His pretensions once. This time, they just withhold belief, so that Jesus can do very little in their midst.

Their mistreatment of Jesus is so typical of the human race that a proverb readily comes to His mind: "Only in his hometown and in his own house is a prophet without honor." Jesus' Nazareth rejection parallels in miniature what He suffered at the hands of His nation and even of the whole world. "He was in the world, and though the world was made through him, the world did not recognize him. He came to that which was his own, but his own did not receive him" (John 1:10, 11). The hometown spirit of this global village had difficulty believing that one who was raised here, who was so much like the rest of us in so many ways, was not like us in all ways. Where such disbelief prevails, He cannot do many miracles.

CHAPTER FIFTEEN

Of Banquets and Boat Rides
Matthew 14

Two Royal Banquets (14:1-21)
(Mark 6:14-46; Luke 9:7-17; John 6:1-14)

Two kings rule in these verses. One is not much of a king, just a puppet monarch, a pretender propped on his throne by Rome. He is Herod Antipas, the son of the tyrant who ruled Judea when Jesus was born, Herod the Great. When "the Great" died, his territory was divided among his three sons, with Antipas receiving Galilee and Perea. He had married the daughter of the king of Nabatean Arabia in a political marriage to buy peace between his little section of Palestine and the neighboring Arabs. His domestic arrangement was disturbed, however, when on a visit to his brother Philip in Rome, he enticed Philip's wife Herodias to run away with him. Of course, he had to divorce his first wife to make room for his new one, a breach of faith that eventually led to war with the Nabateans.

Antipas' tangled love life broke two laws. He violated one by divorcing his wife, and the other by marrying his sister-in-law while his brother was still living. John publicly denounced the king for these transgressions. Herod retaliated by clapping him in prison. Then he eventually had him killed, as Matthew reports.

Herodias is a woman of easy virtue in more ways than one. Beautiful and sensuous, driven by ambition and faithless to her vows, this immoral woman will stop at nothing to get what she wants. What else can you say of a woman who would force her own daughter into playing a cheap show girl in order to get her vengeance? So, doing her mother's bidding, Salome entertains her mother's drunken husband and his drunken buddies.

It is not a pretty picture, this weak king with his immoral wife and conniving daughter, so afraid of the Jews he rules that he does not dare break the oath that even he recognizes as foolish.

The reader turns with relief to another king and another banquet in this passage. Jesus, having healed the multitude, expresses His concern for their hunger. In a foretaste of the great Messianic banquet to come, Jesus hosts the crowd. He miraculously multiplies the fish and loaves so that everyone has ample refreshment.

Corruption and Compassion

Two kings and two banquets. One is marked by corruption, the other by compassion; one is dominated by sensual entertainment, the other by selfless sharing. You can learn a lot about somebody by noting what it takes to entertain him. Does he get his kicks from pornography, or sensuality, or brutality? What can you say about someone who finds it entertaining to view the head of a prophet on a platter?

Can you imagine Jesus in such a setting? His banquet is in the light, and its entertainment is teaching, healing, and feeding the hungry. Bored people demand that their senses be titillated. People who are busy doing good never experience such boredom.

Fear and Love

This is a tale of two banquets, one marked by fear and one by love. Herod, for all his symbols of power, is afraid. He fears the censure of John the Baptist. It was fear that made him imprison John. He is afraid of his wife. He is afraid of the Jews over whom he is supposed to be the ruler. He is afraid of his own courtiers; he does not want them to think he is weak. So he carries out his foolish oath.

Herod is a victim of his guilty conscience. When he hears of Jesus' miracles, his paranoia instantly concludes that John has returned to life to haunt him. He is the male counterpart of Shakespeare's Lady Macbeth in her famous sleepwalking scene: "Out, damned spot." [She isn't swearing. She is stating a fact: that spot was damned, her hand was damned, her soul was damned—condemned, consigned to hell—for killing an innocent man.]

"Will these hands never be clean?
Here's the smell of blood still."

All the perfumes of Araby could not sweeten her foul hand. The physician observing her obsession admitted, "This disease is beyond my practice." Physical medicine can never cure a guilty conscience.

Antipas is the true heir of Herod the Great, who was just as scared. It was he who commanded that all male children two years of age and younger in Bethlehem be slain (Matthew 2:16) in order to prevent any one of them taking over his throne. He reminds us of King Saul, who was proving to be an acceptable ruler of Israel until he was frightened by David (1 Samuel 18); then the king turned killer.

While Antipas cowers, Jesus strides across the pages of the New Testament without fear. His controlling motive is love, and perfect love drives out fear (1 John 4:18). He has no need to be afraid of aspirants for His throne: not many throne-robbers will climb a cross to snatch one.

Greed and Giving

This is a tale of two banquets. Herod's displays the royal couple's greed. Jesus' feast is an opportunity for giving. Herod grabs his throne; Herodias clutches her crown. Jealous of the perquisites of office, they brook no opposition. It is the nature of jealousy to kill.

It kills marriages, kills parents, children, suitors, anybody who threatens. Jealousy does not hate so much as it fears. Afraid it cannot win, it cheats, sometimes fatally. So-called "jealous love" is a contradiction of terms, since genuine love casts out fear.

There is a king above jealousy, who does not grasp anything to himself, even Heaven (Philippians 2:5-11). He is unique, this giving king. He does not send His soldiers into battle to die for their king; He dies for them. What a difference between the kingdom of Heaven and the kingdoms of this world. Jesus forbids His disciples to imitate this world's rulers. Gentiles know how to lord it over people; Jesus wants His followers to serve them instead (Matthew 20:26).

Dr. Karl Menninger of the famous Menninger Clinic in Topeka, Kansas, observed that many of his patients were suffering what he calls "love deformation." Summoning his staff one day, he instructed them to become more loving. No one was to enter a patient's room with an unloving attitude. He kept careful records and within six months discovered that the clinic had reduced the healing time by fifty percent.

Jesus' disciples are also in the healing business. Our medicine is love.

Death and Life

This is a tale of two banquets. One breathed the air of death and the other of life. John the Baptist died at the word of Antipas. A king can do that. Unfortunately, Hamilton (or Madison, whoever of the two wrote *Federalist Paper 51)* was right: "What is government itself but the greatest of all reflections on human nature. If men were angels, no government would be necessary." But we aren't angels, so government is needed. Governors are ordinary mortals writ large, their virtues and vices magnified by the power of office.

Henry David Thoreau wrote in his *Journal* on September 8, 1859:

"I went to the store the other day to buy a bolt for our front door, for, as I told the storekeeper, the Governor was coming here. 'Aye,' said he, 'and the Legislature too.' 'Then I will take two bolts,' said I. He said that there had been a steady demand for bolts and locks of late, for our protectors were coming."

There was no protection from John's protector.

We turn with relief to Jesus' banquet of life. This is He who said, "I am the bread of life" (John 6:35). He is the "stuff" of life. His is a life-giving ministry (John 3:16). Herod's banquet is for Herod; if somebody should die to entertain a king, so be it. Jesus' feast is for the five thousand, with the host's resources freely given for their sake. They eat all they want. He provides more than is needed, a symbol of the abundant life in store for His disciples (John 10:10)

Freedom and Courage (14:22-36)
(Mark 6:45-56; John 6:16-21)

No incident in the life of the Lord is more widely known than this one. Its notoriety does not rest on the miracle of Jesus' walk on the water. What boggles their minds is that someone like themselves could also be given power to do so. Yet here, during the fourth watch (sometime between 3 and 6 A.M.) on a windy night, Jesus invites Peter to join Him on the water. And Peter begins to do so!

This amazing episode is a study in courage and freedom. "Take courage! It is I. Don't be afraid." The disciples are afraid of what they at first think is a ghost. Jesus speaks to calm their fears, of course. But He also teaches them through Peter what freedom there can be in faith-based courage. When Peter takes his eyes from the Lord to study the treacherous wind (and thus insure his own failure), Jesus scolds him for his loss of nerve. Had he continued to have faith, he would not have sunk in the water.

When Jesus and Peter climb into the boat and the wind dies down, the rest of the disciples worship their Lord. It is not their worship He seeks at this moment, however, but their courage. Look at Peter.

Peter has the *courage to be different*. Peter has long been the butt of jokes about walking on water, but the fact is, only Peter walked on water! The rest sat in safe conformity in the boat. He had the courage to be different. Conformity prevails among us because it requires such strength to be different. As some wag has said, "He was a bold man that first ate an oyster." Whoever steps beyond his peers will be noticed—and probably laughed at. Peter's fellow disciples undoubtedly thought him mad when they saw him step overboard. But as the soldier in Shaw's play *St. Joan* replied when he was accused of being almost as mad as Joan of Arc, "Maybe that's what we need nowadays—mad people. See where the sane ones have landed us."

Charles Swindoll (in *Three Steps Forward, Two Steps Back)* tells of a friend who has a bright red birthmark across the side of his face from his forehead across his nose and a large section of his mouth and neck. Yet, the man gives no evidence of feeling inferior. The reason for his self-assurance is something his father told him as a boy. The wise man explained to his son that the scar was the part of his face where an angel must have kissed him before he was born. The angel left a special mark so that his dad would always know the boy was his. Far from feeling inferior because he was different, the boy grew up feeling sorry for anyone who didn't have a birthmark to make him as special! The father gave his son the courage to be different.

Peter has the *courage to venture out* beyond the safety of the boat and the comfort of his group. With his eyes on the Lord, he can defy even the force of gravity. Such courage is the essence of leadership. When Queen Elizabeth I of England addressed a committee of both houses of Parliament with these words, no one doubted her ability to lead: "I am your anointed Queen. I will never be by violence constrained to do anything. I thank God I am endued with such qualities that if I were turned out of the Realm in my petticoat, I were able to live in any place in Christendom." She could venture out of the comfort of the palace and the security of her throne. She would not be afraid to leave; such is the courage needed to lead.

Peter has the *courage to ignore the doubts of the timid.* Were there time to hold a conference in the boat before Peter steps overboard, the majority decision would be for him to remain. Timidity controls most human behavior. Peter's boldness in this instance expresses the combination of faith, impulsiveness, and courage that makes him the leader to whom the Lord can entrust the leadership of the newly forming church. A much later leader, Ulysses S. Grant, discovered in the midst of America's Civil War that he did not need to be afraid of the enemy. After one battle that never took place because the Confederates under Colonel Thomas Harris had retreated from Grant (who was fearfully dreading the contest), Grant recalled in his *Memoirs,* "It occurred to me at once that Harris had been as much afraid of me as I had been of him. This was a view I had never taken before: but was one I never forgot afterwards. From that event to the close of the war, I never experienced trepidation upon confronting an enemy, though I always felt more or less anxiety. I never forgot that he had as much reason to fear my forces as I had his. The lesson was valuable." With Peter's confidence in the Lord who had told him to venture out onto the water, he, too, has no reason to fear the doubts of the timid ones who would have persuaded him not to try it.

Peter has the *courage to believe the promise of his Lord.* Here is the heart of the matter. He believes in Jesus. He knows that Jesus has never played games with His disciples or teased them into trying what He knew they could not accomplish. He had already empowered them to exorcise demons and to heal the sick; it is no more difficult to walk on water, surely. Peter's courage is not foolhardiness; it results from his implicit faith in the Lord.

So Peter has the *courage to be free.* His faith liberates him from fear, from the confines of the boat, from the limitations of prior human experience. He moves beyond the rest of his race. He lives as an example of the truth that freedom depends on keeping faith. When President Franklin Roosevelt addressed a panicky, depression-paralyzed nation on Inauguration Day, March 4, 1933, the polio-crippled leader brought new hope to his eager constituents when he asserted his "firm belief that the only thing we have to fear is fear itself—nameless, unreasoning, unjustified terror which paralyzes needed efforts to convert retreat into advance." A nation afraid was a nation shackled. The new President's first priority was to inject new courage into the American heart.

If only Peter had not taken his eyes from his Lord, the source of his strength, and focused them on the wind! Caution can often cripple. If you wait until all the risks and obstacles to your adventure are removed, you'll never venture. Too much caution can paralyze you; it can foster a pessimism that will, in time, render you immobile. After the Lord has said come, you dare not wait until the winds are favorable. He who is greater than the winds will help you in spite of them. If you obey the winds, what can the Lord do for you?

Will Rogers delighted one of his audiences during World War I when he told them that Germany couldn't understand how the United States could get trained men to Europe so quickly. What the Germans didn't understand, Rogers explained, was that "in our training manual there's nothing about retreating. When you only have to teach an army to go one way, you can do it in half the time." Jesus gives Peter no instructions for sinking, only for walking. He never gives His disciples practice in retreating before persecution, hardships, the devil, or the contrary winds that blow. Doubting He would banish from our experience, to replace it with steady, obedient faith.

CHAPTER SIXTEEN

Free of the Conventional
Matthew 15

The Commands of God and the Traditions of Men (15:1-20)
(Mark 7:1-23)

"Why aren't you like me?" The natural conviction that *you* ought to be like *me* is the breeding ground of all prejudice. It is obvious, one reasons, that since God and I agree on this or that, you should, too. Your ways should be my ways, since my ways are God's. I worship the way God wants us all to. You don't. Why don't you?

The Pharisees have noticed that Jesus' disciples are breaking the traditions of the elders. They do not wash their hands before eating. Hygiene is not the Pharisee's concern; they aren't knowledgeable about germs. What offends them is that the disciples ignore the elders' legalistic regulation with their nice distinctions of "clean" and "unclean."

The Jews hold in reverence two basic sets of teaching: the law of Moses, and the accumulation of explanations of the law which they call the traditions of the elders. These have been handed down from generation to generation, gathering more reverence and greater legal precision along the way. With time, the teachings of the elders have been granted as much respect as the law itself. It is the same reverence that perpetuates certain traditions in Christian denominations. The dictates of the founder or other outstanding leaders become as sanctified as the Bible itself.

Jesus' disregard of the traditions agitates the self-appointed guardians of Jewish "denominational" purity. In their opinion, Jesus and His disciples are tempting fate by their dishonoring of the hallowed practices. In this case, for example, the ritual they are ignoring was designed, the Pharisees believe, to protect people from demons.

One such demon was called *Shibta*. He was reported to perch on the hands of people as they slept; if they failed to perform their ceremonial hand-washing before eating, Shibta could ride on their food and enter their innards and defile them. A certain Rabbi Ranith taught that whoever has "his abode in the land of Israel and eateth his common food with washed hands, and speaks the holy language, and

191

recites his phylacteries morning and evening, he may rest assured that he shall obtain eternal life."[49] The good rabbi reduced requirements for entry into eternity to living in the right place, eating after proper ablutions, speaking the right language, and reciting memorized charms. Such a perversion of God's will Jesus has to reform.

This exchange between Pharisees and teachers of the law and Jesus raises questions that still demand answers.

Why Do You Put Your Traditions Ahead of the Command of God?

Their charge: You break traditions. His counter-charge: You break the commandment of God himself.

The tradition Jesus' disciples ignore has to do with the proper washing of hands before eating. They were to have poured a minimal amount of water over their hands. Most good Jewish homes kept water jars near the table, from which enough water to fill at least one and a half eggshells was taken. It was then poured over the hands held with fingers up, so the water would run off the wrists. Then the hands were turned over, fingers pointing down. Water poured over the hands would then run down and drip off the fingers. The ritualist was then considered ceremoniously clean. A really conscientious observer would perform the ablution not only before the meal, but between courses as well.

Such is the tradition the disciples have violated. Jesus counters with a much more serious charge: "You are breaking the commandment of the Lord himself." He has in mind another tradition, one in which the elders had modified a specific command of God. Regarding filial piety, the command of God has never changed: "Honor your father and mother." This is God's unalterable will. Years earlier, however, the elders had devised an escape clause. If a man had some possessions that he gave to the temple, he could say to his parents, "What I might have used to care for you in your old age, I dedicated to the Lord's temple. Since I gave it to God, I have no further obligation to you." "While you scribes and Pharisees have so punctilliously attended to your favorite man-made traditions," Jesus implies, "you have disregarded one of God's basic requirements. You have dishonored your parents and God. You who do not scruple to violate this commandment have no right to chastize My disciples."

---

[49]G. Campbell Morgan, *The Gospel According to Matthew* (New York: Fleming H. Revell Company, 1929), p. 19.

Wise is the contemporary church that pays close attention to this debate. Nothing is easier than for a congregation to fall into the trap of making its traditions into inviolable commandments of God while at the same time casually disregarding the weightier matters of God's will. In some churches, by-laws and constitutions have effectively replaced the New Testament as guide to church order. A minister in one of the southern states, for instance, delights in telling of a heated discussion in a board meeting when one of his leaders insisted that a proposal be passed and observed as a rule of the church. "But that's not in the Bible," other leaders objected. "Well," he retorted, "it ought to be," and continued to press his demand. It is not easy to put aside prejudices so that we can read with understanding, and accept with obedience, what the Bible actually teaches.

Renewal movements through the more recent history of the church have attempted to return to Biblical precedents for solutions to the ongoing problems of disunity and corruption in the body of Christ. No substitute for God's revelation has yet been devised that can repair the damage done by secondary loyalties and party spirit. John Gardner has wisely written of secular institutions, "Someone has said that the last act of a dying organization is to get out a new and enlarged edition of the rule book."[50] Rule books will finish off any organization, if they are treated as canonized law. Such traditions strangle any body. God's commands are designed to liberate.

Where Are Your Hearts When Your Lips Are Praising God?

Jesus quotes the prophet Isaiah (29:13). At the heart of Jesus' revolution in religion is His desire to bring heart and lips together, thus uniting ceremony with faith. Jesus has no respect for Sunday-go-to-meetin' religion. He appreciates that worship that is as evident in the office on Monday as it is in the church house on Sunday. No lip-service for Jesus. To abuse your children or neglect your aged parents or cheat your customer is to insult God. Let the meditations of your heart and the words of your mouth be in harmony.

Mark Twain offers an oblique example for us. Picturesque but not always polite in his speech, Twain frequently offended his cultured wife by his swearing. Finally, in a desperate attempt to break him of his habit, she decided to use the old "if-you-can't-beat-'em-join-'em"

---

[50] John Gardner, *Self-Renewal* (New York: Harper and Row, 1965), p. 45.

ploy. She memorized some curse words and one day let him have them, hoping to demonstrate how terrible he sounded. She failed. He just laughed and told her, "You know the words, my dear, but you haven't got the tune." Words and tune must cooperate in our worship, also; desire and expression must harmonize.

Christian Standard some time ago included an article by Edwin Hayden, who reminisced about his days in Bible college. He told of the day the fifty boys who slept in the same large sleeping room came into the dorm to find their beds missing. Someone had played a joke on the young preachers. For three days, nobody could find the beds, so the students slept on the floor. Then the beds were discovered—in the students' prayer room. They knew the words, these young preachers, but hadn't got the tune. Where were their hearts when their lips were praising God?

What Comes Out of Your Mouth?

Jesus is not so concerned about what goes in, but what comes out. He resists the human tendency to reduce religious behavior to matters of what you eat and what you drink or how you do either. Such regulations are more easily observed than paying attention to attitudes, for example. So Christian leaders as well as Jewish teachers before them have devoted exaggerated attention to such incidentals. "You can't be a Christian if you drink." "You must eat fish on Friday." "You must never eat pork." Jesus turns everything around. "What comes out?"

It is not that what goes in is completely irrelevant. A pastor's friend just divorced his wife of over thirty years. The pastor, having had some knowledge of the man for many years, could not help asking of him, "Has he been drinking? Is he on some kind of drugs?" He knew that some things that go into the mouth can change what comes out. Habitual use of alcohol or drugs can definitely change your heart. This is a modern application of Francis Bacon's dictum, "It is not what men eat but what they digest that makes them strong; not what we gain but what we save that makes us right; not what we read but what we remember that makes us learned." We could add: not what we preach but what we practice that makes us disciples. Emerson reminds us of the difficulty of guaranteeing that what comes from the heart is good: "It takes a great deal of elevation of thought to produce a very little elevation of life."

What then shall we say about judging religious behavior? Shall we call those good Christians who wash their hands properly, or who worship with an organ in their church building, or without an organ, or who wear no jewelry or don't go to movies or dances, or who observe Old Testament dietary laws, or worship on the Sabbath instead of Sunday, or wear uncut hair, or refrain from any alcoholic beverages or tobacco, or do not play cards or salute the flag or allow blood transfusions? It would be easier to please God if we could just refrain from this or that activity or be certain to perform this or that ritual. But Jesus won't allow us to make a mockery of God in this way.

God desires holy behavior in His people. Holiness begins in the heart: "Out of the heart come evil thoughts" (Matthew 15:19). Here is the Sermon on the Mount (Matthew 5—7) in a capsule. Again Jesus demands Christians' thoughts and feelings as well as proper conduct. For this reason, He lists "evil thoughts" along with adultery and murder. Adultery is a type of murder, of course, born of lust and killing hope, trust, and faith. Sexual immorality is a type of theft, too. If you steal another person's virtue or reputation or character, you have stolen something more precious than money. If you defame another person through gossip, you steal his reputation.

Jesus has effectively silenced the critics who charged that He and His disciples have failed to wash their hands properly. He told them that the mouth, not the hands, should be their concern. What comes out of the mouth, from the heart, must honor God.

Great Faith Wins (15:21-28)
(Mark 7:24-30)

Jesus has gone beyond the borders of Palestine, away from the press of His own people. Matthew does not say so, but Jesus has probably withdrawn into the area to the northwest of Galilee in order to get some richly deserved peace and quiet. He needs the rest. The end of His ministry is approaching and the intensity of the opposition is heightening. To prepare for the final spring of His strenuous race, He needs to refresh himself and complete the training of His disciples.

He can find no solitude in Galilee, so He travels north to the land of Tyre and Sidon, the region of the Phoenicians. His carping critics won't follow Him into this foreign territory, and the great masses will not be able to venture so far from home.

But even here, He is not to be left alone. "Lord, Son of David, have mercy on me!" A Syro-Phoenician woman (she is not even a Jew, but a Gentile living in the area of modern Lebanon) has heard of the Jewish miracle-worker Jesus. In desperation, she begs—and keeps on begging—for Him to work a miracle for her daughter, who is possessed by demons. She is aware that Jews consider people like her to be pagans. Their prejudice does not stop her. She is so persistent Jesus finally grants her request, marveling over her great faith.

Jesus does not often compliment people on their faith. In fact, He does so only twice, and both times He speaks of Gentiles (here and with the Roman centurion, Matthew 8:10). This rare praise makes her faith worth examining. What, exactly, does great faith look like?

Great Faith Looks Like Self-forgetfulness

The woman makes a perfect nuisance of herself. She is so distracted by her daughter's plight that she doesn't give a thought to herself. What ill child hasn't seen the same look of near-panic in a mother's eye? What mother wouldn't make a pest of herself for the sake of her child? "Have mercy on me," she cries, so identifying herself with her child's need that she hurts in her daughter.

Nothing is more beautiful than complete self-disregard. Or more rare. It is humility in its purest form. Strangely enough, humility is often confused with shyness, yet shyness is a form of selfishness. If this mother were merely shy, she could never summon the courage to call Jesus' attention to her daughter's trouble. Self-consciousness is just what it sounds like: being so conscious of oneself that social paralysis sets in. To the contrary, this mother has lost all self-consciousness in her complete identification with her daughter's need.

Great Faith Focuses on a Higher Power

She admits that Jesus has powers she does not. He can do for her daughter what she is helpless to do. With anticipation and relief, she turns from her daughter's need to Jesus' ability to meet her need.

Faith in Jesus. Faith to petition help for her daughter. Hers is a specific request for the sake of someone else. Her faith is other-directed. She differs markedly from the young man Nels Ferre speaks of who died several years ago after drinking poison. He belonged to the famous snake-handling cult in Appalachia. Members believe they must take literally the words of Jesus in the last twelve verses of Mark's Gospel. (This section is not found in the oldest manuscripts of Mark. It apparently was added on in later years by someone other than the original author.) "In my name they will drive out demons; they will speak in new tongues; they will pick up snakes with their hands; and when they drink deadly poison, it will not hurt them at all...." A young deacon thanked God for the certainty of Jesus' promises, drank his cup of poison, and died. At his funeral, his wife said, "My husband died from having too much faith."[51]

No, not of too much faith, but of misplaced faith. He narrowly relied on one verse in the Bible, and a disputed one at that. He wanted to prove his ability to defy God's natural laws. He did not realize that Jesus never promised His disciples power to perform magic. He did not promise them the Holy Spirit so that they could draw attention to their great faith. If anything, He taught that great faith does not call attention to itself but to the Father in Heaven (Matthew 5:16). Handling snakes and drinking poison are of no value to anyone but the performer. This mother focuses on Jesus for the sake of her daughter. Hers is a noble trust.

Great Faith Does Not Quit When Obstacles Interfere

"Send her away, for she keeps crying out after us," Jesus' disciples urge, with an impatience typical of Jesus' followers. We often feel ourselves so pressed with gravely important matters that we do not wish to be disturbed by people with problems.

Jesus does not reject the woman, but neither does He help her, at first. God has sent Him only to Jews. Not until the end of His earthly ministry will He commission His apostles to venture beyond their own kind. For the time being, Jesus is out of His territory, and the woman is beyond His commission.

Telling her this should silence her, but doesn't. Kneeling, with a few simple words, she tries again. "Lord, help me!"

Jesus' answer reads like an insult, but doesn't sound like it to the woman. We can't hear the tone of His voice, or see the twinkle in His eye and the hint of a smile on His face. It is not in His character to use the language of His people for Gentiles, "dog," in anything but a gently teasing manner. He knows His verbal sparring partner. He has probably already begun to admire her spunk. "It is not right to take the children's bread and toss it to their dogs."

This Canaanite woman knows how to take Him. She does not take offense, but gives tit for tat. "Yes, Lord, but even the dogs eat the crumbs that fall from their masters' table." She doesn't want Him to violate His charge from God; she'll be satisfied with leftovers. Her faith is so strong she trusts the crumbs to heal her daughter.

Great faith does not give up easily. History offers inspiring por-

---

[51]Nels Ferre, *God's New Age* (Harper and Brothers, 1962), p. 105.

traits of men and women who refused to give in to what most of us would consider to be overwhelming odds. There were club-footed Sir Walter Scott, fighting back from financial ruin by writing some of England's finest novels, and Louisa May Alcott, who proved the editor who told her she had no writing ability wrong by turning out *Little Women* and other time-honored books. Walt Disney had the same experience with his drawings. "You have no talent," he was told. Thomas Edison's mother was told that her son was too stupid to learn, and Admiral Richard Byrd was retired from the United States Navy as unfit for service. That was before he flew over the North and South Poles. Then there is the famous example of Winston Churchill, who could not pass English classes but who has left us some of the language's most memorable prose. We could add Milton's blindness, Beethoven's deafness, Napoleon's epilepsy, and Lincoln's poverty.

In fact, many successful personalities seemed at one time to be confirmed failures. Ty Cobb and Babe Ruth, two of baseball's best, looked at from another point of view are baseball's worst. Ty Cobb was thrown out more times trying to steal than any other man in baseball; and Babe Ruth, for years the home-run king, also held the record for strikeouts. Albert Einstein flunked in math. Henry Ford, the billionaire, was broke at 40. They all eventually succeeded, however, because they kept at it.

When Henrik Ibsen, the renowned Norwegian playwright, died, his last word was, "Nevertheless." Having devoted his life to dramatically criticizing the stupidities of society, Ibsen could not have chosen a more appropriate final comment. It's as good a word for Christians to live by as for Ibsen to die by. Beset on every hand by obstacles and enemies, Christians utter their "nevertheless" and keep pressing forward. Jesus did not quit, so neither do we. Even through the cross, when defeat seemed certain, when death appeared so final, God was teaching Jesus' disciples to say, "Nevertheless." Even as the end of the world approaches, 2 Peter 3:13 exhorts that "in keeping with his promise we are looking forward to a new heaven and a new earth, the home of righteousness." No reason to quit.

Great Faith Wins

"This is the victory that has overcome the world, even our faith" (1 John 5:4). More specifically, "Who is it that overcomes the world? Only he who believes that Jesus is the Son of God" (verse 5). The Syro-Phoenician mother wins. Jesus grants her request.

Read the catalog of victorious men and women of faith in Hebrews

11. Then add 12:1—"Therefore, since we are also encompassed by so great a crowd of witnesses, let us throw off everything that hinders and the sin that so easily entangles, and let us run with perseverance the race marked out for us." We can win, too.

When Phillips Brooks, the renowned nineteenth-century New England preacher, was growing up in Litchfield, Connecticut, his parents raised their family of eleven children on Mr. Brooks' $800-a-year income. His mother, whom Brooks later remembered as complaining about the overdue bills in her "sweet, refined, gentle, sad way," expected to die in the poor house. But her husband was not worried. He had trusted God for forty years, and He had never let him down, so the elder Brooks was not going to distrust Him now.

Young Phillips never forgot his father's words. Through his own difficult seasons of poverty and sickness, he never lost sight of his father's faith. In time, it became his own. When he failed as a teacher, he remembered. When he later became a famous preacher, he still remembered. He passed the lesson on to his congregation: "You must learn, you must let God teach you, that the only way to get rid of your past is to make a future out of it. God will waste nothing.... Do not pray for easy lives. Do not pray for tasks equal to your powers. Pray for powers equal to your tasks. Then the doing of your work will be no miracle; but you will be the miracle."[52]

Great faith wins. The woman of Phoenicia had no right to ask Jesus for anything. She had no hold on Him but her faith in Him. It was enough.

A Banquet for Gentiles (15:29-39)
(Mark 8:1-10)

No wonder the great crowds come. They know they can count on the Lord's compassion. He cannot bear to look upon the lame, the blind, the diseased, or the prisoners of demons. His healings are not for show, but from sympathy. God created man perfect, so people's infirmities move the heart of His Son. They already know something of Jesus, for He has previously miraculously freed a man bound by demons in this area (Matthew 8:28-34; Mark 5:1-20). In his excitement, the man has broadcast the good news of his healing. His testimony and that of the large number of Jesus' Galilean followers insure

---

[52]Quoted in Margaret T. Applegarth, *Twelve Baskets Full* (New York: Harper and Brothers, 1957), p. 222.

that a curious crowd will throng to Him even after He leaves Galilee. For three days, Matthew writes, they stick to Him, observing every healing, weighing every word. They are so enthralled, they don't leave even to eat.

Their hunger concerns Him. It is remarkable how many instances are recorded of Jesus' eating with or providing food for His followers. (To realize just how noteworthy this fact is, compare the social Jesus with the ascetic John the Baptist. You can scarcely imagine John, who subsisted on locusts and wild honey—Matthew 3:4—providing a feast for his disciples!) Jesus closed His Galilean ministry with the feeding of the 5,000 (Matthew 14:13-21); here He brings His sojourn in the Decapolis (the ten towns on the East of the Jordan and the Sea of Galilee) to a conclusion with the feeding of the 4,000. His ministry in Judea came to an end with the Last Supper (Matthew 26:17-30). The early church continued this emphasis of the Master, making the meal a central focus of their fellowship and worship (Acts 2:42; 1 Corinthians 11).

Jesus seems to have fed the 5,000 in the springtime, on one of those few brief days when the grass is green in Palestine (Matthew 14:19). The 4,000 are most likely fed in the summer. The first occasion cared for the Jews in Galilee; in the Decapolis, most of the followers would be non-Jews, which explains why Matthew mentions their praise of the God of Israel (Matthew 15:31). Barclay's commentary points out an interesting detail that highlights the difference between the groups. In Galilee, the leftovers were gathered up in baskets called *kophinoi,* narrow-necked, flask-shaped baskets Jews used to carry food with them so they would never be forced to eat anything touched by a Gentile; in the Decapolis, the leftovers are gathered in hamper-sized baskets called *sphurides,* large enough to carry a man. These baskets are common among the Gentiles. The Jews in Galilee might have expected to be fed by their generous countryman who called himself the Bread of Life. However, such compassion must come as a surprise to the Gentiles, who have learned long ago that the average Jew will not bother himself with their hunger. In this miracle, Jesus is foreshadowing the meaning of the cross, through which God's love will be made available for all mankind.

Giving thanks for the seven loaves and the few small fish, Jesus then distributes the abundance provided through the disciples, who also pick up the leftovers. Once again, Jesus has demonstrated His power and God's providence. The little becomes more than enough in the Lord's hands.

CHAPTER SEVENTEEN

Signs of True Faith

Matthew 16

Of Signs and Yeast (16:1-12)
(Mark 8:11-21)

It is an honored saying and true, that "politics makes strange bed-fellows." Pharisees and Sadducees were traditional antagonists. The Pharisees were the righteous ones, given to ritual and tradition and scrupulous observance of the law. They believed in Heaven and its angels, and they believed in life after death. They did not believe in compromising anything for the sake of accommodating either king or emperor, which is exactly what the Sadducees believed. They were great compromisers on matters political. Religiously, they would accept nothing but the first five books of the Bible to be the authentic Word of God. As a result, they could not accept the Pharisee's teaching about angels or Heaven or life after death. But the Sadducean strictness in this area gave them more freedom in others. They could justify their cooperation with the modernistic manners of Herod's court and their Roman overseers. Scorning the religious fanaticism of the Pharisees, the Sadducees prided themselves in being the modern, cultured, and of course, wealthy aristocrats of the Jews.

What are these opposing parties doing together in the vicinity of Magadan (Matthew 15:39) on the northwest shore of the Sea of Galilee, so far from Jerusalem? Did the temple authorities (Sadducees) dispatch a contingency of men to Galilee to challenge Jesus? Probably. Like scrapping dogs who will quickly turn together to chase a cat, they forget their natural animosity long enough to interrogate Jesus. They demand "a sign from heaven." (See Matthew 12:38-40.)

His answer at first disarms them. They know how to interpret a red sky in the evening ("it will be fair weather tomorrow") and the same red sky in the morning ("it will be stormy"). Yet these men who can predict weather from the sky cannot read "the signs of the times." The Pharisees, who pride themselves in being Bible scholars and teachers, don't know how to read the events of their day in light of the Bible's predictions. The Sadducees, who are just as proud of their cultural astuteness, cannot discern what is happening all around them. Both groups love this world more than they love God. Therefore, no sign will be given to them to authenticate Jesus' authority. They wouldn't believe anyway.

As Jesus and His disciples sail across the lake, He warns them against the insidious, rebellious (against God) teachings of both Pharisees and Sadducees. He wants to protect them against both religious legalism and easy compromise. "Yeast" is a common Jewish term for influence either evil (see 1 Corinthians 5:6-8) or positive (Matthew 13:33).

The disciples, their mind still on the bread they left behind after the feeding of the 4,000 (15:29-39), think Jesus is referring to bread. Instead of worrying about food, He tells them, they should recall that He was able to feed the two huge crowds and have plenty of food leftover. Faith, not food, is Jesus' concern. Their faith must be solid, grounded in belief in Him and His teachings, and not adulterated with the bad influence of either Sadducee or Pharisee. Political opportunism and materialism are always tempting; so is the self-righteousness of religious legalism. Jesus' disciples must succumb to neither, but with trust in His truth, they should follow Him only.

"Who Are You, Jesus?" (16:13-20)
(Mark 8:27-30; Luke 9:18-22)

To the artist, He is the One altogether lovely.
To the architect, He is the chief cornerstone.
To the astronomer, He is the Sun of righteousness.
To the baker, He is the living bread.
To the biologist, He is the Life.
To the builder, He is the sure foundation.
To the carpenter, He is the Door.
To the doctor, He is the great Physician.
To the educator, He is the great Teacher.
To the engineer, He is the new and living way.
To the farmer, He is the Sower and the Lord of the harvest.
To the florist, He is the Rose of Sharon and the Lily of the Valley.
To the geologist, He is the Rock of ages.
To the judge, He is the righteous judge—the judge of all men.
To the juror, He is the faithful and true witness.
To the jeweler, He is the pearl of great price.
To the lawyer, He is the counselor, the lawgiver, and the advocate.
To the newspaperman, He is the good tidings of great joy.
To the oculist, He is the light of the eyes.
To the philanthropist, He is the wisdom of God.
To the preacher, He is the Word of God.
To the sculptor, He is the living Stone.
To the servant, He is the good master.

Who is He to you? Jesus' question to His disciples won't go away. It forces us to deal with Him, even when we would rather not. "Who do you say I am?" We would rather debate whether He is an actual historical person, or what really happened in His miracles, or how He saw himself. We squirm when when have to tell Him what He means to us. Like the disciples who marveled when He calmed the winds and waves, and the crowds that murmured when He spoke with such authority, and His fellow Nazarenes who doubted that anyone they knew could be so extraordinary, we would far rather ask, "Just who does Jesus think He is, anyway?" than answer what we think of Him.

The Rumors: Who Do *They* Think I Am?

A recurring theme in the Gospels is the dullness of the disciples. They were agonizingly slow to understand. Not until after Jesus' resurrection did they fully comprehend who He was. In their insecurity, they were quick to pick up the rumors circulating about their Master: "Some say John the Baptist; others say Elijah; and still others, Jeremiah or one of the prophets." They had no trouble answering; it takes no commitment to repeat what others say. The setting for this conversation is most appropriate. Caesarea Philippi, at the headwaters of the Jordan River in northern Israel, was a haven for religious shrines. Here Herod the Great erected, in honor of Caesar, a temple to the god Pan, which was later beautified and enriched by Philip the Tetrarch. Its cavern and hillside provided a natural pastoral setting for worship of the gods. The area was scattered with temples for ancient Syrian Baal worship. Here, surrounded by these "competing" lords, Jesus interrogates His disciples.

"Some say John the Baptist." John had captured the imagination of his countrymen. He sounded and looked like a prophet. Jesus' disciples compliment Jesus in comparing Him to John.

"Others say Elijah; and still others Jeremiah or one of the prophets." More compliments. Elijah was the greatest of the prophets, the promised forerunner of the Messiah (Malachi 4:5). Jeremiah was another forerunner (2 Maccabees 2:1-12; 2 Esdras).

The disciples tactfully do not report some of the rumors. They refrain from telling Him that He has been called, among other things, a troublemaker of Israel, a blasphemer, a false teacher, and a traitor. Criticisms of Jesus still abound. The rumor that He was the illegitimate son of a Roman soldier will not go away. Nor will these: (a) He was a political revolutionary whose radical methods failed; (b) He was a mystic dreamer with delusions of grandeur; (c) He was a brilliant teacher of unrealistic social and ethical messages; (d) He was just another of the world's leading religious and philosophical geniuses, like Buddha, Socrates, Mohammed, and Confucius; (e) He was really a homosexual, the evidence being His failure to marry at a time when marriage was universal in His part of the world.

Truths, half-truths, and downright lies dominate discussions about this unique personality. Even believers in Christ often do not know what they are talking about. They believe in Jesus, but the Jesus they believe in may not be the One revealed in the Bible. A little girl in Flagstaff, Arizona, told her one-year-old sister this story of Jesus:

> Once upon a time, a man and a lady lived in Yoldey. They didn't have any babies, but soon God sent them a sweet little baby named Jesus. They named Him Jesus. He grew and grew without sucking His thumb. When He got as big as Mike [a neighbor boy], they went to Igley. Jesus talked to the big men. They gave Him presents. He loved children and told the mothers and daddies to back up and let the little children sit on His lap. They rode to Pondey on a little donkey. The people waved palm branches at Him and called "Hi" at Him. When they ate supper, He stood up and fussed at the men for bad manners. "Don't eat food with your knife." The men began not liking Him, and made Him carry a heavy old wooden cross. It scratched His back and made it bleed.

This rendition does not tell much about Jesus, but it reveals a lot about a five-year-old girl's world view, as the many descriptions in "The Cosmopolitan Christ" (which opened this section) expose the biased perceptions of their describers. Whoever tells what he thinks of Jesus inevitably tells more about himself—his culture, prejudices, emotions, upbringing, and blind spots—than he intends to.

The Truth: "You Are the Christ, the Son of the Living God"

When Peter answers, he says more than he knows. The Father in Heaven makes it possible for Peter to name Jesus the Messiah (the Hebrew word for the Greek word *Christ*). Jews believed the Messiah would be sent from God to rescue God's people from their plight. He would be unlike anyone else in history. There is no human category large enough to include Him. The best our language can do is to offer an approximate description. Peter's confession suggests that Jesus is Lord, Master, King, Priest, and Prophet, all in one.

That Peter does not fully appreciate what he is saying will soon be obvious. Within this chapter, Jesus has to scold Peter for his lack of insight (verse 23). In the next, Peter misunderstands the meaning of the transfiguration (17:1-13). There will be many more failures to grasp the implications of his confession as well.

Jesus is Christ, all right, but Christ on His terms, not Peter's or ours. It is not good enough to call Him Lord, if we then insist He be the Lord we want instead of the Lord He must be. Adolf Hitler, influenced by the antisemitic historian Houston Stewart Chamberlain, had no scruples in killing Jews, Jesus' people, because he refused to admit that Jesus was a Jew. Chamberlain gave him ammunition. While declaring that the personality of Christ "is one of the three great bequests of antiquity to modern civilization," he insisted that Jesus was no Jew, pointing to His Galilean origins ("Galilee of the Gentiles") and His alleged inability to pronounce Aramaic gutterals correctly. "Whoever claimed that Jesus was a Jew was either being stupid or telling a lie," Chamberlain held.[53] So in the name of Jesus, Jews were killed. (This travesty against Jesus' compassion is as hideous as the one effected when the slave ship bearing the first African slaves to the shores of America was dubbed the *Jesus.)*

We must not delude ourselves into thinking Jesus will be subject to our prejudices and manipulative agenda. If Jesus is the Christ, then as Peter adds, He is "the Son of the living God." The Father who revealed this information to Peter is the author of Jesus' commission. He will do what the Father tells Him and nothing else.

In Caesarea Philippi, surrounded by the relics of false gods, the Father announces through Peter that Jesus is His only Son. All others are phony. There is no hint here of any broadminded or tolerant smiling on all religions (e.g., "It doesn't matter what you believe so long as you are sincere"). G. K. Chesterton once noted that "the whole world very nearly died of broadmindedness and the brotherhood of all religions."[54] Jesus came to save the world, not to embalm it. No longer will the world that knows Jesus be able to embrace Jesus and at the same time hug the image of Jupiter, Mithras, Osiris, Atys, Ammom, or any of the other gods of Jesus' day—or any other day. Only one is God's son. He is, as Phillips Brooks has said, "the condescension of divinity and the exaltation of humanity" meeting in one person. He is all of God that humanity can comprehend and all of man that humanity can become.

---

[53]Quoted in William L. Shirer, *The Rise and Fall of the Third Reich* (New York: Simon and Schuster, 1960), p. 107.

[54]G.K. Chesterton, *The Everlasting Man* (Garden City, New York: Doubleday and Company, 1925), p. 181.

Peter has said more than he knows, but he has said enough. His remarkable confession is the foundation upon which Jesus' church will be constructed. This often impulsive, sometimes unstable Simon has become to Jesus rock-like (*Petros*), and on the boulder or ledge or cliff of rock (*petra*) of the truth Peter utters, Jesus will gather and build up the believers who will form His church.

Jesus has not mentioned His church before, but the word is not new to the disciples. It means "assembly," a gathering of persons called together for some purpose. The building blocks Jesus uses to "build" a church are living persons (1 Peter 2:5). Those who believe in Him will be individually built up, and together they will form an indestructible structure that nurtures and protects those who make it up. They have chosen Christ as the only Son of God. Their belief in Him opens the gates of Heaven for them, and their union forms a strong offensive weapon that the gates of Hades (the abode of the dead) are helpless to resist. Death cannot overtake the church; members of the church, united by the same confession that Peter has uttered, will be victorious even over death. Peter has spoken the words that open the way for one to enter the kingdom of Heaven. Whoever hears Peter's words, or the word of another proclaimer of Christ, and grasps them as his own, has access here on earth to the kingdom, here and in Heaven. Whoever refuses to believe in Christ here has no promise of entrance into Heaven: "Whatever you bind on earth will be bound in heaven, and whatever you loose on earth will be loosed in heaven." To Peter has been given the privilege of uttering the confession first. He is thus the first among his peers to do so. But what he has said, others will also confess. Of such persons is the kingdom of Heaven.

Urging His disciples to be quiet about this conversation, because He is not ready for His identity to be broadcast, Jesus then begins to teach them what a Messiah is really like.

Why Are You Working, Anyway? (16:21-28)
(Mark 8:31-38; Luke 9:23-27)

Peter, who has so recently identified Jesus as the Christ, now presumes to instruct the Lord on His future. Like his comrades, Peter has entertained wrong ideas about God's promised Messiah. Instead of the victorious warrior they have hoped for, Jesus speaks of His suffering and imminent death. He also predicts His return from the dead, but the stunned disciples failed to hear Him. When He prophesies death, they hear no more.

206

"Never, Lord!" Peter will not accept such an insult to God's anointed.

"Get behind me, Satan!" Strong words for a strong man who means well. Peter means no disrespect. His is the voice of common sense. A good soldier, he is determined to protect his general from harm. Jesus needs to convince him that his selfless efforts to keep Jesus alive, while well-intentioned, are contrary to God's purposes.

To Stay Alive?

Peter's reason resisted Jesus' death talk for the obvious reason that he can conceive of nothing to be gained by the death of his master. The basic human drive to avoid death and prolong life is a powerful one. The majority of our race lives on the edge of starvation. They will do almost anything to get enough to live one more day. More affluent people are only slightly less driven. They have enough possessions to allow them to think beyond today, but their primary concern is just the same: to prolong life as long as possible. Peter simply wants the same for his Lord.

Bruno Walter, leading American symphony conductor of a generation ago, reports in his *Memoirs* that he had constant pain in his arms, but it mysteriously disappeared when he was conducting. Harvey Cushing, Boston's distinguished brain surgeon, believed that "the only way to endure life is always to have a task to complete." It is frustrating to have too little time to accomplish one's tasks, but how much worse it would be to have no tasks left to do. Both men suggest that purposeful work is essential to, and more important than, the mere prolonging of life.

Jesus leaves no doubt that His purpose for working is far more important than just staying alive. He has in mind the things of God.

To Make Yourself Comfortable?

"If anyone would come after me, he must deny himself and take up his cross and follow me." Jesus moves beyond self-preservation to the normal desire to improve one's circumstances. A cross may symbolize many things, but it never suggests ease. Following Jesus means giving up comfort for the sake of something or Someone far more important than easy living.

When he was eighty-two years of age, the poet Goethe was showing his guests an elegant easy chair he had just purchased at an auction. He had little intention of using it, however. In his chamber was no sofa; only an old wooden chair. He had long ago found that tasteful furniture arrested his thoughts; he became agreeably passive. "Unless we are accustomed to them from early youth," he believed, "splendid chambers and elegant furniture had better be left to people without thoughts." Jesus challenges us to a thoughtful, cross-carrying life.

Such a life requires rigorous training. Crosses aren't light. As World War I was making transatlantic sailing increasingly dangerous, Lord Joseph Duveen, the American head of an art firm of that name, called into his office the young art expert he had planned to send to England to examine some ancient pottery. He was already booked aboard the Lusitania. The German embassy had issued a warning that the ship might be torpedoed. Duveen intended to tell the young man that the trip was off. He did not want to risk his employee's life.

Instead of agreeing to avoid the danger, the youthful expert insisted on going anyway. A strong swimmer, he had been reading about the increased sea warfare, so he knew what lay ahead. He began hardening himself for the crossing by immersing himself every day in a tub of water. At first, he could stay in only a few minutes. That morning he had stayed in the tub nearly two hours.

So he went on his mission. The Lusitania was torpedoed, taking many passengers to their deaths. The art expert survived, however. He was rescued from the frigid Atlantic nearly five hours after jumping into the water. His excellent conditioning had saved his life.

He had deliberately forsaken his ease. Something far more important than his comfort was at stake.

To "Find Yourself"?

"For whoever wants to save his life will lose it, but whoever loses his life for me will find it." The slogan of the tortured 1960s, at least on American college campuses, seemed to be, "I just want to find myself. I've got to be me." This seductive conceit, which led so many youth astray, has done equal damage to older generations as well. A husband walked out on his wife of thirty-seven years with no other justification than, "I have to find myself." According to Jesus, there is only one way to do so, and that is by losing yourself. In another context, He puts it this way: "I tell you the truth, unless a kernel of wheat falls to the ground and dies, it remains only a single seed. But if it dies, it produces many seeds" (John 12:24). Then, to be certain He is understood, He adds, "The man who loves his life will lose it, while the man who hates his life in this world will keep it for eternal life."

Jesus' words could not stand in bolder relief against today's popular ethics. Read the titles on the self-improvement shelves. They advertise that modern readers are vain, selfish, narcissistic—and scared, ugly, and overweight. They pander to our preoccupation with Number One. Not much is said about bolstering the inner man; the ads promise to paint, patch, perfume, pamper, and finally promote the outer person. You'll be slimmer, more stylish, more assertive, and certainly more successful if you just get everything you want.

Jesus turns things around. First comes the losing, then the finding. Like seed falling to the ground, first comes the dying, then the living.

To Be Rich?

"What good will it be for a man if he gains the whole world, yet forfeits his soul? Or what can a man give in exchange for his soul?" When you are tallying up your assets, do you remember to write down, "One soul"? Have you correctly estimated your worth if you have left the soul out? What good will your bulging bank account be to a dead person?

A middle-aged building contractor in Texas got caught in one of the economy's periodic crunches. Many nights, he awakened in the darkness of the night, his body bathed in a cold sweat. He did not know how he would meet payroll or pay his notes. In the midst of his financial troubles, his physician added to his woes: "You have cancer." He did not take the news as a final disaster. Instead, he told his wife that, even if it meant bankruptcy, he would give more time to her, to their friends, to serving the Lord. His precarious physical and financial health made him realize that there was more to life than becoming rich.

He learned something that W. Somerset Maugham, the fabulously wealthy twentieth-century author, never learned. As an old man surrounded by the magnificent things his money could buy, he wrote, "My success means nothing to me. All I can think of now are my mistakes. I can think of nothing else but my foolishness. . . . I wish I'd never written a single word. It's brought me nothing but misery."[55]

What good *is* it to gain the whole world?

To Please God?

Jesus has no other goal than to please God. Peter, with the noblest of intentions, speaks the language of the devil when he tries to dissuade Jesus. Satan has his reasons for keeping Jesus from Jerusalem,

---

[55]*Time,* July 24, 1978, p. 79.

but God wants Him there. So He will go. This time, He will encounter severe opposition and certain death. But the defeat will be temporary. Victory will be His eventually: "For the Son of Man is going to come in his Father's glory with his angels." What peace of mind Jesus has. He knows His vocation is from God and is determined to live to please Him.

In New York City, the Cathedral of St. John the Divine is now under construction. There is nothing new about that. After a thirty-eight year delay (from 1941 to 1979), workmen are once again shaping stones to finish the 153-foot towers. It will take 24,000 pieces of Indiana limestone and another thirty years to finish the job. It takes a long time to build a cathedral, but the workers are willing to spend a lifetime at it. They feel they are part of something permanent. A thousand years from now, people will marvel over what they have done. They are working to please God.

So are Christians everywhere. Nothing can compare with the work they are doing. It will last longer than a thousand years. The souls they work on are designed to last forever. And when the work that Christians accomplish is finished, and the Son of Man (the Lord himself) returns with the hosts from Heaven, He will pay us according to our work for Him.

In one brief paragraph, Jesus has challenged Peter and his fellow disciples to the highest possible standard of living. Starting with Peter's concern for His physical safety, Jesus rebukes Peter for his limited, this-worldly thinking. Some things are more important than merely staying alive (vs. 21-23), and certainly more urgent than making oneself comfortable (v. 24). The secret of real life is not to be found in protecting or "finding" oneself but, surprisingly, in just the opposite: "Whoever loses his life for me will find it (v. 25). Real life is not to be confused with the accumulation of wealth; one can be rich in goods and poor—even dead—in soul (v. 26). What matters more than riches or comfort or even staying alive is to please God and receive the Son's reward for faithful service (vs. 27, 28, 23).

Jesus' reference to His coming "in his Father's glory with his angels" is not clear in this passage. Is He referring to His transfiguration, His resurrection, the Day of Pentecost when the Spirit descended, the destruction of Jerusalem, or His second coming in power and judgment? We do not know for certain. What is undeniable is Jesus' victory over death and Satan and the share His disciples will have in His rule.

That is worth working for.

CHAPTER EIGHTEEN

The Object and Action of Faith
Matthew 17

Three Living Words (17:1-8)
(Mark 9:2-8; Luke 9:28-36)

The record of Jesus' transfiguration carries fascinating overtones of an Old Testament event. Chapters 24 and 34 of Exodus describe the giving of the law of Moses. God calls Moses up into the mountain, and Moses takes along Aaron, Nadab, Abihu, and seventy Israelite elders. As with the transfiguration, this epochal occasion is covered by a cloud and a voice and the glory of God. By the time Moses descends the mountain, he has been transfigured; his face still shines with such brilliance it has to be veiled.

Jesus' transfiguration replays that earlier communication of God with man, but with a difference. Again there are six days and three companions (Peter, James, and John), the ascent of the mountain (traditionally believed to be Mt. Tabor, but more probably Mt. Hermon), and once more the face shining like the sun. Jesus' clothes are white as the light. And above everything and through everything, there is the glory of God. The difference is that this time Moses (along with the great prophet Elijah) fades and Christ is exalted.

In this extraordinary drama, there are three speakers, and they speak three living words.

Peter's Is the Word of Religion

"Lord, it is good for us to be here. If you wish, I will put up three shelters—one for you, one for Moses and one for Elijah." Peter recognizes the supernatural when he sees it. This moment is unlike any other he has experienced. Eternity meets time; supernatural meets natural. Nearly overwhelmed by such an unprecedented event, Peter responds like a genuinely religious man. He speaks with the voice of enthusiastic ignorance. He is dedicated, sincere, appreciative—and wrong. He wants to capture this holy moment, enshrine it, and commemorate it from now on. "Let's do this again next year!"

There is precedent for Peter's proposal. The Jews have celebrated the Feast of Booths (or Tabernacles) for thousands of years. People construct simple shelters of palm branches and other materials to remind themselves of the temporary shelters their ancestors put up as they trod their circuitous route from Egypt to the promised land. Peter, seeing the hand of God himself at work, desires to pay tribute to God in this time-honored fashion. It is incredible: Moses and Elijah are dead, yet Peter has just seen them with Jesus! "I never want to forget this moment," you can hear Peter say. The booths will serve as a constant reminder. It is this same desire to relive a God-filled moment that leads to those testimony meetings that Christians so love: "Tell me about your greatest religious experience!"

There's an old but unforgettable story of a pastor who was calling on one of his church's backsliders. During the conversation, the man started to tell the pastor the story of his religious conversion, and then he excused himself to go into another room where he kept the paper on which he had written out his experience for safe-keeping. After a while, he returned, shamefaced, holding a tattered scrap of paper. "Pastor, I'm sorry, the rats have eaten my religious experience."

Rats do that to a spiritual life gone dead. With such an experience, you may start your Christian growth, but you can never leave it there. Yet don't misunderstand. Peter expresses an important fact of life: human life demands religious expression. No one is exempt. Even the great twentieth-century physicist Albert Einstein considered himself religious. He was not a Christian, nor even a Jew by religion (although by race), but he readily admitted being overwhelmed by the awesomeness of the universe. "What is the meaning of human life, or of organic life altogether? To answer the question at all implies a religion. Is there any sense, then, you ask, in putting it? I answer, the man who regards his own life and that of his fellow-creatures as meaningless is not merely unfortunate but almost disqualified for life."[56]

But the word of religion is not enough. In fact, the Bible consistently presents itself as one of the world's most outspoken critics of religion, at least as it is commonly understood. In the Epistle to the Romans, for example, the apostle Paul does not preach Christianity as religion, but he presents Christ. Paul not only attacks other religions, but he is equally unsparing in his criticism of the Christian religion as it was practiced by legalists and antinomians (people who held that true religion has no laws whatsoever). He puts Christ up

---

[56]Quoted in Hans Kung, *Does God Exist?* (New York: Doubleday and Company, 1978), p. 627.

against every religion, even Christianity. He wants every Christian to know that his faith is in Christ, a person, and not in a system or order. Paul Tillich has written that "the first word to be spoken by religion to the people of our time must be a word spoken against religion."[57] He has taken that idea straight out of the Bible.

Jesus taught the woman at the well that "God is spirit, and his worshipers must worship in spirit and in truth" (John 4:24). He cannot be confined in a temple or on a mountaintop—nor in three shelters.

God's Is the Word of Truth

"This is my Son, whom I love; with him I am well pleased. Listen to him!" God is addressing Peter, James, and John, but Peter most directly because of his earlier confession of faith in Jesus as the Christ (Matthew 16:16). God offers Peter proof of Jesus' Messiahship. Then comes the full impact of Peter's confession: "Listen to him!"

"Peter, if Jesus is who you have said He is, then why would you build *three* booths? God has only one Son. Moses was the great lawgiver, to the orthodox Jew the greatest man who ever lived. But Jesus is greater. Elijah was paragon of prophets. No greater prophet ever spoke—until now."

God offers something better than religion. He offers revelation: Jesus is His Son, God appearing in human flesh. He is not like the many gods worshiped by Greeks or Romans, or even by the Hindus, from among whom worshipers may choose the one that they feel most attracted to. Hermann Hesse, author of *Siddhartha* and *Steppenwolfe,* smitten by the lure of the East, has written that "one religion is about as good as another. There is not one in which one could not become wise, and not one which could not also be practiced as the stupidist idol-worship. . . . I do not think it most important what faith a man has, as that he have one."[58] Hesse would have built at least three booths, so from then on everyone could have a choice among the gods.

Hesse may not think it so important what faith a person has, but God is of another opinion. "Listen to him!" God reserves the right to define what He is like and how He should be worshiped. That is why God sent His Son. It would be to our advantage to listen to Him.

---

[58] Quoted in Harold O. J. Brown, "The Refiner's Fire," *Christianity Today* (November 21, 1975), p. 16.

[57] Paul Tillich, *The Protestant Era* (Chicago: University of Chicago Press, 1957), p. 185.

The third living word is from Jesus. He makes two brief statements. To His prostrate disciples, He says, "Get up and do not be afraid." He asks for obedient faith: "Get up." He expresses concerned love: "Don't be afraid." The disciples respond with faith and love. They have nothing to fear from God's Son, so long as they believe in Him. They have to believe enough to get up, however. There is no faith without obedience.

What began for Peter as a proposal to erect a religious shrine has come to a spiritually logical conclusion. Religion has been replaced by revelation. God had spoken. Revelation in turn has been succeeded by faithful obedience to the word of truth. Instead of more religious devotion, God demands that whoever has heard and seen the truth in God's Son replace religious awe with active obedience.

Elijah Has Already Come (17:9-13)
(Mark 9:9-13)

"See, I will send you the prophet Elijah before that great and dreadful day of the Lord comes. He will turn the hearts of the fathers to their children, and the hearts of the children to their fathers; or else I will come and strike the land with a curse."

Every Jew in Jesus' day knew this promise from Malachi 4:5, 6. Before the Messiah could return, Elijah must come back to life again in order to prepare the way for the coming of the Christ. These simple words of Malachi became overloaded with meaning between Malachi's day (the middle to end of the fifth century before Christ) and the advent of Jesus. Elijah was expected to come to "restore all things," thus reforming the land. This great and powerful reformer would make everything perfect for the Messiah.

Jesus' disciples share these expectations. They are right to anticipate Elijah's return, Jesus tells them, but wrong in looking for him to be a terrible reformer. They can count on God's promise. Elijah will come. In fact, he has already come but has not been recognized, because, like the Christ after him, his way was not that of power and dominion but of suffering and sacrifice. As John the Baptist died at the hands of the king, so would the Son of Man suffer at the hands of His enemies.

Jesus' critics have undoubtedly been using Malachi's prophecy against Him. They can deny Jesus' right to bear the title of Messiah by protesting that Elijah has not yet come. Peter, James, and John have seen him briefly with Jesus and Moses, but this vision can never be used as proof. In fact, nothing can be proved until after Jesus "has been raised from the dead." Only then will the magnitude of this transfiguration experience make sense to them.

What Faith Can Do (17:14-23)
(Mark 9:14-29; Luke 9:37-43)

From the sublime to the mundane. Jesus cannot stay on the mountaintop to enjoy the praise of His Father. He is needed elsewhere, by another father.

The Parent's Prayer

"Lord, have mercy on my son. He has seizures. . . ." Every parent can identify with this harried father. What child has not caused his parents many anxious, prayerful moments? Sometimes the problem is physical; other times social or emotional, or even moral. The source of this father's anxiety is his son's seizures (caused by an evil spirit—Matthew 17:18; Mark 9:14-32; Luke 9:37-45).

Modern science and medicine have been helpless to relieve parental anxiety. It may not be unfair to say that probably no generation of parents in history has been quite so afraid of parenting as our own. Wanting to do right by our children but bombarded by an incredible variety of conflicting advice, we cautiously wend our way, trying this experiment and adopting that technique, hoping against what sometimes seem to be insuperable odds that we can herd our little lambs to maturity without doing too much damage to their psyches. We fear that they'll become victims of drink or drugs or sexual promiscuity or the prevailing phony philosophies that seduce the unwary unto their own damnation. We have no trouble hearing this father's plea, because his prayer is ours. "Lord, have mercy."

The Lord's Purpose

The Gospel writers make no mistake in narrating this quiet incident of healing immediately after telling us about Jesus' transfiguration. Through them, God conveys this supremely vital fact about the purpose of Jesus' ministry: He did not appear among us to be transfigured, but to be a transformer of others. (Look once more at His job description in Luke 4:16-21.) He came to earth to help people, to communicate in unmistakable terms that God is for us, though all else be against us. He wants only our best. He wants to transform our broken bodies and personalities into whole persons. Even His commands are for our sake, not His.

The Disciples' Perplexity

Jesus even trained His disciples for our sake. Often in their training period, He expresses disappointment in their progress, or lack of it. They too frequently let Him down. But you can understand their perplexity, can't you? Jesus has sent them out before (Matthew 10) with the power to heal and cast out demons. They were successful, then, so why have they failed this time? "Why couldn't we drive it out?" is a legitimate question. What has happened to their former ability?

Jesus blames their timid faith. His answer must have deepened their perplexity. It does ours, as well. That is, we are disturbed by the inconsistency of our own faith. Sometimes we feel so full of faith that we are ready to move mountains. At other times, we pray and nothing happens. We try to walk the Christian way and find ourselves resenting it or unable to concentrate our faculties on its requirements. Like this father, we believe even while needing to confess our unbelief (Mark 9:24). So when we read Jesus' complaint about His disciples' lack of faith, we take the rebuke personally and wonder why He tolerates us.

Our hope rests in His patience with the disciples. He puts up with them, even though they repeatedly disappoint Him.

Thank God His reaction is not the same as Moses', in a parallel occasion in the Old Testament. (See Exodus 32.) While Moses was in the presence of the Lord to receive the law (as Jesus was in the presence of the Lord in the transfiguration), the restless Israelites demanded that his brother Aaron usurp Moses' leadership and fashion some idols for them to worship: "Come, make us gods who will go before us. As for this fellow Moses who brought us up out of Egypt, we don't know what has happened to him" (v. 1). They pooled their gold earrings and melted and molded them into the form of a golden calf. Then Aaron foolishly addressed the congregation: "These are your gods, O Israel, who brought you up out of Egypt" (v. 4). When Moses discovered their treachery, his anger took control and he threw down the sacred tablets of the law and broke them. Then he destroyed the calf. When he had chastised his weak brother, he dispatched the Levites to kill about three thousand men!

Jesus kills no one. He simply chastises His disciples for their little faith. Then He heals the boy.

The Living Promise

"I tell you the truth, if you have faith as small as a mustard seed, you can say to this mountain, 'Move from here to there' and it will move. Nothing will be impossible for you." Think about mustard seeds for a moment. If we were not surrounded by so great a cloud of miracles, we would be more impressed with them. Think of the development of the plant from the seed. Or of a human being from the egg and the sperm. From faith that seems as small as a seed can come results as large as the mustard plant, or as complex as a human being.

What this little episode says to us impossibility thinkers! We paralyze ourselves with our reasonable belief that we cannot do most of the things we would like to. Harry Emerson Fosdick put it this way: "Fear imprisons, faith liberates; fear paralyzes, faith empowers; fear disheartens, faith encourages; and most of all, fear puts hopelessness into the heart of life, while faith rejoices in its God."[59] Mark Twain simplifies the whole matter: "All you need in this life is ignorance and confidence, and then success is sure." He is joking, of course, but not entirely. And he is not entirely wrong. Most people have succeeded in some things just because they did not know they couldn't do them. But the real secret of success is the confidence that comes with knowledge. Jesus encourages His disciples to rely on their knowledge of God and the fact that God is for them, working through them.

Jewish thinker Martin Buber has said that "faith is not a feeling in the soul but an entrance into reality, an entrance into the whole reality without reduction or curtailment."[60] Jesus is that reality for a Christian. When we are in Christ, we have stepped into where God is, so we are no longer limited by our own imaginations or abilities, but we have lost our finiteness in God's infiniteness. His power takes over. In this sense, psychologist Gordon Allport is correct: "A man's religion is the audacious bid he makes to bind himself to creation and the creator. It is his ultimate attempt to enlarge and to complete his own personality by finding the supreme context to which he rightly belongs."[61]

That is a psychologist's way of saying, "I am God's. I belong. God's power works through me. I will work the Father's work and

[59]Quoted in Charles Allen, *Life More Abundant* (New York: Pillar Books, 1965), p. 57.

[60]Quoted in Will Herberg, "The Strangeness of Faith," *Sermons to Intellectuals,* Franklin H. Littell, ed. (New York: Macmillan, 1963), p. 30.

[61]Gordon Allport, *The Individual and His Religion* (New York: Macmillan, 1950), p. 161.

will the Father's will. He is for people, I am for people. He wills healing; I will be an instrument He may use to effect healing. He may do whatever He wants through me."

In a couple of his books, Leslie Weatherhead tells of an experiment conducted by his friend Dr. Hadfield involving a dynamometer (gripping machine). He told three men to grip it with all their strength. They produced an average reading on the dial of 101 pounds. Then he hypnotized them, whispered in their ear that they could no longer grip. They had lost their strength. He told them to try, but repeated, "You can't." Their average grip fell to 29 pounds. Then, again under hypnosis, he told them, "You can." That time their average grip rose to 142 pounds. Because they thought they could! More is possible for us than we think, even on our own. Add to our power God's power—what then can be impossible?

Marie Ray in *How Never To Be Tired*[62] recounts the experience of the British Army in France. From March to June, 1918, the army was constantly retreating. Their hospitals were filled with men who were exhausted but suffered no physical injury. Then in June, the army began to advance. The number of cases was reduced dramatically. After their long marches, the men dropped with physical fatigue, but after a brief rest, they were up and marching again. Their condition was good; few needed to retire to the rear. The difference? When they were in retreat, they felt and acted defeated; their bodies reflected their mental states. When advancing, they believed in themselves and their endurance level rose incredibly.

Your direction matters. Are you advancing or retreating? Do you still hear God calling you forward, as you did when you were younger? Are you still making yourself available for His power to work through you? I like John Gardner's counsel. "Men who believe in nothing change nothing for the better. They renew nothing and heal no one, least of all themselves."[63]

So Jesus' words are echoed in secular writers. "Because you have so little faith. . . ." But you must understand that Jesus is no rosy-eyed optimist. He is not promising that faith will rid you of all your problems. It does not do that for Jesus. Look at verses 22 and 23. He predicts His betrayal and death. He also predicts His resurrection,

[62]Quoted in Mack R. Douglas, *Success Can Be Yours* (Grand Rapids: Zondervan, 1968), pp. 118, 119.

[63]John Gardner, *Self-Renewal* (New York: Harper and Row, 1965), p. xiii.

but the disciples do not hear Him. ("And the disciples were filled with grief.") His faith in God will keep Him true to His purpose, however, and He leaves the results in God's hands. He has come to reconcile men and women to God, and He will reconcile them, even through His death if necessary. God is capable of doing anything. What Jesus has to do is to be faithful to His purpose in coming. God will take care of the rest.

Jesus the Taxpayer (17:24-27)

This is a new criticism of Jesus. He hsd been accused of violating the Sabbath by healing and by allowing His disciples to pluck grains of wheat on it. He has been charged with demon possession. He has been unceremoniously run out of His hometown. Every doctrine of His teaching has been challenged. But He has never before been accused of violating Jewish tax laws. Perhaps because He has only just arrived in Capernaum He has not had time yet to pay the temple tax and the tax collectors are just impatient to finish up their work. More likely, His faithful enemies have stumbled onto another way to embarrass Him.

They don't succeed. Peter has no doubt that Jesus regularly pays the temple tax, and Jesus quickly makes arrangements to bring His account up to date. There are four elements in this little drama, though, that make it especially interesting.

(1) The temple tax. Exodus 30:11-16 states the rules regarding provisions for temple worship. Each male over nineteen is to give an annual tax of a half shekel "for the service of the Tent of Meeting" (tabernacle, later replaced by the temple), as an atonement offering. (In the difficult days when Nehemiah was rebuilding Jerusalem—Nehemiah 10:32, 33—the offering was reduced to a third of a shekel apiece). Governed strictly by the calendar, the tax that is due is given on the first of the month of Adar (six weeks before the Passover each spring). By the middle of the month, tax collectors set up their tables in districts away from Jerusalem, and on the twenty-fifth of the month, they set up shop in the temple itself.

As a loyal son of Judaism, Jesus participates regularly in temple worship when He is in Jerusalem, so Peter rightly assumes that the Lord will pay His fair share of its costs. Its worship is not cheap, either. The daily sacrifices of a year-old lamb each morning and evening, the wine and oil and incense and priests' garments and the especially elaborate high priest's robes add up to a sizable annual budget. Jews do not begrudge their temple tax, even though the half-shekel seems to have been the equivalent of about two days' pay for a laboring man. At least it does not go to the hated Romans.

(2) Jesus' exemption. Jesus accepts His share of the cost, even though, as He explains to Peter with a mini-parable about kings and their sons, He is under no obligation to do so. As the Son of the King of the temple, Jesus should not be expected to pay a tax designed to pay the king's expenses.

(3) The principle of avoiding offense. Jesus does not have to pay but is prepared to so that others won't stumble over His actions (*skandalisomen* —a form of the verb meaning "to cause to stumble"). He probably has several things in mind: (a) He does not want to give His critics any reason to attack Him on such a small matter. He'll give them adequate cause to condemn Him later on. (b) He does not want to cause any Jewish disciples to get themselves into trouble with the authorities by following Jesus' example. (c) His disciples will soon come to realize that His true followers have been set free from the obligations of temple worship. Then they, like Jesus, will be exempt from the temple tax. Until then, so there will be no misunderstanding, all of them will pay the tax expected of the Jews.

This principle is akin to Jesus' concern for the children (Matthew 18:6) and the apostle Paul's refusal to exercise all the freedoms that belong to him as a Christian (1 Corinthians 8:1-13, Romans 14:1-23).

(4) The miracle. This may not be a good word choice, since no miracle actually occurs in these verses. The reader is left to infer that Peter does in fact go to the lake, throw out his line, and catch the fish with a coin in its mouth. Some commentators have wondered whether Jesus actually intends Peter to follow His instructions or, with humor in His voice, He suggests to the fisherman what a simple thing it is to pay this tax.

Yet it is in keeping with Jesus to think that He intends this somewhat out-of-character miracle (Jesus deliberately refrains from using miracles to His personal purposes and from ever seeming to play the magician) as a dramatized parable. It may be compared with His denunciation of the fruitless fig tree (Mark 11:12-14, 20-25). On that occasion, Jesus taught a lesson on the power of faith; on this one, a lesson regarding God. God who is worshiped in the temple, and whose worship is made possible through the temple tax, is also the provider of the money with which the worshiper pays the tax. All things that we return to God have come from God in the first place. Even our giving to God is a receiving from God.

CHAPTER NINETEEN

Love and Mercy

Matthew 18; 19:13-15

God Loves *You* (18:1-14; 19:13-15)
(Mark 9:33-37; 42-48; 10:13-16; Luke 9:46-48; 18:15-17)

The Universal Urge

If ever there was a question symbolic of a universal human urge, this one is it: "Who is the greatest ... ?" Everybody wants to be the greatest at doing or being something. James and John are really representative of the human race when they ask Jesus to let them sit on each side of Him in His kingdom (Mark 10:37). A wise parent understands how important it is for children to experience success in something at the earliest possible moment. Without it, they develop a debilitating sense of their inferiority, and they instinctively compare themselves, usually unfavorably, with any potential competitor, hoping to prove themselves superior to somebody somewhere. Much sin and most foolhardiness can be blamed on this need to be "the greatest."

Listen to adults. They say the strangest, most illogical things. "I'm richer than you; therefore I am your superior." "I am more eloquent than you; therefore I am your superior." "I have received a higher education than you, therefore I am your superior." The Greek philosopher Epictetus pointed out the absence of logical connection in this reasoning in the century following Christ's ministry. The true connection, he said, is this: "I am richer than you; therefore my possessions must exceed yours." "I am more eloquent than you; therefore my style must surpass yours." But persons, Epictetus correctly argued, consist neither in property nor in style (nor, we add, in education or any other appendage). What they do seem to consist of, unfortunately, is this urge to be the greatest. The height of absurdity is uttered by the person who boasts, either by word or deed, "I am more religious than you; therefore I am superior to you."

These foolish comparisons should be absent from the church. The New Testament makes a strong case for the diversity of gifts within

221

the body of Christ (1 Corinthians 12; Romans 12), insisting that all the gifts are from the Holy Spirit, and none is to disparage the others. If any comparisons are to be made, they are between one's potential and his actual selves.

Irving Berlin would have smiled to learn how Scriptural his advice to George Gershwin sounds. At the time, Berlin was enjoying enormous success and Gershwin was a thirty-five-dollar-a-week piano player in Tin Pan Alley. Berlin offered the younger man a job as his personal secretary, at three times his current pay, but he added, "But don't take the job. If you do, you may develop into a second-rate Berlin. If you insist on being yourself, someday you will become a first-rate Gershwin."[64]

Jesus' scale of values often surprises His disciples. Nobody is greater, He tells them, than a child. An anecdote from the administration of President Lyndon Johnson, who ranks among modern America's most skillful manipulators of political power, places Jesus' values in perspective. Jack Valenti, one of Johnson's aides, was attending a security council meeting with the President and other council members when Valenti's wife and daughter stopped by so the overworked aide could see them for a few minutes. When Johnson learned they were outside the room, he told Valenti to bring his daughter in. "I want to see her too." When the door was opened and Courtenay spotted Johnson, she cried out, "Prez!" and ran into his arms. "Go ahead, Dean, continue your report," President Johnson said to his startled Secretary of State. Along with this memory, Valenti also treasures a photograph taken on another occasion of the President in his rocking chair in the Oval Office, surrounded by Senators Mansfield and Russell and other senate leaders. By his side is five-year-old Courtenay, holding the President's phone in her hand. "It is a study in democracy," Valenti concludes.[65]

Indeed. It is for the Courtenays of America that presidents and senators labor. In the final analysis, the so-called great ones are merely the servants of the rising generation. Every national leader ought to have such a picture on his desk, to remind him that all the important business of State is for the sake of the children.

---

[64]Mack R. Douglas, *Success Can Be Yours* (Grand Rapids: Zondervan, 1968), p. 24.

[65]Jack Valenti, *A Very Human President* (New York: Pocket Books, 1975), pp. 76, 77.

The Kingdom Standard: "Unless You Turn ... "

Jesus lays down an unprecedented definition of greatness: "Unless you change and become like little children, you will never enter the kingdom of heaven. Therefore, whoever humbles himself like this child is the greatest in the kingdom of heaven. And whoever welcomes a little child like this in my name welcomes me." An amazing reversal of values!

What's so good about a child? Jesus uses the verb "humbles." A child has little to boast about when comparing himself with adults. Adults are bigger, smarter, richer, stronger, more independent, more almost everything else. A child accepts his dependence, since he can't do anything about it; he is inquisitive, and thus teachable. He is trusting, not naturally suspicious—unless betrayed too often. He is in touch with reality but not locked into it; he can still imagine and dream. Unless he is frightened into falsehood, a child is honest. (And to be fair, a child is expensive—but then he should be, if Jesus is right about his value.)

It is hard for Jesus' disciples to accept this standard. That means, for example, that the greatest in the church may not be the preacher or elder, but the janitor who cleans up after everyone else, or the volunteer who totes out the garbage, or the kindergarten teacher who cleans up the carpet after a little one has vomited on it, or the elderly gentleman who arrives much earlier than anyone else in order to scrape the ice off the sidewalk.

Jesus also implies that the newborn child in Christ takes precedence over the longtime member. Nobody is more important in the body of Christ than the latest convert—or the potential convert. Wise, then, is the mature Christian who looks out for young Christians.

Wiser still is the mature Christian who never loses the humility and teachableness he had when he first came to Christ. He does well to remember that no matter how much he thinks he knows, there is an infinite amount yet to learn. He is but a child standing on a starry night before the immensity of the universe. It ill becomes him to boast.

The King's Concern: The Welfare of His Little Ones

"If anyone causes one of these little ones who believe in me to sin. . . ." Jesus shifts His disciples' attention from their potential roles as ministers in His new kingdom to their actual responsibility as overseers of the Lord's children. He is probably thinking of both children and the young in the faith. His disciples were to use their considerable influence for the good of others and not, as so many leaders of the world do, to lead them into temptation and cause them to sin.

Theirs—and ours—is a grave responsibility. We are neither to sin nor be the reason for sinning in others. Every possible source of temptation is to be avoided at all cost. It is better to cripple yourself than to be guilty of causing offense or of indulging yourself in sin.

So be careful, for your sake and the children's sake. You have no cause to feel yourselves superior to anyone smaller or younger (in the faith or otherwise) than you are. God wants all His children near Him, as their angels (their counterparts, or spiritual doubles, or guardian angels) in Heaven are.

The Father's Hope: That None Should Be Lost

A good shepherd cannot rest easy when he has ninety-nine of his one hundred sheep in the fold. Ninety-nine are not enough. Jesus would probably smile with the substitute teacher who left a note for the regular fifth-grade-class teacher to read when she returned: "If I had but one life to give for my country, it would be either Robert's or Sharon's." He would smile, but He could never take the little joke seriously. He came to seek and save the lost—and the ornery! Jesus taught that the good shepherd lays down his life for his sheep (John 10:11).

Jesus' response to His disciples' arrogant discussion of their relative importance in the Master's new kingdom has moved swiftly. He began by urging them to become childlike. He continued by insisting that no one must cause any little one to sin. He concludes here with His unforgettable story of the faithful shepherd who searches for, finds, and rejoices over his lost sheep. God doesn't want anybody lost! Even you and me.

In Studs Terkel's popular account of the American labor force, *Working*, a black reporter tells the author that when he feels the need to have his spirits lowered, he drives out Chicago's Madison Street to look at the crowds of unemployed youth hanging around. They can't read or write; they try to look mean to show they hate others as much as they hate themselves. That hatred, he says, "is one thing that's contributed to the ease with which gangs kill each other. Another nigger ain't nothing."[66] The message of the gospel is just this: God

---

[66]From the review by John Kenneth Galbraith, *Saturday Review* (September, 1980), p. 65.

didn't make any "niggers." The additional teaching of Jesus here is this: whoever causes a little one to think of himself as "nigger," or who causes him to sin, faces a Godly punishment worse than the worst physical calamity you can imagine. God wants His little ones, whatever their color or race or age or status, saved.

When a Brother Offends You (18:15-20)

Repairing broken relationships is sticky business, but no disciple of the reconciling Christ can fail to do everything in his power to restore an alienated brother. In this chapter alone, Jesus instructs us to do nothing to cause a child to sin and to do everything (as the Father does) to find a lost soul. In the same manner and for the same reason, He carefully spells out the steps to take to heal a broken relationship.

The initiative is with the innocent party, the one who has been offended. "If your brother sins against *you*. . . ." Jesus does not hint that the offending brother will be eager to hear from you. To the contrary, His step-by-step instructions suggest how unwilling the brother might be to hear from you. This happened to a young freshman in a Christian college. Apparently, his dorm mates found him a somewhat-less-than-congenial person to live with. At least, that is what one of them came to his room to tell him. "Let me tell you what's wrong with you," is how he worded it. His boldness angered the insecure young student. "That's unfair," he inwardly howled. "He has no right to speak to me like this." When the tactless older student finally left his room, he was so upset that he went immediately to the room of another dorm mate. He told his friend what had happened and asked him whether he agreed with the criticism or not. To his surprise and chagrin, his friend admitted that there was some truth in the criticisms. He said just about the same things that the tactless student had told him. This time, the young student could accept the rebuke, since he had asked for it. When his Gospels class studied this passage a few weeks later, he realized that he had unknowingly been the offending brother. Jesus' advice was for him as well as for his offended dorm mate.

Here are Jesus' steps for healing broken relationships:

(1) "Go and show him his fault, just between the two of you." Your purpose is not to gloat over his shortcoming, but to repair the relationship. He may not even be aware of what he has done, or of the hurt you have experienced. Most breaches are not deliberately caused. This first step, then, will be sufficient in most cases, especially if your motive is right.

225

(2) "Take one or two others along" if he does not listen to you alone. Deuteronomy 19:15 says that "one witness is not enough to convict a man accused of any crime or offense he may have committed. A matter must be established by the testimony of two or three witnesses." So take along others who are aware of the damage he has done. They will also serve as witnesses to the conversation between you and him in their presence; that way he will not be tempted to report it incorrectly later. The witnesses thus can testify (a) about the original wrongdoing, (b) about the fact that the attempt has been made to confront the offender with the offense, and (c) about his failure to make amends, in case step 3 is needed.

(3) "Tell it to the church." This would specifically mean the elders of the church, who are considered the wisest and most judicial persons in it. Jesus assumes, of course, that the offense is of sufficient gravity to warrant this extreme measure. He also assumes that the motive is reconciliation. Only when everything has failed, should he be treated as "a pagan or a tax collector." This is not quite as harsh as it sounds at first. Jesus taught all kinds of people in a spirit of love and respect for them as persons, even though He could not condone their false religion or dishonest business practices. Full fellowship with them was impossible, however, so long as their standards and His were at odds. Likewise, the offender who refuses to accept any efforts at reconciliation remains beyond the reach of the offended party and his friends. He stands outside the circle of love because he has refused to come in. He will be, unfortunately, in the same relation to them as the pagans and tax collectors were to the Jews.

The early church used this formula for disciplining delinquent members. See 1 Corinthians 5:3-5, 9-13 for the apostle Paul's handling of the man living with his father's wife. See also Acts 15 for an account of the Jerusalem Conference, in which a threatened schism in the early church was prevented when Paul and Barnabas presented the case for their ministry to the assembled elders of the Jerusalem church. Then, of course, you can read through the epistles for ample evidence of the growing church's struggle to maintain the unity of the faith. To keep reconciled brothers at peace with one another requires patience, tenacity, courage, forgiveness, and unending love.

Matthew 18:18 echoes 16:19. There Jesus promises Peter "the keys of the kingdom of heaven; whatever you bind on earth will be bound in heaven, and whatever you loose on earth will be loosed in heaven." Apparently, this power was not given to Peter alone, but to the Christians in assembly. Their strength is in their unity with one another and their commitment to put into practice the teaching of their Lord. Jesus underscores the eternal weight of corporate church decisions. Other Scriptures allude to the same earthly/Heavenly power: John 20:23; 14:13, 14; 15:7 (but this verse adds the qualifying clause, "if you remain in me and my words remain in you"—the power presupposes the intimate relationship between the Spirit of Christ and the spirit of unity in the believers).

Some Bible commentators doubt that Jesus actually said these words, since the "church" to which He refers has not been established yet, so any formal hearing of offenses by the church through its leaders could not yet take place. While the criticism has some validity to it, we might ask whether it is not possible that Jesus is speaking of the time when the church will have been established. In the meantime, the principle is valid. The elders of the Jewish synagogue already functioned in the capacity of judge over disputes among the members. Undoubtedly, the same occurred among the disciples of Jesus, who in many ways were a model of what the church was to become. Jesus is presenting another example of the orderly social organization that God has always favored, with the leaders of the people resolving issues that individuals cannot manage among themselves. In the church, the added dimension of the indwelling Holy Spirit (1 Corinthians 3:16, 17; John 16:7-15) will assist the church to judge wisely.

How Far Can Mercy Go? (18:21-35)

Whether Jesus' answer is "seventy-seven times" (as in the *New International Version* of the Bible) or "seventy times seven" (according to older versions—the number in the Greek is debated by modern scholars), His meaning is clear. You are not to limit your willingness to forgive to any preset number of times. Mercy does not keep score. Peter thought he was capturing the spirit of Jesus when he extravagantly offered seven as the limit. Jesus multiplies the seven many times over, to teach the disciples what a really forgiving heart is prepared to do.

When Nikita Khrushchev was Premier of Soviet Russia, he offered the world an insight into Jesus' teaching on forgiveness (specifically in the Sermon on the Mount, Matthew 5:38-42). While visiting Rouen Cathedral in France, Khrushchev mentioned how much he thought Christ had in common with Communists. But he drew the line at Jesus' doctrine of turning the other cheek. Khrushchev followed another principle, he boasted. When he was hit on the left cheek, he hit back on the right cheek "so hard that the head might fall off. This is my sole difference with Christ."

What a difference! It is the difference that keeps the world at war. The Prince of Peace can never effectively do His work among people who refuse to turn the other cheek. Forgiveness is an essential ingredient in peacemaking. Khrushchev's principle, which has been adopted by practically every world leader throughout history, guarantees that of the making of wars there shall be no end!

God's Forgiveness Is Almost Without Limit

The king (God) forgives his debtor an enormous amount (the *Revised Standard Version* estimates the debt at approximately $10,000,000—in pre-inflation money). Jesus' audience could not even imagine such a sum, which is the point Jesus is establishing. The debtor has no choice—if his creditor is not merciful, he is lost. This is the human condition before God. We have sinned (Romans 3:23) and have no means of recompensing God for our sins (debts). Without His mercy, we are doomed. (A Sunday-school teacher, trying to teach her class of little children about confession, asked them what they had to do before they could obtain forgiveness of sin. One bright six-year-old answered correctly, "Sin." This qualification we all meet.)

However, when the forgiven servant confronts his own debtor, who owes him an insignificant amount some five or six hundred times smaller than the debt the king (God) forgave him, he grants no mercy but instead demands immediate full payment. Jesus starkly contrasts the almost limitless forgiveness of God with the mercilessness of the forgiven servant, who is much too typical of the human race for us to be able to read this parable without discomfort.

In the little town of Dover, New Hampshire, E. J.'s Variety Store made national news when Ernest Peters acted to forgive his debtors. Holding $5,000 in bills that the townspeople owed him because of the economic recession, Peters put an ad in the paper: "Your bill is paid in full. Start fresh with us. We will help you through the tough times. Come back and become a customer again." Their debts were cancelled. (Do you hear Romans 5:8 in this? "While we were still sinners, Christ died for us." Or Colossians 2:13-15? Or John 3:16?) Peters has provided a modern parable; he has acted like the king here. Let us hope the townspeople did not behave like the unmerciful servant.

The Forgiveness of God Is Limited—By Our Forgiveness

Just as Jesus couples the love of God with love of neighbor (Mark

228

12:28-31), so He makes our enjoyment of God's forgiveness conditional upon our mercy towards our debtors:

"Blessed are the merciful, for they will be shown mercy" (Matthew 5:7).

"Forgive us our debts, as we also have forgiven our debtors" (Matthew 6:12).

"For if you forgive men when they sin against you, your heavenly Father will also forgive you. But if you do not forgive men their sins, your Father will not forgive your sins" (Matthew 6:14, 15).

The apostle Paul, concerned about internal harmony in the churches, constantly returns to the theme of forgiveness. The basis of his appeal is the fact that Christ has forgiven us: Ephesians 4:31, 32; Colossians 3:12, 13. In 2 Corinthians 2:10 and 11, he adds another reason. When we forgive one another, we handicap Satan and blunt his assaults on us.

An Unforgiving Person Is in Mortal Danger

God cannot overlook cruelty. Even the man whom God has previously forgiven is in danger if he then turns on his fellow sinner without mercy. It is quite apparent that the unmerciful one will be quickly dealt with. He won't have to await the final judgment to get his just deserts. Any physician or minister can tell far too many stories of men and women under treatment for diverse symptoms from which they cannot be cured, because their real disease is an unforgiving heart. Their bitterness has poisoned them. Their illness could very well be fatal. Only if they relent and forgive can they be saved.

Contrast such persons with Abraham Lincoln, whose quickness to forgive his enemies still amazes students of his Presidency. When he was campaigning for the Presidency, one of his bitterest critics was Edwin M. Stanton. For reasons we don't fully understand, he hated Lincoln and spared no effort to degrade him in the eyes of the public. Yet when Lincoln was forming his cabinet, he selected Stanton to be his Secretary of War. His advisers strenuously objected, reminding Lincoln of Stanton's efforts to ridicule and defeat him. Lincoln's answer is classic. He assured his advisors that he knew Mr. Stanton and was fully aware of everything Stanton had said against him. But he then added that after looking over the nation, he remained convinced that Stanton was the best man for the job. When Lincoln was assassinated, it was this same Edwin Stanton who called the President one of the greatest men who had ever lived and added, "He now belongs to the ages." Had Lincoln returned evil for evil, he and

Stanton and the nation would have been the losers. His mercy benefited everyone. He granted Stanton the same mercy that he granted the South during the Civil War. He never became bitter nor vengeful. When a woman asked him how he could speak so kindly of the South, he replied, "Madam, do I not destroy my enemies when I make them my friends?" He had found the way of peace.

At the close of Jesus' ministry, He demonstrates what forgiveness means. His supreme example, of course, is the cross. But in another personal way, He shows Peter what it is all about. When the women come to the tomb on resurrection morning, they are greeted by the angel of God, who announces the resurrection of Jesus. According to Mark's account, the angel instructs the women to "go, tell his disciples and Peter" (Mark 16:7).

At first glance, it might seem strange that Peter is singled out instead of John the beloved disciple or even Thomas the doubter. Peter alone is mentioned by name, and for a special reason: Peter needed this attention the most. Just a short time earlier, Peter had denied that he even knew Jesus. Then, immediately, he regretted what he had done (Matthew 26:69-75). Yet the burden of guilt remained. How could he face God any more? How could he even face his friends? What kind of a friend was he?

Because Peter's guilt is so great, and God's mercy is so generous, the angel sends the women to tell Peter. He will know, then, that he has been forgiven. Peter, who raised the question about the extent of mercy, who forfeited any right to expect mercy through his denial of Jesus, has been mercifully restored. Now he knows firsthand how essential forgiveness is, even to "seventy-seven times."

CHAPTER TWENTY

It's Not Easy

Matthew 19

What God Thinks of Marriage (19:1-12)
(Mark 10:1-12)

Once again Jesus is being tested. The subject of divorce was as controversial in Jesus' time as in our own. Even the Jewish rabbis were divided on the issue. Rabbi Shammai held that divorce could be allowed for adultery only; Hillel held that whenever a wife displeased her husband, he was free to dissolve the union. King Herod and his ilk naturally adopted an easy-divorce stance, since he had replaced his first wife with the more delectable Herodias. The Essenes, an ultra-strict Jewish sect, practiced celibacy, so the issue of divorce did not come up with them. They just never married. Of course, the sect died out in a few years.

In other words, you could take just about any position on divorce that would please you. The Pharisees, religious legalists that they were, had already made up their minds on this issue. They drilled Jesus on a question they knew would divide His followers. "Is it lawful for a man to divorce his wife for any and every reason?"

The Divine Principle

To answer, Jesus returns to the beginning, back beyond the teachings of the rabbis, and of Moses, to what God had in mind for marriage in the first place. He intended that the man and woman should remain together in an indissoluble union. That union should be considered God-joined. God created woman for man (Genesis 2:18). Each without the other is less than what God intended.

Our traditional marriage vows hint at the purposefulness (as opposed to any impulsiveness) of the marriage covenant. The bride and groom promise each other "to have and to hold, for better or for worse, for richer or for poorer, in sickness and in health" for as long as they live. They make their vows because they realize that their marriage cannot be based on emotions. Some days, they will not feel like staying with each other. They may even feel their love is dead. Yet they remain together because they have made promises. They are not like the man who grumbled to his divorce attorney, "I wanted a good deal, I got a raw deal, now I want a new deal."

God created man and woman. He also created marriage—and judged it good: good for the marriage partners (see Genesis 2:18 again), and good for God's purposes (to "fill the earth and subdue it," Genesis 1:28). To this day, the security of society depends on the stability of marriage. What will happen with the galloping hedonism of modern society is anybody's guess, but it does not promise good. If everybody were to subscribe to the axiom, "If it feels good, do it," or to the popular belief that marriage, like everything else, depends on how you "feel" about it, there would be nothing for the human community to build on. Without faithfulness to promises and to God's intent, marriages will crumble—and so will society.

By returning to God's intent to answer the Pharisees, Jesus speaks to our generation as well as to His own. His age debated over what constitutes an acceptable reason for divorce; so does ours, with the added complication of our unrealistic expectations for marriage. We revere romantic love. For centuries, men and women married for social and economic reasons; love was not a necessary qualification for the wedding. It came later. Now, however, Americans especially like to speak of "falling in love," although when pressed, they can't tell you what this high-sounding phrase means. More objective analysis suggests that it means two people have developed some pretty strong "feelings" for each other. Unfortunately, the feelings won't last. Neither will the marriage, unless more sober judgment and more lasting willpower form the basis.

When Abraham Lincoln's mother, Nancy Hanks died, Tom set out from Illinois to Kentucky to bring back a wife. He arrived at Sarah Bush Johnston's and boldly proposed to the young widow, "Miz Johnston, I have no wife and you no husband. I came a'purpose to marry you. I knowed you from a gal and you knowed me from a boy. I've no time to lose; and if you're willin' let it be done straight off."

"I got debts," she told him. She gave him a list of them, he paid them off, they obtained their license, and they were married. Dennis Hanks, the brother of Lincoln's first wife, later remarked, "Tom had a kind o' way with women, an' maybe it was somethin' she took comfort in to have a man that didn't drink an' cuss none."[67]

---

[67]Carl Sandburg, *Abraham Lincoln, The Prairie Years,* Volume 1 (New York: Harcourt, Brace and World, 1926), p. 25.

Theirs is not a particularly romantic love story, but it commends itself to our consideration. They had a purpose in their union: they had children to raise, land to clear, debts to pay, crops to tend, a life to provide for each other and their children. There were no chills, no stars, no lightning and thunder, but the subsequent record shows the steadfastness that spells love. Theirs was an Isaac and Rebekah marriage. (See Genesis 24.) They were not the Mr. Perfect and Miss Right of television's fantasyland, but a quite human man and an equally human woman attempting to make the best of a difficult life, clinging to each other in a relationship they intended to keep together. They understood that to be God's will for their marriage.

The Exception Explained

"Why then did Moses command that a man give his wife a certificate of divorce and send her away?" They are distorting Moses' words, a trick Jesus quickly stops: "Moses *permitted* you to divorce. . . ." He did not command it. And he only permitted it because "your hearts were hard." Again, this violates God's intentions. "I tell you that anyone who divorces his wife, except for marital unfaithfulness, and marries another woman commits adultery."

The Jews had a very high view of marriage. Every Jewish man over twenty was expected to be married. It was his sacred duty. Even so, divorce was much easier for men than women. If Jesus had been speaking to women, He could not have said, "Moses permitted you wives to divorce your husbands." That was specifically forbidden, except upon the consent of the husband. A woman did not enjoy the legal status of a man; she was property. She belonged to her father until she belonged to her husband. Legally, she was a thing, not a person. The typical young woman was usually engaged in childhood, often to a man she did not know. Her husband could divorce her with or without her consent; she only with his. There were few safeguards to protect her because she was not her husband's equal.

This view of women was not peculiar to ancient Israel. Here is an example from Moscow, in the reign of Peter the Great (eighteenth century). There a girl was usually married in adolescence to a man she hadn't met until after the decision was final. Then she was summoned into her father's presence, wearing a linen veil. Her Father took a small whip, struck his daughter lightly on the back, and said, "My daughter, this is the last time you shall be admonished by the authority of your father beneath whose rule you have lived. Now you are free of me, but remember that you have not so much escaped from my sway as passed beneath that of another. Should you not behave as you ought to toward your husband, he in my stead will admonish you with this whip." Then he handed the whip to the groom, who declared that he would have no need of it, but he still accepted it and attached it to his belt. At the wedding, rings were exchanged, after which she fell at her husband's feet, touching her forehead to his shoes to signal her subjugation. Then he covered her with the hem of his coat, acknowledging his duty to support and protect his humble wife.[68]

What a contrast we find in Jesus' attitude toward women. He boldly spoke to them, enjoyed their company, respected their rights, and treated them as human beings of equal value with men. His words in this passage can only be understood if you remember that he was speaking to men who did not value women as He did. "You cannot dismiss them for this or that or the other cause. That is not what God intended." God has always wanted husband and wife to be one flesh.

Marriage therefore cannot be dissolved for this or that trivial cause. Norman Vincent Peale tells of a young couple who came to see him on the verge of divorce. He was angry because she wouldn't bake him the kind of lemon meringue pie his mother always made, and she was furious because he left the bathroom a mess and expected her to keep the house in order by herself. Peale lectured them like a stern father, telling them they had better grow up and grow up fast. They may have looked like adults, but emotionally they were still children. He told them they had to recognize that all persons have flaws, even the two of them. They had to get busy to replace selfishness with selflessness, a task so difficult "that the Bible compares it to being born again."[69]

A middle-aged wife received a birthday card from one of her children. It said, "How do you do it? You have the body of a seventeen-year-old ... but you'd better give it back. You're getting it all wrinkled." What then should her husband do with this wrinkled wife of his? On the other hand, she could question how she should dispose of her pot-bellied, balding, little old husband. Scripturally, the answer is clear: they must keep each other. God intends for them to remain one, to serve Him through their home and family.

---

[68]Robert K. Massie, *Peter the Great, His Life and World* (New York: Alfred A. Knopf, 1980), p. 32.

[69]Norman Vincent Peale, *A Guide to Self-Control* (Greenwich, Connecticut: Fawcett Publications, 1965), pp. 105, 106.

The Exception Illustrated

By this time, even Jesus' disciples are concerned about the strictness of His teaching. "If this is the situation between a husband and wife, it is better not to marry." Jesus admits that His standards are high. "Not everyone can accept this teaching." They need help from the Lord to accomplish it. Eunuchs—that is, males whose genitalia are missing (either through birth defect or because they have been removed)—can live the celibate life. So can some others, having taken a vow to remain single because of their desire to give themselves entirely to God's work. Only those who can accept celibacy should try it. For the rest, God desires marriage—lifelong monogamy. And if you marry, you must not be hardhearted. Understand what the will of the Lord is: if you marry, stay married. The only exception is if your spouse is guilty of adultery. God wants you to have one life partner.

Realism demands the honesty of Socrates. When he was asked whether it was better to marry or not to, he said, "Whichever you do, you will regret it." Neither the single nor the married life can guarantee constant bliss. But the God who created male and female intended that the two should become like one. If God desires it, you can achieve it. If God commands it, He makes it possible.

The Man Who Had Almost Everything (19:16-30)
(Mark 10:17-31; Luke 18:18-30)

"Teacher, What Good Thing Must I Do to Get Eternal Life?"

"I already have everything else—money, possessions, position as a leading young man in my community. All this—and I want Heaven, too. How can I guarantee that I'll get it?" His is the universal yearning of the person who has accomplished all his goals on earth. Earth is already his; he wants Heaven next. Jesus answers his question with another question. "Why do you ask me about what is good? There is only One who is good. If you want to enter life, obey the commandments." Then, to help the young man understand which ones, Jesus enumerates them: "'Do not murder, do not commit adultery, do not steal, do not give false testimony, honor your father and mother,' and 'love your neighbor as yourself.'" Five of them are from the Ten Commandments (Exodus 20) and the sixth from the Code of Holiness (Leviticus 19:18). Jesus has selected the easy ones. Missing from the list are the commandments regarding the primacy of God, the observance of the Sabbath, and the prohibition against coveting, which speaks directly to this man's condition.

The young man has expertly practiced a religion of works, so he can keep an accurate tabulation of his righteous deeds. Meeting the young man on his own ground, then, Jesus gives him one more "work" to accomplish. "You still lack one thing...." The man has asked about Heaven, but Jesus answers concerning perfection, which is actually the man's goal. He wants to be perfect on earth, perfect in Heaven. Jesus accepts his premise, answering in terms that suggest that what leads you to Heaven will perfect you on earth. Upon hearing Jesus, the young man goes away sorrowfully, because Jesus has asked one more work than he is prepared to do. Jesus requires that he conquer his greedy spirit by practicing a generosity that is new to him. He cannot take this courageous step beyond works to faith in God, which is where Jesus is leading him. His trust must shift from his possessions to his God, a transfer of allegiance he is afraid to make.

"What Do I Still Lack?"

He has come to Jesus because something is missing in his life. He leaves Jesus because he will not pay the price to fill the void. Someone has written, "If you want to corrupt a man, first make him rich." It is possible to corrupt some people by offering them enough money that they are willing to compromise their principles, but there is another way. Take the same people and make them rich. Give them enough time to become accustomed to their new luxury—the swimming pool, the prestige automobiles, the stylish wardrobes and country club memberships—then threaten to take everything away unless they compromise this or that principle. What they have never had they could possibly forego, but what they have come to depend on is as important as life itself. You've got them—they're trapped!

Jesus dealt primarily with the poor. Hard times were the norm, not the exception, for them. This wealthy young man is not typical of Jesus' followers. Jesus' counsel is for his specific problem; His challenge for the man to sell everything is not for everyone. The man has cut himself off from most of his peers by his wealth; able to buy himself a higher standard of living than most, he has come to consider himself a superior person. Not without reason: he has, in fact, kept most of the commandments. He does not realize that his many possessions have possessed him. Perhaps it has not occurred to him until this moment that he cannot live without them. What he lacks, then, are genuine faith in God, the ability to endure privation, and genuine love for his neighbors. He has broken the two most important of all commandments: He does not love God with all he has, and he does not love his neighbors as himself (Matthew 22:37, 38).

Why Does Jesus Tie Heaven to Money?

Surely this question must have been in the young man's mind. It certainly occurs to the rest of us as we study his disappointing encounter with Jesus. Think about it for a moment: does anything make a make a stronger statement about our spiritual condition than the way we spend our money? Whenever you pay your monthly bills, you are writing your spiritual biography for the month. Your check stubs testify more loudly than your words concerning what you think is most important, what you really believe in, who matters most to you. Have you ever wondered how on the Day of Judgment the Lord will conduct His court? Perhaps He will simply dispense with all the preliminaries and just order us to "hand over your check stubs. They will tell Me all I need to know."

Someone has taken the time to count how many times Jesus talks about money in the Gospels. Sixteen of the thirty-eight parables concern themselves with how to handle possessions; one out of ten verses (288 in all) deals directly with the subject of money. The Bible offers 500 verses on prayer, fewer than 500 on faith, but more than 2,000 on money and possessions. Apparently, the Lord believes that Heaven and money have a great deal to do with each other.

In a pious moment, Louis XI of France once gave the city of Boulogne to the Virgin Mary. He did not lose his head in his fit of virtue, however; he kept the revenues from the city for himself. Of such is *not* the kingdom of Heaven. More in keeping with Jesus' desires was the benevolence of Miss Emmeline Pye, a frail ninety-five-year-old who sat beside her window watching the residents of her little English town walk by. Her days were filled with joy because she had secretly made out her will. She was leaving seven cents apiece to all the school children in the town, ninety cents to the ones nearby, whose faces she knew. She wanted the postman to have fifteen dollars and the church choir members from $1.50 to $2.80—some were older and more faithful. Her total estate amounted to $270,000. She could hardly wait to die, so eager was she to share it. She made provisions for blankets to be distributed at Christmas to all the poor. Anything left over would be divided among professional people in need. During her lifetime, she had saved, sacrificed, pinched pennies, and planned for the day when she would be able to bless all the people in her English hamlet. She was experiencing Heaven on earth even as she waited for her Heaven beyond earth.[70]

----

[70]Applegarth, *Twelve Baskets Full,* pp. 27, 72.

Jesus knows He is offering a hard teaching. So do His disciples. They have been accustomed, like the rest of their people, to interpreting wealth as a sign of God's favor. When Jesus warns them that "it is easier for a camel to go through the eye of a needle than for a rich man to enter the kingdom of God," they wonder whether anybody can be saved. But Jesus is still thinking of trust. The rich man can hardly avoid the temptation to trust in his money, in his money-making ability, in the things his money can buy for him. His possessions are his hedge against the future; they are his Social Security. Having to choose between the rigors of Heaven-bound discipleship and the comfortable life, you know which he will choose. But if this wealthy young man, a leader in the community and a ruler in the synagogue, cannot get into Heaven, "Who then can be saved?" He has done everything right. Hasn't he earned eternal life?

That is exactly to the point. He has not because he cannot. "With man this is impossible." Heaven is not up for bid. Grace, not goodness, opens the gates of Heaven. "With God all things are possible." What the young man wanted from God is available only to those who admit their poverty (Matthew 5:3) and trust God's grace to save them. To make certain He cannot be misunderstood, Jesus employs His ludicrous image of a lumbering, ungainly camel trying to squeeze through the eye of a needle—as impossible as trying to buy your way into Heaven, and as difficult as trusting God while luxuriating in your riches. The trouble with money is that it distracts you so. You can't concentrate on Heaven, you can't clearly see your neighbor's needs, and you learn to depend upon your bank account instead of your Lord. You might even believe, as the ancient Jews did, that your wealth is the sign that God has specially favored you, a delusion Jesus is at pains to correct. In fact, He goes to the other extreme of praising poverty! (See Luke 6:20.)

Peter, catching on to Jesus' meaning, reminds Him, "We have left everything to follow you! What then will there be for us?" To him Jesus promises an incredible future. Like the judges of old, the disciples will share the role of judges of God's people, and all others who have sacrificed for Jesus' sake will enjoy the blessings of eternal life. A reversal of order is coming: "Many who are first will be last, and many who are last will be first." Heaven has a different scale of priorities. Everyone can be saved through trust and obedience; no one can be saved through works or wealth.

CHAPTER TWENTY-ONE

Seeing Things God's Way
Matthew 20

Is God Always Fair? (20:1-16)

Is God always fair? No, not always. Sometimes He goes beyond fairness to mercy. When He strikes a bargain with His people, He always keeps His side of it, even it that seems unfair. In His kingdom, justice does not decide the fate of His subjects; grace does.

What angers the Pharisees and other religious leaders is Jesus' disregard of their doctrine of God's justice. He seems to be telling people that the very religious among them, who have worked so hard to observe every jot and tittle of the law in order to please God, will get no more from Him than people who have done little or nothing for Him. Furthermore, Jesus is also claiming that the Jews, God's very own people, will have to share God's blessings with Gentiles. Unfair!

In the parable of the workers in the vineyard, Jesus answers His critics. He agrees with them that from their point of view, God does not govern with strict justice. He does better: He governs with mercy.

God's Call to Work

The parable is not strictly about work, but we can profitably look at what it says on the subject. Sometimes, the kingdom of God is compared to a party (see Luke 14:16-24), a happy simile that stresses the celebrating and gaiety that are to be eternally enjoyed in the presence of the Lord. In this parable, however, Jesus uses labor to help explain another aspect of the kingdom. Our understanding requires both comparisons, because genuine joy in life cannot be found apart from meaningful work. Neither can there be any real faith unless it is expressed in action (James 2:17, 18).

In comparing God's kingdom to working, Jesus sounds like a good Jew. If anything distinguished ancient Israel from the other great civilization from which Western culture descends, ancient Greece, it was Judaism's conviction that there is dignity in physical labor. Plato relegated craftsmen to the lowest rungs of the social ladder and

Aristotle sniffed that "the best ordered state will not make an artisan a citizen." A laborer was *just* a worker, nothing more.

In Israel, however, every human being, even a manual laborer, was considered valuable in the sight of God. Everybody worked in Israel, even God (Genesis 2:2; John 5:17). The whole nation was a work field (Isaiah 5:1-7). The Son of God was a carpenter, and His disciples were called builders, farmhands, and fishermen. Paul's inspired instructions to the Thessalonians are in this tradition:

> Make it your ambition to lead a quiet life, to mind your own business and to work with your hands, just as we told you, so that your daily life may win the respect of outsiders and so that you will not be dependent on anybody (1 Thessalonians 4:11, 12; see also 2 Thessalonians 3:11-13 and Romans 12:3-13).

God's Justice

This is the central issue in the parable. Is it fair that those who work only one hour should receive the same wage as those who labor all day? No, not if we are thinking in hours. But if our real concern is to prevent men and their families from starving, and if it takes practically all of a day's wage to buy enough food to feed a family for one day, is it "fair" to pay for only one hour? Does a man have a "right" to live? Does the Master have a "right" to deprive him of life if he has the resources to keep the man from starving?

For as long as man has thought about God, he has questioned His justice. So many things in the world seem unfair, especially so many things that happen to us. We demand justice! Yet to be fair, we have to admit that the justice we demand is more for ourselves than others. We want what's coming to us! Well, not everything. We don't want the punishment we deserve; we don't want to be treated as we treat others. But we do want others to get the punishment *they* deserve. If we were honest, we'd have to admit that we want justice for everybody else, but mercy for ourselves.

The workers in the parable all received exactly what they agreed to work for. That is just, isn't it? What bothered them was that someone else received as much, but for less work. Is that just? You can argue both sides, of course, but Jesus does not. He is concerned about the welfare of the unemployed as well as the employed. That moves the discussion from justice to generosity.

God's Generosity

This is the essence of the story. God's grace explains the Master's treatment of all His workers. He is thinking of the workmen's needs.

If they go home with wages for only a single hour, or three hours, they will not have enough to feed their families. The eleventh hour recruit needed work as much as the first ones selected. He would not have waited all day in the marketplace otherwise. The law provided that a worker should be paid the day's wages at the end of each day (Leviticus 19:13; Deuteronomy 24:15), because most workers lived a hand-to-mouth existence. They had nothing to fall back on: no savings accounts, no unemployment compensation, no food stamps. Nothing. The employer's concern is that each laborer should have food for the day. He hires more workers than he needs and then pays them more than he has to. To do less would be, from his point of view, unfair. In this compassionate person, mercy triumphs over justice.

The landowner in this parable embodies Jesus' teaching elsewhere:

"I tell you the truth, whatever you did for one of the least of these brothers of mine, you did for me" (Matthew 25:40).

"Go back and report to John what you hear and see: The blind receive sight, the lame walk, those who have leprosy are cured, the deaf hear, the dead are raised, and the good news is preached to the poor" (Matthew 11:4, 5).

Jesus echoes the prophets:

> Strengthen the feeble hands,
> steady the knees that give way;
> say to those with fearful hearts,
> "Be strong, do not fear;
> your God will come,
> he will come with vengeance;
> with divine retribution
> he will come to save you."
> Then will the eyes of the blind be opened
> and the ears of the deaf unstopped.
> Then will the lame leap like a deer,
> and the tongue of the dumb shout for joy (Isaiah 35:3-6).

Scripture offers grace, not justice. The word *grace* does not appear often in the Gospels—only in Luke and in John's prologue. *Mercy* as a noun is also missing. But the meaning is there. It is there in this Landlord's overpayment of His workers; it is there in the Father's joyous reception of His prodigal son; it is there in Jesus' forgiveness of the woman taken in adultery, in His healings on the Sabbath, in His acceptance of the unacceptable, in His refusal to condemn persons because of their past sins, in His free gift of a new chance in life, and in His ready welcome of prostitutes and tax collectors.

Grace becomes a more frequent word in Acts and the epistles, because it characterizes the life of the early church. The concordance shows that *grace* is used only fifteen times in the Bible up to the book of Acts, but from then on it appears at least one hundred times. Paul never tires of rejoicing, as he writes in Romans 5:2, that in Christ "we have gained access by faith into this grace in which we now stand." The church at Rome was, like the others, filled with humble, frail, often disappointing men and women. Only grace allowed them into the church, and only grace—God's grace to them and their grace to one another—could keep them there. From God's generosity, we learn the generosity without which no human bonds hold.

God has made the benefits for those who answer His call available to Gentiles as well as Jews, to women along with men, to slaves as well as freemen (Galatians 3:28), and to the late convert as well as the early. God's grace does not discriminate as human justice does.

The Workers' Selfishness

The employer's generosity is under attack. This is Jesus' reason for telling the story. He has to answer God's critics. They resent the whole thrust of His ministry with its reckless embracing of those who do not "deserve" God's favor. The workers' grumbling against their generous employer (so much like the elder brother's resentment of the returned prodigal son—Luke 15) is no uglier than the critics' carping and their hateful, merciless attempts to exclude all but themselves from God's love.

What should we say of such complainers? Perhaps it is enough to repeat this famous story. It indicates the source of their spirit.

The devil was once crossing the Libyan Desert when he came upon a group of small fiends who were tempting a holy hermit. They tried him with the seductions of the flesh: they sought to sow his mind with doubts and fears; they told him that all his austerities were worth nothing. But it was all of no avail. The holy man was impeccable. Then the devil stepped forward. Addressing the imps he said: "Your methods are too crude. Permit me for one moment. This is what I should recommend." Going up to the hermit, he said, "Have you heard the news? Your brother has been made Bishop of Alexandria." The fable says, "A scowl of malignant jealousy clouded the serene face of the holy man."

Jesus Foresees His Death (20:17-19)
(Mark 10:32-34; Luke 18:31-34)

Jesus and His disciples are on their way to Jerusalem for the Passover feast. (See John 12:1.) On their way, Jesus confides His insight into what awaits Him there. He has warned them before (Matthew 16:21; 17:9, 12, 22, 23), but they can't accept His predictions of death. As we shall see, when Jesus is arrested and convicted, they seem to be caught unprepared. Of course, it is one thing to assent to something intellectually and quite another to fully accept and act on it when the moment of crisis comes. The disciples are probably too absorbed in their own dreams for the kingdom Jesus will establish to hear His sober warnings. Anyway, Jesus has promised some pretty wonderful things, including their joint rulership with Him (Matthew 19:28). They cannot take His predictions of suffering and death too seriously in light of the triumph they expect.

Yet Mark reports (10:32-34) that on their way toward Jerusalem, "the disciples were astonished, while those who followed were afraid." Could Jesus be right? Could these dire predictions come to pass? Matthew does not tell us the reaction of the group. From Mark and Luke (18:31-34) it is apparent that astonishment, fear, courage, and determination marked the disciples. They did not fully comprehend what was happening, but they could read Jesus' sense of resolve in His face. He would proceed, in spite of the consequences. Then, after the betrayal, conviction, mockery, scourging, and crucifixion, He would be vindicated in His resurrection. For the victory that lay beyond, He was prepared to endure the suffering that lay between.

How to Get Ahead in This Organization (20:20-28)
(Mark 10:35-41; Luke 22:24-27)

The Request

This passage is a study in ambition. Here the mother of James and John, acting the part of a good Jewish mother, petitions Christ that her two sons be given the chief seats when Jesus establishes His kingdom. In Mark (10:35-45), the young men speak for themselves. From the indignation of the other ten disciples, we can conclude that the idea is theirs. Their mother probably just carries the request message. It is possible that she and they feel that their request is only fair, since Jesus seems to have been a cousin of James and John. (See Matthew 27:56, Mark 15:40, and John 19:25. Jesus' mother and James and John's mother appear to have been sisters.) In any Oriental kingdom, relatives of the ruler could expect preferential treatment.

Of course, ambition is not the exclusive property of the Orient. It is only normal to want to rise to the top of any organization. In *Love in the Ruins,* Walker Percy comments that the eventual downfall of the

243

United States will not have come about because of political or moral or any of the many other anticipated causes, but because "things stopped working and nobody wanted to be a repairman." Everybody wants to rise in power, nobody wants to stoop in service.

At his first inauguration, Richard Nixon placed his hand on his family Bible. It had been opened to Isaiah, to the verse he had chosen to guide his Presidency (Isaiah 2:4, KJV), "They shall beat their swords into plowshares." Charles Colson finds it tragic that neither the new President nor his close advisers could see the warning of things to come, which Isaiah utters just seven verses later: "The lofty looks of man shall be humbled, and the haughtiness of men shall be bowed down . . ." (verse 11). Had these words been heeded, Colson believes, Nixon and his men would not have been run out of office by the Watergate scandal.[71] Had they been humble enough to worry more about serving than preserving power, they would have survived. They could have benefited from the philosophy of America's favorite cracker-barrel philosopher, Will Rogers, who used to say, "I am just an old country boy in a big town trying to get along. I have been eating pretty regular and the reason I have is, I have stayed an old country boy."[72]

The Conditions to Be Met

"You don't know what you are asking. Can you drink the cup I am going to drink?" They do not know, for certain, the nature of His kingdom, or they would not ask for this special treatment. Nor do they know the bitterness of the cup Jesus will drink (in Gethsemane, Jesus asks His Father to take the cup away from Him—Matthew 26:39). When James and John confidently tell Him they can drink it, Jesus agrees. They can and they will. He knows their character. He also is prophesying. James will be the first of the apostles martyred. Herod Agrippa will execute him (Acts 12:2). John, on the other hand, will live a long but eventful life, filled with imprisonments, persecution, and suffering for Christ. They will both desert Jesus, along with the other disciples, when He is arrested in Gethsemane, but their desertion will be temporary. Their later leadership in the early church justifies Jesus' confidence in them.

---

[71]Charles Colson, *Born Again* (Old Tappan, New Jersey: Revell, 1976), p. 257.

[72]Richard M. Ketchum, *Will Rogers, The Man and His Times* (New York: American Heritage, 1973), p. 7.

The Denial of the Request

Even if Jesus wanted to grant their request, He could not. He does not have that authority. Only the Father, who knows everything, has the right to do so. Only He can discern who is worthy to hold the most influential positions in the kingdom. God's standard of judgment, by the way, cannot be expected to conform to this world's. (See Matthew 18:1-5 and 25:31-46.) God does not define greatness as we do. Was it King Alfred who wrote,

> And well may God with the serving folk
> Cast in His dreadful lot.
> Is not He too a servant
> And is not He forgot?

The Quality of Christian Leadership

Jesus takes advantage of the request to guide the disciples away from the dangerous power hunger of the pagans. In Christ's kingdom, service far outranks ambition as a virtue. Even Jesus, who has every right to expect royal treatment, came to serve and to sacrifice himself. He will offer himself as a ransom, to be used like money paid to free hostages. To be ambitious for personal gain is to violate one of the basic tenets of Christian ethics. To enjoy the prerogatives of office or to lord it over one's subordinates is more pagan than Christian.

A lesson from George Washington illustrates Jesus' meaning here. On one of those miserably cold winter days of which the American Revolution seemed to have such an abundance, General Washington came upon some soldiers who were fortifying the camp. His collar was turned up and his hat pulled down, so no one could recognize him when he stopped to watch the work crew. The men pulled together on a heavy log as their corporal barked orders. "All right, up with it! All together now, push." The men gave everything they had, but the log got away from them and slipped back. Once again the corporal shouted his orders, and once more they tried. But they lost it. The third time Washington ran forward, threw himself into the effort, and this time the log dropped into place.

He was displeased with the corporal. Why couldn't he have helped his men? Washington asked. "Why, because I'm a corporal."

"Well," Washington rebuked him, "I'm the Commander in Chief. Next time you've got a log too heavy for your men to lift, send for me."[73] No one doubts Washington's position in the hierarchy of his

---

[73]*Pulpit Digest,* January-February, 1980, p. 59.

country. He did not get there by posturing, but by serving. "Whoever wants to become great among you must be your servant. . . ." What Jesus teaches of His kingdom is practical advice even for the kingdom of this world. There is no better way to rise in any organization than by stooping to serve.

To See Again (20:29-34)
(Mark 10:46-52; Luke 18:35-42)

Matthew speaks of two blind men who receive their sight. Luke and Mark mention only one, Mark giving his name as Bartimaeus, agreeing with Luke in calling him a beggar. The three accounts parallel each other in so many ways that Bible scholars have wondered about the different number, some going so far as to accuse Matthew of deliberately doubling the number. Perhaps he is compensating for not including the healing of the blind man at Bethsaida (Mark 8:22-26).

A simpler explanation is that two men were actually healed, but Mark and Luke concentrate on Bartimaeus in the telling of the story. The Gospel writers are necessarily selective in their narratives of Jesus' numerous healings. In this case, Bartimaeus is undoubtedly the more prominent of the two men, hence he receives "top billing" in the other accounts.

The noise of the large crowd surrounding Jesus naturally stimulates the curiosity of the blind men. When they learn that it is the now famous rabbi from Nazareth, they seize their opportunity. He has already miraculously healed so many others; why not them as well? They call Him by His Messianic title: "Lord, Son of David." (See Matthew 22:42.) From the reports they have heard of Jesus, they may very well believe Him to be the Messiah.

As usual, those around Jesus try to protect Him from the beggars. But Jesus' compassion breaks through the disciples' shield to confront the men. He already knows what they want, of course, as the Lord knows what we need before we pray, but He wants to hear from them anyway. Then He touches them, and they see.

We are impressed with the tenacity of the blind men. The rebuke of the crowd cannot silence them. They are desperate men who will not be robbed of their one chance to be healed. They believe in God; their cries demonstrate that they are true sons of Israel. Having nothing to lose and everything to gain, they ask for the one thing they most need. Not alms, not from this great healer, but sight. Then, having gained everything, they attach themselves to their Deliverer. Gratitude and curiosity take over. They are beggars no longer; neither are they ingrates. They are believers.

246

CHAPTER TWENTY-TWO

What Is God's Will?

Matthew 21

What's All This Shouting About, Jesus? (21:1-17)
(Mark 11:1-11; Luke 19:29-46; John 12:12-19)

As Jesus rides into Jerusalem, the whole city stirs. "Who is this man? Why is everybody shouting about Him?" To answer these questions is to state the purpose to which the four Gospel authors write. They stress the significance of Jesus' triumphal entry and the events of the week following by devoting disproportionate attention to Jesus' final week of ministry. The Gospels indicate that everything up to this point has been preliminary, for without these startling events in Jerusalem, nothing else Jesus did would have mattered.

Jesus enters a stuffed city. One estimate is that Jerusalem, usually populated by a few hundred thousand residents, swelled to two and a half million during Passover week. Into this mass of Jewish humanity, Jesus deliberately and courageously rides, finally allowing His disciples to proclaim Him Messiah. E. Stanley Jones has written that two great streams of longing course through human history, longing for a new leader and for a new order. As Jesus enters Jerusalem, He does so as a new Leader bringing a new order, the kingdom of God. These verses reveal both leader and order.

A Peaceful Conqueror

Jesus has made prior arrangements for His triumphal entry. He dispatches His disciples to fetch the donkey He has asked for. Matthew sees another prophetic fulfillment in this humble animal, quoting Zechariah 9:9, the prophet's vision of the coming of Israel's future king. But what a king. He rides a donkey colt instead of a white horse. A king who conquers through bloodshed and warfare mounts a gallant steed, so the world will praise his triumph. A conqueror who sits atop a humble donkey comes in peace; His mount is a beast of burden.

How unlike the kings of Israel is this new king. There were Saul, high in stature and mighty in valor; David, creative in music, keen of intellect, a natural leader of men; and Solomon, whose wisdom was heralded around the known world. Like other Eastern monarchs, Israel's kings ruled with almost absolute power; they indulged their every fancy while their people shamelessly pampered them. To this day, Eastern tyrants live in a splendor and with an authority that baffles more democratic Westerners. But Jesus' reign departs from them all. He does not just talk peace but is serious enough about it to die to achieve it. Eastern rulers for centuries have ordered their subjects to do battle to protect their princely prerogatives; Jesus sends himself into battle to protect His threatened people. A truly unusual, a genuinely peaceful, conqueror!

An Adored Savior

"Hosanna to the Son of David!"
"Blessed is he who comes in the name of the Lord!"

Most of the people probably did not fully comprehend what they were saying. They most enthusiastically shouted, though they could scarcely define, "Hosanna." It means, "Oh Lord, save us. Oh Lord, grant us success." It combines praise and prayer, as in the Hallel Psalms (113-118) sung on high feast days during the Passover and the Feast of Tabernacles. Christians reading these words today naturally think of the angel's announcement to Joseph (Matthew 1:20, 21), "You are to give him the name Jesus, because he will save his people from their sins." Jesus, Savior. On the day of His entry into Jerusalem, the people hail Him as Savior, but from Rome, not from sin. They quote a Messianic Psalm (118:26), but their anticipated Messiah and the Messiah who has come differ as much as the salvation they seek differs from the salvation He brings. Although they are to be disappointed in Him, at this moment, they shout His praises with the words the priests chant for six days during the Feast of Tabernacles. (Then, on the seventh day, the priests will chant the words seven times as they circle the altar waving branches of willow and myrtle and palm leaves.)

On this day, Jesus replaces the altar, and the people replace the priests around the altar. Instead of the ordained clergy, the common people are now waving branches and chanting the Psalm and imploring their Messiah to save them from oppression and danger. He will save them, but in a way they do not anticipate. He is a Conqueror who conquers people by saving them and a Savior who saves by conquering them. That's something to shout about.

An Indignant Prophet

Jesus does some shouting of His own. Like an Old Testament prophet, He strides into the temple and scatters the disturbers of its peace. Indignant that money-changers and merchandise vendors have corrupted the house of prayer, He overturns their tables and sends them scampering before His rage. This isn't the "Gentle Jesus, Meek and Mild" of children's stories. He is the avenging Lord, protecting His holy place and His worshiping people. The episode takes place in the outer court of the temple, which is the only area in which Gentiles (non-Jews) can worship. They have been shoved aside, however, by the vendors. Temple leaders, who govern in such matters, meant no harm when they allowed these services to be set up in the holy precincts. They just wanted to assist pilgrims coming to the temple without the required temple money or necessary sacrifices. The services were legitimate. The temple required that offerings be made in its own currency. Jews coming from afar would need to exchange their money. But you can see how tempting it would be to abuse this opportunity, adding on exchange charges, hiking up prices, exploiting unsuspecting foreigners. Sacrifices had to be unblemished. Worshipers frequently arrived with no sacrificial bird or animal, or with a blemished one. To accommodate them, temple authorities allowed merchants to sell sacrificial birds and animals that had been stamped with approval by temple inspectors. This service was also abused by some unscrupulous traders. The losers were the poor but earnest worshipers. They were being bilked in the name of God.

Jesus' anger lashes out at the exploiters, extortionists, hucksters, and con artists who traffic illicitly in the name of religion. His Father's house is to be a house of prayer ("for all nations," Mark adds [11:17], quoting Isaiah 56:7), not an open market. The new Leader is taking over and establishing His new order. Many believed that when the Son of God would come, He would cleanse Jerusalem of Gentiles. There would be no non-Jews in the Holy City. Jesus does just the opposite: He cleanses Jerusalem for Gentiles. His new order unites Jew and Gentile; together they will pray in the house of the Lord. (See Ephesians 2—His church is for people of all colors, nations, cultures, and former loyalties. And it is still a house of prayer.) The prophet Jesus confronts the corrupters of the temple like a latter-day Isaiah, who appeared naked and barefoot to warn what God would do to the Egyptians (Isaiah 20), or like Agabus, who bound his feet and hands with the apostle Paul's belt in order to prophecy Paul's fate in Jerusalem (Acts 21:10, 11). His whip is in His hand (John 2:15) and with its snap, He drives cattle, sheep, doves, and their traffickers off the premises.

The Jews have long wanted a Messiah, but now that He has arrived, they discover that they have got more than they bargained for. Their savior has turned on them. He is supposed to attack "them," not "us." He is to wreak God's vengeance on Israel's enemies, not Israel's sins! What kind of a messiah is this? At the moment, He seems more prophet than savior.

A Compassionate Healer

Here is Jesus' most enduring role: the compassionate healer. Even in this critical moment, when His direct challenge to the temple authorities will seal His fate, His mind is on the needs of others. They can think only of their own troubles, of course, as they crowd against Him to be healed. Their little children in the meantime keep on chanting the songs and praises their parents and other adults have only recently stopped singing.

What a complex personality Jesus presents to us in these verses. Conqueror (who conquers to save); savior (who saves by conquering); prophet and healer. The blind and lame press for healing now because they recognize in their besieged Helper one who identifies with them in their need. Religious authorities have at best ignored, at worst opposed, them. Jesus battles for the rights of all people, not just the privileged. The religious leaders take care of their religious institution; Jesus takes care of their people.

Joni Ereckson lost the use of her limbs in a diving accident shortly after graduating as "the most athletic girl" in her Baltimore high-school class. At first, the beautiful quadriplegic caved in to depression and anger when she realized she could never lead a normal life again. She even contemplated suicide. Then she reversed herself, hoping against hope that God would miraculously heal her. He did not. Now, with deeper insight, she says that she can trust a God who began His earthly existence in a stinky stable, who got angry, was lonely, had no place to call His own, and was abandoned by His closest friends. He wept real tears, so He could identify with hers. She has experienced His compassion, and although she remains confined to her wheelchair, her life has become richly varied. She is whole. She will tell you she is healed.

Not everybody rejoices when the Lord heals. "When the chief priests and the teachers of the law saw the wonderful things he did and the children shouting in the temple area, ... they were indignant." Compassion is a quality of the Godly, not necessarily of the religious. The religious often have too great a stake in institutions and structures and the *status quo*. They are afraid of raw spiritual power. It is no wonder, then, that Jesus has never commanded us to be religious. He would rather have us become like Him.

Of Figs and Faith (21:18-22)
(Mark 11:12-14, 20-26)

This episode presents Jesus in an unusual light. The Bible reader is often impressed with Jesus' remarkable control over His temper, even in the most exasperating circumstances. Yet here, He seems almost petulant, cursing a fig tree because it cannot satisfy His hunger. At first blush, He appears to be succumbing to the very temptation He resisted when the devil tried to entice Him to turn stones into bread to satisfy His hunger (Matthew 4:1-4).

After comparing this passage with Luke 13:6-9, however, Jesus' treatment of the barren fig tree does not seem so out of character. There Jesus told a parable of a man who planted a fig tree in his vineyard, which after three years still bore no fruit, so he ordered his vinedresser to cut it down. The servant asked for and received a year's reprieve for the tree, agreeing to destroy it then if it still remained fruitless. The application of Jesus' parable was obvious to His listeners: a fruitless religion was about to be cut down unless the people repented and began doing God's will. What Jesus taught in Luke 13 He acts out in Matthew 21. The cursing of the fig tree is an enacted parable.

A Parable of Judgment on Fruitless Religion

There are leaves on the tree, but no fruit; the promise of figs, but no delivery. Jesus views His people's religion as promising but not producing. He agrees with Jeremiah before Him, "When I would gather them, says the Lord, there are no grapes on the vine, nor figs on the fig tree" (Jeremiah 8:13). Hosea said the same thing: "Ephraim is stricken, their root is dried up, they shall bear no fruit" (Hosea 9:16).

Jesus' Jewish contemporaries can boast of their magnificent temple, their splendid priests, their peerless law, and their rich heritage of religious traditions, but not of their obedience to God's will, at least as Jesus perceives His will. From traditional Judaism there has been the promise of Godliness, but no delivery.

It has failed because what is most needed the Jewish faith cannot give. Mark's Gospel adds a fact missing in Matthew's. It is the wrong season for fruit-bearing. "When he came to it, he found nothing but leaves, for it was not the season for figs" (11:13). The tree is incapable of meeting Jesus' expectations. Likewise, the popular religion of the Jews can produce leaves of law, temple, priesthood, and Sabbath, but it is helpless to bear the fruits of freedom, peace, and personal salvation as Christians will later come to know them. Traditional religion, too, will wither wherever faith in Christ shines on it.

A Parable of the Authority of the Lord

As Matthew 21 opens, Jesus rides in triumph into Jerusalem to the cheers of the excited crowd: "Blessed is he who comes in the name of the Lord!" Into the temple He proceeds, driving out the money changers and perverters of religion, assuming an authority higher than that of the temple bosses who have tolerated the defrauding of people in the name of religion. Then He retreats to the suburbs, where He demonstrates His authority over nature in His cursing of the fig tree, as He much earlier did when He calmed the angry sea (Mark 4:35-41).

A Parable of the Power of Faith

His disciples want to know how the tree could wither at once. Jesus does not explain; He challenges. "What you have seen Me do, you can do—and even greater things you can do—if you have faith." (See John 14:12.) What startling words: "You can say to this mountain, 'Go, throw yourself into the sea,' and it will be done" (Matthew 21:21).

We have no record that Jesus ever moved a mountain himself. Rearranging the terrain was not His purpose on earth. What He did was better: He restored health to the sick, revealed truth to the confused, returned from the grave when His closest friends thought Him gone forever, opened the doors of Heaven for all who would follow Him, and granted His believers miracle-working faith.

Look closely. He is talking about a specific kind of faith—one that is prayerful and fruitbearing. Faith here should not be defined the way the Sunday-school pupil did for his teacher: "Faith is believing what you know isn't so." Nor is it a sure-fire formula for getting everything you want, like the ill-prepared student who prays for a passing paper as he sits down to his exam, or the businessman who prays for the Lord to keep him from losing his company in spite of his poor management. It is complete confidence in the power of the Lord and complete commitment to bear the fruit that the Lord asks from your life. This faith must not be confused with wishful thinking. Rather, it is thoughtful doing. Its essence is not in hoping against hope, but in receiving help from the Lord to help the Lord realize His dreams on earth. It is expecting the Lord to bring our projects for Him to a successful conclusion because, as the pioneering missionary to China, Hudson Taylor, has written, "If we are obeying the Lord, the responsibility rests with Him, not with us." God's answers to our prayers are in keeping with His character and plans for the universe; they do not always satisfy our longings. But if we ask prayerfully for fruit in our lives, we shall receive.

A Parable of the Danger of Fruitlessness

A faithless, fruitless religion, like this fig tree, withers. So does a faithless, fruitless life. It happens to churches. When they forget Christ's commission and become preoccupied with the "purity" and "spirituality" of their members to the exclusion of evangelism and missions, they bear no fruit. They wither.

It happens to persons as well. When their interests are self-centered, when they are not producers but consumers only, when their conversation turns from visions of the future to recollections of past happiness, when their activities benefit no one other than themselves or their immediate family, they wither. (This is the terrifying danger in the current doctrine of looking out for Number One. You do that, and you die!)

By contrast, if your faith is in God and you desire to bear fruit for Him, you prosper. He will infuse you with extraordinary power. Your asking will be in harmony with His will. What He wants, you want. Then you can be certain that He will help you get what you want.

Safety in Ignorance (21:23-27)
(Mark 11:27-33; Luke 20:1-8)

Jesus has been riding roughshod over the prerogatives of the chief priests and elders of the people. The priests are in charge of the temple. The money changers and vendors whom Jesus chased out of their stalls (21:12-16) were there by permission of the priests. You couldn't expect these officials to take Jesus' challenge lying down.

Jesus' action was offensive to the elders as well. The priests and the elders are of different parties. The former are Sadducees, many of the latter Pharisees. The two sects agree on few issues. As Jesus embarrassed the Sadducees by His unprecedented routing of the violaters of temple sanctity, so He caused the Pharisees also to lose face, since they fancied themselves as the guardians of Jewish holiness. They of all people should have been the ones to take action against the temple authorities. They have been criticizing Jesus throughout His ministry for being too liberal with matters of the law. Now in their own backyard, so to speak, He has proved himself more conscientious than they. So together, these usually bickering bodies attack Jesus.

"By what authority . . . Who gave you this authority?" (Matthew 21:23). Luke (19:47, 48) reports that they were prepared to kill Jesus to shut off His teaching, but "they could not find any way to do it, because all the people hung on his words." Here Matthew records one of their futile attempts to shut Him up.

He does not answer their question. Instead, He traps them with His own query about the authority of John the Baptist. He wisely avoids John's teaching, because that would initiate a dispute over words and meanings. Instead, He raises the issue of John's baptism, which had no Scriptural precedent and which had not been practiced (except for non-Jews who were converting to Judaism) by Jews themselves before John introduced his baptism for repentance. In fact, John's practice had also challenged the priests, since they conducted the sacrifices ordered in the Old Testament for forgiveness of sins, the same purpose for which John baptized. They recognized the challenge (see John 1:25; Luke 3:3) and refused to acknowledge the validity of John's baptism, but they were helpless to stop him because of John's great popularity.

As Matthew points out, either way the chief priests and elders answered Jesus, they would lose. If they denied John's right to baptize, they would ignite a rebellion among the masses, who believed him to be a prophet. If they affirmed that John was under divine orders, then they would have to account for their failure to believe him. They can't win, so they lie. "We don't know."

Jesus knows they are lying. Since they will not be honest, He will not waste an answer on them. "Neither will I tell you by what authority I am doing these things" (Matthew 22:27). They choose to pretend ignorance. He chooses not to play into their hands.

Honest to God (21:28-32)

Some people perform what they promise, most people do not perform what they promise, and a few others perform better than they promise. This parable of a father and two sons describes the latter two. Neither son is praiseworthy. One promises, then fails to keep his promise. The other son tells his father he won't do what his father asks, then does it anyway. Jesus would not have us imitate either son, but of the two, he prefers the doer to the promiser. Since we so often prefer dishonesty to truth-telling and irresponsibility to obedience, we may not enjoy, but we certainly need, this parable.

Honesty Is Good

"I will [go], sir" the second son tells his father, but he lies. He may not be intentionally lying, but the results are the same, anyway. If you don't call him a liar, you must at least think him irresponsible. He is not a person with whom you could close a deal with a handshake. His word is no good. There is little to build a relationship on here. In a word, he is not to be trusted.

A popular joke comes out of the Viet Nam war (although it is a revision of a similar one that circulated after World War II—and that one was undoubtedly borrowed from earlier wars). An American general was boasting the latest U. S. victory over the Viet Cong. (This was one week before the fall of Saigon.) A Vietnamese listened to the general politely, then asked, "Yes, General, I understand, but aren't your victories coming closer and closer to Saigon?" The question was carefully phrased, but the accusation came through loud and clear. The general is not to be trusted.

Another general earned a reputation for honesty that has lasted for centuries. Oliver Cromwell, England's dictator during its Commonwealth years (seventeenth century), was forced to sit for his portrait, a necessary evil to which he submitted provided the painter would not try to flatter him. "I desire you would use all your skill to paint my picture truly like me and flatter me not at all," he told the artist. "But remark all these roughnesses, pimples, warts and everything as you see me. Otherwise I will never pay a farthing for it." We still speak of telling the whole truth about someone, "warts and all."[74]

An unflattering fact of human society is that honesty generally flourishes only where there is a strong probability that dishonesty will be discovered. In Flagstaff, Arizona, a woman pulled an old ruse that demonstrates this fact. Having hit another automobile with her own, she conscientiously stopped to write a note to the owner of the parked car. It said, "The people watching me are thinking that I am leaving my phone number so you can call me, since they saw me run into your

---

[74]Antonia Fraser, *Cromwell* (New York: Alfred A. Knopf, 1973), p. 472.

bumper. They are wrong." Believing she could not be found out, she felt no compunction to be honest. No wonder Shakespeare's Hamlet groaned, "To be honest as this world goes is to be one man out of ten thousand."

Jesus' little parable has too many contemporary applications to do anything more than hint at them. Oaths of all kinds—marriage, contractual, purchase agreements, simple promises—depend upon the integrity of all parties. Without such integrity, social relationships break down. During an air traffic controllers' union strike in the early 1980's, many citizens (within the union and without) were forced to examine the meaning of an oath. The controllers had signed an oath when they were first employed that they would never strike. Yet thousands of them did. What did their promise mean? Could they be considered honest? They said they would not, yet they did. William Murray, Britain's Solicitor General in the eighteenth century, wrote, "No country can subsist a twelvemonth where an oath is not thought binding, for the want of it must necessarily dissolve society."

Honesty is good.

Obedience Is Better

The first son at first refused to do what his father asked, then later did it anyway. "Which of the two *did* what his father wanted?" Jesus asks. That's the moral of His story. He tells it for the benefit of the chief priests and elders who are questioning the authority He exercised when He cleansed the temple (Matthew 21:12-17). These good people have scrupulously observed the requirements of their religion, like good Christians today who regularly attend worship services, pay their tithes, sit on the church's committees, and congratulate themselves on what fine Christian examples they are. What Jesus demands, however, is obedience to the Father, which may be quite different from acts of religious piety. Tax collectors and prostitutes will enter the kingdom of God ahead of religious leaders if they more readily obey the Lord.

Jesus wants honest, not blind, obedience. He does not demand that His disciples stop thinking or raising questions. Thoughtless discipleship is a contradiction in terms. From the seventeenth century comes a story that embarrassed the Roman Catholic Church until the late twentieth century, when Rome officially pardoned Galileo for publishing his findings that the earth traveled around the sun (instead of the reverse). When Galileo was an old man, he appeared in the Minerva convent (on June 22, 1633) before the presiding cardinal, dressed in the garb of a penitent, to retract his heretical teaching. "I, Galileo Galilei," he said, "aged seventy, on my knees before you most reverend lords, and having my eye on the Holy Gospel, which I do touch with my lips, thus publish and declare, that I believe, and always have believed, and always will believe every article which the Holy Catholic Roman Church holds and teaches. And as I have written a book in which I have maintained that the sun is the centre, which doctrine is repugnant to the Holy Scriptures, I, with sincere heart and unfeigned faith, do abjure and detest, and curse the said error and heresy, and all other errors contrary to said Holy Church, whose penance I solemnly swear to observe faithfully, and all other penances which have been or shall be laid upon me."

It is reported, however, that when he arose, he whispered to a friend, "It does move, nevertheless."[75] Galileo had chosen to lie and live rather than tell the truth and die. In servile obedience, he yielded to the dictates of men while secretly believing the opposite of what he declared publicly. This is not the obedience Jesus asks.

Jesus teaches a virtue that is not even particularly Christian. The Roman orator Cicero has said, "All our affairs, public or private, civil or domestic, our social transactions, inevitably fall within the province of duty; in the observance of duty lies all that is honorable, and in the neglect of it all that is dishonourable. This is the common ground of all philosophers." Duty, obedience, dependability. These are the common demands of civilization. What Jesus introduces is the appeal of obedience to the Father above all other authorities, even religious ones. The religious leaders have been like the second son in promising obedience but failing to obey; the tax collectors and prostitutes, while not praiseworthy in their general conduct, at least are superior to the religious leaders in that, having never vowed to obey God as the authorities vowed, they have been obedient anyway. Obedience is better.

It Is Not Too Late to Change for the Better

"You did not repent and believe [John]" (Matthew 21:32). When John the Baptist preached repentance, the tax collectors and prostitutes heard and acted. The religious leaders attacking Jesus did not. Yet if prostitutes and tax collectors, who have lived their lives in

---

[75]John Lord, *Beacon Lights of History,* Volume VI, "Renaissance and Reformation" (New York: James Clarke and Company, 1884), pp. 453, 454.

violation of God's standards, can repent in obedience to God's Word and thus become acceptable to God, it is not too late for others, either. Repent: to change from conformity to an increasingly corrupt and dishonest society, and from supreme loyalty to one's own comforts and desires, to conformity with and loyalty to the will of God. To obey the Father. This is what Jesus wants.

Repentance is a change of heart and mind and behavior. It is a turning around toward God. Bible translators often have difficulty with this word, since the concept is foreign to many cultures. Here are some of their attempts:

Kekchi, of Guatemala: "It pains my heart."

Baouli, of West Africa: "It hurts so much I want to quit."

Northern Sotho, of South Africa: "It becomes untwisted."

The Chols of southern Mexico: "My heart is turning itself back."[76]

Tzeltals, of Mexico: "My heart returns because of my sin."

All these translations indicate the sorrow one feels for the direction he is going; they imply the change of behavior that brings relief. The repentant sinner says, "I am not what I ought to be, I am twisted, going in the wrong direction, perverted, incomplete. I want to make myself whole again. I will not say one thing and do another, I will not live a lie, I will not be dishonest any longer. I am changing. I will be honest to God and honest to other people and therefore honest to myself."

When God Doesn't Get His Way (21:33-46)
(Mark 12:1-12; Luke 20:9-19)

"I hate your God! I hate your God!" With doubled fists, the hysterical woman pounded on the chest of the minister. Overcome with the tragic death of her husband, she took her grief out on him and on God. Her alcoholic husband was physically abusing her, something not uncommon in their strife-filled home, when her son shot him. He couldn't stand to see his mother beaten again. Once and for all, he would put a stop to the man's cruelty. The son killed the drunken step-father so that he could never hurt the boy's mother again. But she blamed the death on God. Is God responsible for everything that happens?

A minister stopped in the hospital room to visit a man badly

---

[76]Eugene A. Nida, *Message and Mission* (South Pasadena, California: William Carey Library, 1960), pp. 47, 48.

damaged in an automobile accident. His wife was killed outright, but the doctors told him that his chances of pulling through looked favorable. His mood was anything but favorable, however, as he verbally accosted the minister: "What do you mean, this was God's will?" It seems that another minister had visited earlier and, trying to comfort the bereaved man, he told him that his wife's death was God's will. "Is that true?" the victim's widower now demanded to know. He needed a second opinion.

Is everything that happens God's will? Are what insurance companies persist in calling "acts of God" really acts of God? Is He to be blamed for the damage wrought by tornadoes, hurricanes, floods, and forest fires? Is it wrong to attribute some of these phenomena to the normal interworkings of nature? Is it God's fault that death is caused from a California earthquake, for example, when people persist on building atop the San Andreas Fault, or from drought when they insist on living in the desert? Is everything that happens God's fault? Does He always get His way?

No, He doesn't. Not if Jesus is describing God and the nation of Israel in the parable of the tenants. Let's approach the parable indirectly, by way of the Old Testament:

"The Lord, the God of their fathers, sent word to them through his messengers again and again, because he had pity on his people and on his dwelling place. But they mocked God's messengers, despised his words and scoffed at his prophets until the wrath of the Lord was aroused against his people and there was no remedy" (2 Chronicles 36:15, 16).

"But [the Israelites] were disobedient and rebelled against you; they put your law behind their backs. They killed your prophets, who had admonished them in order to turn them back to you; they committed awful blasphemies. So you handed them over to their enemies, who oppressed them. But when they were oppressed they cried out to you. From heaven you heard them, and in your great compassion you gave them deliverers, who rescued them from the hand of their enemies. But as soon as they were at rest, they again did what was evil in your sight" (Nehemiah 9:26-28).

The New Testament book of Hebrews eulogizes leaders "who through faith conquered kingdoms, administered justice, and gained what was promised; who shut the mouths of lions, quenched the fury of the flames, and escaped the edge of the sword; whose weakness was turned to strength; and who became powerful in battle and routed foreign armies. Women received back their dead, raised to life again. Others were tortured and refused to be released, so that they might gain a better resurrection." How were these servants of God treated? "Some faced jeers and flogging, while still others were chained and put in prison. They were stoned; they were sawed in two; they were put to death by the sword. They went about in sheepskins and goatskins, destitute, persecuted and mistreated—the world was not worthy of them. They wandered in deserts and mountains, and in caves and holes in the ground" (Hebrews 11:33-38).

These Scriptures give a united testimony: God does not always get His way, even with His own people. They knew better than God did; they wouldn't listen to His spokesmen. In the form of a parable, Jesus preaches the prophets' message concerning Israel's betrayal, man's cruelty, and God's determination.

Israel's Betrayal

The chief priests and the Pharisees know Jesus is talking about them—and about himself. He has come from God to His own people and they have rejected Him (John 1). Even now, immediately following His triumphal entry into Jerusalem, the authorities are plotting to kill Him, the Son of the Owner of the vineyard.

Jesus' audience recognizes that He is talking about Israel. In the eighth-century B.C., the prophet Isaiah had used the metaphor of the vineyard for the nation (Isaiah 5:1-7). Israel took pride in its special relationship with God; He had initiated a covenant with them (Genesis 17:2; Deuteronomy 7:9) and with no other nation. But what the Israelites overlooked was that God's purpose in having a covenant nation was so that He would have a channel for blessing the world. That was a responsibility they purposefully forgot. They were far more motivated to be blessed than to transmit blessing. So God had to take drastic measures: He sent His Son.

Victor Hugo, writing in his magnificent novel, *Les Miserables,* of the fall of the French Empire in the nineteenth century, concluded that Napoleon was not defeated by any remarkable skill on the part of opposing generals Wellington or Blucher, but "because of God. . . . Napoleon had been denounced in the inifinite and his fall had been decided on. He embarrassed God." Whether Hugo was right about France may be debated, but his language is appropriate for Israel: The nation had embarrassed God. The tenants of the vineyard had foiled His plans, ruined His harvest, impugned His character, rejected His emissaries, and murdered His own Son. They refused to let God have His way.

Man's Cruelty

You must not misunderstand this parable. You can blame all of God's problems on the Jews, excuse yourself since you are not a Jew, and feel quite comfortable. The Bible won't let you get away with it, however. Neither will history. Not after two world wars, Vietnam, Lebanon, El Salvador, Afghanistan, the Falklands, and the dozens of other big and little wars of this century. No nation can plead innocent to the charge of killing prophets. Why wouldn't nations kill prophets, since they kill everybody else? Cruelty is not the exclusive trait of one race or people. It's inherent in what we mean when we use the universal excuse, "After all, I'm only human."

"Adam was but human—this explains it all," is how Mark Twain accounts for sin. He says that Adam wasn't interested in the apple for the apple's sake, but because it was forbidden fruit. He believes the mistake God made was in not forbidding the serpent—then Adam would have eaten it and not the apple! There's some truth in Twain's cynicism. We will kill rather than be dictated to. We resist anyone in authority, even if He is the Master.

We resist. So Christians dare not speak too blithely of the sovereign will of God in their lives. They do not consistently allow Him such authority. The freedom we have to accept the Lord is also freedom to reject or deny Him. Our resistance is sometimes so vigorous that P. T. Forsythe is right to call us not merely stray sheep or wandering prodigals, but "rebels taken with weapons in our hands." We chase one another around, demanding the right to govern ourselves so we can repress others. We enrich ourselves at someone else's expense. We will be comfortable no matter how many others we discomfort. We protect our seats in the lifeboat while shoving the drowning away to their deaths. We band together in our select "isms," which protect those within and attack those without. It doesn't matter which one we join—communism, capitalism, militarism, feminism, ageism, heathenism, chauvinism, or any other "ism"—they all work for the benefit of those within at the expense of those without. We seem determined not to catch on to the fact that God wants to bless everybody. Everybody.

God's Determination

What does God do with the rebels in the vineyard? The parable makes it clear that God will not give up. He is determined to bless this world, with or without the tenants' help. If they fight Him, He'll replace them. Lest anyone miss the moral, Jesus spells it out: "The kingdom of God will be taken away from you and given to a people who will produce its fruit" (Matthew 22:43). Then, shifting the figure of speech, He returns to the metaphor in the Scripture He has just quoted from Psalm 118:22, 23, "He who falls on this stone will be broken to pieces, but he on whom it falls will be crushed." Jesus, currently the rejected stone, will have the power to wrest the vineyard away from the tenants and give it to new ones. He will send laborers into the harvest (Matthew 9:38).

God's determination is evident in Christ's saving work. "You see, at just the right time, when we were still powerless, Christ died for the ungodly. Very rarely will anyone die for a righteous man, though for a good man someone might possibly dare to die. But God demonstrates his own love for us in this: While we were still sinners, Christ died for us" (Romans 5:6-8). Because the "righteous" nation would not do His work, God raised up unrighteous people like us. "This is love: not that we loved God, but that he loved us and sent his Son as an atoning sacrifice for our sins" (1 John 4:10). Now we, too, may participate in the work of God on earth. We have become the new vineyard—or the new tenants (either metaphor works)—of the Lord. We are the new Israel, we are the new tenant farmers who know and love and are loved by the Owner. We have no inherited rights here. We did not earn our position or have any special connections. But God loved us, Christ died for us, and Father and Son have called us to this work. We are the church, which, as Robert Schuller describes it, is "a group of happy, Holy Spirit-inspired Christians—the body of Christ helping hurting people in the community."[77]

In the early days of the church, another picture was often used: that of an ark. In the Roman catacombs, you can still see on the walls pictures of arks. That's how the early Christians saw themselves. They were sailors in the ark on the sea surrounded by drowning humanity. Their task was to reach out and rescue as many from the sea as possible. The ark is not just for those already aboard; it is for those in the waters. The vineyard is not for the benefit of the tenants; it was planted by the Master to serve those beyond the vineyard. God has not always had His way—but He is determined, even at the cost of His Son's life, to bless. In spite of everything.

---

[77]Quoted by Marshall Leggett, "Reflections," *Christian Standard* (August 23, 1981), p. 4.

CHAPTER TWENTY-THREE

A Day of Questions

Matthew 22

Come to the Celebration (22:1-14)

To give His disciples some insight into the kingdom of Heaven, Jesus tells a little story (parable) of a king and his son's wedding banquet. Immediately Jesus' audience will grasp the importance of the kingdom of Heaven, since His story is about the most important person in a kingdom and the most important event in the life of the king's family. In Jewish culture, families saved for a lifetime to be able to host a huge celebration for the wedding of a son. Nothing else in Jewish experience could compare with a wedding feast.

To just such a feast, the best human life can offer, Jesus compares the kingdom of Heaven. The king's summons to the celebration is like Jesus' invitation to His disciples to enter God's kingdom. But note: the celebration is only for those who accept the invitation. Many more are invited than actually attend. The surprise of the story is that anybody would have the effrontery to reject the king's invitation.

They had been formally invited earlier, of course. The summons comes here to alert them that everything has been made ready for the feast. So the guests aren't caught off guard or surprised by the servants' announcement. They have known it would be coming soon. There can be no other explanation: their refusal to accept the invitation is nothing less than a deliberate snub.

They not only ignore the king; they abuse and kill his servants. What was intended as a festive occasion turns into a violent test of wills. In such a contest, the king will always win. He has the army.

The main thrust of the parable is obvious. Jesus narrates this tale to rebuke His nation, Israel. For centuries, God has been preparing His people for a coming celebration. God will send His Son, a Savior, to announce the kingdom of God, to save the people from their sins. He will be like the servant announcing that all preparations were in order for the king's party. Instead of an eager welcome, however, the Son suffers the same brutal rejection as the king's servants, from the very ones for whom the party has been prepared. The king's hand is forced; he must put down the rebellion and restore order.

But the preparations have been made. The oxen and fatted cattle have been butchered and are ready to be eaten. If the guests refuse to come, the king will replace them with others who, until now, might have seemed less deserving a seat at the king's table. The specific invitation has become a general one: "Go to the street corners and invite to the banquet anyone you find" (Matthew 22:6). So they come, good and bad, from the highways and byways, and the celebration is ready to begin. Others may have missed this opportunity because they were too busy with their fields or oxen or other mundane chores. They could have been feasting on the abundance of God's eternal banquet table, but they have thrown away their chance of a lifetime. Jesus' moral is clear: when God invites, accept!

The king will not be denied. He is determined to have his house filled. If society's bluebloods won't come, he'll take the poor, the crippled, the blind, the rejects and outcasts. Jesus' king belongs in this Bible story, doesn't he, because his character is so much in keeping with the God of the Bible whose burning desire is that the whole world should be saved. He dispatched His Son to search the world over in order to seek and to save the lost. (If the children of Israel reject the King's Son, then the Gentiles will banquet at His table—a recurring theme in Matthew; see 20:1-16, 21:33-46, for example.)

Read this parable in the company of the Great Commission (Matthew 28:18-20) and Jesus' instructions when He first sent His disciples out to "heal the sick, raise the dead, cleanse those who have leprosy, [and] drive out demons" (Matthew 10:5-8). Jesus' proof to John the Baptist, who sent messengers to find out if Jesus was really the Promised One, was that "the blind receive sight, the lame walk, those who have leprosy are cured, the deaf hear, the dead are raised, and the good news is preached to the poor" (Matthew 11:5). The Lord's celebration is for the ones who least expect to be invited. And God urges them to attend. That's what His grace is all about.

In verse eleven, Jesus seems to conclude one parable and begin another. His attention turns from the nature of the invitation to the preparation of the guests. The king spots a man who attends in inappropriate attire. He has just issued a general invitation, inviting persons of all walks of life to attend. But he still expects them to show proper courtesy to him and his palace by wearing clothes appropriate to the occasion. He has had the grace to invite them; they can have the grace to respect the customs of the palace.

For better or for worse, "clothes make the man." The English writer Thomas Carlyle wrote an entire book, which he entitled *Sartor Resartus,* "the tailor re-tailored," in which he explores the effect of clothing on civilization, with results both humorous and sobering. Our uniforms and costumes and styles and fads all testify to the hold of fashion on our social behavior. When we wish to signal respect, we dress accordingly; when we are ignorant or disrespectful, our clothes show it. Students in the rebellious 1960s knew precisely how to demonstrate their rejection of their parents' middle-class values: they let their hair grow long, did not shave their beards (or elsewhere), wore old, dirty, and ill-fitting clothes, and abandoned the suburban comforts of their parents for cheap slum dwellings.

The guest at the wedding feast, either deliberately or inadvertently, has offended the king by his appearance. No wedding clothes. Since many of the guests are too poor to buy their own, the king has undoubtedly supplied garments that are appropriate for the occasion. The guest only had to put it on. Is he too proud to do so? Or too careless? Or resentful? It doesn't matter. What matters is that he has offended the king by failing to do the one thing expected of him. (It is unwise to push a kindly king too far; it is likewise foolhardy to assume that the God of love and grace has no expectations of those whom He graciously invites into His company.)

What began as a story of celebration ends with the warning of eternal punishment. The laughter and joy of the wedding celebration are not for the unprepared. The outer darkness awaits them. Of the many invited, only a relative few will feast at the banquet table. They are (1) those who have no right to expect an invitation, (2) who nevertheless are invited and accept the invitation and (3) who accept also the responsibility to treat the king and his customs with respect.

Of Tips, Taxes, and Tithes (22:15-22)
(Mark 12:13-17; Luke 20:20-26)

"Politics makes strange bedfellows," the old adage goes. It strikes us as strange, indeed, to read of the Pharisees and the Herodians in the same verse. The Pharisees we are well acquainted with. Theirs was the strictest of the Jewish sects, and the most anti-establishment, politically speaking. They opposed the Romans and their puppets, the Herods. Yet here they are teaming up with the supporters of the Herodian dynasty to interrogate Jesus about tax-paying.

Actually, their partnership is more apparent than real. No matter which position Jesus takes regarding paying taxes to Caesar, He is bound to offend one of these groups or the other. The Pharisees hate the Roman tax; the Herodians are in favor of it since Roman money keeps the puppet king on his throne. So Jesus cannot win, it seems. Whichever answer He gives, they think, will mark Him as either a revolutionary (thus pleasing the Pharisees on this issue) or as submissive to Rome and Herod (thus incurring the Pharisees' wrath as much as the Herodians' pleasure).

They begin with flattery: "Teacher, we know you are a man of integrity and that you teach the way of God in accordance with the truth. You aren't swayed by men, because you pay no attention to who they are" (Matthew 22:16). It is the truth, although one wonders how much they believe it. Jesus isn't taken in: "You hypocrites (pretenders, play-actors), why are you trying to trap me?" (22:18).

But He will not be trapped. Instead, He reminds them of a principle fundamental to both Old and New Testaments. That is, that believers in God hold citizenship in two realms, the kingdom of God and the particular nation in which they temporarily reside. Since they are now now in Caesar's territory, and Caesar's image is on the coin of the realm, they have to obey the laws of Caesar's land. But they must not neglect their responsibilities to their God, either. They hold a dual citizenship. In the one, they are forced to pay taxes; in the other, they are expected to pay their tithes and go beyond tithing to generosity. (As Dr. Louis Evans has remarked, "We are born with our hands closed into fists; only when we are born again can we learn to open them.")

Three levels of loyalty are evident in this brief passage—loyalty to self, to government, and to God. These can be represented by tips, by taxes, and by tithes.

Of Tips

The lowest level is tipping, the gratuities we voluntarily give in return for a service rendered. It is not automatic; when we are displeased, we withhold the tip. It is never sent in. If we don't eat in the restaurant, we don't tip the waiter. Unfortunately, some Christians just tip God. If they are in worship Sunday, they put a little something in the offering plate; if they aren't, they don't. No service rendered, no tip offered. This is not giving to God what is God's. Jesus will have both the Herodians and the Pharisees understand that even as they are talking about taxes, they must keep God's portion in mind. He must never be reduced to the position of a servant or waiter who gets a little something when He performs well.

Of Taxes

Jesus' interrogators are good citizens who obey the laws of their land. The denarius Jesus holds (a silver coin about the size of the American dime, worth the equivalent of a laboring man's wage for a day) is Roman; the Caesar's image is on it. To use it is the privilege of those under the Emperor's protection. Such government must be paid for. So "give to Caesar what is Caesar's." Jesus does not advocate revolution against established governments, even one as corrupt as Rome's. Revolution will only replace one corrupt government with another one. Jesus' way is the way of a new kingdom, which transcends all earthly governments. Until they are removed from the dominion of earthly nations, Jesus' followers will enjoy double citizenship—and they will help in the support of both kingdoms. Government costs, and good citizens will pay taxes to meet those costs.

By calling attention to Caesar's image, Jesus diverts the Bible reader's attention to Genesis 1. On the coin is the image of the Emperor; but the Emperor was created in the image of God. On the coin itself, then, two human loyalties are depicted: loyalty to government and loyalty to God, in whose image human beings were created. Give to government what government has coming to it; give to God your Creator what God has coming to Him.

Jesus' answer deals specifically with taxes. But does the nation have the right to expect anything further? Yes. Honor, concern for your fellow citizens' welfare, obedience, loyalty, and patriotism. Then what does God have a right to expect? That we should honor Him with loyalty and obedience, of course, and that we should be concerned about the welfare of His people, the education of His children, and the fulfilling of His purposes.

Of Tithes

This brings us to the highest loyalty. We pledge our highest allegiance to God. If the government has a right to expect our taxes, God certainly has a right to expect our tithes. A percentage of the money that Jesus holds is God's. Since He owns one hundred percent of all we have anyway, He has every right to demand all He wants. He starts with the tithe (Matthew 23:23; Hebrews 7:4; Deuteronomy 14:22; Malachi 3:10). The first Christians went far beyond this minimum (Acts 2:44-46; 4:32-37). They still paid their taxes, but their giving to God exceeded their giving to Caesar.

American coins are stamped, "In God we trust."

If we believe that, we will give to God what is God's.

The Home of the Angels (22:23-33)
(Mark 12:18-27; Luke 20:27-40)

"Suddenly there was with the angel a multitude of the heavenly host . . ." (Luke 2:13, KJV). Where did they come from, these beings who appeared in the sky before the shepherds on the night Jesus was born? Where is the home of the angels?

The Bible defines *heaven* in two ways: (1) the firmament or sky, that which we see above us, and (2) the dwelling place of God and the angels.[78] The questions we have today about the nature and dwelling place of angels have their parallels in the debate on the subject between the Pharisees and Sadducees. Pharisees believed in life after death, in Heaven, and in the reality of angels. Sadducees, on the other hand, denied life after death. Elevating the Pentateuch above all other sacred writings, Sadducees would not subscribe to what the Pentateuch did not teach, and it says nothing about life beyond death. It does, however, include the law of levirate marriage (Deuteronomy 25:5), which requires a man to marry his brother's widow. From this law, they raise the hypothetical question in this passage, hoping to ridicule Jesus. So they fabricate a question about seven brothers who in succession all married the same woman. "At the resurrection, whose wife will she be of the seven?" (Matthew 22:28).

Jesus does not answer them. Instead, He introduces a discussion of the resurrection and life after death.

What is Heaven? G. B. Shaw's definition in *Man and Superman* is a good one: "Heaven is the home of the masters of reality." Angels, by this definition, are messengers from the realm of reality. When they appeared to the shepherds on that night of Jesus' birth, it was to convince them that the darkness in which they dwelt was not all there is to reality. There is more to life than we experience on earth. This world of sin and suffering and paradox is not all there is. The angels announced that for the people who live in darkness, a child has been born, a child whose very being represents reality.

Several years ago, a popular novel was making the rounds on college campuses. Written by British theologian and mathematician Edwin A. Abbot, *Flatland* presents a two-dimensional world. The characters have the attributes of length and width, that's all. No height or depth. From time to time, disturbing gossip circulates among the Flatlanders that there is a third dimension, but since

---

[78]In Standard Publishing's publications, this latter definition is signified by capitalizing the *H: Heaven.*

nobody has experienced that dimension, these reports are dismissed as rumors and nothing more. They are disturbing, nevertheless, like rumors that circulate in our three-dimensional world (or four-, if you take time into consideration) that there is another dimension beyond our experience. But since our scientists and leading thinkers refuse to admit anything that does not fit into their three-dimensioned scheme of things, these reports, too, are peremptorily dismissed.

Jesus frequently speaks of life beyond earth's dimensions. In these few verses, He shares some of His knowledge of it.

Heaven Is Where Life Continues

There will be a resurrection from the dead, and those resurrected will be like the angels in Heaven. There the living God will dwell among His living people. The "place" will not be limited to time and space like our earth, yet we must speak of it in such language because it is all we have. It is called the "city with foundations" (Hebrews 11:10); there God, the Alpha and the Omega, the Beginning and the End, presides over His people (Revelation 22:13) with His Son, who is the same yesterday, today, and forever (Hebrews 13:8). Life is not to be confined to the spatial or temporal limits of our globe, nor to the boundaries of human intelligence. The appearances of angels recorded in the Bible testify to life beyond earth's borders.

A couple of old friends, a clergyman and a professor, were sharing a few minutes together toward the end of the professor's terminal illness. "The doctors tell me that I am near the end," the professor told his friend. "Do you know what I am going to do as soon as I get into the other world? First, I shall salute my blessed Lord, and then I shall hunt up the apostle Paul and tell him just what I think of those predestination passages in the epistles!"

What strikes the eavesdropper to this conversation is the very natural manner in which these believers anticipated the next phase of their life. Death was not the end, but another beginning.

Jesus suggests that the Sadducces are too bound in their definition of life. What they cannot easily conceive, they will not believe. Jesus warns them against reducing God's domain to the limits of their limited intelligence. The sacred writings of the Jews (many of which the Sadducees rejected) held records of previous resurrections: 1 Kings 17:19-23 (Elijah brought back to earthly life the son of the widow of Zarephath) and 2 Kings 4:32-37 (Elisha raised the son of the Shunammite). The disciples have already seen Jesus raise Jairus' daughter (Matthew 9:23-25; Mark 5:35-42) and His friend Lazarus

(John 11). When they were "raised," where did they come from, if life consists of nothing beyond what can be known through the senses?

Heaven Is Where the Living Is Better

"You do not know the Scriptures or the power of God. . . . they will be like the angels in heaven" (Matthew 22:29, 30). The Sadducees make the mistake of thinking that life beyond will be similar to life here. The Scriptures present it in more glowing terms:

> Then I saw a new heaven and a new earth, for the first heaven and the first earth had passed away, and there was no longer any sea. I saw the Holy City, the new Jerusalem, coming down out of heaven from God, prepared as a bride beautifully dressed for her husband. And I heard a loud voice from the throne saying, "Now the dwelling of God is with men, and he will live with them. They will be his people, and God himself will be with them and be their God. He will wipe every tear from their eyes. There will be no more death or mourning or crying or pain, for the old order of things has passed away. (Revelation 21:1-4).
>
> No longer will there be any curse. The throne of God and of the Lamb will be in the city, and his servants will serve him. They will see his face, and his name will be on their foreheads. There will be no more night. They will not need the light of a lamp or the light of the sun, for the Lord God will give them light. And they will reign for ever and ever" (Revelation 22:3-5).

In C. S. Lewis' little book, *The Great Divorce,* the author imagines the difference in magnitude between the immensity of Heaven and the almost imperceptible tininess of Hell. A bus load of tourists from Hell visits Heaven to see whether they would like it. They wouldn't. They have already made their choices and will live with them. When one of the visitors tells his host he is ready to return, the host tries to find the crack in the Heavenly soil through which the Hell-bus had come. The visitor is astonished. He cannot believe that that infinite empty town is down some little crack. His host assures him that all Hell is smaller than a pebble of earth, and smaller than an atom of Heaven. The moral Lewis makes is that "all loneliness, angers, hatreds, envies and itchings that it contains, if rolled into one single experience and put into the scale against the least amount of the joy that is felt by the least in Heaven, would have no weight that could be registered at all. Bad cannot succeed even in being bad as truly as good is good."[79] That is how much better the living in Heaven is.

---

[79]C.S. Lewis, *The Great Divorce* (New York: Macmillan, 1946), p. 123.

Heaven Is Beyond the Limits of Language

We borrow such terms as "streets of gold," or "pearly gates" to indicate the incomparable grandeur of Heaven. But our language does it injustice. The Sadducees presuppose that life beyond goes on quite like life on earth. There is no comparison. Yet our very language misleads, since we are forced to use the only language we know, and all human language is earthbound. (We have enough trouble trying to translate from one human language into another.) Paul tries to describe his vision in what he calls the "third heaven," but words fail him (2 Corinthians 12:1-4).

Again, we have such trouble on earth. When Marco Polo returned to Europe after his thirteenth-century adventures in China and the Far East, his skeptical countrymen dismissed his reports as the ravings of a madman or charlatan. When he lay on his deathbed, some of them urged him to recant and withdraw some of the tales he had told. But he could not, since he had reported the truth. In fact, he assured them, "I have not told half of what I saw." Jesus, the man of Heaven, had similar difficulties.

Heaven Is Within the Compass of God's Love

Jesus implies that Abraham, Isaac, and Jacob, all of whom worshiped God on earth, are alive with Him now, since God "is not the God of the dead but of the living" (Matthew 22:32). This living, loving God holds His own to himself. He counts the hairs of our heads; He notices the sparrows that fall; He hears a baby's cry. One woman, after attending the funeral of her father, said, "Every time the door swings to let a loved one through from the world of the visible to the world of the invisible, I feel more confidence in the divine care." That is a Christian's confidence.

In 1892, James Martineau, one of England's great preachers, went to Dublin University as an honored visitor at the University's three hundredth anniversary celebration. Sixty-three years earlier, he had lived in Dublin. At that time, his wife gave birth to a baby girl, who very soon died and was buried there. Years went by, and everyone but the father and mother forgot the little one who had so briefly lived. Then his wife died, and he alone remembered. At eighty-seven years of age, James Martineau slipped away from the university festivities to stand alone beside a tiny grave in a cemetery. It had been sixty-three years, but he had not forgotten.

Another Parent does not forget, either. Now or forever.

He is the Parent of the living.

Caught in a Triangle of Love (22:34-40)
(Mark 12:28-34; Luke 10:25-37)

Christians are not entirely free from the restraints of law. In fact, they are under the most demanding of all laws, the law of love. When Jesus quotes the greatest commandment in the law of Moses, He combines two separate commands that assume a third element. Love is the greatest commandment, and its elements are three: love of God, love of neighbor, and love of self.

I Love Me

Love begins with self-concern. Love of God or of neighbor is impossible apart from love of self. "Love your neighbor *as* yourself" (Matthew 22:39). The Bible teaches that God loves you and that Jesus gave His life for you and is now preparing a place for you, so it is expected that you should love yourself. It is possible to sin here, of course, and confuse self-love with self-indulgence, which is another matter entirely. Because of this confusion, the Bible urges us not to make gods of ourselves: "There will be terrible times in the last days. People will be lovers of themselves, lovers of money, boastful, proud, abusive, disobedient to their parents, ungrateful, unholy, without love, unforgiving, slanderous, without self-control, brutal, not lovers of the good, treacherous, rash, conceited, lovers of pleasure rather than lovers of God" (2 Timothy 3:1-4). This catalog of sins describes the consequences of self-indulgence. "Lovers of themselves" do not so much build upon self-love as elevate the self to the position of a god to be served without reserve. Their sin is idolatry.

Spinoza's definition of love in his *Ethics* is helpful: "Love is nothing but joy accompanied with the idea of an external cause, and hatred is nothing but sorrow with the accompanying idea of an external cause. We see too that he who loves a thing necessarily endeavors to keep it before him and to preserve it, and on the other hand, he who hates a thing necessarily endeavors to remove and destroy it." Spinoza helps us to understand that much self-indulgent behavior is motivated by hatred, not love, of self.

What Christ calls us to is real self-love. Thomas Wolfe, in his essay, "God's Lonely Man," points out that the writings of the Old Testament combine to produce an image of man's loneliness. The New Testament, on the other hand, produces another unified image, in this case, one of man's loneliness destroyed by the life of love. Your mind thinks of Noah, fending off the barbs of ridicule thrown by disbelieving neighbors; or of Elijah single-handedly combatting the priests of Baal and inviting the wrath of Jezebel; or of Amos, the lonely shepherd, the solitary prophet attacking corrupt luxury in Israel; or of Nehemiah, or Ezra, or any one of multitudes of "God's lonely men." In the New Testament, Wolfe suggests, we do not think of individuals (except, perhaps, John the Baptist, who is really a holdover from the great days of the prophets) so much as groups: disciples, apostles, elders, congregations. Loneliness has been abolished by love. Jesus does not send His followers out separately, but two by two. He does not expect them to invite individual martyrdom. He commands them to love each other, to remain in fellowship with one another, to abide in Him as He abides in them, in love. Jesus' teachings and modeling stress His belief that love of self and love of neighbor are inseparable. In order to preserve myself, I must love another.

I Love You

In the final analysis, I cannot really love me unless I love you. So long as I am determined to save myself, to serve myself, to worship myself, to be my own god, I guarantee my loneliness. But if I can really learn to love you, another person, my best self comes forth in the very act of loving. When Jesus lifts up the commandment to love my neighbor, He assumes the definition of neighbor He has taught in the parable of the good Samaritan (my neighbor is anyone who needs my mercy, anytime, anywhere). His definition of love does not limit it to mere emotion, either. You cannot command an emotion. He treats love as a law to be obeyed. As Hugh Bishop of Mirfield words it in one of his books, "Love is not an emotion. It is a policy."

Martin Niemoller, a Protestant scholar in Europe during World War II, has written about the religious and political persecution of the Jews under Hitler. "In Germany the Nazis came for the Communists, and I didn't speak up because I was not a Communist. Then they came for the Jews and I didn't speak up because I was not a Jew. Then they came for the Trade Unionists and I didn't speak up because I was not a Trade Unionist. Then they came for the Catholics and I was a Protestant so I didn't speak up. Then they came for me—but by that time there was no one to speak up for anyone." He confesses that his failure to act in love on behalf of his neighbors left him without neighbors when he needed help. Self-love and neighbor-love cannot be separated. If you live by a policy of love, you become involved with others who do not agree with you, whose politics and religion may differ from yours. You are not commanded to agree with them— just love them.

In 1979, a young man named Tom Tucker was flying his plane across Oklahoma when its engine failed. He looked for a clearing, but as he landed his plane, he overshot the clearing and crashed into the trees. His forehead was crushed, the roof of his mouth split completely in two, his jaw broken in nine places. He was rushed to the hospital's emergency room, where the attending surgeon gave him about ten minutes to live. Nevertheless, he made a desperate attempt to save him by surgery. The surgeon labored over him for nine and a half hours, and as he completed what turned out to be a successful series of operations, he growled to his nurse as he left the operating room, "If that guy dies now, I'll kill him!"

Why did he care? He was a surgeon, doing his duty, that's all. Or is it? No, something else happened, something Jesus would call love. The dying man brought out the very best in the surgeon. He became obsessed with the man's welfare. He gave his all to preserve. This is why the Bible ties self-love with love of our neighbor. We need somebody, lots of somebodies, to bring out the best in us. So long as we content ourselves with ourselves, we never really discover who we are, what we have, or what we can do or give. Only through love of another—another who cannot repay us—can we become our best.

Love of neighbor is well defined by the apostle Paul in 1 Corinthians 13:4-8. What he describes is not emotion, but willful policy:

> Love is patient, love is kind.
> It does not envy, it does not boast, it is not proud.
> It is not rude, it is not self-seeking, it is not easily angered, it keeps
> no record of wrongs.
> Love does not delight in evil but rejoices with the truth.
> It always protects, always trusts, always hopes, always perseveres.
> Love never fails.

I Love God

We have saved Jesus' first quotation for our last: "Love the Lord your God with all your heart and with all your soul and with all your mind" (Matthew 22:37). Everything in the Old and New Testaments is predicated on the existence of God and His love for man. Apart from that love, we would not exist. Love of God is gratitude for the gift of life. It is becoming attuned to the source of reality. It is essential to being totally alive.

Leviticus 19 is the chapter from which Jesus quotes His second commandment: "Love your neighbor as yourself." The same chapter contains a catalog of little commands to be obeyed just because you love God. Let's look at some of them.

"Each of you must respect his mother and father, and you must observe my Sabbaths. *I am the Lord your God*" (v. 3).

"Do not turn to idols or make gods of cast metal for yourselves. *I am the Lord your God*" (v. 4).

"When you reap the harvest of your land, do not reap to the very edges of your field or gather the gleanings of your harvest. . . . *I am the Lord your God*" (vs. 9, 10).

"Do not curse the deaf or put a stumbling block in front of the blind, *but fear your God. I am the Lord*" (v. 14).

"Do not do anything that endangers your neighbor's life. *I am the Lord*" (v. 16).

"Do not seek revenge or bear a grudge against one of your people, but love your neighbor as yourself. *I am the Lord*" (v. 18).

"When you enter the land and plant any kind of fruit tree, regard its fruit as forbidden. For three years you are to consider it forbidden; it must not be eaten. In the fourth year all its fruit will be holy, an offering of praise to the Lord. But in the fifth year you may eat its fruit. In this way your harvest will be increased. *I am the Lord your God*" (vs. 23-25).

"Do not cut your bodies for the dead or put tattoo marks on yourselves. *I am the Lord*" (v. 28).

Other regulations follow, governing the mating of cattle, the making of clothing, sexual behavior, diet and personal hygiene, and family relations. All of them are interpreted as logical extensions of the fact that "I am the Lord your God." Having the Lord as your God will make a difference in big and little things: the way you treat your neighbors and family, the care you give your animals and grain and clothes. Acknowledging Him as your God includes admitting that He is God of all people everywhere. "If you love Me, you will be what I want you to be and you will treat others and yourself as I want you to. Then you will understand that love of God cannot be divorced from love of others and of self. You will observe that I have created an order to be preserved. You belong to the earth and to your fellow human beings and to Me." Bernard of Clairvaux centuries ago prepared a little ladder of spiritual growth. This is his order:

> Love of self for self's sake. [Here is where we begin. I love me for me.]
> Love of God for self's sake. [I love God for what He can do for me.]
> Love of God for God's sake. [I love Him because He's the Creator, because He gives life, because He is powerful, merciful.]

275

Love of self for God's sake. [He made me. He is my Father. I will make Him proud of me, so that he won't feel He made a mistake in creating me.]

Bernard could well have expanded his ladder, to include our love of neighbors. But we already know about that. And we know how blessed it is to be caught up in a triangle of love.

Son of David or Son of God? (22:41-46)
(Mark 12:35-37; Luke 20:41-44)

Since morning Jesus has been under fire from His critics (Matthew 21:18, 23). Now it is His turn. He challenges them with a question that at first seemed so elementary as to be insulting to men of their religious training. When Jesus asks, "What do you think about the Christ?" He is not inquiring of their opinion about himself. The question is more abstract. What do they believe about the Messiah? They obviously do not accept Jesus as the Christ. What then do they expect of the Christ?

He is "the son of David," they predictably reply. Every Jew would have answered the same. David was Israel's greatest king. God had promised David that He would establish David's kingdom to last forever (2 Samuel 7:16). When Jesus entered Jerusalem to the shouts of the people, He could hear in their praises that they believed Him to be the Messiah, for they called Him the Son of David (Matthew 21:9). For centuries, the oppressed nation had looked for one of David's descendants to reestablish his great kingdom. He would be a political and military giant; under his dynamic leadership, Israel would throw off any other power (currently Rome) that ruled over the nation.

To correct this erroneous assumption, Jesus gives the Pharisees a little Bible lesson. He does not dispute their anticipation that the Messiah will be of the lineage of David. The point of His lesson is that the Christ will be more than simply a nationalistic hero. Even the great David, in Psalm 110:1 (universally accepted by the Jews as a song about the coming Messiah), sang about the Lord (God) speaking to "my Lord" (the Christ). Thus, says Jesus, David acknowledged that the Messiah was his Lord. His Lord could not be his son, could he? That is, just his son? Something more is to be expected of Him, then, than merely the resurrection of David's kingdom. The Pharisees are blind to Jesus' Messiahship because they have too narrowly defined the Messiah's role. His kingdom is vaster than Israel; His is the kingdom of God. He is not only Son of David, but Son of God.

CHAPTER TWENTY-FOUR

The Faith That Can Face the Future

Matthew 23, 24

In Praise of Simple Religion (23:1-39)
(Mark 12:38-40; Luke 11:39-50, 13:34, 35)

Older readers of these pages will fondly remember the great black American singer Marian Anderson, of whom it was said that she had not simply grown great, but she had grown great simply. When a reporter asked her to name the greatest moment in her life, she had many choices. She could have mentioned the time when Toscanini told her that hers was the finest voice of the century, or the evening when she gave a White House concert for the Roosevelts and the King and Queen of England. Then there was the $10,000 Bok Award she received as the person who had done the most for her hometown, Philadelphia. She could have recalled the Easter Sunday in Washington when she stood beneath the Lincoln statue and sang for a crowd of 75,000 that included cabinet members, Supreme Court justices, and most congressmen.

She did not speak of any of these. She said her greatest moment was the day she went home and told her mother she would not have to take in washing anymore.

Hers were the simple virtues that make for great living. Matthew 23, on the other hand, is about people who complicate life, especially religious life. Ever since the Jews had returned to Jerusalem (around 450 B.C.), they thought of themselves as people of the law (Nehemiah 8:1-10). Such people need lawyers, of course, so many Jews made themselves experts in preserving and interpreting the law. (These are the scribes or "teachers of the law" so often mentioned in the Bible.) Between Nehemiah's day and Jesus', fifty volumes of regulations that "explained" or "interpreted" the law had been amassed.

In 175 B.C., Antiochus Epiphanes of Syria did his best to stamp out Judaism and replace it with the Greek religions and practices he favored. During this period, the Pharisees—Separatists—arose. This sect of Jews—at most there were never more than 6,000 of them—were really the best of the best. They revered the law and taught

277

others to do so. Jesus found himself in agreement with most of their teachings, and He regularly urged His disciples to be as serious about their faith as the Pharisees were. They were good teachers.

But many of them were bad examples. They were like a well-known Bible professor of a generation or two ago. In the classroom, he was a brilliant interpreter of the Bible. His influence over his students was almost hypnotic. Few could sit at his feet for long without being inspired by his insights into God's Word and being persuaded to his point of view. But off campus, he often destroyed what he accomplished in class sessions. His rudeness, especially to persons he perceived to be his social inferiors, embarrassed everyone with him. After a few hours in his company on such occasions, many former disciples could not listen to his Biblical expositions again. He was a good teacher, but such a bad example that he canceled his words by his actions.

This is Jesus' opinion of the Pharisees and teachers of the law, who "sit in Moses' seat" (as professors authorized to explain the correct meaning and application of Moses' laws). Jesus' disciples do well to obey their teaching, but would be ill advised to follow their example. Jesus knows them well. They have already made themselves His enemies. They have sought every opening to criticize and heckle Him. In the end, they look for a way to kill Him.

Yet they seem so respectable. Of course they do, because that is one of their chief goals. Jesus castigates them on at least these counts:

(1) You don't practice what you preach (3).

(2) Your rules are a burden to sincere people (4).

(3) You put on a good show to win men's applause (5-7).

(4) You glory in titles and honors (8-12). Jesus' disciples, on the other hand, are not to seek to be honored with titles like "rabbi" or "father" or even "teacher." They are to take nothing away from the Father or the Son. They are to remember they are servants, not masters. If there is to be any exalting, God is to do it!

(5) You are keeping people out of the kingdom of God (13). You are hypocrites, pretending to be serving God but really just using your religious role to puff yourselves up. You won't heed My teaching about the kingdom of God, and you do everything you can to keep others from hearing and obeying. You won't repent and you won't let anyone else repent, if you can help it. (Verse 14 is reduced to a footnote in recent versions of the Bible, since it is not found in the most reliable early manuscripts. It is quite in keeping with the rest of Jesus' denunciations, however. His heart always goes out to widows,

who are often helpless to prevent themselves from being taken by unscrupulous profiteers.)

(6) Your converts are worse, not better, than before their conversion (15). As students often surpass the fanaticism of their teachers, so yours invite an even more disastrous judgment than you do.

(7) You complicate even such matters as oath-taking (16-21). We already know Jesus' opinion concerning oaths: Matthew 5:33-37. The prevailing principle seems to have been to swear by the greater, so the Pharisees thought an oath "by the gold in the temple" would be more binding than swearing by the temple (made of stone) itself. All this does not matter to Jesus, who would do away with the whole system of swearing oaths.

(8) You commendably practice some doctrines—like tithing—while completely ignoring weightier matters like justice, mercy, and faithfulness (22-24). Mint and anise and cummin were garden herbs used in cooking and for certain medicinal purposes. The tithing of herbs was considered the ultimate in religious piety.

(9) You scrupulously observe the external niceties of religion while leaving the inner person unreformed (25-28).

(10) You honor dead prophets but, like true descendants of their murderers, you do as your forefathers did (29-32).

(11) When I send "prophets and wise men and teachers" to you, you will prove yourselves to be as quick to kill as your forefathers killed the prophets who came to them (33-36). The first reference is to Zechariah the son of Jehoiada the priest, who was slain in the court of the temple—2 Chronicles 24:20f. The second is to Abel, son of Adam, who was slain by his brother Cain, the first of a long and inglorious line of murderers—Genesis 4:10.

It is instructive to compare this passage with a similar list of grievances that Moses presents in the so-called "Song of Moses" in Deuteronomy 32. Grieved by Israel's failure to be true to their God, Moses recalls his people to their former relationship with the One who brought them out of slavery in Egypt. Reproach and tenderness mingle together in Moses' song, just as they do in Jesus' catalog of woes.

Jesus is not fooled by the piety of the religious. Nor is He overly impressed with their theological education. One cannot help wondering whether Jesus would have agreed, at least partially, with Walter Kaufmann's scathing critique of theology: "Theology is a comprehensive, rigorous, and systematic attempt to conceal the beam in the

Scriptures and traditions of one's own denomination while minutely measuring the mote in the heritage of one's brothers." It is so easy to twist theology into the service of religious ambition, when it was intended to be the servant of religious truth.[80]

Throughout these seven expressed "woes" and the introductory (2-12) and concluding (37-39) remarks, Jesus implicitly praised the virtues He found so obviously missing in His critics: simple faith and simple honesty.

Simple Faith

"You Pharisees and teachers of the law have complicated what God intended to be simple and within the reach of all His people." In another context (John 6:28, 29), Jesus tries to deliver His followers from the bondage of religion by works. "What must we do to do the works God requires?" The Pharisees and teachers, you remember, had a fifty-volume answer to that question. They had a rule for every occasion, and some for no occasion at all. Jesus' answer is simplicity itself: "The work of God is this: to believe in the one he has sent." That's it. No phylacteries, no tassles, no sales of indulgences, no books of discipline, nothing else.

Just believe. Everything else flows from belief. Believe in Jesus. Do not even place your faith in the miraculous signs He gives you, but in Him.

This is too simple for some people, certainly for the Pharisees and teachers of the law. Even the clothes they wore had to be regulated, they believed. Their phylacteries were especially precious. These were little leather boxes with portions of Scripture inside—Exodus 13:1-10, 11-16; Deuteronomy 6:4-9; 11:13-21—worn on the forehead and arm in accordance with a literal interpretation of Deuteronomy 6:8. From about the second century B.C., male Jews were expected to wear these at morning prayers (except on the Sabbath); on festival occasions, they were to wear them on the forehead and the left arm. Some men invited ridicule (at least from Jesus) by their apparent belief that "the bigger the better," just as they thought that the longer the tassel on their prayer shawl, the greater their virtue.

Faith in God is not expressed in clothes or phylacteries, Jesus insists. It has to do with belief, especially now belief in the Son whom the Father has sent. Not in rabbis or teachers or preachers or

---

[80]Walter Kaufmann, *The Faith of a Heretic* (New York: Meredian Books, 1978), p. 104.

theologians or anyone else! Faith in Christ, as He never tired of saying, is expressed in humble service, not in showy display.

Simple Honesty

Jesus' displeasure with oaths (16-22, 25-28) is rooted in His conviction that oaths are unnecessary among honest people (Matthew 5:33-37). Again, the religious regulators had determined that certain oaths were binding and others were not. But an honest person needs nothing more than his word.

In this respect, Jesus' critics were realists. They knew that most of the world is hypocritical. Honesty does not come easy to us, especially honesty about ourselves. Mark Twain is not the only person to observe that "we do not deal much in facts when we are contemplating ourselves." In Schiller's great biography of Frederick the Great, the monarch's visit to Potsdam prison is recounted. As he questions each of the prisoners in turn, every one assures him of his innocence. They had been framed, each and all. But then he came to an exception. One prisoner looked at the floor and said quietly, "Your majesty, I am guilty, and richly deserving punishment."

Frederick called the warden: "Free this rascal and get him out of our prison before he corrupts all the noble innocent people here."

There is freedom in honesty, although not always the kind that Frederick was authorized to award. Jesus said, "If you hold to my teaching, you are really my disciples. Then you will know the truth, and the truth will set you free" (John 8:31, 32). To know the truth and to speak the truth—these are liberating. Lying, manipulating, pretending, scheming, and game-playing entangle a person in a confusion of rules and regulations and defensive maneuvers that kill genuine spontaneity. How free is the person who has nothing to hide and nothing to prove!

The honest person does not need to utter an oath to be believed. He pays attention to the doctrines governing tithes while not overlooking attitudes that affect his treatment of other people. He takes care to see that what he seems on the outside corresponds to what he is on the inside. He will not kill (29-36) to prove anything; he trusts the truth to take care of itself. He is simply honest.

After all has been said, Jesus cannot wish His critics ill. Often before, He has longed to save Jerusalem (37-39), but Jerusalem's inhabitants (and, by implication, its Pharisees and teachers of the law) have refused Him. Since they have rejected their only hope, their future will be tragic.

What Our Future Holds (24:1-31)
(Mark 13; Luke 21:5-36)

Jesus is in the final week of His pre-crucifixion ministry. He knows what is ahead for Him; His disciples sense it, too. Jesus has been speaking more and more frequently about His future and theirs as He has approached His inevitable capture by His enemies. His vision is not limited to the immediate, however. He looks beyond, to the fall of Jerusalem, to the persecution that will befall His disciples after His departure, and on to His second coming and the end of the age. Matthew weaves several of Jesus' futuristic themes together, so that it is often difficult to know precisely which He is speaking of at any one moment.

It seems that in Matthew 24:4-14, Jesus has in mind all of future history. He warns His disciples that they must not hastily interpret calamities like wars and earthquakes as sure-fire proof that history is about to end. Verses 15-28, on the other hand, appear to be more restricted to the destruction of Jerusalem. With verse 29, He picks up the theme of the second coming.

When the disciples of Jesus mention "the end of the age," they phrase their question in language that their contemporaries would readily understand. Jews divided time into two ages, (1) the present age (which is bad), and (2) the age to come (which will be good). Between the two ages is the Day of the Lord, accompanied by terrible, sudden, universe-shattering upheaval and moral chaos. Jews fervently awaited the Day of the Lord and the age to come. Jesus' disciples are not exceptional, then, in wishing to know what their Teacher has to say on the subject.

Matthew's setting for these teachings is the Mount of Olives, after Jesus and His men have left the temple. The temple, a massive complex of buildings and porches and paved courts, is the Jews' central symbol. It represents God to them (not as an idol but as a place to worship Him) and it signifies permanence and security for the nation. Yet, says Jesus, a destruction is coming that will so devastate the temple that "not one stone here will be left on another; every one will be thrown down." Beware of placing your trust in things, no matter how secure they seem.

"When will this happen?" (Matthew 24:3). Interpreting the temple's fall as the signal of Jesus' return and the end of the age, the disciples ask for a sign so they will be ready. The answer given offers six specific things for the disciples to look for. Some of them indicate the end of the age, others are simple instructions for living in end times. (Some Bible students, by the way, believe that the entire passage has to do with the fall of Jerusalem, a catastrophe so overwhelming to the Jewish people who believed that Jerusalem, the Holy City, was the real capital of the world, that its destruction would usher in the end of the age. It would be an attack on God himself; God would have to retaliate with such force that it would be like nothing less than the end of the world.) Here is what Jesus has to say:

There Will Be False Messiahs (3-5)

The first century abounded in revolutionaries that appealed to Jewish patriotism and religious fervor by announcing themselves as the Messiah. Don't be misled by them, Jesus counsels. It is good advice. A quick survey of church history makes a student wonder whether there has ever been an age since Christ that has not generated a multitude of false messiahs. The first century was beset by them. So is ours. Cults of every description cluster around charismatic leaders who either openly or subtly claim, "I am the Christ." The most blatant phony in many years was Jim Jones, leader of the People's Church in California, who persuaded over 900 of his devotees to follow him to Guyana, where they all eventually died in a mass suicide inspired by Jones. Earlier, this charismatic leader had grumbled that too many of his people were following the Bible instead of him. He succeeded in diverting their loyalty from the Bible to blind faith in him as the reincarnate Christ, even as God. Such demagogues have no trouble in gathering a following. The world is full of scared, timid souls who are afraid of the future and afraid of the present. They seek an authority figure to take over their thinking and deciding. They also want a Christ or a prophet who can detail future events for them.

But that is the difference between true and false prophets, between a Greek seer, for example, and a Jewish prophet. Seers believed that everything was decreed by fate, so man had no freedom. Thus in Sophocles' *Oedipus Rex,* the ancient seer Tiresias could easily foretell events, since he had been granted prophetic insight into a future that was immutably mapped out by the gods. Israel's prophets could never do that. They were limited to proclaiming what God would do if His people refused to change their ways. But God grants people the freedom to act; He does not dictate every detail of their future. So if the people were to change, God would be free to change His plans, also. The message of the prophets, then, was not a preview of coming events, but a call for moral responsibility and a return to God. They did not, like Jim Jones, promise security from all harm if the people would just follow them; they did not even present themselves as authority figures around whom a warm community could gather. The true prophets, like the true Messiah, preached repentance; they sought righteousness. No crystal balls for them.

There Will Be Human and Natural Disasters (6-8)

Do not be alarmed; these things must happen, but they do not signal the end. Uprisings and famines and earthquakes are just the beginning of birth pains. Do not put too much stock in any of these things.

The first century suffered famines (Acts 11:27-30); it was beset by earthquakes. (The Roman writer Suetonius reports that the earth shook so violently in Rome one autumn that 30,000 people died there; elsewhere whole cities were wiped out.) For two thousand years, each generation has enumerated the disasters of its era and announced, "This is it!"

But still the earth survives.

Christians Will Be Persecuted (9-14)

Jesus speaks to the disciples with Him at the moment and through them to all of us who follow Him. From the earliest days of the church (2 Corinthians 11:23-27; Acts 7:57-60; 12:1, 2), some believers in every generation have experienced persecution, or at least hostile opposition, because of their faithfulness to Christ. At its heart, the Christian message—as well as the Christian life—invites hostility. We cannot fully participate in the life-style or values of our society. As Christians take a stand against evil in any form, you can bet your life there will be persecution.

A powerful Christian woman in a major American city has recently been frightening her friends because of her bold stand against evil. Her section of the city has been suffering urban blight for several years. Its most pernicious form has been the proliferating of topless bars, pornographic book stores, prostitution solicitation, and other unsavory businesses. Single-handedly, this woman, a widow and retired businesswoman, has taken them all on in her effort to clean up her neighborhood. She has stormed their businesses, recruited city officials to accompany her on her raids, enlisted her church leaders to assist her, and has raised the level of her neighborhood's consciousness. Her friends are frightened because she is courting opposition. She isn't afraid, though. "I'm 76 years of age. I've had a good life. If it ends, it's O.K." She is a realist; she knows you cannot fight evil without paying a price.

You will be hated by nations; you will be deserted and betrayed and hated by fellow Christians; you will be in danger of being deceived by false prophets. The love many people now feel for God and for fellow believers will grow cold. Only steadfast believers, who may have to endure persecution for their faith, will be saved. In the midst of all this turbulence, the good news of the kingdom of God will continue to be preached, eventually reaching throughout the whole world. The end will not come until then. (If Jesus is thinking of the end of Jerusalem here, His words have been literally fulfilled, since the Gospel was preached to the "known" world of the Roman Empire before A.D. 70, when Titus entered Jerusalem.)

Evil Will Apparently Triumph (15-22)

"So when you see standing in the holy place 'the abomination that causes desolation....'" Jesus is referring to Daniel (9:27; 11:31; 12:11). One hundred fifty years earlier, Antiochus Epiphanes of Syria overran Jerusalem and Judea. A typical conqueror, this despot then made moves to replace the God of Israel with his own god. He desecrated the temple by erecting an altar to Zeus in the temple court. Then he insulted God and Israel by sacrificing swines' flesh on the altar and transforming the priests' rooms and temple chambers into brothels. "When you see such things, get out of here."

To their great regret, when Jerusalem was besieged in A.D. 70, its citizens did just the opposite of what Jesus told them. They fled *into* the city from all over the countryside, presenting themselves in huge numbers to Syrians eager for the slaughter.

False Rumors and False Saviors Will Abound (23-28)

Twice in this chapter, we read the same warning against false Christs. This warning naturally follows the warning about evil's apparent triumph. When it appears that evil has triumphed, people will desperately seek a messiah to lead them. Note also that Jesus does not deny that these phonies will be able to work miracles with their magical abilities and prophecies that sound like truth. They will quickly amass a following of gullible disciples. Beware of them.

Many contemporary cults flourish in these tense days because they pretend to predict the exact date of the end of the world. One such cult has published several dates for the Battle of Armageddon, each one proving as wrong as the former one. *Eternity* magazine (October, 1980) quotes the predictions of Jehovah's Witness officials during the past century:

> 1889: Armageddon, "which will end in 1914 ... is already commenced."
> 1914: "The present great war in Europe is the beginning of the Armageddon of the Scriptures."
> 1918: "We may confidently expect that 1925 will mark the return of Abraham, Isaac, Jacob, and the faithful prophets of old."
> 1922: "The date 1925 is even more distinctly indicated by the Scriptures than 1914."
> 1931: "There was a measure of disappointment on the part of Jehovah's faithful ones on earth concerning the years 1914, 1918, and 1925, which disappointment lasted for a time ... and they also learned to quit fixing dates."
> 1941: "... work in the remaining months before Armageddon."
> 1968: "Why are you looking forward to 1975?"
> 1975: "We never predicted when Armageddon would come. We said 6000 years of human existence will terminate in 1975."

It is a precarious business, this basing of a religious movement on the fixing of God's dates. Since He will come "as lightning that comes from the east and flashes to the west," it makes little sense to fuss over the specific moment. For the believer, there is nothing to fear in the Lord's appearing.

The Lord Will Come (29-31)

Jesus borrows the language of Isaiah (13:10; 34:4—and Ezekiel 32:7, 8) to picture the heavenly transfiguration that will accompany the Son of Man's return. There is nothing for a believer to fear. If you are in the Lord, who is Lord of today and tomorrow, of this earth and its universe, of history and the future, then you have nothing to be afraid of. He will gather His elect together to be with Him.

What, then, can be concluded from this first portion of Jesus' address on the future? At least this much is certain:

—Wickedness is not going to win, regardless of appearances.

—You have no reason to lose hope, even in the midst of persecution.

—Judgment is coming for the whole human race.

—So keep faithful. In your faithfulness is your salvation and your peace. Jesus offers just enough information about the future to prevent our giving way to speculation while offering encouragement for living courageously in the present.

No One Knows the Hour (24:36-51)
(Mark 13; Luke 21:5-36)

The entire twenty-fourth chapter of Matthew answers the disciples' question, "Tell us, when will this happen, and what will be the sign of your coming and of the end of the age?" (Matthew 24:3). In this final section of the chapter, Jesus repeatedly returns to a theme that is one of the constants of His ministry. No one knows the hour.

The Hour of the Lord's Return

Not even the Son knows, only the Father. Since the moment is unknown, Jesus' disciples must live a life that is prepared for His return at any moment.

Like a good teacher who approaches his lesson from several angles, Jesus employs a number of examples to emphasize this point. He reaches back to Genesis, to Noah and the flood. "As it was in the days of Noah, so it will be at the coming of the Son of Man" (Matthew 24:37). Noah was ready. He had heeded the voice of the Lord and he had built his ark, so he and his family were saved when the waters rose. His neighbors must have had great sport laughing at this eccentric man who built his ark on dry land. But while they scoffed, Noah kept at his calling. Then it was his turn to laugh, although he probably didn't. (See Genesis 6-9; Hebrews 11:7; 1 Peter 3:20.)

Jesus next takes a couple of examples from daily life. "Two men will be in the field.... two women will be grinding ...one will be taken and the other left" (Matthew 24:40, 41). Jesus does not hint that they should be doing anything other than their usual work. He does not propose that they run to a mountaintop and wait for His appearing. For centuries, so-called prophets have emotionally bullied their followers into fleeing homes and employment for a desert or mountaintop to await the coming of the Lord. That is exactly what Jesus does not encourage us to do. His return will be so swift you will have no time to prepare. So live that, no matter when He comes, you will be found faithful.

> Happy are those whom [judgment] finds laboring in their vocations, whether they were merely going out to feed the pigs or laying some good plans to deliver humanity a hundred years hence from some great evil. The curtain has indeed now fallen. Those pigs will never in fact be fed, the great campaign against white slavery or governmental tyranny will never in fact proceed to victory. No matter; you were at your post when the inspection came.[81]

---

[81]C.S. Lewis, quoted by Robert G. Clouse, *The Meaning of the*

To these very simple illustrations of everyday life, Jesus adds two equally simple parables. The first, of the thief in the night, elicits a sympathetic response from most readers today. Probably the majority of us have been robbed at one time or another. Upon discovering the theft, we have blurted out, "Oh, if only I had known. I'd have...." What is that famous little saying we have? Something about closing the barn door after the horse has run away? If only we had known! Such will be the lament of those surprised by the Lord's return.

The second has the same moral: wise is the servant who is always busy about his appointed tasks, because he cannot predict when his master will return. If he should not be faithfully serving, his fate is gruesome. The parable needs no explanation. All employers understand it immediately. In an organization of any size, there are faithful and unfaithful workers. You can count on some to do the job even when the boss isn't looking; others won't give their best even when he stands right beside them.

Our Heavenly Master is away temporarily. He cannot give us the precise minute or hour—or day or year—He'll return. Wise is the Christian who does not gamble that he has plenty of time. Instead, he adopts the policy of this little poem from William Barclay's commentary:

> There's a king and a captain high,
> And he's coming by and by,
> And he'll find me hoeing cotton when he comes.
> You can hear his legions charging in the regions of the sky,
> And he'll find me hoeing cotton when he comes.
> There's a man they thrust aside,
> Who was tortured till he died,
> And he'll find me hoeing cotton when he comes.
> He was hated and rejected, He was scorned and crucified,
> And he'll find me hoeing cotton when he comes.
> When he comes! When he comes!
> He'll be crowned by saints and angels when he comes.
> They'll be shouting out Hosanna! to the man that men denied,
> And I'll kneel among my cotton when he comes.[82]

Millennium: Four Views (Downers Grove: Intervarsity Press, 1977), p. 212. This is an unusually helpful book on this subject.

[82]William Barclay, *The Gospel of Matthew,* Volume 2 (Philadelphia: Westminster Press, second edition, 1958), p. 351.

The Hour of Death

The passage is about the unknown hour of Jesus' return, but its overtones of preparation for death are too loud to be passed over. The Lord will return only once, but in every generation, everybody dies; sometimes death strikes with terrible suddenness. Blessed are those who are ready.

On November 26, 1982, an article appeared in the Phoenix, Arizona, newspaper. "Woman Killed on Freeway," its headline read. It reported that in the heavy evening traffic, a woman struck a dog on the freeway. She immediately pulled her car over to the median and stopped, then darted across the highway to offer the dog what help she could. An oncoming car hit her and killed her instantly. Then several more hit her.

The newspaper article did not report that Laura K. Hubka was a Christian.

This last fact made all the difference to the man whose car killed her. A member of my church, he was deeply shaken by the unavoidable tragedy. There was no way he could have avoided her. A sensitive person, he was paralyzed by what he had done. He suffered inescapable pangs of guilt. He was concerned about her family and about her spiritual condition. I was able to contact her pastor and learned, much to everyone's great relief, that she and her husband were dedicated Christians. Her death was still a shock, but now everything could be accepted in a new perspective.

A few days following her funeral, I found a hand-delivered letter on my desk. It was from Laura's husband. It contains a couple of factual errors, but its Christian content is memorable:

> "Dear Loved Ones in Christ: It was my wife's funeral yesterday. I was talking with my pastor concerning the love you all displayed at the news of my wife's death. All through the service I kept thinking of what Paul wrote in I Thessalonians 4:13, in which he told those in Christ not to be overcome with sorrow as the unbelievers who have no hope, for we have the hope of the resurrection of Christ and the assurance that one day we in Christ will all be reunited with our loved ones in Him. The Lord has sustained me with His strength, comforted me with His love, and encourages me with His word.
>
> During these past days of dark sorrow, the Lord showed me that even though we yearn so eagerly to be with the Lord, He yearns even more eagerly for us to be united with Him in fullness, where never again would we have to feel pain or sorrow. It was Lori's time to be united with Him, and knowing what a beautiful woman Lori was inwardly as well as outwardly, I can certainly understand why He wanted her with Him. If she had to die, I am just thankful that death

came quickly and mercifully, for the highway patrolman who brought me the news of Lori's death told me that she never knew what hit her.

As I understand it, the woman whose car struck Lori is a member of your congregation. I want to assure her that there is absolutely no bitterness on my part towards her. Bitterness is absolutely foreign to the nature of our Lord Jesus Christ, and His nature dwells in me. Let this woman be assured that I love her with the love of Christ, and my prayers go up to God for her, as I know that this is a difficult time for her also.

I am very proud of Lori in the way she died, for there is no doubt in my heart that if Jesus were driving on the Superstition freeway and hit a dog, that Jesus, like Lori, would have stopped and tried to save that dog, taking no thought for His own life. I know from the Scriptures that when He was in Gethsemane, He did not want to go to the cross, but He also knew what would become of the whole human race if He did not go. He knew His Father's will, and became obedient unto death so that through death He could give life to all who would receive Him as savior. Jesus, like Lori, cast aside His concern for His life in order to save those in danger. Lori certainly demonstrated the fullness of Christ in her life by her death. . . ."

She was ready. She was doing what Christ would do. She was beautiful inside and out. Therefore, she can never be taken from her husband, even by death. And he was ready for her death, understanding the heart of Christ. What his letter meant to the family of the man whose car hit her is past description. Her readiness, her preparedness, brought peace to her husband, her family, her church, and the family and church of the man whose swerving still could not prevent the accident. The man himself, upon receiving this letter, could leave his house for the first time.

Jesus certainly does not promise in this twenty-fourth chapter that His disciples will escape all of life's problems. In fact, He predicts suffering, persecution, betrayal, and deception. But He does urge them—and us—to be prepared for any eventuality, including His return. We don't know the day or hour when He will come, nor the day or hour when we shall leave. But we can be ready every day.

CHAPTER TWENTY-FIVE

Parables on the Second Coming and Judgment

Matthew 25

Always Prepared (25:1-13)

The moral of this simple parable, the first of three on the coming Judgment, is this: "Be prepared for the return of the Lord." It follows without a break Jesus' teaching in the twenty-fourth chapter on the suddenness and certainty of the end of the age and the Day of the Lord. The parable's application, however, is much broader, as its readers quickly discern. How many sermons on preparation for living have included this tale? The five wise and foolish maids are outstanding examples (good and bad) of the necessity of planning ahead.

Be Prepared for the Lord's Coming

Once again Jesus uses a wedding celebration to describe something of the kingdom of Heaven. (See Matthew 22:1-10 and Luke 12:35-38.) This is not a new idea to Jesus' audience. The Old Testament uses the same language for God's relationship with Israel. God is the bridegroom or husband and Israel is His bride or wife (Hosea 2:16; Isaiah 54:6; Ezekiel 16:8f), although not always a faithful one. In the New Testament, the analogy is applied to Christ and His church. He is the "husband" and the church is to be a "pure virgin" for Him (2 Corinthians 11:2). "Christ loved the church and gave himself up for her" so that she might be a perfect wife (Ephesians 5:25f). The church is a bride ready for her husband, the Lamb of God (Revelation 19:7).

In Jesus' parable, the bride awaits the groom, according to Jewish custom, at her home with her friends. The wedding itself is just the final stage of Jewish marriage customs. First comes the engagement, when the formal agreement is reached by the fathers of the bride and groom. Next is the betrothal, a ceremony that takes place in the bride's home; there is an exchange of promises sealed by the giving of gifts to the bride-to-be by her intended husband. Although they do not yet live together as husband and wife, the bond is so strong that if a wedding does not ensue at the end of the betrothal period (usually about a year) either because of a death or cancellation for some reason, the woman (if she is the one left) is treated as a widow or divorcee. To be betrothed is to be bound. The final step is the wedding itself, which takes place in the groom's parents' house.

The bridesmaids in the parable will join the friends of the groom in escorting the couple back to the groom's house, where the wedding feast will begin. Jesus does not mention the bride, by the way. Departing slightly from the usual Biblical language, in this case, He treats the bridesmaids as members of the church. In this respect, they resemble the wheat and weeds or the good and bad fish in other parables (Matthew 13:24-30, 36-43, 47-50). The bridesmaids are not necessarily good and bad, however, just prepared and unprepared.

All the maids sleep, although the moral of the story is watchfulness. *Preparedness* might be a better word, perhaps, since Jesus uses *keep watch* to mean *be prepared,* so when you see the groom and his party coming, everything will be ready. His words are akin to the prayer offered by a concerned Christian man at the church's weekly prayer meeting. He asked the Lord to bless those at home on beds of sickness—and on sofas of wellness. Theirs may be the graver danger.

Lawyer Karen DeCrow, past president of the National Organization for Women, recently waxed enthusiastic about the joys of being single and forty. Writing in the *New York Times,* she boasted, "You eat, sleep, make love, watch television, listen to music, go out, come in, read, use the telephone, write, type, talk, work, sing—when you want to."[83] She's a good candidate to be one of the foolish bridesmaids in Jesus' story, isn't she? She relaxes on her bed of wellness, unconcerned about any obligations or the possibility that at any moment the Lord may come.

Be prepared for another reason. The careless bridesmaids do what all thoughtless people do in a moment of crisis: they try to force their friends to bail them out. "Give us some of *your* oil; our lamps are going out." *You* assume responsibility for *us.* It is the cry of the weak and immature of every generation: smokers who expect insurance policies or government assistance to pay their self-incurred medical bills; chronic drinkers who expect family and employers and everyone else to take over their responsibilities; addicts who seek escape through drugged reveries, leaving the running of society to others; simple careless people who have learned that there is always someone

---

[83]Quoted in *Evangelical Newsletter,* June 16, 1978.

else to pick up the ball when they drop it. Jesus is not disposed to coddle the irresponsible. "No," the prepared maids answer. "You take care of yourselves. Our provisions are not ample enough for us and for you as well."

Jesus does not invite speculation on the day or hour of His return. In fact, He specifically forbids it (Matthew 24:36-44). He insists that His followers experience normal lives, living expectantly but without anxiety about tomorrow. Let the believer use his talents for God's glory, let him busy himself in feeding the hungry, clothing the naked, and doing other acts of mercy in Jesus' name (Matthew 25:1-46), but let him never fall into idle speculation about times and seasons. It is sufficient to live so that whenever Christ comes, the believer is prepared. If he has not planned for the Lord's return, for him as for these foolish maidens, the door will be shut (verse 10).

Be Prepared — Period

Old Benjamin Franklin was right: "For want of a nail the shoe was lost; for want of a shoe the horse was lost; and for want of a horse the rider was lost, being overtaken and slain by the enemy; and all for want of care about a horseshoe nail." Former Secretary of State John Foster Dulles, preparing for a critical meeting in Geneva, adds a more contemporary flavor to Franklin's saying. Desperately battling cancer, Dulles hoped to muster strength for this one last conference. He wasn't certain he would be released from Walter Reed Hospital in order to attend. If he found that he could not go, he would resign as Secretary of State. He would not shirk his duty. "I have found out," he told his associates, "that a man's accomplishments in life are the cumulative effect of his attention to detail."[84] When the details are cared for, you are prepared.

Preparation is not attractive to the careless. They are too preoccupied with the present to pay any attention to the future. They are unlike successful sportsmen, who put themselves through present agony in the hope of winning the future contest. Paul compares Christians with athletes (see Philippians 3:12-14) straining to win the victory. Preparation in Christian endeavors, no less than in athletics, means discipline, tedium, study, steadfastness, and scrimmages to get ready for the big contest. These are hard words for a success-oriented society like ours. We want instant accomplishment, immediate glory.

---

[84]Leonard Mosley, *Dulles* (New York: The Dial Press/James Wade, 1978), p. 447.

We even blaspheme to the point of claiming that something that succeeds must necessarily be of God. We don't discuss failure.

Jesus urges preparation. He does not promise that everything will always go our way. Our business is to prepare, to do right, to love the Lord and our neighbors, to be diligent in God's purposes for us. We don't have to worry about the outcome. God has not asked us to guarantee the victory, only the preparation. The end of the matter is this: "Since everything will be destroyed ... what kind of people ought you to be? You ought to live holy and godly lives as you look forward to the day of God and speed its coming" (2 Peter 3:11, 12).

Be prepared.

God's Personal Investment Program (25:14-30)
(Luke 19:11-27)

This is a very modern parable. Jesus has His nation Israel in mind, of course, and as they listen, His disciples will make that application. They will also take it to heart themselves, just as we do. We quickly assess our potential and identify with the five-, two-, or one-talent man. Then we look at what God expects of us, what He gets from us, and what He does when He is disappointed in us.

What God Expects

He expects a good return on His investment. Every servant in the parable receives something to manage for his landlord. Each was expected to invest profitably for the master. His distribution of assets among the servants is the landlord's investment program. God has similarly distributed His assets among His people: He has talented us, gifted us, and empowered us to manage a portion of His estate on earth. No one of us can honestly pretend, then, that "I am my own. I can do what I want to. It is nobody else's business what I do." The Scriptures insist that God owns us and everything else on earth, even our talents. (This is the origin of our English word *talent* by the way, which was a measure of money in the Bible, often thought of as approximately $1,000—although with the impact of inflation, that is undoubtedly too low a figure now.)

In the parable, the businessman distributes the money on the basis of his assessment of each servant's ability to manage. From each, he expects the same: a proportionate return on the investment. Every one is thus important to the master. This stress on the responsible assignments the servants receive makes this a very personal parable. No reader can fail to ask, "What is God realizing from His investment in me?"

What God Gets

From two servants, the master gets results. From the third one, he receives excuses and blame. As his reaction demonstrates, there is no substitute for results.

Yet what God often gets are excuses. The excuses quickly turn into blame. It's God's fault that I have not done better! Like the third servant, our excuses usually prove us to be cowardly, negative, and dull. How unfortunate it is that we often have trapped ourselves in a web of our own weaving. We have not produced, we have not succeeded, we have not even managed a good beginning. So we retreat into our protective web of alibis. We become expert at quickly spotting scapegoats on whom we can blame our failure.

When we hide our talents (literally, our money; figuratively, whatever God has invested in us to "turn a profit" for Him), we pervert their purpose. The late Teilhard de Chardin wrote somewhere that gold is "blameless so long as it is busy in service and so long as it helps along the current of humanity," but it "becomes corrupt as soon as it stands still. It is lack of motion that makes gold—a thing good in itself—first fester and then infect other things."[85] This servant's "gold" infected him. His master intended that the money—which was not his any more than anything we "possess" is ours—should produce a profit. The servant defied his master, denied the true purpose of his master's investment in him, and in the end fatally damaged himself.

God is not very patient with these substitutes for obedience. From the experience of Adam and Eve (Adam: "It is her fault, Lord." Eve: "It is the serpent's fault, Lord.") to my miserable failure yesterday, the human race has been perfecting the fine art of explaining our failure to do God's will. The old retelling of Noah's problems says it all:

> The Lord said to Noah, "Where is the Ark I commanded you to build?"
> And Noah said: "Verily, I had three carpenters off sick. And the gopher wood supplier hath let me down, even though gopher wood hath been on order for nigh on twelve months."
> And God said to Noah, "I want the Ark finished before seven days and seven nights." And Noah said, "It will be so." And it was not so.

---

[85]Quoted in Garry Willis, *Bare Ruined Choirs* (New York: Delta Books, 1971), p. 98.

The Lord said to Noah, "What seems to be the trouble this time?"

Noah said: "My sub-contractor hath gone bankrupt. The pitch for the outside hath not arrived. The glazier departeth on holiday, yea, even though I offered him double time. Lord, I am undone."

The Lord grew angry and said: "What about the animals, two of every sort I have ordered? Where are the giraffes?"

And Noah said, "They have been delivered to the wrong address but should arrive on Friday."

The Lord said to Noah, "How about the unicorns?"

Noah wrung his hands and wept. "O Lord, they are a discontinued line. Thou canst not get unicorns for love or money. Thou knowest how it is."

And the Lord said, "Noah, my son, I know. Why else dost thou think I cause a flood?"[86]

Excuses. Abraham Lincoln almost despaired of finding a general who had the ability to lead the Union forces to victory. After studying Ulysses S. Grant's string of successful battles in the Western theater, the President decided he had found his general, and ordered him to Washington. Grant had earned a reputation for saying little but producing much. He refused to play games with journalists, who consequently gave him bad press, but they didn't worry him; he was willing to lose skirmishes in the papers but unwilling to fail on the battlefield. Someone told him he should give the press a statement of the objectives in his maneuvers around Vicksburg before the siege began. Grant refused, saying he believed life to be too brief to be frittered away with explanations. The taciturn general then went ahead to win his victory.

Everyone's life is too short to be spent explaining. The faithful servants could have accused the master of being demanding and unfair also, just as the weak one did, but they didn't. They just produced results.

What God Does

The parable is about judgment. Two men returned an investment on what the master had entrusted to them. The third man returned excuses. God judged all three. The two men received commendations and the privilege of sharing their master's happiness. (We forget that God's judgment can result in joy as well as sorrow.) The third was stripped of what little he had and was cast out.

---

[86]From *The United Church Observer.* Quoted in *Pulpit Digest,* January-February, 1980, p. 23.

Napoleon Hill (in *How to Sell Your Way Through Life)* encourages his readers to play "a good joke" on their employers by getting to work earlier and staying there longer than required, handling their boss's tools with the same care they would give their own, being kind to their fellow workers, and volunteering for extra work that needs to be done. Then, he adds, they should not be surprised when they are offered oversight of a department or partnership in the business. He confesses that, "This is the best part of the joke."[87] Jesus would call Hill's advice going the second mile. Paul would say that it is working as if to serve the Lord and not just to please men (Ephesians 6:5-8). All this advice means returning a profit on the employer's investment in the employee.

The moral of the parable comes at the end, in the judgment against the faithless servant. Jesus clearly implies in this second of the three parables on judgment that His disciples are to live active, productive lives until He comes again. We are to use everything the Master has given us to produce results for the kingdom of Heaven. If we don't, then whatever we have will be taken from us and given to someone else who knows what to do with it.

The apostle Paul later picks up the theme from Jesus in his several treatments of the gifts of the Spirit (see Romans 12, 1 Corinthians 12, and Ephesians 4:11-13). God has obviously invested heavily in the church. His gifts differ from person to person, yet every gift is important and is intended to help the Christian make his contribution to God's purpose in the church. He wants no excuses.

Life Is Full of Surprises—And So Is Death (25:31-46)

"Nothing is certain but death and taxes," Benjamin Franklin opined. About taxes, there is no doubt we shall pay. About death, there is no doubt we shall die. But there are some other doubts, or at least questions, about death that will not go away. When will I die? What will death be like? Will there be a Judgment?

Jesus does not dodge the question of Judgment when He discusses death. Yes, there will be Judgment. No, God's standard of judgment will not be the one we are accustomed to in human society. There will be surprises. "When the Son of Man comes in his glory, and all the angels with him, he will sit on his throne in heavenly glory" (Matthew

---

[87]Napoleon Hill, *How to Sell Your Way Through Life* (Cleveland: Ralston Publishing Co., 1958).

25:31). Many surprises: Jesus glorified, angels on earth, the Son on the throne!

Many People Will Be Surprised at the Judgment

Prince Machiavelli, contemplating the afterlife from his deathbed, long ago said, "I desire to go to Hell, not to Heaven. In Hell I shall enjoy the company of popes, kings and princes, but in Heaven are only beggars, monks, hermits and apostles." The Heavenly company seemed too tame for him; he had been accustomed to consorting with the world's shakers and movers. Mark Twain's Huckleberry Finn hoped for a similar destination. The Widow Douglas' sister had told him all about the bad place. He said he preferred it to the other place, which made her mad. "She said it was wicked to say what I said; said she wouldn't say it for the whole world; she was going to live so as to go to the good place. Well," Huck concluded, "I couldn't see no advantage in going where she was going, so I made up my mind I wouldn't try for it." Miss Watson might have been surprised at the Judgment.

According to Jesus' parable, many will be surprised at their final disposition. They will not be asked to give evidence of their Bible knowledge or their Sunday-school attendance or of their doctrinal orthodoxy. The King will decide on the basis of their assistance to the needy. He will consult records of deeds done or left undone that they have long forgotten.

They will be surprised, but they shouldn't be. Jesus is not propounding any new teaching here. He is simply picking up the teaching of the prophets and telling in story form what they had repeatedly preached to Israel. Look at Isaiah 58, for example:

> Is not this the kind of fasting I have chosen:
> to loose the chains of injustice
>   and untie the cords of the yoke,
> to set the oppressed free
>   and break every yoke?
> Is it not to share your food with the hungry
>   and to provide the poor wanderer with shelter—
> when you see the naked, to clothe him,
>   and not to turn away from your own flesh and blood?
> Then your light will break forth like the dawn,
>   and your healing will quickly appear;
>   then your righteousness will go before you,
> and the glory of the Lord will be your rear guard.
> Then you will call, and the Lord will answer;
>   you will cry for help, and he will say: Here am I (vs. 6-9).

These things are what the Lord wants His people to attend to. He always has. Jesus, on more than one occasion, placed the acts of love in an eternal dimension. On one such occasion, a lawyer demanded, "What must I do to inherit eternal life?" Jesus asked him what the law required, and the astute lawyer correctly summarized all its tenets in two: "Love the Lord your God with all your heart and with all your soul and with all your strength and with all your mind," and, "Love your neighbor as yourself" (Luke 10:25-27). The clever lawyer, seeking a loophole by which to justify himself, went the next step: "And who is my neighbor?" (verse 29). Then Jesus told His parable of the good Samaritan. There could be no mistake, as the lawyer had to admit, that a neighbor is anyone who needs or shows mercy. In the parable, by the way, neither the priest nor the Levite (who took care of the temple) showed any compassion on the man. Jesus wants no misunderstanding: religious reputation or position will count for nothing on the Day of Judgment.

On another occasion, a rich young man asked Jesus the same question (Mark 10:17-22). This time, Jesus interrogated the young man and found that he had faithfully observed the Ten Commandments. Then, to the man's amazement, Jesus pointed out the one thing that he had neglected: he must sell what he possessed and give to the poor. Then he could follow Jesus into eternity. The man could not comply. He was too rich. Jesus would have had the man come to Alexander Pope's conclusion:

> Thus God and nature linked the general frame,
> And bade self-love and social be the same.

The Jewish *Talmud* teaches that all Israelites are mutually responsible for one another. Self-love apart from social-love is strongly discouraged, as this little story teaches. In a boat at sea, a passenger began boring a hole in the bottom. When he was scolded for endangering their lives, he protested, "But I am only boring under my own seat." His fellow passengers were quick to point out that when the sea water rushed in, all of them would be drowned with him. "So it is with Israel. Its weal or its woe is in the hands of every individual Israelite." So, Jesus would add, it will be with His disciples.

"Love each other as I have loved you," Jesus told them. Then He explained what this means: "Greater love has no man than this, that one lay down his life for his friends" (John 15:12, 13). John adds, "Whoever does not love does not know God, because God is love. This is how God showed his love among us: He sent his one and only

299

Son into the world that we might live through him" (1 John 4:8, 9). This is why there will be surprises at the Judgment. Many who have considered themselves true believers will be appalled that the Judge does not ask them about their belief. He wants to know, "Did you take care of people who couldn't take care of themselves?" He does not allow us to reduce discipleship to a narrow concern for personal "spirituality." Jesus believes that a "spiritual" person becomes involved in a very physical world, where people are hungry and naked and politically abused and frightened by their superstitions and troubled in their families. "What did you do for them?"

Then They Will Be Surprised by the Nature of Love

Love gives. "God so loved the world that he gave . . ." (John 3:16). Even after the world rejected God's Son, neither the Father nor the Son stopped loving and giving. Love does not have to be reciprocated. Love "always protects, always trusts, always hopes, always perseveres. Love never fails" (1 Corinthians 13:7, 8). Even when it is not returned, love never fails. The surprise for the sheep and the goats is that they would not have defined what Jesus is speaking of as love. A little bit of charity, perhaps, giving alms to the poor, perhaps, but not love. Yet love is not a feeling, Jesus insists, but the human equivalent of God's love in action. Love as defined in our songs, soap operas, magazines, and movies is as far from *agape,* God's love, as it can be.

John Hinckley, Jr., shot and tried to kill President Ronald Reagan. He said he committed this felony because he was "in love with" actress Jody Foster. In order to prove just how much he loved, he would kill for her. Hinckley was hospitalized for insanity, yet he was only applying in extreme the prevalent romantic notion of love. Jesus' love, on the other hand, doesn't kill. It dies for love.

Jesus' love is a far cry from the self-love that governs most lives. One father, devasted by his family's involvement with cultist Jim Jones, decided to become a hedonist, since all his important relationships (except the one with his mother) had ended in disaster. Rejected by his family and facing a lonely future, he decided "the only thing left for me is to try to enjoy the time I have; to attend parties, to dance, to travel, to seek love. These are things through which I can forget."[88]

---

[88]Min S. Yee and Thomas Layton, *In My Father's House* (New York: Berkley Books, 1981), p. 302.

Thinking that he is serving his best interests, this man is actually further destroying himself. He wishes to save what is left of his life, a certain way to lose it (Matthew 16:25). Many psychologists and psychiatrists have written that Jesus' is the only prescription for mental health. Depression, for example, can be quickly banished through service to others. Dr. Karl Menninger used to say frequently that if you know someone heading for a nervous breakdown, you should tell him to head straight for his front door, turn the knob, cross the tracks, and find somebody who needs him. Only in looking past himself and his troubles can he find wholeness.

This love is not sentimental; it is not mere "do-goodism." It does not keep score of its good deeds, hoping in time to accumulate enough to be judged a sheep rather than a goat some day. It is generally interested in others; it forgets about its own happiness, to wake up one day to the surprising discovery that happiness has sneaked up on it. Love is justice and more than justice. It is mercy. It is compassion. It is taking another's burden upon oneself. A young disciple of a Jewish rabbi said to the old man, "My Master, I love you!" Instead of answering, the rabbi asked, "Do you know what hurts me, my son?"

Offended, the disciple scolded. "I don't understand your question, Rabbi. I am trying to tell you how much you mean to me, and you confuse me with irrelevant questions."

The rabbi did not believe his question irrelevant. He was trying to teach his young student that if he did not know what hurt his rabbi, he could not truly love him.[89]

Jesus teaches the same lesson in His parable of the sheep and goats. Unless His disciples can know what hurts the Lord—and do something to ease that hurt—they cannot claim to love Him. "Not everyone who says to me, 'Lord, Lord,' will enter the kingdom of heaven, but only he who does the will of my Father who is in heaven" (Matthew 7:21).

The Examinees Will Be Surprised by the Knowledge of God

It will not take Him long to administer the test. He already knows what He needs to make His judgment. His eye is on the sparrow—and our treatment of the sparrow. The famous medieval mystic St. John of the Cross wrote, "There is nothing in the world to be compared with God and he who loves any other thing together with Him wrongs

---

[89]L'Engle, *Walking on Water,* pp. 70, 71.

Him." Where did he get this idea? Certainly not from Scripture. "If anyone has material possessions and sees his brother in need but has no pity on him, how can the love of God be in him?" (1 John 3:17). Love God and others. "No one has ever seen God; but if we love one another, God lives in us and his love is made complete in us. . . . For anyone who does not love his brother, whom he has seen, cannot love God, whom he has not seen. And he has given us this command: Whoever loves God must also love his brother" (1 John 4:12, 20, 21).

We love God, then, through loving others. In this way, we avoid the danger of concentrating exclusively on God, fashioning a "me and God and nobody else" religion. Jonathan Swift once grumbled, "We have just enough religion to make us hate, but not enough to make us love, one another." True religion, religion that is of God, loves. It is quite unlike that expressed by a Chinese pastor, who asked the famous missionary who was to address a convention of pastors, "Please do not preach to us to love our enemies, but preach to us spiritually."[90] He was making impossible demands on the missionary. Nothing is more spiritual than loving one's enemies or caring for the unlovely.

It is quite possible in the affluent sections of our country to avoid unpleasant meetings with the poor and hungry and naked and imprisoned. That is precisely what concerns Jesus. Real love goes out of its way to be bothered by people that other people can't be bothered with.

The biggest surprise of all about the Judgment is that God has kept no secrets from us. He will be exactly what His Word has revealed Him to be. He will be like Christ. His judgments will be according to Christ's word (John 12:48). It pays to take Him seriously. If we are surprised, it will not be His fault.

---

[90]E. Stanley Jones, *Christ's Alternative to Communism* (Nashville: Abingdon, 1935), pp. 48, 49.

CHAPTER TWENTY-SIX

Conspiracy, Communion, and Cowardice

Matthew 26:1-35; 69-75

The Crisis Looms (26:1-5)
(Mark 14:1, 2; Luke 22:1, 2; John 13:1)

Three times before, Jesus has predicted His death in Jerusalem (16:21; 17:12; 20:17-19). Then the event seemed far away and unreal. But now the air is charged with tension. Even as Jesus prepares His disciples, Caiaphas (high priest from around A.D. 18 to 36) presides over an extraordinary session of the Sanhedrin (Israel's Supreme Court, composed of priests, scribes, and elders). The subject under discussion is the best way to dispose of this troublemaker. John's Gospel notes that several times before, the religious leaders have taken either counsel or definite steps toward the same goal: John 5:18; 7:1, 32; 8:59; 10:31-39; 11:47-53. (See also Matthew 12:14.) Jesus is popular with the people but hated by the people's leaders, especially the authorities of the temple. He had embarrassed them when He boldly drove out the money changers and vendors. In their fury, however, these vengeance-bound leaders are cool enough to do nothing to encite a riot among the masses who regarded Jesus as a prophet. (The word here for *riot* is *thorubos,* which Jewish historian Josephus used when he meant "bloody insurrection.") Caiaphas, especially, is prepared to do anything to prevent a riot. In an era in which Rome appoints the high priests frequently (no fewer than twenty-eight of them between 37 B.C. and A.D. 67), Caiaphas is a survivor. He knows that Rome will tolerate almost anything except social upheaval. He wants Jesus done away with, but quietly.

Matthew carefully notes that Jesus' death takes place during the Passover Feast. With his eye on Jewish history, Matthew cannot overlook the obvious parallel. For the Jews, the passing over of the angel of death on the night when the firstborn of the Egyptians was slain (Exodus 11 and 12) was the most memorable event of their history, for it led to their freedom. For Christians, Jesus' crucifixion is the significant Passover. God has again delivered His people, and again the sacrificial lamb is the instrument of deliverance. Paul calls Christ

303

"our Passover lamb" (1 Corinthians 5:7). This is "the Lamb of God, who takes away the sin of the world" (John 1:29).

How to Give Yourself Away (26:6-13)
(Mark 14:3-9; John 12:1-8)

A simplified Internal Revenue Form 1040 made the rounds this last tax season. It has a place for you to fill in your Social Security number. There is no line for your name, since a name is unnecessary in this computerized age. There are just two lines for the required financial information. Line One: "How much money did you make last year?" Line Two: "Send it in." Not even the most ardent patriot, who is ready to do just about anything his for country, will send in everything he makes. That would be too extravagant.

Yet love isn't really love if there isn't something extravagant about it, something of the spendthrift in the lover. This rare and wonderful moment in the last tension-filled week of Jesus' ministry pictures love in action. What is so beautiful is that for once Jesus, who always so freely gave, is on the receiving end.

The drama occurs in the home of Simon the Leper in Bethany, a little suburb just outside Jerusalem.

But what is Jesus doing in a leper's home? Lepers were unclean, forbidden entrance into polite society (Leviticus 13). Yet here is Jesus relaxing in the home of one. Our best guess is that Jesus is a guest of Simon because Jesus has earlier touched and healed him. This meal is undoubtedly Simon's opportunity to express appreciation to Jesus. Because he *was* a leper, he still has the name, but he *is* a leper no more, thanks to Jesus.

Others of Jesus' friends are present, including Mary, the sister of Martha and Lazarus (John 12:1-8). John's Gospel identifies her as the woman who Matthew says "came to him with an alabaster jar of very expensive perfume" (Matthew 26:7). There is something extravagant about close friendships. Mary's anointing of Jesus has all the marks of totally selfless love. When Mary pours the enormously expensive perfume ("pure nard") over Jesus, she is "squandering" the most precious item in her household. It represents her fortune, the equivalent of the annual wage of a working man. Matthew reports that the disciples are indignant; John says that Judas especially resented her act, but then he adds, as if this reaction was to be expected, "because he was a thief" (John 12:6). Very often those who protest that such and such should not be done, that the money should instead be given to the poor, have less interest in the poor than in the money.

She Has Done a Beautiful Thing

While Judas has in mind the monetary value of the perfume, Jesus thinks of the sheer, simple beauty of Mary's act. Impulsive, yes, but motivated by love. Judas was like those hordes of social critics who delight in running other people's business. Jesus, on the other hand, refuses to be trapped into translating everything into cash equivalents. He values persons more than things—certainly more than money. "She has done a beautiful thing to me" (Matthew 26:10). Such beauty was rare in His life. He constantly gave but seldom received. He appreciates the kindness.

In a mountain grotto near the ancient capital of the Ching dynasty, Kyung Ju, is Korea's largest statue of the Buddha. While only Buddhists worship there, even non-believers cannot help marveling over the beauty of the statue and the extravagant act of worship that carved the stone. Equally impressive is the attention given the grotto's grounds. In Bangkok, Thailand, you can find similar evidence of religious devotion in the capital's temple and palace grounds. Again, even non-believing tourists will be smitten by the dazzling beauty of the temple area. The buildings and grounds are carefully tended. No matter how impatient a Christian may be with some of the misleading teachings of Hinduism, you can't help being impressed that some Hindus love their religion enough to give sacrificially to adorn their temple in splendor.

Two Americans visiting these grounds entered into a lively debate over the apparent wealth of the temple. One argued that much good could have been done for Thailand's poor if so much money hadn't been squandered on the temple. His colleague suggested to him that Americans have difficulty understanding corporate ownership. In the Hindu religion, the people, all of the people, could identify with "their" temple and claim it as their own. They could boast, "That is our temple; our money helped to build and helps to maintain it. We give because we love our religion." Their feeling for "their" temple is comparable to the pride the common people of Europe in past centuries took in their cathedrals. Visiting Americans wonder about "squandering" so much money on buildings when it could have been given to the poor. But our medieval forefathers were also not the extreme individualists we have become. They labored through their various guilds and in their offerings to make the cathedrals possible. Then they could say, "That's our cathedral. We have built it to the glory of our God." In that light, the cathedrals take on new beauty.

"Well, we wouldn't do this now in America," his friend retorted. "Times have changed."

"True, but neither do we give our money to the poor in any manner to boast of. Instead, we build cathedrals to the gods we believe in, just as these others have done. No, our cathedrals are not for the worship of the God of Christ, but the god of football. These 100,000-seat shrines sit vacant most of the year, but without counting the cost, football's devotees have erected scores of them around the country, to say nothing of the thousands of smaller ones. Salaries upwards of a million dollars a year for some of the more outstanding player/priests are becoming commonplace. Our gods have changed, but the nature of love has not." He was making the point of this passage: When we love, we pay; we give—extravagantly.

She Has Seized Her Opportunity

"The poor you will always have with you, but you will not always have me" (Matthew 26:11). Some of Jesus' modern critics have misread these words and scorned His disregard for the poor. They are unfair. How many times Jesus encouraged His disciples to care for the needy! How many times He himself healed and fed and comforted them. His surprising vision of the Judge separating the sheep from the goats on the basis of their service to the needy (Matthew 25:31-46) gives the lie to any charges of unconcern. What He says here has nothing to do with the poor. He is simply answering the charge that she is squandering what could have been given to them. "She did it to prepare me for burial," He tells them (26:12). She has listened to Him with the understanding of love. She has believed His predictions that He will die in Jerusalem, even though the rest haven't. In her generous, impulsive act of sheer friendship and love, she has seized the opportunity to do something for Him.

Rich is the person who is alert to opportunities to do something in love.

She Has Given Herself to Something Permanent

"I tell you the truth, wherever this gospel is preached throughout the world, what she has done will also be told, in memory of her" (Matthew 26:13). The Gospel will last. So will her memory, because she hsa given herself to something lasting. Implied in Jesus' response is that her devotion to Jesus is far more abiding than anything she could have bought with what the perfume cost. For two thousand years, her simple act has been honored. "What," we can't help but ask, "can we do that will be remembered with respect after we have died?" Think of your grandparents, their parents, and their parents. What do you know about them? What memory has outlived them? Now, generations hence, what will be known of you? What will you have contributed? What beautiful thing will you have done?

In 1 Corinthians 15, the apostle Paul devotes a long chapter to the subject of life beyond the grave. Then, after fifty-seven verses on the subject, he abruptly concludes his presentation with these words, "Therefore, my dear brothers, stand firm. Let nothing move you. Always give yourselves fully to the work of the Lord, because you know that your labor in the Lord is not in vain." Give yourselves to God, give yourselves to what really matters, to what lasts!

Give yourself to something permanent. The sensitive disciple of Jesus cannot read of this brief moment in Jesus' final week without some introspection. "What does this have to do with me?" Even a casual reading forces one to take inventory of what he has given to the Lord recently. Or ever. When placed beside the supreme sacrifice Jesus offered on the cross, Mary's gift seems small. Yet Jesus is quick to point out the beauty of her act, since she has done what *she* could do. What, then, can I do for the Lord? More broadly, what is the will of the Lord for my life? As this passage hints, the answers to these questions may not be as profound or difficult as we like to make them. We answer them with two more questions:

"What Has God Given Me to Give Away?"

Scripture makes it clear that God has given gifts to us in order that we can give them away. Love is His command, and love gives—extravagantly. To some, He has given money—not to be hoarded, but shared. To others, talents for singing or speaking or leading. These are not to be objects of boasting, but instruments of service. So we must ask, "What has God given me to give away?" In the Academy Award winning film *Chariots of Fire,* the great Scottish runner Eric Liddell's father tells his son, "Run to God's glory and let the world stand back and wonder." Later Eric himself says, "He [God] made me fast, and when I run I feel His pleasure. To not run is to hold Him in contempt." God had gifted him to run, so he gave that gift away.

I cherish a letter that arrived shortly after my return from a trip out of the country. The writer wished me a "welcome home" and let me know I was missed. She praised God for a good Lord's day at our church, with the choirs singing well and everything seeming to be filled with God's goodness. I kept the letter, though, for her

307

salutation: "His servant, too." When I read these words, I knew she understood the priesthood of all believers, a theme I frequently stress in my preaching. The writer was a sponsor of the church's college age youth group. I know of no more tireless, selfless worker than she. Having a high regard for my ministry, she had a similarly healthy regard for her own service. She was "His servant, too." (See Romans 12, 1 Corinthians 12, and Ephesians 4.)

"Who Needs It?"

This is the second question. God has gifted you for the sake of others. Seize your opportunity to bring what God has given you to the service of others who need you. That is His will for your life.

Two Hands in a Common Dish (26:14-30)
(Mark 14:10-25; Luke 22:3-23; John 13:2, 18)

They were reclining at table, trying to concentrate on the Passover Feast they were eating, but their minds were on other things. The Passover reminded them of God's miraculous delivery of the slave-nation Israel from Egypt, but they quickly forgot those ancient days to think about their more immediate troubles. Tension filled their days in Jerusalem. Jesus' enemies were everywhere. Even He seemed subdued that night, in that borrowed room, as He hosted their meal. He had no doubt that His time (*kairos,* appointed time) was at hand. The purpose for His earthly life was about to be fulfilled.

It was undoubtedly not an elaborate setting; more likely, it was a humble room that matched the simplicity of Jesus' birthplace. As the disciples partook of the lamb, the herbs, the wine, and the Passover ritual, they could participate without much thought. They had eaten such a meal every year of their lives. But then, at the end of the meal, Jesus did something unprecedented.

Before we discuss His institution of what we call the Lord's Supper, however, we need to listen in on the conversation between Jesus and Judas. All the disciples heard Jesus say, "I tell you the truth, one of you will betray me" (Matthew 26:21). Only Judas and one or two others seem to have heard Jesus' direct answer to his question, "Surely not I, Rabbi?" "Yes, it is you" (26:25). Some Bible students think that Judas was sitting next to Jesus on one side, John on the other, Peter across. Maybe only those three heard.

But everybody had seen Judas' hand. They had all been dipping into the same bowl. But two hands stand out: Jesus', the hand that gives; and Judas', the hand that takes.

308

The Hand That Takes

For two thousand years, Christians have speculated about the hand that takes. Why did Judas betray Jesus? What possessed the man? Is the explanation the fact that he was a Zealot, a member of the fanatical party working to overthrow the Roman Empire and free the Jews? If so, did Judas join Jesus in the hope that this remarkable man had the capacity to lead the revolution and set the Jews free? Did he then become disillusioned when it seemed that Jesus was not a political revolutionary, or at least not a competent one? Is the answer simpler? Perhaps Judas was a competitor, a Type A, who had to be on the winning side. When he saw Jesus headed for certain defeat by the accumulating hosts of opponents, he decided to switch allegiance before it was too late. Is that it? Whatever explanation, you have to agree that he was a self-server. He looked out for his own interests. In this regard, he is a perfect model of modern man! John is quite blunt: he says that Judas was a thief who had filched some of the disciples' money that had been entrusted to him as the group's treasurer (John 12:6). If so, he was just acting in character when he pocketed the thirty pieces of silver for betraying Jesus. His cynical, calculating mind figured the advantage: "What are you willing to give me if I hand him over to you?" (Matthew 26:15). "What's a betrayal worth these days?"

What disturbs today's reader of this passage is that we hear ourselves asking, "Surely not I, Lord?" There's a bit of Judas in the best of us. What would be our motive for betrayal? Money? Disappointment? Would we turn Him in because He had failed to live up to our expectations? Have we treated Him like a cosmic bellhop who has been dilatory in carrying out our commands? Is it possible that we view God as the guarantor of our success? If so, are we ready to turn against Him when success eludes us?

Do our prayers give us away? "Lord, I pray that You will help me find my lost earrings." "Lord, I know I haven't studied as much as I should have, but help me pass this exam." "Lord, I ask You to help me find exactly the right house in exactly the right location of town at exactly the right price." "Lord, deliver me from pleurisy." "Lord, deliver to me that red Corvette." "Lord, deliver me from the prying eyes of the auditors." "Lord, Lord, Lord!" Jesus taught us to ask freely, of course, but He also taught that we should pray, "Your kingdom come, your will be done" (Matthew 6:10). That means, "Lord, help me do Your will." If we are to be delivered, it is from our "me first" mentality.

That was the ethic of Benedict Arnold. A loyal patriot until 1779, Arnold was a prosperous businessman, a natural leader, an obvious choice to be captain of the Connecticut State Militia. He proved to be a good military leader. He joined Montgomery in the attack on Quebec. The offensive failed, but Arnold was promoted to Brigadier General. Other victories followed. But when Congress created five new generalships, Arnold was passed over for political reasons. Only General George Washington's pleading kept Arnold from resigning his commission. Smarting from this or that slight, Arnold switched his allegiance to the British. As the American, he was to obtain command of West Point and then deliver it over to the British. His asking price was 20,000 pounds for betraying this post, half of it if he failed. He failed. His British contact was captured by the Americans, who then discovered the plot. Arnold escaped in time, aboard the British ship appropriately named the *Vulture*.

When General Washington learned of Arnold's betrayal, Washington at first showed no emotion. He sent Alexander Hamilton off with a detachment of soldiers to try to intercept Arnold at Verplanck's Point. He gave orders to his staff to defend the fort. Then, taking Lafayette with him, he left the room. Only when he was out of sight and earshot did he give vent to his emotion. He threw his arms about Lafayette's neck and wept. Only Lafayette saw this and, to his knowledge, it was the only time during the war that Washington wept.

He wept because he had been betrayed. He wept because he had completely trusted Arnold. If Arnold would betray him, who could be trusted?

Betrayal is the logical conclusion of self-service. If you are Number One, the best anyone else can be is Number Two. Whenever you must choose, you will lay down someone else's life for your own. And there is just enough of the Judas in us to make us ask, "Surely not I?" Undoubtedly Arnold felt justified in selling out his country. Judas felt equally justified—at first. They owed it to themselves!

George MacDonald provides the answer to such rationalization. "I owe myself nothing. What has myself ever done for me, but lead me wrong! What but it has come between me and my duty—between me and my very Father in heaven—between me and my fellow man!"[91]

[91]Rolland Hein, ed., *The World of George MacDonald* (Wheaton, IL: Shaw Publications, 1978), p. 107.

The Hand That Gives

If Judas' hand is on the take, Jesus' is on the give. It is He who gives the meal, He who gives thanks. "While they were eating, Jesus took bread, gave thanks and broke it, and gave it to his disciples" (Matthew 26:26). A profitable study could be made of the several instances that the Gospel writers have recorded of the times Jesus gives thanks. His giving to others begins with His thanksgiving to His Father. It always does. The grateful person is almost inevitably a generous one. The person who acts as if the world owes him a living can never find it in his heart to give to others, but the grateful person easily shares what he has received with others.

Jesus' is the hand that gives thanks. First, Jesus gives thanks; then He gives the bread and the cup. "This is my body.... This is my blood of the covenant, which is poured out for many for the forgiveness of sins" (Matthew 26:26, 28). The hand on the take never forgives, because it can never assume the point of view of the other person. The taking person is self-centered. He cannot forgive because he thinks only of his hurt, his pride, his prerogatives. Everyone else must meet his needs; he has nothing left for another.

Jesus' is the hand that gives self. What a contrast between Judas, who is willing to kill, and Jesus, who is prepared to die in the supreme act of forgiveness. The Judas in us will kill a relationship in order to serve self. We stand upon our dignity and insist on our rights; we will not allow ourselves to be spoken to rudely; we will not tolerate this or that. Of course, we will not have many lasting relationships, either. Friendship demands forgiveness.

Jesus' is the hand that forgives. "I'm doing this," Jesus says, "in spite of all that is happening to Me. I am doing this so that you will know you are forgiven." On the cross, He will pray for those who kill Him, asking the Father to forgive them. Here, in preparation for that event, He tries to teach His disciples that His blood is not being given in vain. Like the blood of the sacrificial animals in the Old Covenant, Jesus' blood effects forgiveness in the New. Bible writers return again and again to the mystery of Jesus' inexpressible gift: Romans 3:23-26, 5:6-9; Hebrews 2:17, 7:26, 27; 1 John 2:2; 4:10.

Jesus' is the hand that gives hope. There will be a new kingdom based on forgiveness, love, and Jesus' sacrifice. Its characteristic will be giving, not taking. What a contrast to this world's style. What a contrast with most religions! Archeologists in Mexico City have been learning more about the Aztec civilization than has previously been known. In their digging, they have discovered that an annual ritual

311

was observed, known as the Raising of Banners. Their chief war god was appeased by the killing of prisoners and slaves. Records have been found indicating that up to 20,000 victims were sacrificed in one year! Without such offerings, the Aztecs were convinced, the world would end. Theirs was a god on the take.

We continue to sacrifice to war gods. The current century has been the most violent in world history. We have slaughtered millions upon millions to the god of war. And he has not yet given us peace.

But Jesus promises a new kingdom, where peace and love and forgiveness will reign. The new covenant will ask for no more blood, since Jesus' blood is enough.

A few years ago, Supreme Court Justice Hugo Black celebrated his eighty-third birthday. He received many letters of congratulations, and many gifts, but one letter meant more to him than anything else. It was handwritten by his friend on the bench, Justice John Marshall Harlan. Justice Harlan was practically blind. To sign his name on court documents, he ordered a powerful overhead light installed above his desk. Using a large magnifying glass and the powerful light, he was able to see just enough to sign his name, painfully. When Justice Black read Harlan's letter, he folded it, put it in his pocket, turned his back on his clerk, and stared into the distance. When he turned around, there were tears in his eyes. He said to his clerk, simply, "He wrote it himself." He knew what it had cost his friend to write the letter.

Jesus' disciples do not yet know with what pain Jesus will write the New Covenant. They accept His cup and drink. Only later, after the crucifixion and resurrection, will they fully understand what it cost Him to bring us the forgiveness of God.

Jesus' is the hand that reconciles. The taking ways of a Judas alienate; the giving ways of Jesus reconcile. Judas went out and hanged himself. Jesus was hanged on a cross. Both men died. Both are remembered, one for being on the take, the other for being on the give. The giving hand still reaches across the void that separates man from God and man from man, giving access, providing reconciliation.

The Peter Principle Revisited (26:30-35, 69-75)
(Mark 14:26-31, 53, 54, 66-72; Luke 22:31-34, 54-62;
John 18:15-18, 25-27)

Dr. Laurence J. Peter became famous a few years ago when he propounded his cynical but accurate Peter principle: "In a hierarchy every employee tends to rise to his level of incompetence." After a careful study of the way organizations work, he concluded that "for every job that exists in the world there is someone, somewhere, who cannot do it." With enough time and the usual promotions, the incompetent will naturally make his way to that job and there he will remain, "habitually bungling the job" to the frustration of his co-workers and the detriment of the organization.[92]

These two passages concern the Biblical Peter. Unfortunately, he demonstrates a type of spiritual incompetence that shows that the Peter principle has a broader application than Dr. Laurence Peter gave it. It implies a spiritual truth as well.

Jesus and the disciples are on the Mount of Olives, where Jesus desires to pray to prepare himself for the certain agony of the morrow. Having appraised His followers and assessed the strength of the forces arrayed against Him, He predicts, "This very night you will all fall away on account of me" (Matthew 26:31). He quotes from the prophet Zechariah (13:7) to underscore His prediction: "I will strike the shepherd, and the sheep of the flock will be scattered." Then He further mentions His resurrection, but once again, His disciples do not hear Him out.

Instead, Peter, bristling with the self-confidence of someone who does not know himself very well, insists, "Even if all fall away on account of you, I never will" (26:33). Others may be weak or timid in the hour of trial, but not Peter. He is prepared to stand alone in defense of Jesus. Jesus believes that Peter believes what he is saying, but Jesus does not believe it. "This very night, before the rooster crows, you will disown me three times" (26:34).

Incensed, Peter again blusters, "Even if I have to die with you, I will never disown you." Then the other disciples chimed in with similar promises (26:35).

Jump from verse 36 to verse 69. This is the same Peter. Jesus is before the Sanhedrin. His "trial" is not going well. It is apparent that He will be convicted. Peter, warming himself by the fire in the courtyard, has witnessed his leader's fall. He is so dismayed by this unexpected turn of events and so unsure of himself that when a girl, a servant girl, accuses him of being an associate of the condemned man, Peter swears, shouts, and lies, "I do not know the man!"

---

[92]Laurence J. Peter, *The Peter Principle: Why Things Always Go Wrong* (New York: William Morrow and Co., 1969).

Now we are ready to state the Biblical Peter principle: "*Because we are not as strong as we think we are, we must have a leader to believe in and a group to belong to.*"

We Are Not as Strong as We Think

Look at the first part of the principle: "Because we are not as strong as we think. . . ." If there was anyone in Jesus' company who should have stood by Him, it was Peter. A powerful man physically, a courageous adventurer, a committed believer, and a strong natural leader, Peter has every reason to promote the power of positive thinking. Today, he would fit the image of the self-made, aggressive, prosperous executive. But for all his ability, Peter has not realistically appraised himself. It is not entirely his fault: he has never been so sorely tested as here. Further, his confidence is not exactly self-assurance; it is derived assurance, the result of so closely identifying with his leader. When his leader stumbles, Peter's faith crumbles. He loses his courage and denies his Lord.

Peter's behavior is so typically human as to be called a principle. Henry David Thoreau remarked that "the mass of men lead lives of quiet desperation." We despair because of our inconsistency, our frequent feelings of helplessness, our spiritual emptiness, our inability to withstand temptation. We become thoroughly disgusted with ourselves. Dag Hammskjold, meditating in his *Markings* on our propensity for self-revulsion, sounds a necessary alarm: "Is your disgust at your emptiness to be the only life with which you fill it?" No, it isn't enough to chastise yourself. We all need something more—Someone more. We have to have a leader to believe in. Peter had reason to be confident when he was in the presence of Jesus. Having accepted Jesus as the Son of God, the Messiah, he thought his Lord invincible. Seeing Him now, a bound prisoner before the supreme court, Peter doubts his earlier allegiance and panics as he feels Jesus' strength drain from him. He has lost faith in his Lord and in himself.

We Must Have a Leader to Believe In

Because we are not as strong as we think we are, we must have a leader to believe in. The amazing partnership of General Ulysses S. Grant and General John Sherman has left a sterling testimony to the leader's role in war. Upon hearing that his commanding general had been called to Washington to assume command of all Union troops in the Civil War, Sherman wrote to Grant. He praised his commander: "I believe you are as brave, patriotic & just as the great prototype

Washington; as unselfish, kind-hearted & honest as a man should be
. . . the simple faith in success you have always manifested I can liken
to nothing else than the faith a Christian has in a Savior. . . ." Then
Sherman spelled out the quality in Grant that made it possible for
Sherman to dare to follow him so loyally: "When you have completed your last preparations, you go into battle without hesitation—
no doubts, no reserves; & I tell you it was this that made us act with
confidence. I knew wherever I was that you thought of me, & if I got
in a tight place you would come if alive."[93] In this confidence, Sherman could lead his troops. He wasn't alone. He had a leader to
believe in, who would come if necessary.

Everybody has to have somebody. We admire the courage of the
apostle Paul, but Paul openly admitted there was no secret to his
bravery. It came from his leader. He put it this way: "To me, to live is
Christ" (Philippians 1:21). And this way: "I have been crucified with
Christ and I no longer live, but Christ lives in me. The life I live in the
body, I live by faith in the Son of God, who loved me and gave
himself for me" (Galatians 2:20, 21). Paul totally identified himself
with his leader. Because of Christ's power, Paul could do amazing
things, face any danger, endure any hardship.

Peter had come close to such partnership. Earlier, when many disciples were leaving Jesus, the Master asked His disciples, "You do not
want to leave too, do you?" It was Peter who answered, "Lord, to
whom shall we go? You have the words of eternal life" (John 6:67,
68). So he stayed and toughed it out with a commitment to Jesus he
fully intended would last forever. But he had counted on Jesus' triumph, not His defeat.

God understands that about Peter—and the rest of us. We cannot
be expected to follow a fallen leader. What makes Peter's experience
so helpful is that we can read his subsequent career in the book of
Acts, after the resurrection through which God said to Peter and
anyone else paying attention, "Jesus is My Son, indeed. You were
right to follow Him. Death was but a temporary pause in Jesus'
victorious march Heavenward. You were right to believe in Him."
Once Peter becomes convinced that Jesus has really arisen from the
tomb—and has forgiven him for his desertion—from that moment on
there is no turning back for him. He can stand before the huge crowd
on the day of Pentecost (Acts 2) and preach Jesus without fear; he

---

[93]Carl Sandburg, *Abraham Lincoln, The War Years,* Volume II (New
York: Harcourt, Brace and Company, 1939), p. 542.

can provide steady leadership for the church in Jerusalem; he can speak up to governmental and religious authorities and insist that he must obey God rather than men. Once again, he has his Leader.

We Must Have a Group to Belong To

Because we are not as strong as we think we are, we must have a leader to believe in and a group to belong to. We need both the shepherd and the flock, a fact that independent Americans prefer to ignore. We praise the strong, silent, solitary type. We want to believe that Peter could have withstood all the enemies, as he said he would. He couldn't, however, and neither can we. This is not to speak disparagingly of ourselves; it is just to admit a human characteristic. We were created social beings, to need other people. Families need parents to hold them together. Nations need presidents or kings or other leaders to hold them together. Groups require strong leaders to give the group cohesion. Churches need pastors. Every human community needs leadership—and it also needs fellowship. This is how we are built. In fact, as Dr. Samuel Johnson expressed it, "The solitary mortal is probably superstitious, and possibly mad." He is trying to deny his nature. We need each other. When Jesus left the earth, he did not leave His disciples as a disparate collection of individuals; He left a church, a group of interrelated persons. Call it the body of Christ, the household of faith, or the assembly of believers, these Scriptural names indicate the communal nature of the church. Jesus knows we need Him and we need one another. Peter thought he could stand against the group, but when the others left, he could not.

Jesus is still under attack. How well are Christians standing up for Him? When He is tried in the newspapers and found guilty, are they defending Him? When movies promote a morality contrary to Christian standards and make a mockery of all that Jesus represents, are they defending Him? When the nation drifts further and further from the Lord, are they speaking out? Solitary Christians are seldom able to raise a voice on Jesus' behalf. Churches are more effective, because the members have both a leader and a group.

In Ephesians 6, Paul writes, "Be strong in the Lord and in his mighty power" (verse 10). This he writes in a book that has as one of its major themes the nature and essentiality of the church. In the very next paragraph, he exhorts his Christian readers to pray for each other and "pray also for me." Even the peerless apostle needed the prayers of the group. He was no stronger than Peter. He also needed a group to belong to.

CHAPTER TWENTY-SEVEN

Sorrow and Despair

Matthew 26:36-68; 27:1-10

We Walk Today Where Jesus Walked (26:36-46)
(Mark 14:32-42; Luke 22:39-46)

In the Garden of Gethsemane, Jesus once again wrestles with His mission. At the beginning of His ministry, immediately following His baptism, He overcame the almost irresistible seductions of the tempter (Matthew 4). On that occasion, His temptation came from without. He defended himself by leaning heavily upon the Word of God to overpower the words of Satan. This time, the urge to give up His appointed destiny comes from within, from the quite human drive to stay alive. The olive grove on the Mount of Olives (*Gethsemane* means "oil press") to the east of the Kidron valley becomes for Jesus another wilderness, even though His disciples are near and Jerusalem is just across the way. Here, in the depths of His being, His final cosmic struggle with God's adversary ensues.

Peter, James, and John are close at hand, the same companions who were present to see their Lord transfigured. They were with Him in His glory; now they wait while, unknown to them, their glorified Lord struggles with His fiercest temptation. Their presence comforts Jesus; it also comforts us. We are not alone in our need for companionship in life's critical moments. The Lord himself relied on His friends.

His words should have alerted them to the momentousness of this occasion. *"My soul is overwhelmed with sorrow to the point of death. Stay here and keep watch with me" (Matthew 26:38).* He has reason for His sorrow. He shall die, of that He is certain. But that is not the prime cause of His hurt. He has come into the world to His own people, and His own people have rejected Him (John 1:10). He offered them love and they returned hatred; He came to save them from their sins and they preferred their damnation. To die on a cross is humiliation enough, but to die an apparent failure is almost unbearable. He who has cried over Jerusalem (Matthew 23:37) will now be assassinated by the city He came to deliver.

As the body of Christ, the church walks today where Jesus walked.

We, too, walk into the Garden of Gethsemane, where our souls are "overwhelmed with sorrow." We cannot even view the evening news with indifference. Disaster, destruction, and death dominate the reports. While we sometimes sing, "I am happy in the service of the King," and we mean it, we certainly cannot be happy about the condition of our fellow human beings. We Christians smile a lot, but we smile through tears, as Jesus did. You find Christians smiling because in the name of Jesus, they are able to bring a little comfort to refugees in Thailand, the orphaned in Korea, the diseased in India, the terribly poor in Brazil. They are happy in the service of their King, but inwardly, they ache for the wretched existence that is the lot of too much of humanity.

Our sorrow is not only for the lost of mankind, but for the terrible price Jesus paid to save them. Church business can never be taken lightly by anyone who has walked into Gethsemane with Jesus. We bristle whenever we find a Christian "playing church," majoring in minors, busy about a million things that don't really matter. Some offended disciple, unable to tolerate this violation of Christian purpose any longer, composed a mock litany to register his protest:

> We have the handsomest minister. Isn't that nice!
> He preaches the sweetest sermons. Isn't that nice!
> He never angers anyone. Isn't that nice!
> Our church serves the best bean suppers. Isn't that nice!
> We oversubscribe our budget every year. Isn't that nice!
> Our Lord was crucified on a cross. Isn't that nice!

To reduce Jesus' awful agony to a level of social busy-ness is as unnice as it can be to the Christian whose soul, like his Savior's, is overwhelmed with sorrow.

"My Father, if it is possible, may this cup be taken from me" (Matthew 26:39). Jesus does not want to die, but knows He must. His "cup" is the cross, soon to become such a powerful symbol for Christians. It represents the supreme sacrifice of One who comprehended completely what it was going to cost Him to do His Father's will.

The cross still represents the readiness of Christ's body to take up the cup of suffering, even when we would rather not. To the extent that the church identifies with the mission of Christ, it cannot be indifferent to any form of human suffering and cannot opt out of serving Christ's cause just because we would rather that the cup would pass. In the providence of God, Jesus has to die. He has to take man's sins upon himself. In the providence of God, if there is any hope for this tragic world, the church must hold the same cup.

Obviously, national governments have proved they cannot help the world. Something greater than government is needed. A spiritual solution will save the world or nothing will. Only a cross-bearing church will right its wrongs. Only Christians who drink from Jesus' cup are prepared to do anything—and everything—to bring God's love to loveless men.

"Not as I will, but as you will" (Matthew 26:39). Jesus is simply practicing what He has earlier preached to His disciples (Matthew 6:10). He has said as much on other occasions as well: Matthew 7:2l; John 4:34; 6:38-40. Nothing is easier than for believers to pray, "Your will be done," except after uttering such a prayer to forget it completely when it no longer seems so easy to do what God wants. Everybody has at least one friend who will gladly do almost anything, except his duty. That's hard, he has found, and he would rather not.

One of the twentieth century's heroes is Conrad Adenauer. After World War II, at the age of 73, Adenauer became the Chancellor of West Germany, and he remained the dominant leader of his nation fourteen years. That great and straight old man said of his stewardship, "My hope is that when mankind looks beyond the dust and clouds of our day, it can be said of me that I have done my duty." Duty. "If it is not possible for this cup to be taken away unless I drink it, may your will be done" (Matthew 26:42). Jesus was prepared to do His duty. Do we walk where Jesus walked?

"Could you men not keep watch with me for one hour?" (Matthew 26:40). Three times He has returned to find them sleeping. They do not have the energy to enter into true communion with Him. They sleep, but the betrayer is wide awake. "Rise, let us go! Here comes my betrayer!" (Matthew 26:46). The betrayer never sleeps. While casual Christians sleep comfortably on our *Beauty Rest* mattresses in our air-conditioned bedrooms, and drive to worship in our air-conditioned automobiles and hurry in to nod contentedly on our padded pews, the betrayer is wide awake, "looking for someone to devour" (1 Peter 5:8).

What Killed Jesus? (26:47-68)
(Mark 14:43-50; Luke 22:47-53; John 18:3-14)

When someone dies, the curious always ask, "What killed him?" The chief killers come immediately to mind: heart attack, cancer, accident. When Jesus died, the immediate source of death was obvious. The cross killed Him. But what preceded the crucifixion? Which of the many contributing causes was the critical one?

Treachery and deceit (47-50)? The kiss of Judas would be enough to kill a person. According to Luke, Jesus asked, "Judas, are you betraying the Son of Man with a kiss?" (Luke 22:48). Are you, My trusted disciple, really a traitor?

His is the heartbroken question of Caesar, betrayed by his trusted ally, Brutus. *"Et tu,* Brutus?" Even you? Such treachery was, as Mark Antony said, "the most unkindest cut of all."

Yet it was not Judas' treachery that killed Jesus. He was prepared for it. When Judas kissed Him with the traditional greeting of a disciple for His master, Jesus quietly told him, "Friend, do what you came for" (Matthew 26:50). He had earlier told His dining disciples that one of the group would betray Him (26:21).

The police and other armed forces (51-56)? Temple police arrested Jesus, accompanied by Roman soldiers. Why there were so many is anybody's guess. Perhaps the priests did not trust Jesus to come peacefully; perhaps they were afraid of ambush or uprising. The number probably grew as the detachment tramped its way toward Gethsemane. They were a threatening number at any rate, armed for combat. Matthew says one of Jesus' disciples met force with force, drawing his sword and clipping off the ear of the high priest's servant. (Luke reports that Jesus immediately restored the ear—Luke 22:51.) According to John, it was the impetuous Peter who charged forward against the servant (John 18:10). He did not understand the true nature of Jesus' power.

Jesus did, however. "Put your sword back in its place, for all who draw the sword will die by the sword," He said to Peter (Matthew 26:52). More instructively, John adds that Jesus asked Peter, "Shall I not drink the cup the Father has given me?" (John 18:11). The sword could only harm, not help, His cause. Having just promised to do whatever the Father wanted of Him (Matthew 26:39), He would not now take things into His own hands. He could have summoned thousands of angels to rush to His rescue (Matthew 26:53), but He would not. He had something more important to accomplish than walk away from Gethsemane unharmed.

The desertion of His allies (56-58)? Did Jesus wonder, as He caught a glimpse of His fleeing disciples, whether it was worthwhile after all to endure what lay ahead? He had devoted himself to them for three years and now, in His hour of need, they deserted Him. Jesus told the arresting officers to leave His disciples alone (John 18:8), but He surely did not intend to give blanket permission for them to run out on Him. But run they did. They may have disappointed Him, even keenly, but they did not kill Him. He had long ago learned the lesson of the loneliness of leadership.

The lies and twisted truths the witnesses told (59-61)? It was a rigged trial. "The chief priests and the whole Sanhedrin were looking for false evidence against Jesus" (Matthew 26:59). They had nothing else to go on. He had broken no laws worthy of death.

A word about the Sanhedrin. This was the Supreme Court of Jewry, with power to decide all political and religious questions for the Jewish nation. Its membership consisted of seventy members and the presiding high priest. The seventy were scribes (lawyers), Pharisees, Sadducees, and elders, the recognized leaders of local Jewish synagogues. As the top court of the Jews, the Sanhedrin decided criminal cases as well as civil disputes. Their regulations prohibited any meeting to decide criminal cases during Passover Week and any criminal trial in other than daylight hours at any time. A criminal could never be condemned on the same day as the trial. Further, the decision was not valid if rendered anywhere else than in the regular meeting place of the Sanhedrin in the temple precincts.

Jesus' trial violated many of the Sanhedrin's own rules. It was further disgraced by the employment of false witnesses. You can always find someone willing to lie for a price. Probably nothing is more common than perjury. An English authority on antiques once declared that eighty percent of all of them sold in the English market were fakes. Another art authority, Dr. Wilhelm Bode, once stated that in Rembrandt's lifetime he painted 700 canvases, of which 10,000 can be found in America. Lying for a price is a practice as old as human history. Jesus had to listen to the witnesses lie, or at least twist the truth. He had never said He would destroy the temple, as the witnesses charged. He had said, "[If you] destroy this temple ... I will raise it again in three days" (John 2:19). That is not the same thing. When He spoke these words, He was not referring to the temple anyway, but to His own body. His words could easily be twisted, however, so they were. But their lies did not kill Him.

His religious enemies (62-66)? The high priest Caiaphas and his father-in-law, the former high priest Annas, wanted Jesus done away with. Earlier, Caiaphas had vented his cynicism when he remarked, "It is better for you that one man die for the people" (John 11:50). Kill Jesus and keep the peace. That was Caiaphas' philosophy. More importantly, kill Him to protect our political positions. Caiaphas was only a slightly more hardened politician than Harold Macmillan was when he served as Britain's Prime Minister in the mid-twentieth century. Trying to appease a restless constituency, Macmillan sacked several of his Cabinet officers and moved others to new posts. A reporter waggishly observed, "Greater love hath no man than this, that a man lay down his friends for his life." Thus Caiaphas.

He was good at his work, though. He forced Jesus to admit His true identity. He could not make Jesus defend himself against the absurd charges of the false witnesses, but he could goad Him to admit the truth. The key words were "Christ" and "Son of God." To get Jesus to admit these was, in his mind, tantamount to eliciting blasphemy from His lips. (See John 5:18.) "[Are you] the Christ, the Son of God?" (Matthew 26:63).

"I am," His "yes" affirmed. But He affirmed more than Caiaphas asked. "You may condemn Me for what I have said, you may kill Me, but let Me assure you of something: No matter what you do to Me, 'in the future you will see the Son of Man sitting at the right hand of the Mighty One and coming on the clouds of heaven.' I may appear temporarily down, but I'll not be out!"

Thus with deliberate intent, Jesus signed His death warrant. But these religious enemies did not kill Him (John 10:17, 18).

The physical and psychological abuse (67, 68)? They spit in His face, they struck Him with their fists, they taunted and mocked Him. Before long, they would hold a mock coronation, complete with crown (of thorns) and royal robe. Indulging themselves in the cruel entertainments of petty men, they heaped indignities on Him. But their abuse did not kill Him.

His death can be traced to only two sources: *God's purpose and Jesus' love (54, 56).* Once more Matthew calls attention to one of his major themes: these things are being done to fulfill Scripture.

> Surely he took up our infirmities,
>   and carried our sorrows,
> yet we considered him stricken by God,
>   smitten by him, and afflicted.
> But he was pierced for our transgressions,
>   he was crushed for our iniquities;
> the punishment that brought us peace was upon him,
>   and by his wounds we are healed....
> He was oppressed and afflicted,
>   yet he did not open his mouth;
> he was led like a lamb to the slaughter,
>   and as a sheep before her shearers is silent,
>   so he did not open his mouth.
> By oppression and judgment, he was taken away
> (Isaiah 53:4, 5, 7, 8).

Here is the heart of Christian faith. We affirm that through Christ's death we have been drawn close to God. He allowed Caiaphas and Pilate and their minions to deal Jesus the death blow so that through the cross, God could defeat death. What reads like a terrible travesty of justice surprises us into a new insight into the character of God himself. Almighty God has assumed the role of a lamb.

Revelation 7:17 pictures Him as a sacrificial lamb. As paradoxical as it sounds, on the throne of the universe sits a lamb. What religion would dare make such a claim? The Greeks placed Zeus on the throne, tossing his lightening bolts and flexing his thunders. Power is on the throne. Buddhists bow before the Buddha as the embodiment of undisturbed peace, utter absence of desire. The Jews could imagine nothing but an almighty Jehovah (Yahweh) on the throne. The Muslims worship a God so dictatorial that nothing happens in the universe except as Allah wills it. Science places scientific law, unbreakable and completely deterministic, on the throne. But the gospel? Its incredible claim is that the God who rules the universe is a God of Love, so loving as to sacrifice himself like a lamb on an altar to rescue wayward humanity. This loving God goes so far as to submit himself to the savagery of power-mad, self-serving human judges in the hope that even the dishonest judges will repent and be saved.

This teaching offends many, of course (1 Corinthians 1:23). A God who would stoop and suffer for unworthy man cannot be a perfect God, they object. E. Stanley Jones quotes a Hindu's criticism: "If Brahma would suffer, he would be unhappy; and if he were unhappy, he would be imperfect; and if he were imperfect, he would not be God."[94] But the gospel retorts, God *is* unhappy with humanity's unhappiness. He loves enough to take the unhappiness upon himself. He stoops to save.

Here, then, is why Christ died: because He believed the purpose of God required Him to and because His own love, which He shared with the Father, led Him to. He chose to die. He did not have to journey to Jerusalem in the first place, or cleanse the temple, or defy powerful religious antagonists, or remain in Gethsemane until the troops came for Him. He died by choice. For love.

Dr. Royal J. Dye was a pioneering missionary in what was still called, in the first half of the twentieth century, the Belgian Congo. As an old man, he loved to reminisce about the breakthrough that

---

[94]E. Stanley Jones, *Christ at the Round Table* (Abingdon, 1928), p. 246.

came as he and his comrades were trying to explain the meaning of the cross to Africans whose superstitious, hate-filled culture made it very difficult for them to grasp it. After what seemed an interminable time, Dr. Dye heard a folk story of a long-ago incident that gave him his opening. Two villages in the distant past had been at war for a long time, and peace seemed an impossible dream. Finally, the son of one chief, unable to stand the tension any longer, presented himself to his father. "I shall go and offer myself to the other village. They can have me and then there will be peace." His father consented. He went alone through the jungle to the village, where his people's enemies immediately hanged him on a tree. He gave himself to establish peace.

That is what killed Jesus. God sent Him into a hostile global village so that by His death, there could be peace.

When You've Gone Too Far (27:1-10)

Judas' remorse was real. Why he had betrayed Jesus remains a puzzle, but there is no doubt that he regretted his actions. Some people believe he was just trying to corner Jesus into having to declare himself the Messiah in a majestic display of power. Perhaps he never thought Jesus could actually be convicted and sentenced to die. Or perhaps he just didn't think. At any rate, along the way he opportunistically picked up some money—thirty pieces of silver, to be exact.

Whatever his motive, he went too far. Of that he was now convinced. Jesus was going to die and it was Judas' fault.

The money burned in his hand; shame burned in his heart. He ran to the temple, hurried through the court of Gentiles, through the women's court, through the court of the Israelites, up to the court of priests. He couldn't go in, but he could yell to the priests. "I have sinned. I have betrayed innocent blood. Take your money back."

They had no sympathy for him. "What is that to us? That's your responsibility." Judas was alone in his sin. He had deserted his fellow disciples and now he was being deserted by his fellow conspirators.

Flinging his money at the priests, he tore out of the temple and raced away to his death. (See Matthew 26:3-5.) Suicide. In his attempt to control events, he had gone too far. Restless, despairing, he had turned against Jesus. Tired of waiting for Jesus to make His move, perhaps, Judas had taken matters into his own hands. He knew better than Jesus; he could run things. So he ran them, too far.

The priests, who had no scruples about using temple money to secure the arrest of Jesus, displayed newly sensitive consciences about its dispensation now that it was back in their hands. Matthew reports that they felt they could not return it to the temple treasury, so they bought a field with it. Once a potter's field (providing clay for the pottery), it had probably been stripped of usable clay down to the limestone, which provided a natural burial place for poor aliens.

As usual, Matthew reaches into the Old Testament to show that everything is going according to God's prophesied plan. This time, however, the Gospel writer leaves readers in a bit of a quandary. The Old Testament as we now have it does not contain a passage like the one Matthew cites (27:9, 10), and the one we do have which is most like it is not from Jeremiah, but from Zechariah 11:12, 13. Perhaps Matthew took his quotation from a single scroll containing most of the prophets; if so, he could very easily have attributed the words of one to the other. (It has been pointed out that Zechariah is never quoted by name in the New Testament, even though his prophecies are referred to eighteen times). Perhaps he was simply combining the substance of Jeremiah 32:7-9 and Zechariah 11:12 and 13. If so, then Judas, in returning the blood money, imitates Zechariah, and the priests, in purchasing a field, repeat the precedent of Jeremiah.

While there may be some confusion over the prophecies, there is none about Judas' treachery. As far as he was concerned, he had killed Jesus. He saw only one course open to him. What he had caused to happen to Jesus he would do to himself. His fellow Jews might regard suicide as murder, but perhaps by murdering himself he could offer some kind of atonement for his heinous sin.

What can be said of Judas? At least this much: (1) He was a manipulator. (2) He was a loner. He isolated himself from friends and foes alike. No one loves a traitor. (3) He was sorry. (4) He was helpless to undo what he had done. He had gone too far. (5) Thinking there was no way back, he succumbed to his despair.

That was his fatal mistake. Peter, whose denial of Jesus in the courtyard of the high priest's dwelling was also a form of treachery, deserted his Lord as surely as Judas did. Both were flawed men. One we honor as the leader of the early Christian church; the other wears a name so odious no parent would burden his child with it. The difference between Judas and Peter is in what they did after they found they had gone too far. If only Judas had not succumbed to his despair. If only he had stopped taking things into his own hands. What a different story this would be if he had only placed himself once again in the hands of the Savior.

Everyone can readily identify with Judas. Not a believer among us has not at some time or other been profoundly discouraged because we have gone too far and hated our stupidity, cursing ourselves for the damage we have done someone else. We need to have someone tell us, *"When you've gone too far, go no further. Come back."*

Peter wept bitterly when he realized what a fool he had been. But he returned to the disciples, which made it possible for the risen Lord to restore him to His fellowship. Judas also wept bitterly when he realized the extent of the damage he had done. But he ran away and kept on going. He didn't turn back; he couldn't face the disciples. Once more, he took matters into his own hands. And it killed him. If only he had remembered some simple facts about Jesus.

The Lord Is Alive

When Judas killed himself, Jesus had not yet even been sentenced. Judas gave up on Jesus too soon. How could he know whether Jesus, who had promised to return after three days, would or would not be able to do what He had predicted?

There is a story about Reformation leader Martin Luther that is helpful here. In a period of depression, when his dark moods were making life at his home miserable for everyone around him, his wife appeared at the breakfast table dressed in her black mourning clothes. When Luther asked who had died, she replied, "Martin, the way you've been behaving lately, I thought God had died, so I came prepared to attend His funeral." Luther repented his display of unbelief. He had given up on God too soon.

It is so tempting to quit too soon. One wonders what would have happened to Great Britain had Churchill and other English leaders listened to the counsel of United States Ambassador Joseph Kennedy in the early days of World War II. Kennedy sent cables to President Roosevelt predicting that only "a miracle can save the BEF from being wiped out. . . ." He faulted Churchill, Attlee, and other leaders for not realizing that "physical destruction of men and property in England" could not compensate for their pride. Privately, Kennedy told Mary Hemingway that British resistance against Hitler was madness. "They haven't got a hope," he told her.[95]

That is how Judas would have said it. "I haven't got a hope." His enemy was not someone else, like Hitler, but himself. Having taken everything into his own hands, he had made such a mess of it that

---

[95]Herbert S. Parmet, *Jack: The Struggles of John Kennedy* (New York: The Dial Press, 1980), p. 80.

he had no hope of straightening things out himself. And he would still trust nobody else, certainly not Jesus, to correct the situation.

If only he would have reminded himself that Jesus was not yet dead, and that the other disciples were still alive, and that the cause to which they had all committed themselves was not yet aborted. It was not as dark as it seemed. If only, like Peter, he could have held on a little longer, to give God a chance.

The Lord Still Forgives

Judas' crime was terrible—but not unforgivable. He lives in infamy not so much for betraying Jesus as for depriving Jesus of any chance to forgive and restore him. If only Judas had given some more thought to Jesus' character and His frequent teaching on forgiveness. If he had, he could have lived to hear Him say on the cross, "Father, forgive them, for they do not know what they are doing" (Luke 23:34).

When Gerald Ford was President, the press took delight in exaggerating reports of his so-called clumsiness. Ford had the last word. "We skiers know that falling down isn't important; it's getting up again."[96] His stance resembles that of a coach who charged his team (trailing 20 to 0 at halftime) to forget all about trying to play catch-up. "Just start all over this half and play to win." You really can't catch up in life, undoing the mistakes you have already made. What has happened has happened. But you can start over.

That is what Charles Edison said he learned from his father, the famous inventor. When Thomas Alva Edison's West Orange, New Jersey, industrial plant went up in flames one night in 1914, the sixty-seven-year-old inventor shouted enthusiastically to his son, "Find your mother and bring her down here. She'll never see such a magnificent sight as long as she lives!" The fire did not cast him into despair. He later told Charles, "There is great value in a catastrophe like this. All our mistakes have been burned up. Now we can start all over again!"[97] Within ten weeks, he was in full production again.

The fire burned up the past errors. When John the Baptist preached and baptized at the Jordan River, he promised the Jews that somebody greater than he was coming, and this Great One would bring fire. "I baptize you with water for repentance. But after me will come one who . . . will baptize you with the Holy Spirit and with fire"

---

[96]*Time,* January 7, 1980.
[97]Peale, *A Guide to Self-Control,* pp. 142, 143.

(Matthew 3:11). He will burn up your mistakes. He will give you a chance to start over again. If only Judas had remembered that the Lord still forgives!

The Lord Still Helps Us in Our Weakness

If Judas had not insisted on doing everything himself, Jesus could have helped. Do we have any tougher battle than this one, to allow the Lord to have *His* way? Dr. Paul Tournier tells in *The Meaning of Persons* of a patient whose faith in God was genuine and who was respected in religious circles for his obvious devotion. Everyone admired him—and expected the best from him at all times. He worked hard to live up to their expectations. Always helping others, no one thought to help him. When Tournier saw him, however, the doctor discovered that the truth about this man was far different from his appearance. He was lonely and depressed. So depressed, in fact, that he had tried to commit suicide. He had been religious, all right, but not trusting the Lord to help him in his admitted weaknesses.

This was the lesson Buzz Aldrin has helped many people to understand. Aldrin was one of the first two astronauts on the moon. Basking in the fame this moon landing brought him, he thought for a while that he could do no wrong. But before long, the hero seemed much less than heroic to himself. From the landing in 1969 to his hospitalization for alcoholism three years later, his was a swift descent and a hard landing. Now he had to say of himself, "I'm no longer a he-man; I'm no longer a superhuman." He confessed his weakness in the hope that he could help others as deluded as he used to be.[98]

Thank God he did not keep running. When you've gone too far, come back. Let your prayer to God be something like this:

"Father, it is a terrible thing to be profoundly discouraged. But it is wonderful to know that You still live and still forgive and still want to help us in our weakness. You have taught us that when we are weak, then You are strong. Your Word reminds us that life is not over for us when we seem to have gone too far—if we will just come back to You. Help us not to be so proud that we refuse Your help or the help of Your loving church. Draw us into Your circle of love and keep us there. Help us to resist the strong temptation to take things into our own hands. Help us to trust You, to love You, and to leave the results to You. In Christ's name, amen."

---

[98]*The Tribune* (Mesa, Arizona, July 17, 1979).

CHAPTER TWENTY-EIGHT

The Crucifixion

Matthew 27:11-61

"What Shall I Do With Jesus?" (27:11-26)
(Mark 15:1-15; Luke 23:1-25)

Pilate's quandary is as contemporary as today. The problem of what to do with Jesus will not go away. No other person in human history forces a decision from us the way Jesus does. Pilate, the religious leaders, Barabbas, and the crowd cannot escape.

Pilate

Jesus stood before the Roman governor accused of three things, according to Luke 23:2.

"We have found this man subverting our nation."

"He opposes payment of taxes to Caesar."

"He claims to be Christ, a king."

For their purposes, the Jews did not scruple to translate *Christ,* which would have no meaning to Pilate, into *king,* which would force him to take notice. There could be no king but Caesar. Their charge, then, was treason.

Pilate was Caesar's appointed governor (procurator) in Judea, A.D. 26-36. It was the duty of procurators to oversee tax collections and other financial matters of the province. Things were not that simple in Judea, where the independent and rebellious Jews required a firmer hand. Pilate had judicial authority as well. He could take or save life in the name of the Emperor.

Secular historians have not been as kind to Pilate as the Scriptures are. They depict him as a stern, even cruel governor. He never fully understood the Jews in his charge. He thought their religion was fanaticism of the worse kind. Luke mentions his having his soldiers slay men even as they sacrificed in the holy place (Luke 13:1), but in his treatment of Jesus, Pilate seems to have been uncharacteristically benign.

His was no little dilemma. His emperor was Tiberius, who was severe with governors who mistreated his provincial subjects. (It was just such maltreatment that eventually cost Pilate his position.) Yet Tiberius was also ruthless with traitors. If Pilate should pardon Jesus and discover Him really to be a traitor, Tiberius' wrath would not be turned away. But if Pilate should order Jesus killed and later His innocence were established, Pilate's fate would be just as bad.

In the ancient Greek city of Locris, when a man proposed a law in the popular assembly, he did so on a platform with a rope around his neck. If his law passed, the rope was removed. If it failed, the platform was. Pilate must have felt like a citizen of Locris as he made his decision. Treading his way cautiously, the governor from Rome confronted the King of the Jews. And what a king! No armies, no political standing, no defenders—He seemed harmless enough. Yet somehow He had stirred the imaginations of His followers as only a genuine leader could. There He stood, only without defenders, yet offering no self-defense.

Pilate vacillated. He pleaded with the accusers, he stalled, he listened carefully to the warnings of his wife ("I have suffered a great deal today in a dream because of him"—Matthew 27:19), and finally, in an act of supreme political cowardice, he turned the decision over to the crowd, washing his hands of his responsibility.

Pilate, the stern ruler of secular historians, is more accurately displayed here in all his weakness. Finding no fault in Jesus, he lacked the strength to resist the demanding crowd. He epitomizes the kind of political leadership that the late United States President Harry Truman deplored. He said once that if America had been blessed with stronger Presidents in the pre-Civil War days, instead of the succession of five weak ones who dallied while the slavery issue burned, America might have been spared its terrible War Between the States. He was convinced that our national troubles have never been caused by the strong men who have led us, but by the weak ones who just sat twiddling their thumbs in the White House.

A stronger Pilate could have saved Jesus. Instead, he answered his own question, "What shall I do with Jesus?" by deciding not to decide.

The Religious Leaders

They knew what they wanted to do with Jesus. They wanted to kill Him. But Roman law, which granted surprising freedom to the colonies, did not grant the Jewish leaders the right to take life. They had to appeal to the governor to get what they wanted. Matthew says Pilate was aware that their motive was envy. They envied Jesus' popularity, His miraculous powers, His brilliance in teaching. They not only envied, but they feared Him as well. There was no compromise with His teaching. If He was right, they were wrong. If He were to win, they would lose. He had to be stopped.

There is no fanaticism more deadly than religious passion. It is impossible to number the assassinations attempted and accomplished in the name of religion. One such attempt was against Peter the Great of Russia. He labored valiantly to bring his backward people up to the standards of Western Europe in the early eighteenth century. Along the way, he offended many of his subjects. When a stranger nearly succeeded in stabbing the Czar in his summer palace on the Fontanka, Peter asked his would-be assassin what he intended to do. "To assassinate you."

"But why? Have I done you any harm?"

No, the man admitted, but Peter had harmed the man's brethren and his religion. Devoted to the old ways, he hated Peter for the changes he was introducing. The assailant would rather murder than suffer such indignities to his faith.[99]

He would have understood Jesus' enemies. In a sense, they meant Him no harm personally, but they had to stamp Him out because He embarrassed their religion and threatened their sacred institutions. How could they allow a man who successfully violated the Jerusalem temple (Matthew 21:12, 13) to live to do more damage?

Jesus was and has always been a threat to religious and political institutions. On the side of freedom and justice, of persons against systems and of the downtrodden against the overbearing, He smokes out the real persons hiding behind the trapping of office or piety. Such people have always known what to do with Jesus.

Barabbas

If Barabbas had been able to overhear the shouted debate between Pilate and the crowd, he would have asked, "What will *they* do with *me?*" He had a stake in the debate, after all. What they decided about Jesus would seal Barabbas' fate.

Barabbas was a bit player in this drama. Not much is known about him. He appears to have been a revolutionary, a killer, but he would have denied the charge that he was a murderer. If he killed, it was only to promote the cause of Israel's freedom from Rome.

---

[99]Massie, *Peter the Great, His Life and World,* p. 798.

There is not much suspense in the drama. When given a choice between a violent and a non-violent revolutionary, the crowd will choose the violent one every time. Non-violence requires sacrifice and suffering; no crowd is prepared to adopt such a strategy. Mohandas Gandhi's incredible movement for India's freedom from British sovereignty was but a temporary detour in the world's long history of violent upheaval. Jesus' methods have never been popular. Barabbas is the people's choice.

Take another look at Barabbas. He is a prisoner. As such, he symbolizes the majority of mankind, on whose behalf Jesus now stands charged before Pilate. He came to set the captive free and to release the oppressed (Luke 4:18). The masses, always played as pawns in the hands of the powerful, have long been manipulated and mistreated for the benefit of their overlords—but always in the name of religion or government or economics. Even democracies have perpetrated grave injustices against the weak. Against all such arrayed power, and on behalf of all the oppressed and imprisoned, Jesus stands before Pilate.

Barabbas would shout for Jesus' crucifixion right along with everyone else, because it seems to his advantage. And it is, for the short term, just as it seems to Pilate's advantage to kill Jesus to buy peace and to the leaders' advantage to kill Him to secure their positions.

But Jesus allows them all to win their skirmish with Him so that He can give Barabbas and all other sinners a greater and much more enduring victory.

The Crowd

As we have repeatedly noted, the crowd knows exactly what to do. "Crucify him!" Flogging is not enough (Luke 23:16, 18). They want Him dead.

Pilate hesitates, and rightly so. Nothing is more frightening than a crowd with its mind made up. Crowds always know more than individuals, because no one in the crowd has to be responsibile for his actions. What everybody does, nobody feels responsible for. He is a wise man who fears crowds.

During the American Civil War, a senator went to the White House to deliver a mandate from the conference of Northern States governors. Lincoln listened with respectful silence, then told the senator he was aware of the governors' authority, but he was not quite ready to follow their advice. "Go home and think the matter over," he countered. "Come to me tomorrow morning at nine o'clock and I will promise to do anything that you have then determined upon as right and proper. Good night."

The senator left quite pleased with himself. The interview had gone well. All night he thought about the course of action he would recommend to the President. However, when the appointed hour arrived the next morning, the senator did not arrive with it. He did not see Lincoln for three weeks. Then, at a reception, the President confronted him with his failure to appear. "I had an appointment with you for one morning about three weeks ago." He asked the senator where he had been all this time.

"To tell the truth, Mr. President, I have decided never to keep that appointment."

"I thought you would not when I made it for you," Lincoln told him.[100] Groups, crowds, know exactly what to do. Individuals who must be responsible for their decisions are more cautious.

Pilate's consulting the crowd for the decision is equivalent to modern politicians reading their opinion polls before taking a stand. (And like the cartoon depicting the housewife who says to the pollster, "Put me down for 'No Comment' on that one. I really haven't read enough polls on the subject to form an opinion."[101]) So Pilate "polls" the crowd, and the crowd, like all mobs, shouts its choice. Pilate has found no fault in Jesus (Luke 23:4, 14; John 18:38; 19:4, 6), but he yields to the crowd's demands.

And Jesus is crucified.

If you are a Christian, do not expect that yours will ever be a popular majority religious movement. If you are a Christian, do not expect to be understood and appreciated—by political leaders, by religious leaders, certainly by the majority. If you stand with Jesus, you will not win the crowd's approval. But, of course, you will be right.

He Was Crushed for Our Iniquities (27:27-50)
(Mark 15:16-39; Luke 23:26-48; John 19:17-30)

Russian novelist Dostoevsky describes a man gazing at a picture of the crucifixion. "Don't look at that picture, you fool," another character warns him. "Don't you know a man can lose his faith by looking at that picture?"

---

[100]Sandburg, *Abraham Lincoln, The War Years,* p. 238.

[101]Stayskal, *Chicago Tribune,* 1980. Reprinted in *Christianity Today,* November 12, 1982, p. 33.

"Yes, that is just what is happening to me."

It has happened to many. The cross that draws men to Christ also drives them from Him (1 Corinthians 1:23). They want a powerful, vengeful God, an omnipotent Lord who will force His will upon this evil world, overthrowing godless dictators, ridding humanity of incurable diseases, banishing suffering. "Oh God, if there is a God, why don't You do something about all these problems?"

He does. He did. He suffered with us. He suffered so that we would not always have to. He died so we might live. He experienced sorrow that we could experience joy. He emptied himself so that we might become rich.

Suffering is not the world's greatest evil; otherwise He would not invite us to imitate His experience. "If anyone would come after me, he must deny himself and take up his cross daily and follow me" (Luke 9:23); "To this you were called, because Christ suffered for you, leaving you an example, that you should follow in his steps" (1 Peter 2:21).

Christ brought new meaning to the cross. His disciples have followed Him through the ages, denying themselves, carrying their personal crosses in imitation of His example. But why did God not stop the torture just short of death? Why did the Lord have to experience the tomb? Of the many answers given in Scripture and elsewhere, Albert Camus offers the one indisputable reason: "Men are never convinced of your reasons, of your sincerity, of the seriousness of your sufferings, except by your death. So long as you are alive, your case is doubtful; you have a right only to their skepticism."[102] An almost-dead Christ, who nearly died to deliver us from sin, is not good enough. A tortured Christ, rescued at the eleventh hour by a God who could not bear to see His Son in agony, could never have convinced cynical mankind that He had borne their iniquities.

So He had to die. The Roman governor, Pontius Pilate, ordered a notice prepared and fastened to the cross: JESUS OF NAZARETH, THE KING OF THE JEWS. It was printed in three languages, so no one would miss their meaning. Whether in mockery or admiration, Pilate would use the words that so infuriated Jesus' enemies. They wanted the sign down, but Pilate would accommodate them no longer. "What I have written, I have written" (John 19:19-22).

Jesus died a king. But what a unique king!

---

[102]Albert Camus, *The Fall* (New York: Random House [Vintage Books], 1956), p. 74.

A Mocked King (27-31)

"They stripped him and put a scarlet robe on him, and then wove a crown of thorns and set it on his head" (Matthew 27:28). Then the staff in His right hand, the soldiers' mock obeisance, the hailing and spitting and beating. Then the crucifying.

Mockery. They hailed Him with hoots that echo in our century. Christian discipleship is not for the thin-skinned. You can't expect to be treated better than Jesus was. The world is no more hospitable to Jesus' followers than it was to Jesus. The oldest crucifix in existence (third century A.D.) was found on the Palatine hill in Rome, the imperial residential district during the years of the empire. The inscription under the crucifix says, "Alexamenos worships his god." On the cross is a human body; on the body is the head of an ass.

The crucifix is somebody's idea of a joke. As humor, it belongs in a class with the crown of thorns and the scarlet robe. Modern Christians need to realize, however, what the cross represented before Jesus transformed it. The Roman orator Cicero declared that "the very name of the cross should never come near the body of a Roman citizen, nor even enter into his thoughts, his sight, his hearing." Nothing was more heinous to a Roman than crucifixion. Hans Kung writes, "The *cross of Jesus* was bound to strike *an educated Greek* as *barbaric folly, a Roman citizen* as *sheer disgrace,* and *a devout Jew* as *God's curse."* [103] (See Deuteronomy 21:23.)

But God can turn mockery into victory.

A Helpless King (32-44)

After World War II, some German paintings were exhibited in London. A painting that attracted a great deal of attention was by an artist named Gruenwald. It depicted a man horribly beaten, eyes swollen, cheek torn; he was obviously near death. British viewers immediately thought of the Gestapo and grieved again for the victims of Naziism. It came as a shock to them to discover that this was Gruenwald's conception of what Jesus looked like after He had fallen into the hands of the soldiers.

If He is king, He is a helpless king. Simon of Cyrene, undoubtedly in Jerusalem from his country in order to celebrate the Passover Feast, an innocent observer of this "parade of criminals," is

---

[103]Hans Kung, *On Being a Christian* (Garden City, New York: Doubleday and Company, 1976), p. 397.

unceremoniously yanked from the crowd and forced to help the exhausted Jesus carry the cross. (Simon's experience may very well have made a Christian of him. Mark 15:21 calls him the father of Alexander and Rufus, obviously Christians whom the readers of Mark's Gospel know by name.) Callous soldiers, impervious to human suffering, gamble at the feet of the cross for Jesus' clothes. Casual strollers, ambling by Golgotha to see the show, jump into the spirit of things by joining their insults to the shouts of the agitated crowd. "You who are going to destroy the temple and build it in three days, save yourself! Come down from the cross, if you are the Son of God!" (Matthew 27:40).

At least the soldiers have enough heart to offer Him some drugged wine to ease His pain (Matthew 27:34). Of course, this is a routine custom; they mean nothing personal by it. Jesus twice (see verse 48) refuses it, wishing to bear our pain consciously as He bears our sin. His companions are robbers; He is, as Isaiah said He would be, "numbered with the transgressors" (Isaiah 53:12).

He saved others. But He cannot save himself—for our sake.

In India, a swami was baptized and became a fervent disciple of Christ. While talking with a group of Hindu lawyers one day, he took offense when one of them referred to Jesus as the illegitimate son of Mary. In fury the swami, a huge man, took off his shoe and struck the lawyer several times across the shoulder. Then he stormed away, proud that he had so ably defended his Lord.

That night as the swami lay thinking about the matter, he saw Christ come to him. The Master spoke no word, but quietly removed the robe from His shoulder and showed him the marks of his shoe upon His own skin.[104]

Jesus' way is not the way of vengeance. "He was pierced for our transgressions, he was crushed for our iniquities; the punishment that brought us peace was upon him, and by his wounds we are healed" (Isaiah 53:5). He was helpless because He chose to be, for our sake. Perhaps Malcolm Muggeridge is right: "The world would have to destroy him in order that henceforth the nature of the world should be made manifest."[105] He was helpless, because if He rose to defend himself, He would become like the world that was killing Him. His

---

[104]E. Stanley Jones, *Christ and Human Suffering* (New York: Abingdon Press, 1933), p. 159.

[105]Malcolm Muggeridge, *Jesus Rediscovered* (London: Collins [Fontana Books], 1969), p. 84.

willingness to submit to the worst the world could do to Him revealed the nature of its hatred and of God's redeeming love.

An Apparently Abandoned King (45-50)

"My God, my God, why have you forsaken me?" (Matthew 27:46). His disciples had fled from Him earlier. Now it seems that even God is gone.

How do we explain His sense of abandonment? Scholars like to point out that Jesus is here quoting Psalm 22. That hymn begins with this cry, but it ends on a resounding note of victory:

> You who fear the Lord, praise him!
>   All you descendants of Jacob, honor him!
>   Revere him, all you descendants of Israel!
> For he has not despised or disdained
>   the suffering of the afflicted one;
> he has not hidden his face from him
>   but has listened to his cry for help (Psalm 22:23, 24).

Jesus may be borrowing the opening words of this Psalm, but the words nonetheless genuinely express His feelings in this terrible moment. His is certainly, as other scholars point out, a very human outcry. To some, Jesus' words are the first utterance of so-called "modern man," man alone against the universe. Jesus' outcry must have pierced the hearts of the few believing witnesses who heard it. He told them He had come from God. But where was God now? What could they hope for, if the person in whom they had hoped had no hope himself?

Yet could Jesus' experience have been otherwise? He "who has been tempted in every way, just as we are—yet was without sin" (Hebrews 4:15) could not have been completely human had He not experienced what it means for a person to be alone, terribly alone, without friend or guide or God.

It is a fleeting sensation. Soon comes the resurrection with its stunning affirmation that Jesus was never outside the embrace of His Father's love. It only seemed so.

His abandonment by God was only apparent. Unfortunately, His desertion by His disciples was and is real. Peter, Judas, the rest of the disciples, were gone. The faithful few remained (Matthew 27:55, 56), but the key ones had fled. Man's treachery, not God's, remains the grave concern of Christendom to this day.

When Jesus came to Golgotha they hanged Him on a tree,
They drave great nails through hands and feet and made a Calvary;
They crowned Him with a crown of thorns, red were His wounds
   and deep,
For those were crude and cruel days, and human flesh was cheap.

. When Jesus came to Birmingham they simply passed Him by,
They never hurt a hair of Him, they only let Him die;
For men had grown more tender and they could not give Him pain.
They only just passed down the street and left Him in the rain.

Still Jesus cried, "Forgive them for they know not what they do,"
And still it rained the winter rain that drenched Him through and
   through;
The crowds went home and left the streets without a soul to see,
And Jesus crouched against a wall and cried for Calvary.
                                              —Studdert-Kennedy[106]

Standing by God (27:51-61)
(Mark 15:38-47; Luke 23:47-56; John 19:31-42)

After the agony of Gethsemane, after the mockery of the trial, and
after Jesus' sense of being abandoned on the cross, these verses re-
sound with affirmation.

God Has Not Abandoned Jesus

"My God, my God, why have you forsaken me?" Jesus cried from
the cross (Matthew 27:46). Now from the bowels of nature, God
provides this rumbling answer. Jesus has not been alone, but through
His dark passage, God has been rearranging the relationship between
Heaven and earth.

(1) "The curtain of the temple was torn in two" (Matthew 27:51).
This massive veil (Josephus reports in his *Jewish Wars* that it was sixty
feet high) was the one separating the Holy Place (where the priests
burned incense to God) from the Holy of Holies, the inner sanctuary
that symbolized God's presence (which was entered only by the high
priest and by him only once a year). Christ's death tore away this
barrier between man and God, giving Jesus' disciples "confidence to
enter the Most Holy Place by the blood of Jesus, by a new and living
way opened for us through the curtain" (Hebrews 10:19, 20). The
incredible message of the New Testament is that through Jesus'

---

[106]This famous old poem I have quoted from Robert E. Speer, *Five
Minutes a Day* (Philadelphia, Westminster Press, 1929).

crucifixion, man's way to God has been permanently opened up. No longer is any intermediary required; no more are mysteries perpetuated by a priesthood operating on behalf of ignorant devotees. God's embrace is for us all.

(2) "The earth shook and the rocks split" (Matthew 27:51). The foundations of the world were shaken by a power greater than anything in this world, including death. The earth learned anew of the mysterious connection between moral and physical worlds (Genesis 3:17, 18—"Cursed is the ground because of you . . ."). The apostle Paul speaks of creation's being "subjected to frustration" in a "bondage to decay" and a "groaning as in the pains of childbirth . . ." (Romans 8:19-22).

(3) "The tombs broke open" (Matthew 27:52). When God decides to break the grip of death, then death no longer has the victory. As Paul proclaims in 1 Corinthians 15 (read the entire chapter), Jesus' resurrection is but the firstfruits of the raising of the dead. Matthew grants this amazing phenomenon just a passing glance, however, because it pales into insignificance before the world-changing gospel (good news) of Jesus' death and resurrection.

God could not have made a stronger statement to the watching world: He has not forsaken Jesus. He has changed the world through Jesus. The centurion and other witnesses are catching on: "Surely he was the Son of God" (Matthew 27:54). What exactly the centurion (commander of a hundred Roman soldiers) means by this title, we do not know. At the least, he is acknowledging that Jesus has supernatural connections! Earthquakes and grave openings do not accompany just anyone's crucifixion. What the centurion observes is the power of God announcing that He has been standing by Jesus all along.

God Has Not Abandoned Us, Either

Like a long-suffering parent or a rebellious child, God has not given up on the human race. He is instead working out His ultimate plan to rescue His children from their folly. "For Christ died for sins once for all, the righteous for the unrighteous, to bring you to God" (1 Peter 3:18). He did not do this because we deserved such consideration; to the contrary, "God demonstrates his own love for us in this: While we were still sinners, Christ died for us" (Romans 5:8). "This is love: not that we loved God, but that he loved us and sent his Son as an atoning sacrifice for our sins" (1 John 4:10). For our sakes, then, God became one with us (Philippians 2:5-11), suffering for us, that we might through His grace live with Him.

When David was king of Israel, he suffered a rebellious child. Absalom killed his brother Amnon for raping Absalom's sister Tamar. This was the start of a career of defiance, one that culminated in a final armed rebellion against his father. When news of Absalom's death reached David, the wronged father did not rejoice that the troublemaker had been silenced forever. Instead, he cried out in anguished love, "O my son Absalom! My son, my son Absalom! If only I had died instead of you—O Absalom, my son, my son" (2 Samuel 18:33).

The Heavenly Father cried the same cry. On Jesus' cross, He "died" in place of His rebellious offspring (John 3:16, 17). He has not abandoned us.

Some Disciples Have Not Abandoned Jesus

"Many women were there, watching from a distance" (Matthew 27:55). The leading disciples aren't around. Judas betrayed Jesus, Peter denied Him, and the rest have fled. But these courageous women remain nearby. They have followed Him to Jerusalem from Galilee, in order "to care for his needs." Some of them have been regular financial supporters of Jesus' ministry (Luke 8:1-3). Others could prepare food and in other ways assist the master and His band of disciples. Three of them are spoken of by name.

Mary Magdalene is mentioned first. Her name indicates that she came from Magdala along the western coast of the Sea of Galilee. Jesus healed her of demon possession (Luke 8:2; Mark 16:9), and in gratitude, she became one of His most devoted followers. In the popular imagination, Magdalene is portrayed as a loose woman before Jesus healed her, probably a prostitute. There is really no Scriptural basis for this reputation. It probably stems from the fact that Luke mentions her immediately after telling the incident of the sinful woman who anointed Jesus (Luke 7:36-50; 8:2). Luke does not connect that woman with Magdalene. We should not do so, either.

Mary the mother of James and Joses. We cannot speak with too much certainty about her identity, although she seems to be the same person who is called the wife of Clopas (or Cleopas) in John 19:25. Some students also think that Clopas and Alphaeus (Matthew 10:3) are the same person.

The mother of Zebedee's sons. We first met this assertive woman in Matthew 20:20 when she petitioned Jesus for special favors for her sons, apostles James and John. She probably was Salome, the sister of Jesus' mother. A comparison of Matthew 27:56 with Mark 15:40

and John 19:25 suggests this, since each verse mentions Mary Magdalene, Mary the mother of James and Joseph, and another woman. That woman is "the mother of Zebedee's sons" here, Salome in Mark, and Jesus' mother's sister in John. Her husband was a Galilean fisherman of some substance. Mark refers to his hired servants (1:20), leaving the impression that Zebedee's was a family of means.

There they are, these three women and the others, standing by their Lord even though their leaders have fled. They call to mind some lines written by Dietrich Bonhoeffer in his prison cell, just months before the Nazis killed him. This is the second stanza of his poem, "Christian and Unbeliever."

> Men go to God when he is sore bested:
> find him poor and scorned, without shelter and bread,
> whelmed under weight of the wicked, the weak, the dead.
> Christians stand by God in his hour of grieving.

Like these women.

The two Marys and Salome can be found in thousands of churches around the world. How many little congregations are alive only because of some faithful, devoted women. Men may be elected to positions, but women more often do the jobs. They clean, they pray, they teach, they cry, they visit, they care.

In the early part of the nineteenth century, Alexis deTocqueville left France for an extensive visit of America. He documented his findings in his classic work, *Democracy in America,* which is required reading for any student of American history. He must have met the spiritual descendants of these women in his visits, because this is his conclusion about American womenfolk:

> As for myself, I do not hesitate to avow that although the women of the United States are confined within the narrow circle of domestic life, and their situation is in some respects one of extreme dependence, I have nowhere seen women occupying a loftier position; and if I were asked, now that I am drawing to the close of this work, in which I have spoken of so many important things done by the Americans, to what the singular prosperity and growing strength of that people ought mainly to be attributed, I should reply: To the superiority of their women.

There was also one superior man at the cross. Joseph of Arimathea stepped forward and declared himself a disciple of Jesus, and in a most daring manner. He requested an audience with Pilate himself in order to seek the privilege of burying Jesus in his own new family tomb (a very generous gift, since no one else could be buried in the tomb of an executed criminal). Joseph's town was probably to the northwest of Jerusalem, where he was one of the leaders. He was rich, a member of the Sanhedrin (Mark 15:43), and, according to Luke, a righteous man who was looking for the kingdom of God (23:50, 51). In addition, for some time, he had been a secret disciple of Jesus. He did not make his belief known, because a man of his position and wealth had a lot to lose (John 19:38). With his colleague Nicodemus (who had secretly visited Jesus by night—John 3), he prepared Jesus' body for burial and placed Him in his own tomb, which had been hewed out of the rock on the side of a hill. (See John 19:38-42.)

You cannot help wondering what thoughts must have crowded the minds of all the disciples, these who stood by and the others who fled. It was a dark day for every one of them, undoubtedly. They had placed their trust and hopes in Jesus. Now He was dead. Joseph buried Him just as any mortal would be buried. Gone was the hypnotic hold of Jesus' eyes, the magnetic tug of His unique personality, the persuasive voice that swept all other authorities aside with a simple, "But I say to you." What plans were these leaderless disciples making? Could they return to their old ways after consorting with the Master? What would their neighbors say, when they returned in defeat after having left in such hope?

We don't know, of course, what they thought. We only know what these women and Joseph did. They stood by. They did not abandon their Lord.

CHAPTER TWENTY-NINE

The Resurrection and Its Results
Matthew 27:62—28:20

"Do Not Be Afraid" (27:62—28:10)
(Mark 16:1-8; Luke 24:1-12; John 20:1-10)

Fear so dominates the actions in these verses that nothing short of God's direct intervention can overcome it. Frightened men hounded Christ to the cross; frightened men spare no effort to guarantee that the dead Jesus stays dead.

Do Not Be Afraid of a Tomb

Without man's nearly universal fear of death, there would have been no cross for Jesus. The worst punishment His enemies could imagine was to snuff out His life. They were afraid to die; they were certain that He, too, was frightened. They did not count on His unnerving calm. He had nothing to be anxious about, however, because He already knew what the New Testament would shout from the highest, that God is Lord of life *and* death. Try whatever they could to destroy Jesus, they would fail. Goldsmith's *Traveller* says it well:

> How small of all that human hearts endure,
> That part which laws or kings can cause or cure.

Pilate and the chief priests could interrogate, try, torture, ridicule, and crucify Jesus, but they were helpless to alter God's plan for Him. Through all the agony of His passion week, when Jesus even asked His Father to spare Him the pain of the cross, Jesus never once uttered a word of fear.

His equanimity before dying is not typical. Man has always been afraid to die. From as long ago as ancient Sumer (important from 3300 B.C. to 1800 B.C.), we have received the early Sumerian epic *Gilgamesh*. The writer develops the theme of the hero's quest for a means to break death's power over him. But immortality literally slips through his fingers. He finds a branch of the tree of life, but it slips down into the water where a snake snatches it. Gilgamesh is thus condemned to mortality. One day he, too, must die.

The ancient Greek gods were not always admirable—they were too human in their loves and lusts—but at least they were immortal. That was good enough for the Greeks: immortality was sufficient for divinity!

We moderns tend to scoff at these primitive myths, but for all our sophistication, we still have difficulty facing death head on. We prefer to say someone has "passed on" or "gone to his reward" to saying, "He died." We seem more reluctant to talk about death than sex, which death has replaced as the leading taboo subject in polite conversation. Corpses are treated to the finest cosmetic facials in an attempt to make them appear "lifelike"; ministers are sometimes denied access to a dying parishioner because the family fears the minister's presence will signal to the patient that death is imminent. Fear of the grave still haunts humanity. To such anxious souls, Jesus' resurrection is God's promise: "You do not have to be afraid any more. Even a sealed tomb, with guards on duty, cannot hold a person that God's wants out of it. Do not be afraid."

Do Not Be Afraid of a Messenger From God

The angel's reassurance to the women takes us back to the beginning, when the angel spoke the same words to calm the shepherds (Luke 2:10). Billy Graham calls these words "the divine hush for God's children." In his *Till Armageddon,* he lists the many times God hushed His troubled children with these soothing words:

> To Abraham: "Do not be afraid, Abram. I am your shield, your very great reward" (Genesis 15:1).
> To Joshua: "Do not be afraid; do not be discouraged" (Joshua 8:1).
> Elisha to his servant: "Don't be afraid ... those who are with us are more than those who are with them [the enemy]" (2 Kings 6:16).
> David to the Lord: "I will fear no evil, for you are with me" (Psalm 23:4).
> Another Psalm: "The Lord is with me; I will not be afraid. What can man do to me?" (118:6).
> The Lord to Israel: "So do not fear, for I am with you" (Isaiah 41:10).
> Jesus: "Do not be afraid, little flock, for your Father has been pleased to give you the kingdom" (Luke 12:32).
> Jesus: "Do not be afraid. I am the First and the Last. I am the Living One; I was dead, and behold I am alive for ever and

ever! And I hold the keys of death and Hades" (Revelation 1:17, 18).

When covered bridges still dotted the American countryside, a farmer was driving his herd of cattle over one of them. That is, he was trying to. The cattle were not afraid of the dark bridge. What scared them were the shafts of light cutting the darkness. The bridge's siding had some knotholes in it, and several of the boards did not quite meet. The cows were afraid of the light that these openings allowed in to penetrate the darkness. They shied away from it, tried to turn around and go back, bucked and lunged in their attempts to leap over the light. They finally made their way through, emerging at the other end worn out from their crossing. Not the darkness, but the light in the darkness, frightened them.

They were like the vermin that dwell in the darkness on the underside of leaves and boards on the grass. They seem to be unafraid of being trampled, but turn the leaves or boards over and watch them scramble for the dark.

> The people walking in darkness
>   have seen a great light;
> on those living in the land of the shadow of death
>   a light has dawned (Isaiah 9:2).

But not everyone living in the shadow of death welcomes the light. John speaks of Christ as the light: "In him was life, and that life was the light of men. The light shines in the darkness, but the darkness has not understood it" (John 1:4, 5). The Light came from "the Father of the heavenly lights" (James 1:17). The angel addressing the women also came from the Father, and "his appearance was like lightning, and his clothes were white as snow" (Matthew 28:3). And the women were afraid. But the angel spoke the "divine hush" to calm their fears.

Do Not Be Afraid Of Belief

The women "hurried away from the tomb, afraid yet filled with joy" (Matthew 28:8). A disturbing mix of emotions warred within them. They could scarcely take in what they had seen and heard, yet they wanted with all their hearts to believe. They were afraid, because it seemed too good to be true. It is an altogether too human response, isn't it? One man said of his troubled father, "The real tragedy of Dad's life is that he had it all, but he never realized it." Always

345

expecting the worst, never giving in to the beauty of the moment, such people rob themselves of the full joy of their blessings. If only they could learn to trust the message from God, they could be like the bird Victor Hugo describes:

> Be like the bird
> That, pausing in her flight
> Awhile on boughs too slight,
> Feels them give way
> Beneath her and yet sings,
> Knowing that she hath wings.

The wings of faith bring joy; the doubts summon fear. Like the father of the seizure-stricken (or demon-possessed) son (Mark 9:14-29; Matthew 17:14-21), each of the women could have cried out, "I do believe; help me overcome my unbelief" (Mark 9:24). Remembering what Jesus had taught them and trusting God to bring His plans to a successful conclusion, they could have banished their fears.

William Inge reports that in the days of the British Commonwealth, Bulstrode Whitelocke, Ambassador to The Hague, was tossing through a sleepless night, anxious about his country's safety, when his old servant, trying to get some sleep in the same room with the ambassador, asked permission to ask a question. His question was whether God had governed the world well before the ambassador was born. "Undoubtedly." Then he wanted to know whether God would govern the world well after the ambassador was gone. "Undoubtedly." "Then, sir," he asked, "can you not trust Him to rule the world well while you are in it?" The reminder did its work, and the tired ambassador turned over and slept.[107]

Trust in the Lord brings that kind of peace. But here a disclaimer must be inserted. The word is belief (trust), not wishful thinking. The women would have no cause for joy if they were just wishing Jesus had arisen. Their trust had to be based on the evidence they have seen and their belief in the God who can raise the dead. Belief is misunderstood by too many. They act as if they think "wishing" could make something happen. "When you wish upon a star, your dreams come true." Such sentimentalism does far more damage than good. In an episode in the popular television mini-series *Backstairs at the White House,* Emmett Rogers tells his lame daughter Lil'yan that, in spite

---

[107]*Lay Thoughts of a Dean* (Garden City Publishing Company, Inc., 1926), p. 215.

of her polio-inflicted paralysis, she can be anything she wants to be, "don't you let nobody tell you you cain't." Her one dream above all dreams is to become a dancer. "That what you want sweetheart? Well, you jus' keep on believin'."

When his wife Maggie scolds him for misleading their daughter, whose leg will never be able to hold her without a crutch, Emmett defends himself. "It's all I got to my name to give the child. Had to give her somethin'." But all he gave her was some wishful thinking. He hadn't been able to wish himself well, either. He remained a hopeless alcoholic.

Wishful thinking doesn't produce. But belief, belief that is trust in God, can banish fear and introduce joy into one's life. "Every tomorrow has two handles," someone has said; "we can take hold by the handle of anxiety or by the handle of faith." Take the handle of faith—not wishful thinking—and don't be afraid.

Do Not Be Afraid of Jesus

"Suddenly Jesus met them" (Matthew 28:9). With awe, they approached Him and clasped His feet. His greeting was the now familiar divine hush: "Do not be afraid" (28:10). These repeated words need to be memorized by every believer. Too much religion is shrouded in fear. Paralyzed by a fear of sinning or of a vengeful God, some people sharpen their conscience until it cruelly stabs them. They take no pleasure in serving God; they doggedly pursue their duties, anxious lest He discover some of their spiritual furniture undusted. They cannot enjoy their faith; enjoyment seems a sin to them, as if God demands that His subjects take on only unpleasant tasks. Afraid of God, they are equally afraid of His Son. Their anxiety grows in ignorance; they do not know who they are or to whom they belong. If they did, they would realize that they are the loved children of a loving Father, of whom they have no cause to be afraid. They must respect Him, they may be in awe of Him, they will worship Him, but they will not be terrified by Him.

Having comforted His friends, Jesus dispatches them to their home territory where, He tells them, He will meet with His disciples again. No time for casual conversation or explanations of the resurrection. They must carry the incredible announcement: God has acted; Jesus is triumphant. Now, before He leaves them again, He has some final business with His followers. When they meet in Galilee, He will issue His last orders to them. They have nothing to fear. What God started with Jesus, He will continue through Jesus' disciples.

A Lie, the Truth, and the Consequences (28:11-20)

At the end of the Gospel, the enemies of Jesus are still lying, but their lies are unable to thwart God's plans.

The Lie

Money is a powerful persuader. It must have taken a large chunk of change to bribe the guards to swear that Jesus' disciples stole His corpse while they were asleep. The lure of the hush money coupled with the chief priests' promise to arrange things with the governor was enough to persuade the guards. They took the money and lied. The lie, Matthew says, was still widely circulated as he was writing.

Arguments against the reality of Jesus' resurrection have usually fallen into one of three categories:

(1) The disciples were simply mistaken. What they thought had happened did not happen. Period. They believed they were telling the truth, but they were deceived.

(2) The writers of the Gospels merely repeated myths that had quickly grown up about this unusual Nazarene. While alive, Jesus was larger than life, so it is only natural His followers would exaggerate events surrounding His death. Stories of His supernatural escape from the grave are the logical consequence of the exaggerated stories of miracles wrought during His life.

(3) There was a so-called "Passover plot," a clandestine spiriting away of the body by His conspiring disciples who, after stealing the corpse and disposing of it, maintained absolute silence about their crime until they were all dead. This last option is what the chief priests decided to push as their account of what happened to the missing body. It's a pretty weak story, however, since it is impossible to believe that this lie could have originated with the disciples and the five hundred additional persons who saw the risen Lord (1 Corinthians 15:6). That many people can't keep quiet about something as extraordinary as a human resurrection. They certainly would not have died for the lie. To the contrary, men would ordinarily do almost anything to keep from losing their lives. What did they have to gain by stealing the body?

But the lie does not change reality. The fact is, Jesus arose.

The Truth

Matthew does not bother to refute the lie. The living Christ, addressing His disciples in their final meeting, is refutation enough. The subsequent developments in the young church are proof enough. In

Acts, the disciples, invigorated by their encounter with the risen Lord, are changed persons. They had been dispirited, confused, and hurt by their Master's death. Now they appear confident, enthusiastic, and filled with joy. They do not pause to present reasoned treatises on the possibility of resurrection; they hail their risen Lord.

Students of Christian art have admired a certain pre-medieval cross (before crosses had become crucifixes, with the body of Christ hanging on them). This one has two guards beneath it, one of them fast asleep. Above the cross is a laurel wreath, the symbol of victory. Doves on the arms of the cross are pecking at its berries. Within the wreath is the monogram of Christ. Altogether, the artist has given a picture of Jesus' passion and resurrection. What begins in suffering ends in victory. Here the truth in general about God has become very specific: His love sacrifices, His will conquers, His mercy forgives, His power suffices. Men no longer need to speculate about theology: they can see God in action. The Lord has entered the battlefield against the Great Liar himself and has defeated him. It is no theoretical defeat: God has taken action against him once and for all. He can lie all he wants to, but he cannot destroy the evidence. The dead is now alive.

On the truth of Jesus' resurrection pivots the entire Christian faith. We cannot respect Jesus as merely "a good man" if this claim to the resurrection is untrue. If He did not rise again as He promised He would, then He could not produce what He promised. If He, in fact, did rise from the dead, however, then we would be pretty foolish to call Him "a good man" like other good men. Of whom else in all history have such claims been made?

The Consequences

The logical conclusion, then, is that if Jesus did rise from the dead, then He is of God. And if He is of God, then He really does have the authority He claims. And if He truthfully claims all authority "in heaven and on earth," then He must be obeyed. When He says, "Go," we must go; when He says, "Disciple," we must disciple; and His orders to baptize we must also carry out (Matthew 28:18-20).

This undistinguished band of eleven disciples was to commence a mission that has not yet been completed: they were to carry the gospel to the whole world. Without formal education, with no social standing, with their membership in the Jewish community a definite liability in the Roman world, with their homes far away at the extreme Eastern outskirts of the Roman empire, the Eleven seemed highly unlikely candidates for effecting any change on their world. They must have been astonished when they heard Jesus' words. Even His promise to be with them must have seemed less than adequate assistance in so huge an undertaking. Yet He is Lord—a risen Lord at that—and He must be obeyed.

He must be obeyed because only Jesus holds the keys of life and death. Only Jesus can save. This conviction of the uniqueness of Jesus as Savior separates Christianity from other world religions. For example, Hinduism accepts all religions as equally true and believes that their adherents have an equal chance of being saved if they will honestly follow their religion's tenets. "God is one though the sages call it variously," Hinduism's Vedas proclaim. The Bhagavad Gita agrees: "Howsoever men approach Me, even so do I accept them, for on all sides whatever path that they choose is Mine." This broad tolerance directly contradicts the exclusive claims of Jesus that the way to God is through Him (John 14:6).

If Jesus is telling the truth here, then His commission is of utmost importance. The whole world must be told about Him. It is unfair for only the privileged few to have a chance to be saved. The disciples must get the word out, in the spirit of David Livingstone. On this remarkable missionary's simple slab marking his burial place in London's Westminster Abbey are the words, "Other sheep have I." To rescue those sheep, Livingstone penetrated the heart of Africa. His was the spirit of the earliest Christians. They took up Christ's challenge and went everywhere making disciples. They told what they had personally experienced with Christ. Some of them died talking about Him, for then as now Jesus' enemies were powerful. By their words and by their deeds, they let the world know about Christ. (See 1 John 1:1-3.) They felt they had no choice. Jesus had told them to go.

The scene of this commissioning service is Galilee. Matthew treats this moment as the climax of his entire Gospel, the moment and the setting toward which he has been writing. This is Galilee of the Gentiles, the meeting place of Jew with Gentile, religious with pagan. Other Gospel writers include visits of the risen Lord to Jerusalem, but Matthew concentrates on Galilee, so there will be no misunderstanding that Jesus, having completed His own mission to the lost sheep of Israel, is now ready for His saving mission to be extended to all peoples everywhere. He who began His earthly life as the baby King of the Jews whom the Magi sought now concludes it as the risen Lord of the universe in whom all authority resides. As Lord of all, He cares ⋯ ˡˡ. He thus commissions His chosen assistants to go to all peoples everywhere with the divine solution to their problems. In Christ, they can be saved.

Not long ago, columnist William F. Buckley, Jr., was berated by an advertising executive for publishing material on the Shroud of Turin (which some believe to have been the grave clothes Jesus wore in the tomb) in his magazine, *The National Review*. Buckley, a devout Roman Catholic, offended the executive, who wrote, "Keep your faith to yourself as every well-bred man does."

Buckley took on his antagonist. There was a principle at stake that mattered more to him than good breeding. He responded that it would be selfish of him to keep his faith to himself. What a pity if someone like Thomas Aquinas had kept his faith to himself. The advertising executive should feel quite free to tell the world "the virtues of Grape Nuts—or whatever else it is you devote yourself to." But he should also leave to others "the freedom to advertise their own enthusiasm."[108]

When you have discovered the truth you must broadcast it, even to unbelieving ears. In the fourteenth century, Marco Polo traveled to Central Asia and China. Returning to his native Italy, he wrote articles describing the wonders he had seen and the magnificent cities he had visited. He was accused of lying, of course, since what he described lay so far beyond the imagination of his readers. Disbelief turned to ridicule. Polo was in disgrace. When he lay dying at the age of 70, priests asked him to confess his lies. They did not wish him to face God with these wild tales on his conscience. His last answer was, "I never told the half of it."

This is the spirit of the Gospel writers. John speaks for all of them when he says, "Jesus did many other miraculous signs in the presence of his disciples, which are not recorded in this book. But these are written that you may believe that Jesus is the Christ, the Son of God, and that by believing you may have life in his name" (John 20:30, 31).

> So the disciples are to go—
> under Christ's authority
> to make others disciples of Christ like themselves
> baptizing them
> teaching them to obey all Christ's teachings
> with full assurance that in so doing, Christ will never leave them on
>   their own.

---

[108]Quoted by E. Ray Jones, "Minister Muses," *Clearwater Christian* (April 21, 1982).